GLOBAL ENVIRONMENTAL CONSTITUTIONALISM

Reflecting a global trend, scores of countries have affirmed that their citizens are entitled to healthy air, water, and land, and that their constitutions should guarantee certain environmental rights. This book examines the increasing recognition that the environment is a proper subject for protection in constitutional texts and for vindication by constitutional courts. This phenomenon, which the authors call environmental constitutionalism, represents the confluence of constitutional law, international law, human rights, and environmental law. National apex and constitutional courts are exhibiting a growing interest in environmental rights, and, as courts become more aware of what their peers are doing, this momentum is likely to increase. This book explains why such provisions came into being, how they are expressed, and the extent to which they have been, and might be, enforced judicially. It is a singular resource for evaluating the content of, and hope for, constitutional environmental rights.

Jim May is a professor of law at Widener University School of Law in Delaware, where he codirects the Environmental Law Center, and adjunct professor of graduate engineering at Widener University in Chester, Pennsylvania. He has served as a delegate to the United Nations and as a consultant to the Hungarian government concerning constitutional reform in environmental matters. He is the editor of, and a contributing author to, *Principles of Constitutional Environmental Law* (2011) and has written or cowritten more than eighty articles and book chapters relating to environmental and constitutional law. He is a former federal litigator, NGO founder and director, and nuclear weapons engineer.

Erin Daly is interim dean and a professor of law at Widener University School of Law in Delaware. She has served as a delegate to the United Nations concerning constitutional reform in environmental matters. She is the author of *Dignity Rights: Courts, Constitutions, and the Worth of the Human Person* (2012) and coauthor, with Jeremy Sarkin, of *Reconciliation in Divided Societies: Finding Common Ground* (2006) and of numerous articles and book chapters on comparative constitutional law and transitional justice.

Reviews

"In their new book, May and Daly rigorously and comprehensively analyze one of the most remarkable developments in constitutional and environmental law in the last fifty years: the explosion of constitutional environmental rights. They clarify every aspect of this sea change in the law, and provide an indispensable resource for anyone interested in constitutional law or environmental law."

John H. Knox
UN Independent Expert on Human Rights and the Environment
Henry C. Lauerman Professor of International Law
Wake Forest University School of Law

"The constitutionalization of environmental norms witnessed in the last two decades represents a significant but not very well-understood trend. This important new book by May and Daly offers an impressive and considered yet critical examination of the usefulness of constitutional environmental provisions. It ought to be essential reading for anyone with an interest in environmental rights."

Ole W. Pedersen
Senior Instructor
Newcastle Law School

"James May and Erin Daly provide a superb global tour d'horizon *of environmental constitutional rights. Their comparative legal analysis is insightful and makes clear the congruent emergence of a rights-based environmental constitutionalism across most regions of the Earth. Their research is an essential complement to studies of both national and international environmental laws, which are incomplete until read together with this innovative book."*

Nicholas A. Robinson
Kerlin Professor Emeritus of Environmental Law
Pace University School of Law

"Global Environmental Constitutionalism *fills an important space in the literature on human rights and environmental protection, addressing the increasing inclusion of environmental rights in constitutions around the world. Over the last four decades nearly three-quarters of the world's countries have adopted constitutional provisions that address environmental matters in some way. This book expertly examines the legal issues and practice surrounding such provisions, which may address substantive rights, procedural rights, directive policies, reciprocal duties, or a combination of them. As the book notes, environmental constitutionalism is growing at the subnational level too, filling gaps in federal systems. The enforcement of these widely varying provisions through litigation is itself a major subject well-examined in the volume. This will be an indispensible volume for those interested in a rights-based approach to environmental protection."*

Dinah Shelton
Manatt/Ahn Professor of Law (emeritus)
The George Washington University Law School

"May and Daly provide a sophisticated survey of the jurisprudence of 'third generation' constitutional rights in the environment. Their discussions of the conceptual foundations of such rights and of the issues of standing, procedure, remedies, and enforcement (and much more) will be of great interest to students of comparative constitutional law as third generation rights become an important part of domestic constitutional law worldwide."

Mark Tushnet
William Nelson Cromwell Professor of Law
Harvard Law School

Global Environmental Constitutionalism

JAMES R. MAY

and

ERIN DALY

CAMBRIDGE
UNIVERSITY PRESS

CAMBRIDGE
UNIVERSITY PRESS

32 Avenue of the Americas, New York NY 10013-2473, USA

Cambridge University Press is part of the University of Cambridge.

It furthers the University's mission by disseminating knowledge in the pursuit of education, learning and research at the highest international levels of excellence.

www.cambridge.org
Information on this title: www.cambridge.org/9781316612842

First published 2015
First paperback edition 2016

A catalogue record for this publication is available from the British Library

Library of Congress Cataloguing in Publication data
May, James R., author.
Global environmental constitutionalism / James R. May, Erin Daly.
     pages cm
ISBN 978-1-107-02225-6 (Hardback)
1. Environmental law.   2. Constitutional law.   I. Daly, Erin, author.   II. Title.
K3585.M383 2014
344.04'6–dc23   2014012950

ISBN 978-1-107-02225-6 Hardback
ISBN 978-1-316-61284-2 Paperback

Contents

Acknowledgments

This book would not have been possible without contributions from many others. We are grateful to Carl Bruch, Sylvia Bankobeza, and Elizabeth Mrema for suggesting that we write a book on the topic, and to John Berger for agreeing to publish it. A draft of the manuscript benefited from editorial comments from Richard Hiskes, Rebecca Bratspies, Nick Robinson, John Knox, Ole Pedersen, Josh Gellers, Itzchalk Kornfeld, and an anonymous reviewer. The book, and parts of it, enjoyed input and encouragement from participants at workshops and speaking events at Widener University, including Mark Tushnet, Edith Brown Weiss, Bob Percival, Josh Gellers, Daniel Bonilla, Jacqueline Hand, Tracy Hester, Angel Oquendo, Jessica Owley, Dinah Shelton, and William Weeks, and our colleagues David Hodas, Andy Strauss, and Patrick Kelly. Daniel Bonilla, David Boyd, Marcelo Buzaglo Dantas, Josh Gellers, and Maria Antonia Tigres also shared research and input. We were inspired too by discussion at various conferences at which we were invited to present our findings, including those sponsored by the International Union for the Conservation of Nature, the International Association of Constitutional Law, the American Bar Association, and the International Bar Association, and law schools at the Universities of Hawaii, Mexico, Nairobi, Oregon, Pace, South Africa, Vermont, and Widener. Janet Lindenmuth provided research on constitutions. Student research assistants included Katharina Earle, Holly Frey, Brittany Giusini, Marie Hobson, Nadiia Loizides, Adam Stallard, and Andrew Yarnell. The Young family provided additional financial support to both of us by naming us consecutive H. Albert Young Environmental Law Fellows at Widener University. Widener University provided financial support for summer grants and research assistance. Debbie Dantinne and Debbe Patrick helped with preparing the typescript. We appreciate everyone and everything that had a hand in making this book happen in more ways than words can convey.

James R. May and Erin Daly
Wilmington, Delaware

Introduction

Such a right belongs to a different category of rights altogether for it concerns nothing less than self-preservation and self-perpetuation ... the advancement of which may even be said to predate all governments and constitutions. As a matter of fact, these basic rights need not even be written in the Constitution for they are assumed to exist from the inception of humankind.

Juan Antonio Oposa et al. v. The Honorable Fulgencio S. Factoran, Jr.[1]

So it was that in *Oposa v. Factoran, Jr.* the Court stated that the right to a balanced and healthful ecology need not even be written in the Constitution for it is assumed, like other civil and political rights guaranteed in the Bill of Rights, to exist from the inception of mankind and it is an issue of transcendental importance with intergenerational implications.

Metropolitan Manila Development Authority v. Concerned Residents of Manila Bay[2]

Environmental constitutionalism is a relatively recent phenomenon at the confluence of constitutional law, international law, human rights, and environmental law. It embodies the recognition that the environment is a proper subject for protection in constitutional texts and for vindication by constitutional courts worldwide.[3] This book explores the evolution, deployment,

---

[1] *Juan Antonio Oposa et al. v. The Honorable Fulgencio S. Factoran, Jr.*, G.R. No. 101083, 224 S.C.R.A. 792 (Supreme Court of Philippines, July 30, 1993), reprinted in 33 I.L.M. 173, 187 (1994) [hereinafter *Minors Oposa*].

[2] *Metropolitan Manila Development Authority v. Concerned Residents of Manila Bay*. G.R. Nos. 171947–48 (Supreme Court of Philippines, December 18, 2008) [hereinafter *Manila Bay*].

[3] See generally, May, James R. and Erin Daly. "Global Constitutional Environmental Rights." In *Routledge Handbook of International Environmental Law*, by Shawkat Alam, Jahid Hossain Bhuiyan, Tareq M.R. Chowdhury and Erika J. Techera (eds.). Routledge, 2012; May, James R. and Erin Daly. "Vindicating Fundamental Environmental Rights Worldwide." *Oregon Review of International Law* 11 (2009): 365–439; May, James R. and Erin Daly. "New Directors in Earth

and potential of environmental constitutionalism at national and subnational levels around the world.

Environmental constitutionalism is evolving globally. The constitutions of about three-quarters of nations worldwide address environmental matters in some fashion: some by committing to environmental stewardship, others by recognizing a basic right to a quality environment, and still others by ensuring a right to information, participation, and justice in environmental matters. Dozens of nations and many subnational governments have adopted constitutional guarantees to environmental rights in recent years. Indeed, most people on earth now live under constitutions that protect environmental rights in some way. And environmental constitutionalism continues to emerge and evolve in courts all around the globe, although many constitutionally embedded environmental rights provisions have yet to be energetically engaged. Despite remarkably progressive language in South Africa's constitution, for instance, there have been decidedly few significant decisions from that country's constitutional court interpreting the ample right to environmental well-being.[4] This book explores evolutionary trends, as well as why some forms of environmental constitutionalism have tended to be more consequential than others.

Much has been written about the linkages between human rights and the environment,[5] between human and environmental rights,[6] and whether there

---

Rights, Environmental Rights and Human Rights: Six Facets of Constitutionally Embedded Environmental Rights Worldwide." IUCN *Academy of Environmental Law E-Journal* 1 (2011a); May, James R. and Erin Daly. "Constitutional Environmental Rights Worldwide." In *Principles of Constitutional Environmental Law*, by James R. May (ed.). ABA Publishing, Environmental Law Institute, 2011b; May, James R. "Constituting Fundamental Environmental Rights Worldwide." *Pace Environmental Law Review* 23 (2006): 113.

[4] See *Fuel Retailers Association of South Africa (Pty) Ltd. v. Director-General Environmental Management Mpumalanga and Others*. 2007 (10) BCLR 1059 (CC) (South Africa Constitutional Court, June 7, 2007), available at www.saflii.org/za/cases/ZACC/2007/13.html. See generally, Kotzé, Louis J. and Anél du Plessis. "Some Brief Observations on Fifteen Years of Environmental Rights Jurisprudence in South Africa." *Journal of Court Innovation* 3 (2010): 157.

[5] See generally, Shelton, Dinah. "Human Rights and the Environment." *Yearbook of International Environmental Law* 13 (2002): 199; Kravchenko, Svitlana and John E. Bonine. *Human Rights and the Environment: Cases, Law and Policy*. Carolina Academic Press, 2008.

[6] See, e.g., Gormley, Paul W. *Human Rights and the Environment: The Need for International Cooperation*. Sijthoff, 1976; Thorme, Melissa. "Establishing Environment as a Human Right." *Denver Journal of International Law and Policy* 19 (1991): 301; Merrills, J.G. "Environmental Protection and Human Rights: Conceptual Aspects." In *Human Rights Approaches to Environmental Protection*, by Alan E. Boyle and Michael R. Anderson (eds.). Clarendon Press, 1996 (reconciling environmental and human rights).

is a fundamental right to a quality environment.[7] There is a growing corpus of scholarship about embodying environmental rights constitutionally,[8] and the emergence of such rights in the global order of environmental law.[9] The discussion about environmental rights also internalizes related concepts of intergenerational equity and the precautionary principle.[10] What distinguishes this book from other works is that it deploys principles of comparative constitutionalism to examine whether, and the extent to which, global environmental constitutionalism is occurring, and why. It is intended to serve as a comprehensive guide to, and examination of, current trends in environmental constitutionalism, rather than as a normative argument for environmental constitutionalism as a human or other right, or necessarily as an exponent of environmental protection in particular contexts. It is not an exegesis that contends that environmental constitutionalism does or should predominate over other legal regimes, including environmental human rights or international and domestic environmental laws. It does not argue *ipse dixit* that environmental constitutionalism suffices for achieving the dual purposes of advancing environmental protection and promoting human rights. Instead, it demonstrates that environmental constitutionalism is an important and complementary tool for advancing these aims. Moreover, we do not seek to litigate

[7] See generally, Turner, Stephen J. *A Substantive Environmental Right: An Examination of the Legal Obligations of Decision-makers Towards the Environment.* Kluwer Law International, 2008; Bruch, Carl, Wole Coker, and Chris VanArsdale. *Constitutional Environmental Law: Giving Force to Fundamental Principles in Africa.*, 2nd edn. Environmental Law Institute Research Report, 2007; Hayward, Tim. *Constitutional Environmental Rights.* Oxford University Press, 2005: 12–13; Pallemaerts, Marc. "The Human Right to a Healthy Environment as a Substantive Right." In *Human Rights and the Environment: Compendium of Instruments and Other International Texts on Individual and Collective Rights Relating to the Environment in the International and European Framework*, by Maguelonne DéJeant-Pons and Marc Pallemaerts, 11–12, Council of Europe, 2002. (discussing the extent to which international law recognizes the existence of a substantive individual right to a healthy environment).

[8] See, e.g., Brandl, Ernest and Hartwin Bungert. "Constitutional Entrenchment of Environmental Protection: A Comparative Analysis of Experiences Abroad." *Harvard Environmental Law Review* 16 (1992); Shelton, Dinah. "Human Rights, Environmental Rights, and the Right to Environment." *Stanford Journal of International Law* 28 (1991): 103 [hereinafter Shelton I]; Symposium. "Earth Rights and Responsibilities: Human Rights and Environmental Protection." *Yale Journal of International Law* 18 (1993): 215–411; Sax, Joseph L. "The Search for Environmental Rights." *Journal of Land Use and International Law* 93 (1990); *cf.* Fernandez, José L. "State Constitutions, Environmental Rights Provisions, and the Doctrine of Self-Execution: A Political Question?" *Harvard Environmental Law Review* 17 (1993): 333 (objecting to enforcement of constitutional environmental rights).

[9] Yang, Tseming and Robert V. Percival "The Emergence of Global Environmental Law." *Ecology Law Quarterly* 36 (2009).

[10] Hiskes, Richard P. *The Human Right to a Green Future: Environmental Rights and Intergenerational Justice.* Cambridge University Press, 2008.

the *exact* number of constitutional provisions to enshrine a substantive, procedural, or other environmental right at the national or subnational level. There is no question that the number of such provisions is substantial and ever expanding. For example, and as examined in Chapter 2, in the mid-1990s there were about 50 constitutional provisions globally that had explicitly recognized a fundamental right to a quality environment. By 2004, one of the authors of this book reported that this number had grown to around 60. By 2008, we noted the number had increased to at least 65. By 2009, another study placed the number at 70. By 2011, our number had climbed again to about 75. And in 2012, yet another study placed the figure at about 95, including countries that impose a duty on the *government* to provide or protect a quality environment, in addition to those that guarantee an *individual* right to a quality environment. In this book, Appendix A lists 76 countries that explicitly recognize an individual right to a quality environment. It does not include countries that are *considering* whether to adopt explicit provisions, or countries that arguably have done so *implicitly* or as a constitutional function of *incorporating* other legal paradigms. Nor does it include countries that impose duties on the state to uphold environmental rights. We include these in Appendix C. Nor does Appendix A include duties imposed on individuals to protect the environment, which we list in Appendix B. Appendices D–G delineate hundreds of other manifestations of environmental constitutionalism. The exact figures are subject to both the influence of events and divergence in categorization, and will remain dynamic. The constant is that environmental constitutionalism exists in just about every nook and cranny on the globe, with growing significance.

Comparative constitutionalism plays an important role in analyzing and contextualizing environmental constitutionalism's emerging influence. Comparative constitutionalism – that is, the practice by constitutional courts of comparing and contrasting texts, contexts, and outcomes elsewhere – is a growing field. Indeed, while this has been called a "founding moment,"[11] it is probably more accurate to call it a *renaissance* in the discipline and the methodologies of comparative constitutional law, propelled by two principal factors. The first is the increasing number of constitutional democracies around the world in the past 40 years, with most new constitutions incorporating extensive catalogues of individual and social rights, including environmental rights. The second is the worldwide growth in independent judiciaries, or at least courts that have jurisdiction to hear constitutional questions.

---

[11] Fontana, David. "Refined Comparativism in Constitutional Law." *UCLA Law Review* 49 (2001): 539.

Indeed, many constitutional courts take seriously Justice Kennedy's reminder that "persons in every generation can invoke [constitutional] principles in their own search for greater freedom."[12] With more courts engaging in constitutional review, and issuing more opinions, the import of comparative constitutionalism grows. For instance, while Israel, South Africa, and Colombia have radically different histories, each has constitutional courts addressing the multivariate challenges of balancing public and private power, of interpreting entrenched constitutional texts, and of maintaining institutional legitimacy while ensuring the progressive development of rights.

But comparative constitutionalism may have other appeal as well. As the societies around the world evolve at an ever-faster rate, courts are increasingly faced with problems of first impression, problems that are answerable less by recourse to each country's own history and constitutional origins than to contemporary experience and reason. A single nation's own past practice is unlikely to guide a court's judgment with regard to diminishing privacy, or the threat of terrorism, or, especially, to the challenges of environmental degradation and climate change. These challenges must be answered by reference to the best practices among nations. And the development of the internet – with ready access in multiple languages to primary and secondary jurisprudential sources from around the world – has facilitated this research.

Theorists see a number of other overlapping benefits in comparative constitutional methodologies: former President of the Israeli Supreme Court Aharon Barak argues that looking to other constitutional cultures "expands judicial thinking"[13] while Vicki Jackson argues that looking abroad can produce better law at home by enhancing "one's capacity for self-reflection."[14] In particular, Jackson says, seeing differences in other constitutional cultures reveals the "false necessities" in our own system and, further, encourages us to develop "what are the normatively preferable best practices."[15] To these we add that comparative constitutional methodologies can help fill in gaps when a nation's own history and experience do not resolve the question; this is particularly likely to be useful when courts confront challenges of the modern world that constitution-drafters of even a previous generation might not have anticipated.

Comparative constitutionalism is of such unquestioned utility that neither scholars nor judges typically see the need to justify it. Within the United

---

[12] *Lawrence v. Texas*, 539 U.S. 558 (2003).
[13] Barak, A. "Response to the Judge as Comparatist: Comparison in Public Law." *Tulane Law Review* 80 (2005): 195, 197; see also Jackson, V.C. "Methodological Challenges in Comparative Constitutional Law." *Penn State International Law Review* 28 (2009): 319.
[14] Jackson, "Methodological Challenges," 320.   [15] *Ibid.*, 321.

States, the debate rages both on and off the bench, but it is a mostly rhetorical debate:[16] since its inception, the Supreme Court has looked to the experience or law of other nations for insight and guidance, and all the members of the current Supreme Court have done so, including those most vociferously against the practice.[17] The concerns raised in the American debate – that it threatens American sovereignty and superiority in constitutional matters,[18] or that it allows for cherry-picking,[19] or that it evinces an implicit progressive bias – seem largely unproblematic elsewhere. It is widely accepted that comparative constitutionalism contributes to the development of a body of best practices.

Comparative constitutionalism is particularly appropriate in the field of environmental protection and governance. Since environmental law, like human rights law, emerged at the international level, there is no inherent incompatibility between the environmental norms of a nation and those of the global community. Developing the former, therefore, may well benefit from attention to the latter, and vice versa. Because each nation is now implementing a common set of environmental principles and values derived from international agreements and conventions, comparisons among national experiences are likely to reveal relevant and valuable lessons. While each nation's particular environmental problems are distinctive – because they concern unique ecosystems put at risk by particular concatenations of political, economic, and cultural threats – the need to balance environmental protection against development is common to all parts of the globe.

If the controversy within the United States has any salutary value, it is to offer reminders of the potential misuses of comparative constitutionalism. Judges should not feel bound by approach or the outcome in a foreign case because the constitutional court's obligation is, of course, to interpret and apply its nation's own constitution.[20] And judges should be especially cautious in order to avoid misreading or failing to contextualize decisions of a peer court. But

---

[16] See Confirmation Hearing on the Nomination of John G. Roberts, Jr. to be Chief Justice of the United States Before the S. Comm. on the Judiciary, 109th Cong. 200 (2005) (statement of Sen. Jon Kyl, Member, S. Comm. on the Judiciary) [hereinafter "Roberts Confirmation Hearing"]: "It's an American Constitution, not a European or an African or an Asian one. And its meaning, it seems to me, by definition, cannot be determined by reference to foreign law. I also think it would put us on a dangerous path by trying to pick and choose among those foreign laws that we liked or didn't like." See also, e.g., Fontana, David. "The Rise and Fall of Comparative Constitutional Law in the Postwar Era," *Yale Journal of International Law* 36(1) (2011); Jackson, Vicki C. *Constitutional Engagement in a Transnational Era.* Oxford University Press, 2010.

[17] http://dianemarieamann.com/2013/07/08/justice-scalia-cites-foreign-law

[18] See Roberts Confirmation Hearing.   [19] *Roper* v. *Simmons*, 543 U.S. 551 (2005).

[20] "This Court should not impose foreign moods, fads, or fashions on Americans." See http://dianemarieamann.com/2013/07/08/justice-scalia-cites-foreign-law

most courts intuitively avoid this mistake and require little guidance. Moreover, we note here that the task of the jurist differs fundamentally from the task of those who seek to comment on, understand, and elucidate judicial opinions. Because the law takes into account judicial reasoning, it is important to know what sources influenced or inspired the judge; whether he or she borrowed from foreign or international sources or relied exclusively on domestic experience determines how the opinion is interpreted and applied in later cases and affects its expressive significance. It is, for that reason, especially important for the court to understand the nature and the character of the foreign or international source.[21] The borrowing jurist must pay particular attention to the reasoning of the foreign opinion to ensure that he or she is appropriating it fairly and accurately. By contrast, when scholars survey global jurisprudence, the very fact that a judicial opinion has construed a constitutional environmental provision or applied it in a particular way is itself worthy of note, whether or not the reasoning is particularly persuasive.

The evidence is that the trend in global environmental constitutionalism is positive and powerful, given the increasing attention that constitutions are giving to environmental rights and the growth of constitutional jurisprudence generally in all regions of the world. And the ambit of constitutional law is growing too. The cases address both collective and individual rights and emanate from common law, civil law, and mixed traditions. They concern all aspects of the environment – air, water, and soil – and many forms of environmental degradation: pollution, clear-cutting, exploitation of natural resources, over-use and over-development, as well as recklessness and simple negligence of the rights of others and of the environment. And they seamlessly implicate civil and political rights as well as social, economic, and cultural rights at both textual and subtextual levels: while some cases discussed in this book vindicate an explicit right to a quality environment, other cases demonstrate that the right can be inferred from the rights to life, health, dignity, property, family, cultural integrity, and even the right against cruel and unusual punishment. Indeed, courts are incorporating into their national jurisprudence

---

[21] There is an abundant and growing literature on how courts should engage in comparative work. See, e.g., Hirshl, Ran. "The Question of Case Selection in Comparative Constitutional Law," *American Journal of Comparative Law* 53 (2005): 125; Jackson, "Methodological Challenges," 319; Fontana, "Refined Comparativism"; Saunders, Cheryl. "The Use and Misuse of Comparative Constitutional Law," *Indiana Journal of Global Legal Studies* 13 (2006): 37; Frankenberg, Günter. "Comparing Constitutions: Ideas, Ideals, and Ideology – toward a layered narrative." *International Journal of Constitutional Law* 4 (2006): 439; Annus, Taavi. "Comparative Constitutional Reasoning: The Law and Strategy of Selecting the Right Arguments," *Duke Journal of Comparative and International Law* 14 (2004): 301.

international norms – thereby contributing to the hardening of otherwise soft international law. And because the cases come from every region of the world including cases from both developed and developing countries, environmental constitutionalism has given rise to borrowing from national and transnational common law and other general principles of environmental law, some of which have been codified at the national level, while others remain subject to development and elucidation by constitutional courts.

While comparative constitutionalism is a legitimate means for evaluating the emergence of global environmental constitutionalism, it is not without its limitations. First, because the jurisprudence is global, describing and respecting the integrity of localization can be challenging. Throughout this book, we examine in detail the arguments that favor and disfavor adjudication of environmental claims in domestic constitutional fora; we suggest at this juncture simply that national courts are better suited to implement the norms that have been articulated at the international level, given their ability to translate those universal values into the local vernaculars and to do so with authority and impact. National courts offer each country the opportunity to determine for itself the appropriate balance of development and sustainability, the ways in which the nation will mitigate or adapt to climate change, the means it will use to protect the environment for the benefit of mankind or for nature itself, and the particular ways it will balance the often competing needs of present and future generations. Although most countries adhere to international declarations and conventions affirming their commitment to environmental protection, one country might do so by treating environmental protection as a public good, while another might prefer to use the revenues produced from private exploitation of natural resources for education or social security. These are complex policy choices that are best made at the national level by institutions that are operating within the local society, familiar with local conditions, and accountable within the local political climate. And courts, more than the tribunals and commissions that operate regionally and internationally, are more accessible to the local population and more able to effectively enforce their orders against local officials.

Localization of environmental protection is particularly important for several additional reasons, too. It is undoubtedly true that, although some environmental problems transcend national borders, most are rooted in local spaces, whether a bay, a forest, or a particular part of a mountaintop. And the manifestations of environmental degradation are experienced by the local residents as loss of access to nature, deterioration of health, and so on. Likewise, the solutions are most likely to be implemented locally. Responsibility for the choices made must be taken by actors who are politically accountable.

The ability to implement environmental values in a local context also helps to avoid some of the most contentious charges made against international environmental law – namely, those embodied in claims of western hegemony and cultural imperialism. Judiciaries in countries that resist the global environmental ethos can move more slowly or not at all, while others can push the boundaries of international law into new and unchartered territories, as, for instance, Ecuador and Bolivia have done in protecting the rights of nature, and many countries have done in explicitly encouraging environmental rights litigation and in tying environmental protection to the protection of life and human dignity.

But while the situs of environmental issues are ordinarily contextually specific, their implications are transcendent, involving almost all aspects of life. National courts, like international summits, have recognized that pollution can affect individual and social health: lack of water can diminish girls' opportunities to attend school; climate change can produce environmental refugees; irresponsible exploitation of natural resources can devastate entire cultures; and, as the water wars of the 1990s in Bolivia suggest, failure to balance environmental and human needs can even threaten rule of law and democratic governance. The Rio+20 United Nations Conference on Sustainable Development recognized the inextricable link between sustainable development and the eradication of poverty. "We therefore acknowledge the need," the outcome document, *The Future We Want*, said, "to further mainstream sustainable development at all levels, integrating economic, social and environmental aspects and recognizing their inter-linkages, so as to achieve sustainable development in all its dimensions."[22] But to recognize the social and economic implications of a problem is to admit that it is primarily a national issue: the causes of environmental degradation are often rooted in national political and economic history and in the choices that have been made at the national level, whether to develop land, to privatize water, to allow mining or clear-cutting, and so on. These are questions of national policy that should be made within each country's unique political and legal culture. Comparative constitutionalism thus allows one to keep an eye on the generality of cases, while appreciating the local context of each.

Another limitation to comparative constitutionalism is that it assumes that different constitutions are legitimately subjects of level comparison. But, as we shall see, comparative constitutionalism assumes the existence of positive law and available case law to a great extent. Every constitution is the result of years

---

[22] UN Conference on Sustainable Development. "The Future We Want, A/CONF.216/L.1*." June 20–22, 2012, para. 3.

and sometimes generations of customs, traditions, and social structures that are anything but homogenous. They can encapsulate principles that can evade precise exposition, like socialist law, Islamic (and other theocratic) law, and customary (such as indigenous) law. Official translations can be non-existent or inconsistent. And of course oral constitutions passed down through millennia that are common in indigenous traditions are largely out of reach to a study such as this.

The challenges inherent in any comparative approach have particular salience with regard to emerging (and what can be evanescent) ideals like environmental protection. For example, because the legal boundaries of environmental protection are often not well defined, courts engaging constitutional claims may find themselves not only defining the scope of legally enforceable rights but also propounding social values. Values, more than rights, may inform public discourse and infiltrate social consciousness that, in turn, can help to change the behavior of both public and private actors. A court that persistently emphasizes the importance of sustainability and of maintaining a balance with nature will help to inculcate environmental values into the culture: people will demand that public officials act in ways that respect nature, and will do so not only through litigation but in all forms of political discourse and even private activity. As a result, judicial articulation of environmental values may be as instrumental in promoting environmental protection as the legal pronouncements on the scope of the rights asserted.

Comparing the constitutional environmental jurisprudence of countries around the world yields insights into the ways different legal cultures have responded to similar problems. The panoply of cases discussed in these pages illustrates the profound commitment to environmental protection that some courts have shown, and the inexhaustible creativity that they have evidenced in trying to resolve complex, polycentric problems that implicate these diverse interests. Through the comparative project, we can see how, by borrowing and learning from one another, courts are developing a rich and varied set of responses to the challenges of environmental protection through the means of environmental constitutionalism.

Some limitations of the comparative constitutional project partake of both practical and theoretical considerations. We emphasize decisions issued by apex or constitutional courts in certain countries; with few exceptions, we have not analyzed decisions by lower courts in most countries, nor those of green courts or other specialized tribunals because these decisions are less accessible in a medium that can be cite-verified, they are subject to subsequent revision by apex courts, and they are less likely to have a social impact that is as profound. And because we are most interested in the *constitutional* dimensions of domestic environmental rights, we have not generally considered decisions involving common or civil law environmental issues, nor the decisions of regional bodies, such as the African Commission on Human and People's Rights, the Inter-American Commission on Human Rights, or the European Court of Human Rights (ECHR), except to the extent they engage environmental constitutionalism.

Other limitations of comparative constitutionalism are epistemic. Most constitutions lack a constitutional record that might help to explain what the framers of a provision had in mind. Only rarely does one gain a glimpse into the machinations of constitutional reform. For example, in 2012, Fiji considered adopting a constitution with various environmental provisions. In an explanatory document, the framers wrote that: "Fiji's natural beauty and its clean environment are not just important for the well-being of the people but for its economy as well, especially because of the importance of tourism to the country. Like other rights, this one applies not just against the state but against other people and against companies and businesses. The Constitution also makes it clear that the environment is an important responsibility of everyone."[23] Similarly, Nepal's Constituent Assembly Committee for Fundamental Rights and Directive Principles is the primary source of the explanations behind the wording of its recently amended constitution.[24] These sorts of evidentiary footprints of intent are exceptions, however.

Moreover, a constant of environmental constitutionalism is how quickly it changes. Indeed, in the past decade alone, more than a dozen countries have adopted or substantially modified substantive environmental rights provisions in their constitutions, including Armenia, Bolivia, Dominican Republic, Ecuador, Egypt, France, Guinea, Hungary, Jamaica, Kenya, Madagascar, Maldives, Montenegro, Myanmar, Nepal, Rwanda, Serbia, South Sudan, Sudan, and Turkmenistan.[25] And at any given point, environmental constitutionalism is

---

[23] Fiji, *Draft Constitution: The Explanatory Report.* The Constitution Commission 527 (2012), available at www.fijileaks.com/uploads/1/3/7/5/13759434/thursday_the_explanatory_report_two-4.pdf

[24] See generally, Nepal's Constituent Assembly Committee for Fundamental Rights and Directive Principles: "A Report on Thematic Concept Paper and Preliminary Draft 2066 (2009–10 AD)," available at www.constitutionnet.org/files/concept_paper_fundamental_rights_directive_principles.eng_.pdf

[25] See generally, May, "Constituting Fundamental Environmental Rights Worldwide," 113 (sixty countries affording subjective fundamental rights to a quality environment as of early 2005); Boyd, David R. *The Environmental Rights Revolution: A Global Study of Constitutions, Human Rights, and the Environment.* UBC Press, 2012 (ninety-two countries with constitutional recognition of rights to a quality environment as of early 2012).

under consideration (or was until very recently, as of this writing) elsewhere, including Fiji, Iceland, Sri Lanka, and Tunisia. It is a moving target.

The final caveat is that, given that the scope of this book is the global landscape of environmental constitutionalism rather than an in-depth study of any particular country, we focus on what the constitutional texts and judicial opinions *say*. We generally do not presume to explicate what each judicial decision can *mean* in a particular political and cultural context or the social implications of each case. It is a separate question, and one that we generally avoid, as to whether or not a particular case has resonated throughout society or become an icon of the potential for judicial engagement (for good or ill). Nor as a general matter do we presume to analyze the political ramifications and sequelae of each case: How was it received? Was it implemented? Has the river or forest or mountaintop returned to a pristine state? Because of the fragility of the environment and the enormous forces that militate against protection (development, population growth, conflict, culture, corruption or greed, and so on), it is likely that the environmental interest that is protected in a given case may not remain protected for long. Depending on location, circumstances, timing, and other factors, a judicial pronouncement can contain powerful, showy but unenforceable prose that ultimately advances the human condition in unremarkable ways, if at all. On the other hand, some judicial opinions that appear to advance justice only parochially or incrementally can ultimately harbor emerging rights for present and future generations.

In fact, environmental constitutionalism can hardly on its own cause wholesale transformation of domestic environmental policy. In most countries, constitutional and apex courts have spoken seldom if at all about environmental constitutionalism. And yet, it is our contention that even these sporadic assertions are important because they are indicative of a growing worldwide awareness of the potential of environmental constitutionalism. The mere fact that top national courts are focusing on the constitutional dimensions of environmental issues makes it more likely that environmental awareness will seep into the cultural consciousness here and now for the living, and there and then for generations to come. Viewing these developments comparatively keeps their ramifications in perspective. Thus, despite all the caveats, comparative constitutionalism is important in and of itself, particularly when it ventures into new territory like environmental constitutionalism.

Part I explains the nature of environmental constitutionalism, the advantages and disadvantages of express constitutional rights to a quality environment, and the extent to which countries have adopted them. What we see is that environmental constitutionalism can serve as a proxy to most matters affecting the human condition, including rights to life, dignity, health, food, housing, education, work, poverty, culture, non-discrimination, peace, children's health, and general well-being – as well as the quality of the earth's water, ground, and air. It encompasses both human and non-human phenomena and therefore draws from both environmental rights movements and human rights movements. And we explain the vast extent to which nations around the globe have chosen to embody environmentalism constitutionally.

Part II examines judicial outcomes in constitutional environmental cases and special issues that arise in the litigation and enforcement of such claims. It examines pronouncements by apex and constitutional courts in cases vindicating environmental claims of constitutional pedigree. It provides an overview of this evolving judicial culture across the globe and suggests ways to capitalize on the energy that courts so far have expended on constitutional environmental claims. Indeed, national courts have issued rulings to protect the last stands of ancient forests in the Philippines, remaining cold-climate forests in Patagonia, the Ganges River in India, the Acheloos River in Greece, the celebrated woodlands of Hungary, and rare water supplies in Africa, among many other valuable natural resources worldwide. Yet courts in some countries are reticent to engage constitutional environmental rights. This may be due to concerns about the absence of a limiting principle entailed in enforcing such a right, or about their own impotence in forcing compliance with orders to remedy environmental degradation. Nonetheless, courts play a necessary if not sufficient role in implementing environmental constitutionalism.

Part III considers emerging issues in environmental constitutionalism, such as procedural environmental rights, water rights, and subnational environmental rights, as well as less common constitutional issues concerning rights of nature, sustainability, climate change, and the relationship of environmental rights to other emerging constitutional norms on the horizon. What we see is that environmental constitutionalism is branching out into new and unexplored constitutional territory.

The book ends with final thoughts about environmental constitutionalism's potential to advance environmental and human conditions in an ever-changing planet. We conclude that environmental constitutionalism is worth the coin for present and future generations. This is a normative claim, but it is a limited one. We do not advocate *for* the constitutionalization of environmental rights across the globe both because there is still insufficient evidence that their existence *ipso facto* enhances the environment, and because many countries without constitutional environmental rights have managed to promote environmental protection and basic rights to a quality environment. Nonetheless, we intend for this book to help demonstrate the value of environmental constitutionalism in the slow but steady entrenchment of environmental values worldwide.

PART I

EVOLUTION AND EXISTENCE OF
ENVIRONMENTAL CONSTITUTIONALISM

1

The nature of environmental constitutionalism

Man has the fundamental right to freedom, equality, and adequate conditions of life, in an environment of a quality that permits a life of dignity and well-being, and he bears a solemn responsibility to protect and improve the environment for present and future generations.

UN Conference on the Human Environment, Stockholm, 1972[1]

Throughout human history and all over the world, humans have sometimes lived in tension with nature and at other times in harmony with it, alternatively reforming and revering the natural environment around them. The constitutional law of nations around the world has recently taken note of this legacy: in one case from Sri Lanka, for example, the court referred "to the irrigation works of ancient Sri Lanka, the Philosophy of not permitting even a drop of water to flow into the sea without benefiting humankind," and emphasized that for several millennia sustainable development had been already consciously practiced with much success in Sri Lanka.[2] On the other side of the globe, the same sentiment is echoed in the 2008 constitution of Ecuador, which guarantees the rights of nature by recalling the values of the local indigenous civilizations, referring to nature as Pacha Mama, or Mother Earth, in the language of the Achuar people of the Amazon.

What is new too – at least in the past few decades – is growing concern about severe and deepening environmental challenges, including increased pollution, loss of speciation and biodiversity, and global climate change, to name just a few. And with it, greater attention to how to protect the environment

---

[1] Declaration of the United Nations Conference on the Human Environment, Stockholm Conference, Princ. 1 at para. 2, UN Doc. A/CONF.48/14/rev.1 (adopted June 16, 1972).

[2] *Bulankulama and Six Others* v. *Ministry of Industrial Development and Seven Others.* S.C. Application No 884/99 (F.R.) (Supreme Court of the Democratic Socialist Republica of Sri Lanka), published in *South Asian Environmental Reporter* 7(2) (June, 2000).

through law, and, in particular, through law that is most deeply entrenched in the legal system of nations.

Environmental constitutionalism offers one way to engage environmental challenges that fall beyond the grasp of other legal constructs. It can be coalescent, merging governmental structures and individual rights modalities in furtherance of "an overarching legal-normative framework for directing environmental policy."[3] It can be deployed to protect local concerns, such as access to fresh food, water, or air, or global concerns like biodiversity and climate change that share elements of both human rights and environmental protection. Environmental constitutionalism offers a way forward when other legal mechanisms fall short.

The potential reach of environmental constitutionalism is staggering: it implicates most matters affecting the human condition. These include rights to life, dignity, health, food, housing, education, work, poverty, culture, non-discrimination, peace, children's health, and general well-being – as well as the quality of the earth's water, ground, and air.[4] It encompasses both human and non-human phenomena and therefore draws from both environmental rights movements and human rights movements, both of which have ballooned over the last few decades; both areas of law, it has been said, "house . . . a hidden imperial ambition; both potentially touch upon all spheres of human activity, and claim to override or trump other considerations."[5] The grand scope of environmental constitutionalism suggests that it offers complex and multilayered constitutional value. But environmental constitutionalism's ambition may also be its greatest weakness: the nearly limitless application of

---

[3] Hayward, Tim. *Constitutional Environmental Rights.* Oxford University Press, 2005.
[4] See UN Commission on Human Rights, Sub-Commission on Prevention of Discrimination and Protection of Minorities, Human Rights and the Environment, *Review of Further Developments in Fields with which the Sub-Commission has been Concerned: Human Rights and the Environment* prepared by Fatma Zohra Ksentini, U.N. Doc. E/CN.4/Sub.2/1994/9 at para. 248 (July 6, 1994), concluding:

> Environmental damage has direct effects on the enjoyment of a series of human rights, such as the right to life, to health, to a satisfactory standard of living, to sufficient food, to housing, to education, to work, to culture, to non-discrimination, to dignity and the harmonious development of one's personality, to security of person and family, to development, to peace, etc.

See also MacDonald, Karen E. "Sustaining the Environmental Rights of Children: An Exploratory Critique." *Fordham Environmental Law Review* 18 (2006): 5. "Others have even argued that environmental harm can result in a breach of the right to security of the person (non-intervention)."
[5] Anderson, Michael R. "Human Rights Approaches to Environmental Protection: An Overview." In Boyle and Anderson, *Human Rights Approaches*.

human and environmental rights makes it difficult for constitutional drafters to choose appropriate language by which to protect the environment, and may dampen judicial enthusiasm for their vindication.

Several questions present themselves at the outset: because the environment exists in our immediate environs *and* all over the globe, is it best protected at the international or domestic level? Both offer means to address environmental protection. Is the best strategy to build on environmental or human rights legal frameworks to promote environmental interests? Indeed, human and environmental rights are distinct yet synergistic. Arguably, environmental and human rights are complementary and synergistic. And whatever the appropriate paradigm, how do we best define the environment that merits legal protection? The "environment" has any number of interpretations and applications. And how can courts, with their carefully bounded but often tenuous authority, vindicate these important yet amorphous interests? Each judicial system is the product of distinct structural, practical, and philosophical frameworks. Some countries have a strong rule of law tradition, which can lend credibility to environmental rights, while others do not, which can render them ephemeral.

This chapter examines the extent to which international environmental and human rights laws, and common domestic legislative and regulatory legal mechanisms, address environmental rights. It posits that environmental constitutionalism can serve to fill gaps left by these legal regimes and help to move forward a worldwide yet locally grounded environmental agenda.

THE LIMITATIONS OF INTERNATIONAL LAW

At first glance, the international level may seem best suited to addressing environmental challenges because they so often transcend national boundaries. The allocation of water resources often straddles national frontiers, the consequences of climate change affect people from the equator to both poles, minerals and other natural resources have international markets, just as certain specific places, such as the Amazon River basin and the Great Barrier Reef, enjoy global economic and environmental significance. These are just a few examples to demonstrate the environment's global dimensions. As the Indian Supreme Court has said, "To meet the challenge of current environmental issues, the entire globe should be considered the proper arena for environmental adjustment. Unity of mankind is not just a dream of the enlightenment but a biophysical fact."[6] Relegating environmental protection

---

[6] *Karnataka Industrial Areas Development Board v. C. Kenchappa and Others.* AIRSCW 2546 at para. 71 (Supreme Court of India, 2006).

to the national level could limit its efficacy and result in haphazard and conflicting rules and responses to the same core issues.

Typically, there are two strands of argument that environmental rights are better protected at the international level under existing international environmental law accords or under human rights regimes.[7] The first argument is that environmental rights are adequately protected under the existing environmental law framework of international treaties and agreements that already address environmental issues like biodiversity, climate change, desertification, and marine pollution. Collectively, this body of international environmental law is a loose affiliation of treaties, principles, and customs that define and describe norms, relationships, and responses among and between states to meet these many global ecological challenges.[8] International environmental law is influenced by many stakeholders, including nation-states, international institutions, such as the United Nations Environment Programme (UNEP); non-governmental organization (NGOs), such as the World Wildlife Fund; hybrid international intergovernmental organizations like the International Union for the Conservation of Nature (IUCN);[9] corporate associations; individuals and academics concerned for future generations.[10] On the other hand, skepticism about the efficacy of international treaty systems is abundant. Anne Peters, for one, remarks:

> The international legal order is overall *minimalist and soft*. In important issue areas, such as in environmental protection, including global warming and animal rights, the international legal standards are too low, too vague, formally nonbinding, or are altogether lacking. Especially the increasing resort to international soft law in the form of summit declarations and the like instead of binding covenants is a symptom of lacking political consensus and a lack of commitment. ... *Enforcement* of international law is deficient. Moreover it is often handled unevenly in the sense that weaker states are forced to comply with international law, for example human rights or

---

[7] See Abate, Randall S. "Climate Change, the United States, and the Impacts of Arctic Melting: A Case Study in the Need for Enforceable International Environmental Human Rights." *Stanford Journal of International Law* 43A (2007): 3, 10 (discussing the relationship between human rights and environmental protection).

[8] See generally, Sands, Philippe. *Principles of International Environmental Law*, 2nd edn. Cambridge University Press, 2003.

[9] The IUCN is composed of more than eighty sovereign states (including the United States), some 120 governmental ministries and about a thousand international and national NGOs. See www.iucn.org/about

[10] See generally, Weiss, Edith Brown. *In Fairness to Future Generations: International Law, Common Patrimony, and Intergenerational Equity.* United Nations University, 1989.

investment law, notably through economic sanctions. In contrast, stronger states can hardly be pressured by sanctions ..."[11]

International environmental law is especially soft.[12] The congress of international environmental accords has fallen short of expectations for protecting environmental rights. Despite the abundance of treaties and conventions, there is no independent international environmental rights treaty. The Stockholm Declaration, Rio Declaration, and Ksentini Report are hortatory. The Aarhus Convention provides for procedural but not substantive rights. Other regional instruments have experienced only idiosyncratic substantive traction at the domestic level.[13] Nor is there, as of yet, any global environmental constitution.[14] Thus, existing international environmental law regimes do not afford an enforceable right to a quality environment. Moreover, as Ben Cramer observes, "multilateral or regional agreements that do exist are also largely lacking in enforcement mechanisms and rely on signatory states to enact their own internal legislation, which has only occurred in some countries," although, he notes that at the domestic level, "some components of environmental human rights activism have found their way into national statutes and constitutions."[15] Various international environmental accords recognize human rights to a healthy environment. These include the Stockholm Declaration on the Human Environment,[16] the Rio Declaration

---

[11] Anne Peters. "Are we Moving towards Constitutionalization of the World Community?" In *Realizing Utopia: The Future of International Law*, by Antonio Cassese (ed.), 126. Oxford University Press, 2012, available at http://law.huji.ac.il/upload/Peters_Constitutionalization_in_Cassese.2012.pdf. See also, J. Klabbers, A. Peters, and G. Ulfstein. *The Constitutionalization of International Law*. Oxford. Oxford University Press, 2009.

[12] Burhenne, W.E. (ed.). *International Environmental Soft Law. Collection of Relevant Instruments*. International Council of Environmental Law. The Netherlands. Kluwer Academic, 1993.

[13] Pedersen, Ole W. "European Environmental Human Rights and Environmental Rights: A Long Time Coming?" *George Washington International Law Review* 21 (2008): 73, available at SSRN: http://ssrn.com/abstract=1122289

[14] Kotzé, Louis J. "Arguing Global Environmental Constitutionalism." *Transnational Environmental Law* 1(1) (2012): 199 (arguing in favor of global environmental constitution).

[15] See Cramer, Benjamin W. "The Human Right to Information, the Environment and Information About the Environment: From the Universal Declaration to the AARHUS Convention." *Communication Law and Policy* 14 (2009): 73, 86.

[16] "Both aspects of a man's environment, the natural and the man-made, are essential to his well-being and to the enjoyment of basic human rights and the right to life itself." Declaration of the United Nations Conference on the Human Environment; "Man has the fundamental right to freedom, equality, and adequate conditions of life in an environment of a quality that permits a life of dignity and well being ..." *Ibid.*, at Principle 1.

on Environment and Development,[17] the United Nations' and the Aarhus Convention.[18] With the exception of the Aarhus Convention, none of these conventions, however, is designed to be enforced to resolve disputes concerning human rights to a healthy environment.

Indeed, enforcement of international environmental law is often lackluster: the major transgressors often do not agree to the terms, and the patchwork of enforcement mechanisms can have limited jurisdictional authority and are chronically underfunded. Furthermore, because interest in environmental issues can be diffuse, relegating them to international resolution can make it less likely that individuals or coalitions of interested groups will assert the rights that these treaties ostensibly create.

Next, international human rights laws are often enlisted as a proxy for protecting environmental quality.[19] Forty years ago, the Universal Declaration of Human Rights (UDHR) first recognized that human rights are worthy of protection at the international level.[20] More recently, the Ksentini Report addressed the intersection of human and environmental rights as a global concern.[21] Furthermore, regional instruments have drawn a line from human to environmental rights. For example, the African Charter on Human and

---

[17] "Human beings are at the centre of concerns for sustainable development. They are entitled to a healthy and productive life in harmony with nature." UN Conference on Environment and Development, *Rio Declaration on Environment and Development*, Principle 1, UN Doc.A/CN.17/1997/8 (1992); "States shall enact effective environmental legislation. Environmental standards, management objectives and priorities should reflect the environmental and developmental context to which they apply." *Ibid.*, Principle 11.

[18] Convention on Access to Information, Public Participation in Decision-Making and Access to Justice in Environmental Matters, 2161 United Nations Treaty Series (UNTS), 447 (opened for signature June 25, 1998).

[19] See, e.g., Gormley, *Human Rights and the Environment*; Thorme, "Establishing Environment"; Merrills, "Environmental Protection and Human Rights," 25 (reconciling environmental and human rights); Anderson, "Human Rights Approaches: An Overview." In Boyle and Anderson, *Human Rights Approaches*, 1–24; Boyle, Alan E. "The Role of International Human Rights Law in the Protection of the Environment." In Boyle and Anderson, *Human Rights Approaches*, 6, 43–70; Pallemaerts, Marc. "The Human Right to a Healthy Environment as a Substantive Right." In *Human Rights and the Environment: Compendium of Instruments and Other International Texts on Individual and Collective Rights Relating to the Environment in the International and European Framework*, by Maguelonne DéJeant-Pons and Marc Pallemaerts, 11–12, Council of Europe, 2002.

[20] Universal Declaration of Human Rights, GA Res 217 (AIII), UN GAOR, UN Doc. A/810 (December 10, 1948), 3rd session., 1st plenary meeting; see generally, Weiss, *In Fairness to Future Generations*; Churchill, Robin. "Environmental Rights in Existing Human Rights Treaties." In Boyle and Anderson, *Human Rights Approaches*, 89.

[21] See UN Economic and Social Council [ECOSCO], U.N. Commission on Human Rights, Sub-Commission on Prevention of Discrimination and Protection of Minorities, Human Rights and the Environment, *Review of Further Developments*.

Peoples' Rights and the Protocol on Economic, Social and Cultural Rights to the American Convention on Human Rights[22] both promote environmental rights as an incident of basic human rights. The member states of the Association of Southeast Asian Nations adopted the ASEAN Human Rights Declaration, which declares that citizens of member states have "a right to an adequate standard of living, including the right to a safe, clean and sustainable environment."[23] The Arab Charter also explicitly creates a right to a healthy environment.[24] Only the European Convention on Human Rights does not explicitly provide for a right to a healthy environment.[25] Anderson notes:

> As a result of these and other multilateral treaties, some have argued in recent years that while the environment should be protected primarily at the international level, it should be pursued under international human rights law instead of international environmental law.[26]

Hayward, Boyle, and others argue that protecting environmental rights within the architecture of international human rights laws has the primary advantage of making environmental rights actionable by individuals through some of the mechanisms of international human rights law enforcement. Indeed, the global and regional human rights frameworks involve elaborate enforcement infrastructures that have been growing exponentially over decades. The Human Rights Council has some responsibility over matters relating to the environment, including food, water, indigenous peoples' rights, and the obligations of transnational corporations. The Committee on Economic, Social and Cultural Rights (which protects social and solidarity rights, including the right to water) has a new optional protocol that allows for individual enforcement of the latter convention rights, which tend to bear more closely on environmental issues.[27]

---

[22] African (Banjul) Charter on Human and Peoples' Rights. *I.L.M.* 21 (1982): 58, available at www.achpr.org/instruments/achpr

[23] ASEAN Human Rights Declaration (adopted November 18, 2012), available at www.asean.org/news/asean-statement-communiques/item/asean-human-rights-declaration

[24] Article 38: "Every person has the right to an adequate standard of living for himself and his family, which ensures their well-being and a decent life, including food, clothing, housing, services and the right to a healthy environment. The States parties shall take the necessary measures commensurate with their resources to guarantee these rights."

[25] See Pontin, Ben. "Environmental Rights under the UK's 'Intermediate Constitution.'" *Natural Resources and Environment* 17 (2002): 21. The UK has incorporated this interpretation to a certain extent through domestic legislation. *Ibid.*, 22–3 (discussing the UK Human Rights Act's incorporation of the ECHR).

[26] Anderson, "Human Rights Approaches: An Overview." In Boyle and Anderson, *Human Rights Approaches*, 1.

At the transnational regional level, there are active adjudicative bodies, such as the ECHR and the European Court of Justice, the Inter-American Court of Human Rights and the African Commission on Human and Peoples Rights, all of which have decided important cases respecting the environment.[28] Beyond these hard law obligations, some, including Hayward, argue that customary international law envelops a fundamental human right to an "adequate environment," and amounts to *opinio juris* and accepted state practice because so many countries recognize it as a normative principle.[29] Weston and Bollier argue that environmental rights would be advanced if the legal framework and institutions of international human rights, as well as their moral suasion, were used to greater effect.[30] Whether or not these views are correct, there is still, as Boyle contends, much potential for international human rights law to protect environmental norms.[31]

The availability of human rights bodies has led to a boom in legal activity at the juncture of human rights and environmental protection: "The late twentieth century has witnessed an unprecedented increase in legal claims for both human rights and environmental goods. Never before have so many people raised so many demands relating to such a wide range of environmental and human matters. And never before have legal remedies stood so squarely in the centre of wider social movements for human and environmental protection."[32] This trend has contributed to some early landmark decisions, such as *Lopez Ostra* v. *Spain*, in which the ECHR seemed to accept the notion that the Convention's protection of human rights incorporates a right to a healthy environment.[33]

---

[27] GA resolution A/RES/63/117, Optional Protocol to the International Covenant on Economic, Social and Cultural Rights (December 10, 2008), Article 2: "Communications may be submitted by or on behalf of individuals or groups of individuals, under the jurisdiction of a State Party, claiming to be victims of a violation of any of the economic, social and cultural rights set forth in the Covenant by that State Party."

[28] Kravchenko and Bonine, *Human Rights*; Pedersen, "European Environmental Human Rights," 73.

[29] See Hayward, *Constitutional Environmental Rights*, 25–58. But see, e.g., Daniel Bodansky, *The Art and Craft of International Environmental Law*. Harvard University Press, 2009: 198–99 (explaining the difficulties of establishing customary law.)

[30] Weston, Burns H. and Bollier, David, *Green Governance: Ecological Survival, Human Rights, and the Law of the Commons*. Cambridge University Press, 2013 (Table of contents and Prologue), University of Iowa Legal Studies Research Paper No. 13–13, available at http://ssrn.com/abstract=2207977

[31] Boyle, Alan E. "Human Rights and the Environment: Where Next?" *European Journal of International Law* 23 (2012): 613–42.

[32] Anderson, "Human Rights Approaches: An Overview." In Boyle and Anderson, *Human Rights Approaches*.

[33] *Lopez Ostra* v. *Spain*. 20 Eur. Ct. H.R. 277 (European Court of Human Rights, 1995).

The growth of human rights case law has been accelerating recently, providing some familiar content and boundaries to the enforcement of claims deriving from environmental degradation. As a conceptual matter, linking human and environmental rights makes sense insofar as environmental rights *are* human rights; they exist for the benefit of humans and the harms caused by environmental degradation are violations of well-recognized human rights, such as the right to life, to health, and to dignity. In the human rights context, environmental concerns are not the cause of action or the injury itself, but the source of the injury: illegal dumping becomes actionable not because it endangers the environment but because it causes cancer in the local population and therefore implicates the right to health; clear-cutting a forest becomes actionable not because of the harm to the trees but insofar as it diminishes the property values of the local residents; using water for irrigation or development is actionable when the diminution in the available supply for personal consumption and sanitation impairs a person's right to live in dignity.

Adjudicating environmental harms as violations of human rights requires no controversial extensions or distortions of established human rights law because most rights implicated by environmental degradation are already protected against infringement, *however* the violations occur.[34] Given the existing broad protection for human rights, the argument goes, there is no need to create additional environmental human rights, lest these new rights dilute the efficacy of existing rights.[35] Furthermore, limiting recognition of environmental interests to these instances of actionable human rights violations will avoid the primary objection to environmental rights – that their definition is "too uncertain a concept to be of normative value."[36]

Another advantage of using the established human rights framework to protect environmental rights is that, in the words of Alan Boyle, it focuses attention on the core problem: "The virtue of looking at environmental protection through other human rights, such as life, private life, or property, is that it focuses attention on what matters most: the detriment to important, internationally protected values from uncontrolled environmental harm."[37] This is true – assuming that what matters most is the well-being of human beings. But advocates of pursuing environmental rights protection through international environmental treaties would, of course, argue that "what matters most" is not necessarily the already recognized *human rights* values, such as life and property, but *environmental* values including sustainable

---

[34] Boyle, Alan E. "Human Rights and the Environment: A Reassessment." *Fordham Environmental Law Review* (revised 2010): 471.
[35] *Ibid.*   [36] *Ibid.*   [37] Boyle, "Human Rights and the Environment," 33.

development, biodiversity, and protection against or mitigation of climate change. Simply put, if the purpose of environmental protection exists solely because of its utility and meaning to humans, using a human rights framework might be sufficient; however, if the end is conceived more broadly in terms that are not exclusively anthropocentric, then a human rights framework can be limiting.

Even with this limited ambit in mind, international human rights mechanisms have proven to be ineffective at protecting environmental rights more than idiosyncratically.[38] As Hill *et al.* observe:

> [W]hile there appears to be a growing trend favoring a human right to a clean and healthy environment – involving the balancing of social, economic, health, and environmental factors – international bodies, nations, and states have yet to articulate a sufficiently clear legal test or framework so as to ensure consistent, protective application and enforcement of such a right.[39]

And even to the extent that frameworks exist, human rights regimes are incomplete means for advancing environmental protection and environmental human rights. As Peters observes:

> The main problem of the current international human rights protection scheme is not a lack of formal acceptance but its deficient enforcement. Many states have ratified human rights covenants mainly for opportunistic reasons, in order to gain standing in the international community and obtain material benefits, without a real intention to implement them domestically. The international monitoring mechanisms, including the Universal Periodic Review through the UN Human Rights Council, are very weak.[40]

There are many reasons that human rights regimes that are truly international and trans-regional do not necessarily protect environmental rights effectively. The first is that international human rights regimes are not designed to address environmental rights. Dorsen notes that global (as distinct from regional) "human rights systems do not include any direct right to a healthy or satisfactory environment. In fact, most important global human rights treaties were put

---

[38] Dorsen, Norman, Michel Rosenfeld, András Sajó and Susanne Baer. *Comparative Constitutionalism: Cases and Materials*. St. Paul, MN: West Group, 2003, 1313–14; see also, Hodkova, Iveta. "Is There a Right to a Healthy Environment in the International Legal Order?" *Connecticut Journal of International Law* 7 (1991): 65, 67 (skeptical); Thorme, "Establishing Environment," 317.

[39] Hill, Barry E., Steve Wolfson and Nicholas Targ. "Human Rights and the Environment: A Synopsis and Some Predications." *Georgetown International Environmental Law Review* 16 (2004): 361.

[40] Peters, "Are we Moving towards Constitutionalization of the World Community?" 121.

into force prior to the institution of environmental protection nationally or globally."[41] Ansari et al. observes that "early human rights instruments were drafted at a time when environmental issues were not a matter of universal concern, and thus they did not have adequate explicit provisions for protection of right to pollution free environment and other environment-related rights, e.g. right to information pertaining to the environment, right to participation in environment-related matters, and access to justice."[42] Indeed, the right to a clean or healthy environment is one of the few rights widely recognized in constitutions today that have no ancestral claim in either of the human rights covenants and only a tenuous claim to the UDHR.

Second, as a practical matter, to be taken seriously in existing human rights regimes, environmental rights must be tethered to another recognized right. As Shelton observes, "the scope of protection for the environment based on existing human rights norms remains narrow because environmental degradation is not itself a cause for complaint but rather must be linked to an existing right."[43] For example, the ECHR has held that a state's failure to control industrial pollution, like excessive noise pollution resulting from the expansion of Heathrow Airport, may impact not environmental rights *per se*, but the privacy and family rights protected by the European Convention.[44]

Third, international human rights regimes, although formally enforceable, "suffer . . . from weak institutional and compliance mechanisms."[45] Domestic courts have largely declined to find that human rights are customary normative law subject to domestic enforcement,[46] although there are some exceptions. In fact, many commentators conclude that global human rights regimes are underperforming as means to achieve traditional human rights ends, let alone environmental protection ends.

Last, even incorporating human rights conventions by reference does little to advance environmental rights. For example, because the ECHR lacks

---

[41] Dorsen *et al.*, *Comparative Constitutionalism*, 1313–19.

[42] Ansari, Abdul Haseeb, Abdulkadir B. Abdulkadir and Shehu Usman Yamusa. "Protection of Environmental Rights for Sustainable Development: An Appraisal of International and National Laws." *Australian Journal of Basic and Applied Sciences* 6 (2012): 258–72.

[43] Shelton I, 112–113, 116.

[44] *Lopez Ostra* v. *Spain* (European Court of Human Rights, 1995). But see *Hatton and Others* v. *the United Kingdom*, 36022/97 Eur. Ct. H.R. 338 (European Court of Human Rights, 2003) (no violation).

[45] Dorsen *et al.*, *Comparative Constitutionalism*, 1313–19.

[46] See, e.g., *Flores* v. *Southern Peru Copper Corp.*, 343 F.3d 140, 160 (2d Cir. 2003) (finding customary international law does not include a "right to life" or "right to health").

explicit environmental rights, the UK Human Rights Act of 1998 – which gives it "further effect" – does not explicitly advance environmental rights.[47]

Thus, despite good intentions and salutary objectives, human rights instruments do not obviate the need for constitutionally recognized rights to a quality environment, although they may support and promote them.

If we care about the environment for its own sake and for the sake of future generations, independent of its value to living humans, a legal framework to protect the environment *per se* would seem worthwhile. Arguing that rights reflect how we structure relations, Nedelsky observes:

> [T]he process of discernment of wise relations with our environment will be inadequate if it is driven entirely by instrumental reasoning, that is, by asking only the question what is good for humans. ... Insight into the complex web of interdependence that characterizes human interaction with our environment (as with each other) will be fostered by the kind of attentiveness and responsiveness that comes from care and respect, and is much less likely to be yielded by objective, instrumental reasoning that treats the rest of the world (universe) as objects to serve the needs and pleasures of humans.[48]

Thus, it may be essential to develop a body of enforceable environmental law at the international level, building on Stockholm and Rio and other manifestations of an international consensus to protect the world's environment. Only in this way, it is contended, can the international community give environmental protection the attention it deserves. A body of international environmental law also highlights important environmental issues, such as biodiversity or climate change, because they matter in and of themselves, not necessarily because or when environmental degradation implicates specific human rights that have been recognized in other contexts.

In one sense, the debate between protecting the environment as a matter of environmental law or as a matter of human rights law is of little consequence – as long as it gets *some* recognition in one framework or the other. But the two strands are not necessarily coextensive. They have different political bases and different adjudicative mechanisms. And there are situations when a particular harm is protected under one framework and not the other. The draining of a wetland that neither threatens life nor constitutes a violation of the right to

---

[47] Morrow, K. "Worth the Paper that They are Written on? Human Rights and the Environment in the Law of England and Wales." *Journal of Human Rights and the Environment* 1 (2010): 66; Pedersen, O. "A Bill of Rights, Environmental Rights and the British Constitution." *Public Law* (2011): 577.

[48] Nedelsky, Jennifer. *Law's Relations: A Relational Theory of Self, Autonomy and Law.* New York: Oxford University Press, 2011: 197.

health or property or other human right should nonetheless be cognizable as a violation of an environmental right. To limit environmental claims to established human rights defines them in purely anthropocentric terms. Defining claims in terms of their environmental harms may enlarge the range of enforceable claims beyond the already expansive reach of human rights law but reinforces the independent importance of nature, thereby focusing attention on what many say matters most – that is, the global environment. On the other hand, international law does not reach every situation of environmental damage: the diminution in access to clean water may have environmental causes, but its significance is to the human right to life, health, and dignity.

Regardless of the outcome of this debate, there are problems with the international regulation of the environment that appertain to whether the rights are protected through environmental law or through human rights law. First, there is the problem of cultural relativism: environmental protection, "particularly from a North-South perspective [lacks] the universal value normally thought to be inherent in human rights."[49] Although it cannot seriously be maintained that developed nations are unilaterally imposing progressive environmentalist values on the rest of the world (because they do not appear to have particularly robust environmentalist values), it may well be that the cultural influence of the North is nonetheless affecting how, and to what extent, environmental values are promoted in the rest of the world. Indeed, it seems clear that the terms of the global debate have to a significant degree been shaped by Northern priorities: the fast pace of global environmental degradation and the slow pace of its protection reflect the Northern commitment to industrial development, its addiction to non-renewable resources, and its cultural disconnection from the natural world. Moreover, the cultural values of the world's richer countries are being felt in the rest of the world through such instrumentalities as the International Monetary Fund and the World Bank, which have so far favored privatization and development over ecological and cultural values.

A second problem with the internationalization of environmental interests concerns the locus of the problem. Although the environment is global, it is experienced locally and, ultimately, the argument goes, protection should happen most energetically at the local or national level. In his examination of landmark environmental litigation, Oliver Houck has written, "there is little doubt that the real concern, for both lawyer and client, was always the place. The fight was really about protecting some part of nature – a river, a forest or a

---

[49] Boyle, "Human Rights and the Environment," 33.

landscape – representing a remnant of paradise."[50] What is at stake is always a particular corner of the earth that has special significance to someone. The particularity of environmental litigation suggests that localization is essential to the protection of nature.

Other arguments are made in opposition to further development of the internationalization of environmental rights. One problem is indeterminacy or the difficulty of defining the scope of the environmental right or interest. "Indeterminacy is an important reason, it is often argued, for not rushing to embrace new rights without considering their implications."[51] Kiss and Shelton "accept the impossibility of defining an ideal environment in abstract terms" but would alleviate the problem by having "human rights supervisory institutions and courts develop their own interpretations, as they have done for many other human rights."[52] But the record of implementation at the international level is not reassuring. Individual enforcement of social and economic environmental rights is only now becoming possible, and, while individual enforcement of international civil and political rights has been available for decades, this has rarely extended to environmental rights outside Europe. On the other hand, the ECHR has issued dozens of binding environmental decisions, and as of this writing the Aarhus Compliance Committee has received nearly ninety communications.[53]

Nonetheless, global institutions charged with giving meaning to and defining the content of environmental rights have hardly been effective in developing a common international environmental law that reaches environmental rights. While the situation is better at the regional level, particularly in Europe and the Americas, other areas of the world have not been enthusiastic or effective protectors of the environment. The involvement of some national courts in these areas – including especially those in Africa and parts of Southeast Asia, as well as Israel – has thus been essential for many people living in these regions of the world.

Other problems are borne out of the practical challenges and costs associated with implementation. Implementation of the Aarhus Convention, for example, has left something to be desired. As Reid and Ross observe about the UK:

---

[50] Dannenmaier, Eric. "Environmental Law and the Loss of Paradise." *Columbia Journal of Transnational Law* 49 (2011): 463, 467, reviewing Oliver A. Houck, *Taking Back Eden: Eight Environmental Cases that Changed The World*, 1st edn. Washington: Island Press, 2011.

[51] Boyle, "Human Rights and the Environment," 33.

[52] *Ibid.* (citing A.C. Kiss and D. Shelton, *International Environmental Law*, 2nd edn. New York: Transnational Publishers, 2000, 174–8.)

[53] See www.unece.org/env/pp/pubcom.

Complying with the Aarhus Convention is at the heart of the shared difficulty across the UK. Whereas the Convention requires that the public should have access to remedies that are fair, equitable, timely and not prohibitively expensive, the cost of litigation in the UK is notoriously high, exacerbated by the rule that the losing party must pay the costs of the successful opponent. The high cost of preparing one's own case, plus the risk of being liable for the other side's costs if one loses is a major disincentive to litigation. ...The Aarhus Convention Compliance Committee has already stated that the position in the UK does not meet the required standards.[54]

Even if implementation were adequate, the question would remain whether the responsibility for defining an ideal environment and protecting it should, as a theoretical and normative matter, lie primarily with supervisory institutions and courts at the international or national level. Courts around the world are showing that environmental rights are better advanced through constitutional law at the national level.

DOMESTICATING ENVIRONMENTAL RIGHTS

The line between national and international law is, of course, increasingly blurred, as international law exerts an ever-more powerful influence on domestic constitutional law in both hard and soft ways. Several countries have adopted constitutional environmental rights provisions at least in part in response to international law; perhaps the most prominent examples are those provisions in furtherance of the principles set out in the Aarhus Convention relating to procedural environmental rights.[55] Other constitutions, such as South Africa's, adopt international environmental law values and language or require courts to adhere to, or at least consider, relevant international law.

But, in many countries, international norms are followed not because they are obligatory but because they reflect a growing global consensus on a particular issue. The Israeli Supreme Court has explained that, even with regard to an international covenant that has "not been incorporated into our legal system through legislation, it comprises a guiding and directing value not

---

[54] Reid, C. and Ross, A. "Environmental Governance in the UK." In *Environmental Protection in Multi-layered Systems: Comparative Lessons from the Water Sector*, by M. Alberton and F. Palermo (eds.). Leiden: Martinus Nijhoff 2012: 161–85 (Studies in Territorial and Cultural Diversity Governance) (internal quotations and citations omitted).

[55] Boyd, *Environmental Rights Revolution*, 106. For a general assessment of the incorporation of international human rights norms into domestic constitutions, see Zachary Elkins, Tom Ginsburg and Beth Simmons, "Getting to Rights: Treaty Ratification, Constitutional Convergence, and Human Rights Practice," *Harvard International Law Journal* 54(1) (2013): 61–95.

only on an international level but also in the interpretation of internal legal matters."[56] The Pakistani Supreme Court in 1994 was even more elaborate about the powerful influence of international law on domestic institutions:

> Without framing a law in terms of the international agreement the covenants of such agreement cannot be implemented as a law nor do they bind down any party. This is the legal position of such documents, but the fact remains that they have a persuasive value and command respect. The Rio Declaration is the product of hectic discussion among the leaders of the nations of the world and it was after negotiations between the developed and the developing countries that an almost consensus declaration had been sorted out. Environment is an international problem having no frontiers creating transboundary effects. In this field every nation has to cooperate and contribute and for this reason the Rio Declaration would serve as a great binding force and to create discipline among the nations while dealing with environmental problems.[57]

Thus, domestic constitutional law is increasingly absorbing the values and principles of international law, including both environmental and human rights law.[58] Conversely, and in part because of this convergence, international and supra-national tribunals are increasingly looking to domestic constitutional practice in interpreting their own charters and conventions. That many countries and their subnational instruments have robust environmental statutory schemes, regulations, and common law traditions does not mean constitutional entrenchment of environmental values is superfluous.[59] Rather, the international and regional turn toward environmental protection may buttress and help to promote these values at the national level. This may be done, of course, through legislative and regulatory efforts, but, for numerous reasons, environmental constitutionalism offers advantages over non-constitutional means of advancing environmental protection.

---

[56] *Abu Masad v. Water Commissioner.* Civil App. No. 9535/06, 26 (Israel Supreme Court, 2011).
[57] *Shelhla Zia v. WAPDA.* Human Rights Case No. 15-K of 1992, P L D 1994 Supreme Court 693 (Supreme Court of Pakistan, February 12, 1994).
[58] See, e.g., J.L. Larsen. "Importing Constitutional Norms from a 'Wider Civilization': *Lawrence* and the Rehnquist Court's Use of Foreign and International Law in Domestic Constitutional Interpretation," *Ohio State Law Journal* 65 (2004): 1283, and Ralph G. Steinhardt. "The Role of International Law as a Canon of Domestic Statutory Construction," *Vanderbilt Law Review* 43 (1990): 1103.
[59] These include Australia, Austria, Belarus, Bermuda, Canada, China, Czech Republic, France, India, Italy, Jamaica, Japan, Mexico, the Netherlands, Poland, Russia, Singapore, South Korea, Ukraine, the United Kingdom, the United States, and the European Union. See generally, Schlickman *et al.* (eds). *International Environmental Law and Regulation.* Butterworth Legal Publishers, 1995, Vol II (discussing the national environmental statutory and regulatory laws in these countries).

First, constitutionally embodied environmental provisions are more durable than non-entrenched rights. Brandl and Bungert observe that:

> Constitutional implementation enables environmental protection to achieve the highest rank among legal norms, a level at which a given value trumps every statute, administrative rule or court decision. For instance, environmental protection might be considered a fundamental right retained by the individual and thus might enjoy the protected status accorded other fundamental rights. In addition, addressing environmental concerns at the constitutional level means that environmental protection need not depend on narrow majorities in legislative bodies. Rather, environmental protection is more firmly rooted in the legal order because constitutional provisions ordinarily may be altered only pursuant to elaborate procedures by a special majority, if at all.[60]

Second, environmental constitutionalism provides a normative function that is superior to other domestic legal approaches because "as supreme law of the land, constitutional provisions promote a model character for the citizenry to follow, and they influence and guide public discourse and behavior."[61] As Brooks explains:

> The fundamental purpose of a constitutional right to a healthful environment is to frame the description of the pollution event in terms of a public assault upon an individual's substantive right to life and health. [These] values are nationally shared. From this point of view, a federal constitutional right to a healthful environment makes sense.[62]

Third, and perhaps because of constitutionalism's normative superiority, the public is more likely to respond to environmental constitutionalism than environmental regulation: "On a practical level, the public tends to be more familiar with constitutional provisions than specific statutory laws. Citizens tend to identify with, and in turn are identified by, the form of their national constitution."[63] Because constitutionalism bespeaks of shared national values rather than more narrowly conceived limitations on the activities of private enterprise, the likelihood of compliance with constitutional directives increases while the resistance and challenges to such obligations may decrease.

Fourth, the existing legal architectures of many countries do not protect a broad individual right to a quality environment. As Bruch et al. note: "Even

---

[60] Brandl and Bungert, "Constitutional Entrenchment," 4–5.   [61] *Ibid.*
[62] Brooks, Richard O. "A Constitutional Right to a Healthful Environment." *Vermont Law Review* 16 (1992): 1109.
[63] Brandl and Bungert, "Constitutional Entrenchment," 4–5.

countries with advanced environmental protection systems find that their laws do not address all environmental concerns." Although, as Bruch et al. say, "this problem is more pronounced in nations that are still developing environmental laws and regulations,"[64] it is prevalent worldwide. None of the vaunted environmental laws in the United States, for example, guarantee a right to a quality environment. Even the United States' most heralded environmental law achievements, the National Environmental Policy Act or "NEPA,"[65] falls short in this regard. NEPA has been widely copied,[66] finding analogues in national and subnational statutes and regulations worldwide and in some international environmental accords.[67] The purpose of NEPA is:

> to declare a national policy which will encourage productive and enjoyable harmony between man and his environment, to promote efforts which will prevent or eliminate damages to the environment and biosphere and stimulate the health and welfare of man; to enrich the understanding of the ecological system and natural resources important to the Nation.[68]

Notwithstanding this expansive language, NEPA does not promote substantive environmental rights. Among other things, NEPA requires federal agencies to assess the environmental impact of activities likely to significantly affect the quality of the human environment. While the US Supreme Court has said that NEPA requires federal agencies to take a "hard look" at environmental consequences,[69] and has acknowledged that the statute is intended to be "action forcing,"[70] the Court has interpreted NEPA to be primarily a procedural statute, allowing for a process prior to decision making but not one that provides a cause of action to vindicate environmental rights. This renders it void of substantive moment. As a general matter, statutory and civil code laws worldwide concerning environmental protection are not designed to protect substantive environmental rights, and those that are concerned only with selected environmental problems.

Fifth, even in countries that have robust statutory environmental protection laws, litigants must still satisfy a retinue of procedural or constitutional requirements (such as standing) and demonstrate the matter is justiciable.

---

[64] Bruch *et al.*, "Constitutional Environmental Law," 134.   [65] 42 U.S.C. § 4321–4347 (NEPA).
[66] Nicholas Yost writes: "NEPA may well be the most imitated law in American history." *The Nepa Litigation Guide*, 2nd edn. American Bar Association, 2012.
[67] See, e.g., the Antarctic Environment Protocol, 30 ILM 849 (1992).   [68] *Ibid.*, section 2.
[69] *Kleppe* v. *Sierra Club*. 427 US 390 (Supreme Court of the United States, 1976).
[70] *Robertson* v. *Methow Valley Citizens Council*, 490 US 332 (Supreme Court of the United States, 1989).

Last, such common law measures are subject to legislative preemption.[71] For example, the UK Constitution's "principle of legality" envelops common law "natural" rights and is applied on a case-by-case basis.[72] Indeed, the UK has enacted a Human Rights Act that embraces rights provided under the ECHR.[73] This law, however, "preserves the Parliament's discretion to authorize any interference with environmental rights."[74] Thus, a fair observation is that national and subnational legislation and regulation do not necessarily displace the need for such environmental constitutionalism.

Nor does the existence of environmental provisions in subnational constitutions argue against nationalized environmental constitutionalism. As is discussed in Chapter 7, at least thirty states in the United States address environmental matters.[75] Of these, five explicitly and eleven implicitly recognize a right to a clean environment.[76] Yet, as we shall see, subnational constitutional environmental rights have proven to be perhaps the least enforceable constitutional environmental right.[77]

Accordingly, when these international and domestic mechanisms fail, environmental constitutionalism can provide a "safety net" for addressing environmental issues,[78] and can be an efficient and effective national mechanism for inculcating environmental ethics: "A thing is right," wrote Aldo Leopold, "when it tends to preserve the integrity, stability, and beauty of the biotic community. It is wrong when it tends otherwise."[79] As such, constitutional environmental rights can be the last best hope for protecting both basic human rights and biodiversity.[80]

---

[71] See Douglas-Scott, S. "Environmental Rights in the European Union: Participatory Democracy or Democratic Deficit?" In Boyle and Anderson, *Human Rights Approaches*, 109–28.

[72] Pontin, "Environmental Rights under the UK's 'Intermediate Constitution,'" 21.

[73] *Ibid.*, 21–3, 64–5.   [74] *Ibid.*, 64.

[75] See Tucker, John C. "Constitutional Codification of an Environmental Ethic." *Florida Law Review* 52 (2000): 299 (discussing development in Florida).

[76] See Weiss, Edith Brown. *International Environmental Law and Policy*. Aspen Law and Business, 1998: 416 (identifying Illinois, Hawaii, California, Florida, Massachusetts, Montana, Pennsylvania, Rhode Island, and Virginia.).

[77] For a discussion of the interconnectedness between human rights and the environment at the subdivision level, see generally, Deimann, Sven and Bernard Dyssli (eds.). *Environmental Rights: Law, Litigation and Access to Justice*. Gaunt, 1995.

[78] Bruch *et al.*, "Constitutional Environmental Law," 134.

[79] Leopold, Aldo. *A Sand County Almanac*. Random House Digital Inc., 1986, 224–5.

[80] Wilson, Edward O. "The Current State of Biodiversity." In *Biodiversity*, by Edward O. Wilson, 12–13. Washington: National Academic Press, 1988 (noting that humans have multiplied current rates of species extinction by 1,000 to 10,000 times the pre-human-intervention rate).

That environmental constitutionalism can serve to fill gaps left by existing international and national legal orders raises the question as to which rights constitutions should recognize and whether environmental rights are among them.

THE VALUE OF CONSTITUTIONALISM

In turning to the value of constitutionalism, one must concede that the absence of constitutionalism does not mean the absence of environmental protection. For example, environmental law across the UK – which lacks a formal written constitution – is predominantly a statutory matter.[81] Moreover, the absence of constitutionalism does not mean the abject absence of means to achieve overarching policy norms in the service of environmental values, such as sustainable development.[82] The absence of a constitution does, however, suggest a void, particularly as applied to environmental rights. Reid and Ross sum it up this way:

> The absence of a written constitution means that there is no place for broad statements of objectives or individual rights in relation to the environment (or indeed any other pervasive social objectives), and the British tradition in legislating is to avoid establishing general purposes or goals. Thus, although there are provisions setting out the purposes and functions of the environment agencies of National Parks and of other authorities and legal regimes, these are not of general application and do not provide a coherent set of environmental goals. Instead there is a patchwork of detailed provisions relating to individual authorities and their specific powers and duties.[83]

Moreover, as Reid and Ross observe about the UK: "Although some common law doctrines such as tort and delict can apply in environmental contexts, especially the law of nuisance, the role of the courts has predominantly been one of statutory interpretation or of determining the limits of the discretionary powers conferred by statute on a range of authorities, especially in relation to the impact of EU law."[84]

---

[81] Bell, S. and D. McGillivray. *Environmental Law*, 7th edn. Oxford University Press, 2008: 94–5.

[82] For example, for role of legislation in pursuit of broad and pervasive objectives regarding sustainable development, see Ross, A. "Why Legislate for Sustainable Development?" *Journal of Environmental Law* 20 (2008): 35–68; Ross, A. "It's Time to Get Serious – Why Legislation is Needed to Make Sustainable Development a Reality in the UK." *Sustainability* 2 (2010): 1101–27, available at www.mdpi.com/2071–1050/2/4/1101

[83] Reid and Ross, *Environmental Governance* (internal quotations and citations omitted).

[84] *Ibid.*

Constitutionalism has been around since antiquity. Schochet explains:

> The *veneration* of "constitutionalism" is among the enduring and probably justified vanities of liberal democratic theory. Struggles for personal freedoms and for escape from arbitrary political rule have been among the conspicuous features of the history of Western Europe and America since the sixteenth century. Constitutionalism's fundamental principles of limited government and the rule of law ... emerged as the operative ideals of these struggles.
>
> The *tradition* of constitutionalism is much older, extending through the Middle Ages to antiquity ... The "constitution" – in all its historical forms – has always been a standard of legitimacy, for it has been seen as embodying the defining character of its civil society ... [Constitutions are] related to conceptions of human nature, for the constitution can never be divorced from human capacities, needs, and deficiencies.[85]

Constitutionalism has various advantages, particularly in capturing emerging concepts like environmental constitutionalism. In describing the structure of government, constitutions distribute power and allocate authority among governing bodies. In many countries, governing bodies consist of coordinate branches that make, enforce, and interpret laws. Constitutions also describe individual and collective political rights, such as rights to vote, speak, or assemble, and civil rights, such as those to life, liberty, and property; increasingly, they also describe social and solidarity rights, such as rights to medical care, pensions, work, and, most recently, rights to a healthy environment. The import of constitutionalism lies in the supposition that the other constraints on power have failed to prevent political overreaching.[86] Constitutionalism also reflects human nature, inseparable from human capacities, needs, and deficiencies. While constitutionalism is not the answer to every question, having written rules for society is thought to be an improvement over the absence of them. In the end, as Buchanan observes, "we are all constitutionalists ..."[87]

The composition and adoption of a constitution can be a singular national achievement. Written constitutions can memorialize society's most ineluctable relationships and rules.[88] As Borgeaud wrote in the nineteenth century, "The typical written constitution, as conceived by those who adopted it as the

---

[85] Schochet, Gordon J. "Introduction: Constitutionalism, Liberalism, and the Study of Politics," in *Nomos* XX 1, edited by J. Roland Pennock and John W. Chapman. New York University Press, 1979: 1–2.

[86] *Ibid.*, 5.

[87] Buchanan, James M. "Why do Constitutions Matter?" In *Why Do Constitutions Matter?*, by Niclas Berggren *et al.* (eds.), 1, 12. New Brunswick, NJ: Transaction Publishers, 2000.

[88] Bryce, Viscount James. *Constitutions*. Oxford University Press, 1905: 37–8.

basis of the modern state, is democratic, the expression of the sovereign will of the nation."[89] Constitutions can embody the "fundamental and paramount law,"[90] and can declare priorities of rights, obligations, and responsibilities.[91] As Finer et al. said, "Constitutions are codes of norms which aspire to regulate the allocation of powers, functions, and duties among the various agencies and officers of government, and to define the relationship between these and the public."[92] Most importantly, constitutions have "always been a standard of legitimacy."[93] As Borgeaud summed up, "A Constitution is the fundamental law according to which the government of a state is organized and the relations of individuals with society as a whole are regulated. ... They are the great pages in the life of the nations."[94] Indeed, capturing the essence of constitutionalism, the preamble of the Algerian constitution declares that the constitution assures "the juridical protection and the control of action by the public powers in a society in which legality reigns and permits the development of man in all dimensions."[95]

Written constitutions, however, reflect paradoxes. While they can be the product of a convulsive reform advocated by the political or popular majority, rights provisions can contain anti-majoritarian features designed to protect certain individual rights against the tyranny of the majority. And while constitutions usually emerge from a particular historical moment, they often seek to embody principles and values that are meant to endure over time and benefit future generations. Constitutions ultimately describe relationships, between the parts of government and between governments and people, in the present and in the future.

Constitutional rights promote liberty and freedom and are ordinarily intended to offset action taken without the consent of underrepresented individuals or interests. They tend to protect abjured rights and grant to "the individual a subjective or personal guarantee," including rights to speech, religion, education, health, and dignity.[96] Buchanan notes that:

---

[89] Borgeaud, Charles. *Adoption and Amendment of Constitutions in Europe and America.* Edited by John Martin Vincent. Charles Downer Hazen trans. New York: Macmillan, 1895: 35.

[90] *Marbury v. Madison,* 5 U.S. (1 Cranch) 137, 177 (Supreme Court of the United States, 1803).

[91] Bruch *et al., Constitutional Environmental Law,* 138.

[92] Finer, S.E., Vernon Bogdanor and Bernard Rudden. *Comparing Constitutions.* Oxford University Press, 1995.

[93] Schochet, *Introduction,* 1–2.   [94] Borgeaud, *Adoption and Amendment,* xv–xviii.

[95] Algeria Constitution, Preamble.

[96] Brandl and Bungert, "Constitutional Entrenchment," 9–15 (explaining classical–liberal, institutional, value-oriented, or objective, democratic, and social theories supporting fundamental rights).

Support for the imposition of constraints on the operation of the political process may stem exclusively from the fear that a coalition of other persons may act, in the name of the collective unit with powers of enforceability, in ways that harm her own interests. Constitutional constraints are, in this setting, aimed at limiting the range and scope of actions that may be taken by others without the consent of the person in question but actions to which the person is locked in by the fact of collective unity. This reason for rules arises in any collective organization that allows actions to be taken without any explicit consent of the individuals who are affected.[97]

On the other hand, there are arguments opposing constitutionalism, or at least taking a more skeptical view. Some maintain that prefiguring constitutional rights, such as environmental rights, can be normatively ineffective and economically inefficient.[98] As Buchanan observes, "Constitutional rules have the effect of increasing the costs of taking certain actions … Constitutional structure and strategy must be informed, first, by a definition of those patterns of outcomes that are deemed undesirable, and second, by an implementation of limits on the procedures or results designed to forestall such patterns."[99]

Critiques of general complaints about constitutionalizing rights begin with accepting that written constitutional responses to societal challenges matter most when fatigue with other legal approaches descends: "In one sense, constitutions must be seen to matter because, otherwise, we find ourselves, willy-nilly, in a setting of constitutional drift, where inattention to rules and rules' structures may allow patterns of results to emerge that are preferred by no one, then, now, and in the future."[100] On the other hand, Boyd has shown that the reverse is more likely: constitutional protection for the environment tends to foster statutory and regulatory frameworks for managing environmental resources.[101]

Other arguments disfavoring constitutionalizing rights, including environmental rights, also fall short. Some contend that reducing rights that are innate to the human condition trivializes the right.[102] But the ubiquity of rights-containing constitutions belies this concern: it cannot be said that the inclusion of due process, equality, and free speech rights trivializes them or diminishes their significance. There is also an argument that constituting rights has the

---

[97] Buchanan, "Why do Constitutions Matter?" 3.   [98] See *ibid.*, 21–50.

[99] See *ibid.*, 14.

[100] Peczenik, Aleksander. "Why Constitution? What Constitution? Constraints on Majority Rule." In Berggren *et al.* (eds.). *Why Constitutions Matter*, 36.

[101] Boyd, *Environmental Rights Revolution*, Chapters 6–10.

[102] See Dicey, Albert Venn. *Introduction to the Study of the Law of the Constitution*, 10th edn. Palgrave Macmillan, 1959.

anti-majoritarian effect of elevating individual rights over the interests of others. A principal criticism of constitutionalism is "that it represents power given to the majority against a polluting minority, rather than a guarantee of minority rights."[103] But this argument conflates political minorities with economically powerful minorities that already have a hold of the levers of power that environmental constitutionalism serves to balance. Peczenik says, "[I]t can be said that constitutions can, should, and often do include rules making it difficult for the parliamentary representation of the majority to restrict political and human rights. Such rules are the constraints on the power of the majority."[104]

Further, some contend that the amount of light each constitutional right catches is inversely proportional to how many other rights the constitution confers; the more "rights" there are, the less enforced each, including environmental rights, becomes.[105] "The weakness and fragility of a written constitution vary directly as the number of its articles."[106] But, again, there is no empirical support for this claim, and the increasing number and length of constitutions would seem to suggest the opposite. Moreover, this concern would seem to apply to all of law, especially in countries that operate under a civil code system. Constitutions are "a set of instructions for making decisions about the design and operation of society"; one either has rules or one does not.[107] Thus, the issue is whether a right should be recognized under the constitutional framework the country has established. Borgeaud responds to criticism of constituting fundamental rights this way: "The error [with arguments against constitutionalism] ... that there is any incompatibility between what is fundamental and what is written ... When a people frame for itself a constitution, it formulates its public law ... so as to render it a real safeguard against all attempts to undermine popular liberties."[108]

Environmental rights skeptics also argue that all constitutional rights lose their normative value when they are underenforced or unenforceable. And yet, this all-or-nothing approach does not reflect current reality. It is undeniable that some constitutional rights are more amenable to enforcement than others,

---

[103] Brandl and Bungert, "Constitutional Entrenchment," 88.
[104] Peczenik, "Why Constitution?" 17, 21–2.
[105] J.B. Ruhl relays the following tale: "A woman is seated in a restaurant in Moscow, during Soviet rule, and is handed a menu. After a few minutes she orders the roast pork, but is told they no longer serve that dish. She orders the chicken and is told it has sold out. She orders the fish and is told it has gone bad. She orders the beef and is told it has been overcooked. Exasperated, she asks whether she has been handed the menu or the constitution." Ruhl, J.B. "The Metrics of Constitutional Amendments: and why Proposed Environmental Quality Amendments don't Measure up." *Notre Dame Law Review* 74 (1999): 245.
[106] Borgeaud, *Adoption and Amendment*, 36–7.   [107] *Ibid.*
[108] *Ibid.*, 37–8.

and all constitutional cultures protect some rights more robustly than others. But to the extent that a constitution reflects national values, it is of some utility for a constitution to provide substantive rights, even if it cannot, perhaps yet, make them enforceable. The constitutionalization even of underenforced rights may be valuable, if only because some enforcement is likely to be better than none at all, and this is as true of environmental rights as any other rights. Moreover, if rights are in the constitution, they may stay underenforced only for a time and soon enough gain the attention of litigants and judges, or get developed as adjuncts to more robustly protected rights. This is indeed what is happening all over the world with respect to environmental and other rights. And there is no evidence that the amplification of constitutional rights has resulted in a reduction in enforcement; indeed, we are undeniably in a period of burgeoning enumeration *and* enforcement of human rights.

Another concern is that enshrining certain rights, such as environmental rights, can contribute to a degree of discursive dissonance when multiple rights conflict. Lazarus describes the problem this way:

> [T]here are individuals on both sides of the environmental protection debate who summarily reject any characterization of environmental lawmaking as the attempt to balance competing economic interests. Each camp views their position as being supported by absolute, not relative, rights. The right to human health. The right to a healthy environment. The rights of nature itself. The right to private property. The right to individual liberty and freedom from the will of the majority ... Each side tends to view the other as beginning from an unacceptable moral premise.[109]

But while this may be descriptively true, a proper understanding of rights necessarily rejects absolutism and entails instead a healthy respect for balancing competing rights and accepting burdens on rights that are proportionate to the need. As Sax explains:

> the limit of one's rights is measured by the ability of his neighbor to make a reasonably productive use of his own property. Ultimately, environmental constitutionalism helps us to discern which values should be (1) enshrined in fundamental law, (2) left to negotiation and renegotiation in the democratic forum, (3) protected from majoritarian depredations, and (4) secured even for only a small or unrepresentative minority of the population.[110]

---

[109] Lazarus, Richard J. *The Making of Environmental Law*. London: University of Chicago Press, 2004.
[110] Sax, Joseph L. *Defending the Environment: A Strategy for Citizen Action*. New York: Alfred A. Knopf, Inc., 1971 at 159.

One last objection to the constitutionalization of environmental rights is that, perhaps ironically, it is not necessary to mention environmental rights at all because, as the Philippine Supreme Court said in the celebrated case of *Minors Oposa*, certain rights, including "the right to a balanced and healthful ecology" "need not even be written in the Constitution for they are assumed to exist from the inception of humankind."[111] The argument here is that constitutionalizing rights is superfluous because what is most essential to orderly society is a matter of intuition, not composition. But few are willing to do without them. Even in the Philippine case, the constitutional commitment to environmental protection was not at all unnecessary but gave the court the support it needed to order the cancellation of the timber licenses at issue there. As the court explained:

> If they are now explicitly mentioned in the fundamental charter, it is because of the well founded fear of its framers that unless the rights to a balanced and healthful ecology and to health are mandated as state policies by the Constitution itself, thereby highlighting their continuing importance and imposing upon the state a solemn obligation to preserve the first and protect and advance the second, the day would not be too far when all else would be lost not only for the present generation, but also for those to come, generations which stand to inherit nothing but parched earth incapable of sustaining life.[112]

The fact of constitutionalization was, this language suggests, critical to the court's resolution of the controversy, even if it only restated what was already evident. Given the thriving rights culture in which we live, we conclude that there is no compelling reason to exclude environmental interests from the benefit of rights protection that other important civil, political, and social interests receive.

THE LEGITIMACY OF ENVIRONMENTAL CONSTITUTIONALISM

Environmental constitutionalism can help fill interstitial gaps left by international and national law and be incorporated into constitutional structures. As Shelton notes, "recognizing a right to environment could encompass elements of nature protection and ecological balance, substantive areas not generally protected under human rights law because of its anthropocentric

---

[111] *Minors Oposa* (Philippines, 1993), in his capacity as the Secretary of the Department of Environment and Natural Resources, and the Honorable Eriberto U. Rosario, Presiding Judge of the RTC, Makrati, Branch 66, respondents.

[112] *Ibid.*

focus."[113] Still, some dismiss constitutional environmental rights as magical thinking, reflecting a "combination of political idealism and scientific naivety ... given the substantial disagreement [that] remains over the socially appropriate levels and types of environmental protection."[114] For some, the real challenge with environmental constitutionalism is with definition: "In the context of environmental rights, the more important element of constitutional review is designing an objective test to determine when constitutional review is triggered."[115] To be sure, environmental rights can induce syntactical gymnastics. Bruckerhoff remarks that "only a few national courts have held that their constitution's purported environmental right is actually enforceable. In many cases, the problem of enforcement is a product of the constitutional language itself – when the provision is passive or vague, it is difficult for courts to determine both if and how to interpret the right."[116]

One question concerns whether, as a constitutional *right*, environmental protection is necessarily defined by its impact on people; that is, whether constitutional environmental rights follow in the tradition of international human rights or of the international and regional agreements on the environment. Some maintain that international and domestic law support an exclusively anthropogenic approach. Abate observes: "Existing sources of domestic and international law embrace a human-centered approach to environmental protection and recognize the connection between human rights and environmental protection."[117] Onzivu sees environmental rights as a means to protect human health: "An emerging right to a healthy environment favors the protection of public health."[118]

Others argue that environmental rights ought to be stretched to include non-human harms and biodiversity. Bruckerhoff, for one, maintains that a "less anthropocentric interpretation of constitutional environmental rights could be one, albeit small, component of national and international efforts to protect the wonders of nature."[119]

[113] Shelton, Dinah. "Human Rights and the Environment: What Specific Environmental Rights Have Been Recognized?" *Denver Journal of International Law and Policy* 35 (2006): 163.

[114] Thompson, Barton H., Jr. "Constitutionalizing the Environment: The History and Future of Montana's Environmental Provisions," *Montana Law Review* 64 (2003): 57, 87.

[115] Bruckerhoff, Joshua J. "Giving Nature Constitutional Protection: A Less Anthropocentric Interpretation of Environmental Rights." *Texas Law Review* 86 (2008): 638.

[116] *Ibid.*, 625–6.   [117] Abate, "Climate Change," 10.

[118] Onzivu, William. "International Environmental Law, The Public's Health, and Domestic Environmental Governance in Developing Countries." *American University International Law Review* 21 (2006), 667.

[119] Bruckerhoff, "Giving Nature Constitutional Protection," 645.

Others suggest environmental rights can serve a variety of objectives. Mac-Donald, for instance, writes:

> [E]nvironmental rights are those rights related to environmental standards or protection that are safeguarded so as to benefit someone or something. That someone or something could be the environment itself, humans, or combinations thereof. Environmental rights thus concern the right to protect human health and private or common property (including the "natural" environment) from damage or potential damage sourced through the environment.[120]

Definitional ambiguities are shared at the national and subnational levels, particularly in the United States. Hill *et al.* note that "[w]ith the exception of the State of Hawaii, which defines 'healthful' using standards established by state and federal law, state constitutional provisions affording a right to a clean and healthy environment provide little specific guidance."[121]

To some, the ambiguities inherent in environmental constitutionalism suggest that environmental rights are so laden with policy as to be not justiciable, and therefore best left to legislative bodies. Moreover, adjudicative challenges include problems of precedential value, political will, enforcement, individual or collective standing, standing for natural objects, judicial standards, and jurisdiction, as discussed in Part II.

And yet, a growing number of countries in all parts of the world are amending their constitutions in environmentally protective ways, and a commensurate number of courts are overcoming the conceptual and political challenges and finding ways to enforce these new provisions. Indeed, it is becoming increasingly apparent that national constitutions are peculiarly appropriate loci for environmental rights. Environmental rights possess the hallmarks of universally accepted constitutional rights. To be sure, the vast majority of literature in the field endorses the legitimacy of constitutional environmental rights, maintaining that they are a natural outgrowth of canonical liberal constitutional philosophies, and thus have the same weight as other constitutional rights.

By protecting political minorities, environmental rights serve basic civil rights in the same vein as rights to life, free speech, religion, due process, and equal protection. Brandl and Bungert note that the "strongest argument in favor of an environmental fundamental right is that such a right is a mechanism for resolving conflicts ... Inclusion of environmental rights in the constitution amounts to a declaration that such rights stand on an equal

---

[120] See, e.g., MacDonald, "Sustaining the Environmental Rights of Children," 1, 7.
[121] Hill *et al.*, "Human Rights and the Environment," 395.

footing with other fundamental rights and freedoms ... [It] indicates that a nation bestows upon environmental protection the same respect it grants the right to life and physical integrity."[122]

Environmental rights also advance social norms much like other socio-economic rights including rights to education, food, shelter, and dignity.[123] Sometimes, as we explain in Chapter 2, environmental rights are inextricably intertwined with other rights, offering symbiotic opportunities to advance complementary norms.

Other arguments favor environmental constitutionalism as well. Hiskes suggests that environmental constitutionalism satisfies the benchmarks of constitutionalism insofar as it creates and fosters political communities, defines cultural identity, and is generationally timeless.[124] These features distinguish constitutional from other types of domestic law including regulatory and statutory law. First, environmental constitutionalism helps to define a political community largely in terms of geographic markers of land and water: those who live on this side of the river or mountain range are within the political community, to the exclusion of those who live on the other side (with some variance for mobile and expatriate populations). Members of the political community are not only those who have a voice in the community's affairs but those who have the most at stake in the integrity of the physical environment – those who use the rivers for fishing and commerce, or who breathe the air, or swim in the bays. It is these people whose lives depend on their environment for their work, their dignity, their enjoyment of other rights, their very lives. Conversely, it is also these members of the political community who are most likely to have an impact on their local environment, who are most likely to use its resources and develop it for their own benefit.

For the political community, then, the environment is highly valued but also potentially at risk – the two perhaps paradoxical features that Nedelsky has argued characterize constitutional rights.[125] Values that are important but not seen as being at risk are not typically constitutionally enshrined (like dignity until World War II), nor are values that are at risk but not particularly important. Environmental rights paradigmatically satisfy both requirements. They are inherently and instrumentally valuable, and since the 1970s, when they started to appear in constitutions, have been seen to be at risk by political communities around the world due to overdevelopment and overpopulation

---

[122] Brandl and Bungert, "Constitutional Entrenchment," 87.
[123] Hayward, *Constitutional Environmental Rights.*
[124] Hiskes, *Human Right to a Green Future,* 133.   [125] Nedelsky, *Law's Relations,* 253.

and the risks associated with climate change. By that measure, environmental rights are quintessential candidates for constitutionalization.

Environmental constitutionalism is also appropriate because constitutional law is interpreted, applied, and given life by judges who are part of the political community. And although judges in most countries are notoriously immune from accountability, there is in the domestic sphere at least the greater possibility or threat of accountability than exists with international and regional tribunals. Moreover, given the enhanced concern that international tribunals have for uniformity and the deference they owe to their national constituencies, constitutional courts may be better able than their international counterparts to adjust requirements for standing, or develop different evidentiary requirements, or standards of proof for environmental claims. Domestic judges are also more likely to understand the significance of a particular environmental claim – or of the countervailing claims – because they are part of the culture from which the claims emerge.

This relates to a second feature of constitutionalism identified by Hiskes: constitutions help to create the cultural identity that distinguishes members of one constitutional community from another. Communities define themselves through the values they seek to protect in their laws and in particular their constitutions. Constitutionalizing the environmental debate (as opposed to relegating it to the international level) avoids the problems of cultural bias that internationalization presents by allowing each nation to develop its own discourse with its own vocabulary and based on its own priorities and commitments. While local control is often beneficial, it is particularly pertinent in the context of environmental regulation because many environmental questions bear on core concerns of state sovereignty and security (such as control over waterways and access to and development of mineral resources), as well as on important economic and policy matters, such as the balance between development and environmental protection or the allocation of revenues from natural resources. Each nation will want to calibrate these matters in its own ways, according to its own political calculations, cultural and economic history, and contemporary needs; each nation has a slightly different commitment to development, and ways of protecting against excessive privatization on the one hand and nationalization on the other. And each nation has its own political discourse, so the valence of environmental protection varies from country to country, even within a single global region. Every political system is its own experiment, including notions of separation and sharing of powers, federalism, and individual rights and responsibilities. Naturally, this affects public and political discourse concerning environmental protection. Ecuador (constitutionally) and Bolivia (legislatively) have recognized the rights of nature, while Venezuela and Uruguay have not been particularly protective of environmental values, and the courts in Colombia, Chile, and Argentina fall somewhere in between. While international environmental and human rights law will inform, to some degree, the terms of the debate, the debate itself should be defined by these local distinctions.

Whether or not they explicitly protect the environment, modern constitutions typically establish judicial institutions to give effect to constitutional rights and norms, whether in specialized constitutional courts, environmental tribunals, or through diffuse systems of judicial review. More than their international counterparts, these tribunals tend to be more easily accessible to putative plaintiffs, who are more likely to have better access to local lawyers who, in turn, are more likely to have expertise in the relevant legal fields and to know the legal and political landscape against which judges make their decisions. National courts are dedicated to enforcing constitutional values and yet, as noted, operate within their national political culture rather than outside of it, as is the case with international or regional bodies. As a result, the judicial response to an environmental claim, even if on some occasions it is outside the mainstream, is likely to be within the realm of local political possibility. This contributes to a more coherent and culturally relevant development of the law that in turn is more likely to be followed by other judges and to be accepted by the relevant stakeholders. Consequently, constitutionalism's promise of cultural resonance means that constitutional courts are more likely to be able to enforce environmental rights than are international tribunals, although even at the domestic level enforcement of environmental norms remains a challenge. But enforcement by international tribunals is even less certain: international enforcement of environmental rights can be easy for national authorities to ignore or discount in part because the tribunals are remote, their rulings are compromised by incomplete knowledge of local conditions, and their ability to enforce their judgments is limited by fiscal and political constraints.

The third essential feature of constitutions identified by Hiskes is that they are, quintessentially, intergenerational compacts. They are agreements that one generation makes both to bind and benefit future generations. To give the most well-known example, the United States constitution is ordained and established for the explicit purpose of securing the blessings of liberty "to ourselves and our Posterity."[126] Many other constitutions make the same point in implicit and explicit ways. The very purpose of a constitution is to bind

---

[126] US Constitution, Preamble, available at http://constitutionus.com

future generations to the values identified by the present one. This is not unique to constitutions, and, in fact, intergenerational equity can be found in many parts of the law, which not uncommonly speak across the ages with the intent to bind one to the values of another. Respecting a will simply means that the present generation is bound to the values of a past one; creating a pension system binds one generation of workers to the next. In the case of environmental rights, Hiskes shows that this effort is especially apt because future generations are particularly – and uniquely – vulnerable in terms of their ability to secure environmental rights. The present generation has already shown itself capable of inflicting significant and quite likely irreversible environmental harm on generations yet to come; indeed, this is the dominant way we leave our mark on the future. Future generations cannot protect themselves against these harms except by recourse to the present to protect them by entrenching limits on what their predecessors can do to the environment. Constitutional environmental rights are the best defense that future generations have against the harm that is being done presently.

Even if we view constitutions as constraining democratic practice, we can see that they temporalize these constraints. To constitutionalize a right is to express a preference for long-term values over the decisions that a majority or a minority may make for short-term gain. The value of free speech is guaranteed over time against the short-sighted inclinations of those who transiently hold power to punish unpleasant or threatening epithets; the value of due process holds even against those who would, for short-term gain, convict without trial. Likewise, the health of the global environment is a long-term value that should be held to constrain those who would allow environmental degradation to gain a perceived short-term benefit. Indeed, provisions in certain constitutions that are unamendable are called "eternal" to emphasize their power for all time. As Hiskes maintains, combining the attributes of political community and cultural identity with constitutionalism's intergenerational quality reveals that "constitutions provide this link across time that connects all citizens both to their enduring governmental institutions and to the community they share with all past and future citizens. ... [They are] what makes citizens recognize themselves and each other across time as fellow members of the same community."[127] Thus, environmental constitutionalism "offers an opportunity to promote environmental concerns at the highest and most visible level of legal order, where the impact on laws and the public could prove to be quite dramatic."[128]

[127] Hiskes, *Human Right to a Green Future*, 128.
[128] Brandl and Bungert, "Constitutional Entrenchment," 4–5.

THE VALUE OF ENVIRONMENTAL CONSTITUTIONALISM

Environmental constitutionalism is an essential node in the web of national management of the environment, along with national statutory schemes such as environmental impact assessments and water framework legislation, adherence to international, multilateral, and regional treaties and norms, and dialogue with subnational and local governments. As a result, it can provide an imprimatur to ensure and promote complementarity of different regimes at the various levels of governance.

Beyond its role in connecting disparate legal regimes, environmental constitutionalism suggests a *new way of thinking* about the relationship among individuals, sovereign governments, and the environment with the overall goal of prompting governments to more aggressively protect environmental resources for the benefit both of humans, present and future, and of the environment itself. Constitutional law provides a holistic approach to the challenge of environmental protection because it encompasses almost every tool of which law can avail itself. It can hold government officials accountable and even increase the political pressure on them; it can use procedural rights to give people more access to information and to judicial and political process; it can impose fines and award damages; it can require action or forbearance; it can punish for harm done or prevent threatened harm; it can entrench common law principles, promote values, or establish new rules of engagement. Its legal responses can be structural and systemic or individual and incremental. It thus makes available to individuals and organizations the full range of legal process to ensure governmental responsibility for the protection of the environment.

Constitutionalism encompasses law creation, law implementation, and enforcement. And its reach is plenary because it brings together all the constituencies within and sometimes outside the nation: it can speak for one majority or minority group, or speak for the plurality; it can listen to indigenous and marginalized communities, for corporate or development interests, or to lower, middle, or upper classes of the nation. It can influence and is in turn informed by structural features outside of environmental regulation such as civil and political rights that exist in name or in practice in the country, as well as social and economic attributes of the population within the nation. And it speaks in the language of constitutionalism generally, invoking ideas about the respect for human dignity, principles of separation of powers and parliamentarism, rule of law and due process (however understood in the particular nation), public participation and democratic legitimation, and so on. Flavored by the power of politics on the one hand and claims of justice on the other, it occupies all the spaces in which law exists. All of these influences inform how the government and others may be held to account for responsible and sustainable management of the environment. And because constitutionalism speaks mainly through a supreme, apex, or constitutional court, it speaks with all the authority and legitimacy of the sovereign. It thus puts the sovereign entity at the center of the conversation among all the different voices speaking about environmental protection.

This, of course, begs the question of just what the impact of environmental constitutionalism might be. There can be little question that the constitutional incorporation of environmental rights, protections, and procedures has salutary effects that transcend judicial outcomes. Boyd, for example, concludes "that nations with constitutional provisions related to environmental protection have superior environmental records," including leaving smaller per capita ecological footprints, ranking higher on several indicators of environmental performance, being more likely to ratify international environmental agreements, and lowering pollutant emissions, including greenhouse gases.[129]

There is also some evidence that environmental constitutionalism promotes domestic environmental laws and regulations. Boyd concludes that a majority of nations with substantive constitutional rights to a quality environment have "taken the important step of incorporating" such rights into domestic legislation aimed at environmental protection.[130] For example, South Africa enacted Section 24 of its post-apartheid constitution in 1996, which provides that everyone has the right "[t]o have the environment protected, for the benefit of present and future generations, through reasonable legislative and other measures that … [s]ecure ecologically-sustainable development and use of natural resources while promoting justifiable economic and social development." This provision no doubt informed legislative enactment of Section 1 of the National Environmental Management Act 107 of 1998 (NEMA), which provides: "[d]evelopment must be socially, environmentally and economically sustainable."

Yet there is also evidence that environmental constitutionalism is the culmination of, and not the precursor to, domestic environmental laws. For example, Brazil has been home to a fairly extensive retune of environmental protection legislation since the 1970s. Nonetheless, in 1988 it adopted among the world's most intricate and complex constitutional features for advancing environmental protection. The capstone is Article 225 of the national constitution, which both recognizes an individual's right to "an ecologically

---

[129] Boyd, *Environmental Rights Revolution*, 276.   [130] *Ibid.*, 251.

balanced environment," and imposes a duty upon the government and its citizens to "defend and preserve it for present and future generations." The constitution then fortifies these rights by acknowledging environmental concerns as an economic consideration (Article 170), and the value of ecosystem services (Article 186). Subnational environmental constitutionalism in Brazil is also among the most sophisticated in the world. And then in 1991, Colombia followed suit by recognizing rights to a healthy environment, and by requiring governmental institutions to adopt policies that promote sustainable development, despite the existence of a substantial structure of federal environmental laws.

Moreover, the experience of Zimbabwe shows how environmental constitutionalism in post-colonial Africa can serve as a culmination of prior environmental protection measures. Prior to colonialism, natural resources were managed sustainably at the subsidiary level in Zimbabwe.

> Management of natural resources was centrally vested in the chiefs and village heads. Through customary beliefs and metaphysics, concepts of the sacred forest and totems which regulated the consumption of wildlife products, citizens conserved the environment. Thus, the utilization of environmental resources was achieved in a sustainable way.[131]

During the period of European rule, however, natural resources were viewed more as commodities for the benefit of the colonialists:

> In the nineteenth-century, the scramble and partition of Africa began. The colonialists were guided by philosophies of dispossessing the indigenous black populations of their resources while exploiting these resources for selfish ends. . . . In essence, environmental representation during the colonial period was based on racial grounds, always aimed at making sure that only the Europeans benefited from the use of natural resources.[132]

While the entrenched colonial regime enacted environmental laws, these laws largely underserved traditional interests:

> Although it created modern environmental administration and legislative structures, the colonial regime brought about environmental suppression upon

---

[131] Chirisa, Innocent and Muzenda, Archimedes. "Environmental Rights as a Substantive Area of the Zimbabwean Constitutional Debate: Implications for Policy and Action." *Southern Peace Review Journal* 2(2) (September 2013): 104–21, available at www.researchgate.net/publication/258299172_Environmental_Rights_and_the_Zimbabwean_Constitutional_Debate_Implications_for_Policy_and_Action

[132] *Ibid.*

the black majority who consequently lost control over the environment and their natural resources which they had been using for their survival.[133]

Following independence in 1980, the majority government instituted wide and varied legislative measures to re-institute traditional means of environmental management. These efforts culminated in the Environmental Management Bill of 2002, which, among other things, recognized an individual's right to a quality environment, and to have access to information on environmental matters.

Yet these legislative efforts were viewed to fall short, and auger in the push for constitutional reform:

> Service delivery failure has been cited as one condition that led to the violation of environmental rights of the local people in Zimbabwe in the post-colonial times. . . . There is no doubt, that the eventualities of outbreaks of cholera and related diarrhoeal diseases (typhoid, dysentery and diarrhoea) created a serious awareness among citizens for inclusion of the agenda in the constitution-making.[134]

Thus, the push to constitutionalize environmental rights gained force throughout Zimbabwe, aided by "outside forces," and influenced by constitutional developments elsewhere, particularly in South Africa:

> In the environmental rights lobbying platform the outside forces have been acting as watchdogs assessing transparency and equality of participation in comparison to global practice. Local participation in debates and fora has been facilitated by members of parliament, state bureaucrats and councillors, at least from the side of modern institutions. Village Development Committees and Ward Development Committees as grassroots structures have organised their communities in participating in the constitution making process that ultimately saw the inclusion of environmental rights. With respect to traditional institutions, the traditional leadership – village heads, headman and chiefs have played a vital role especially in rural areas. Ideally, the chiefs are overseers of resource management at local level.[135]

Buoyed by these external and internal forces, Zimbabwe amended its constitution to afford a right to a quality environment, and to afford participatory rights in environmental matters. Whether this provision will withstand the test of time in the courts remains to be seen. As the experience in Zimbabwe evinces, environmental constitutionalism can serve as a means of restoring traditional sustainable practices.

---

[133] *Ibid.*   [134] *Ibid.*, 7.   [135] *Ibid.*, 6–7.

Environmental constitutionalism seems to be the culmination of environmental protection efforts elsewhere. New Zealand has recognized environmental rights legislatively since 1991. Common law there recognizes indigenous Maori traditions whereby humans are considered part of and descended from the (personified) natural world, and therefore are seen as having a duty of guardianship towards it.[136] Despite these existing laws and traditions, as of this writing New Zealand is considering amending its constitution to recognize an environmental right either as a new instrument, along the lines of the French Charter for the Environment, or as a Bill of Rights. These case studies suggest that the relationship between constitutional environmental rights and environmental laws and regulations is often correlative rather than causative.

There is also the argument that environmental constitutionalism can *thwart* environmental protection. Despite the thrust of global environmental constitutionalism over the past four decades, it is also fair to observe that it has not been the corrective to an ever-growing body of environmental challenges. Gatmaytan argues in fact that while environmental constitutionalism is intellectually and emotionally fulsome, it has had little practical effect on advancing either environmental protection or advancing the human condition. He contends that it can be counterproductive because it can lull legislators and agencies into a false sense of complacency, feeling as though courts will address transgressions.

Yet the thrust of environmental constitutionalism is that it is diffuse across the population (such as rights relating to climate change or air pollution) but may not otherwise affect any particular individual or group strongly enough to justify the effort and expense of lobbying or litigation. Certain types of environmental rights – particularly those relating to environmental justice – can set a constitutional floor that helps to secure basic conditions necessary for everyone to live with dignity, while constitutional protection from environmental racism and toxification is especially important for those who lack resources and who are politically and socially marginalized because they are more susceptible to the adverse effects of environmental degradation. Indeed, environmental claims are starting to be made on behalf of interests that have no possibility of protecting themselves politically, including children, future generations, and nature itself.

---

[136] For example, the NZ Resource Management Act 1991 includes a duty to consider the Maori concept of *kaitiakitanga* (guardianship) and the "ethic of stewardship" in making all decisions under the Act.

In sum, there is much to commend the human rights protection scheme, the international legal order, domestic legal structures, and global environmental constitutionalism. We do not attempt here to resolve whether one legal paradigm ought to predominate over another. Instead, we conclude that environmental constitutionalism is integral, not substitutive: it supports and scaffolds existing international and national legal systems. It advances constitutionalism generally and is a fitting subject in the evolution of national constitutions around the globe.

2

Textualizing environmental constitutionalism

With such a high percentage of Nepalis totally dependent on the land for survival, a healthy environment and continued supply of natural resources are vital. Activists are now pushing for environmental rights to be enshrined as a fundamental right in the new constitution.

Nepali Times[1]

In Latin America, environmental rights have been expressed in most of the region's constitutions, a phenomenon that can be traced back to the 1972 Stockholm Conference on Environment and Development where the linkage between human rights and the environment began to evolve. Some countries have devoted whole chapters of their constitutions to environmental rights. Moreover, lawyers are asserting the right and courts are developing constitutional jurisprudence around it.

Tom Ankersen[2]

As we have seen, environmental priorities cannot be achieved by virtue of established international law and domestic statutory and regulatory laws alone. Environmental constitutionalism can help to bridge the gaps left by these other legal regimes. In what has been called an environmental rights "revolution," the constitutions of about three-quarters of nations worldwide – inhabited by the majority of the planet's inhabitants – address environmental matters in some fashion.[3] Boyd reports that, as of 2012, 147 of the world's

---

[1] Rai, Dewain. "Naturally Nepal: Protecting the Natural Environment is Protecting the Nation." *Nepali Times* (May 22–28, 2009).

[2] Ankersen, Thomas T. "Shared Knowledge, Shared Jurisprudence: Learning to Speak Environmental Law Creole (Criollo)." *Tulane Environmental Law Journal* 16 (2003): 820.

[3] See, e.g., Turner, *A Substantive Environmental Right*, and Hayward, *Constitutional Environmental Rights*, 12–13 (advocating constitutional incorporation of environmental rights); Hiskes, *Human Right to a Green Future* (arguing for constitutional consideration of future generations); see Boyd, *Environmental Rights Revolution* (reporting on the many countries

193 United Nations members contain constitutions that address environmental matters in some form.[4] The constitutions from about 76 nations specifically recognize some kind of right to a quality environment (Appendix A). Several dozen impose corresponding duties on individuals (Appendix B) or the state (Appendix C) to protect the environment. Dozens more recognize environmental protection as a matter of national policy (Appendix D). Dozens of others recognize specific rights concerning topics like sustainability and climate change (Appendix E), miscellany (Appendix F), and rights to water (Appendix G). Constitutional provisions from subnational units in several countries recognize environmental rights in some fashion (Appendix H). And lastly, about three dozen establish special procedural rights in environmental matters (Appendix I). Some countries do all of these things, while others do none of them. Most fall somewhere in between.

There is room for interpretation in each category. Boyd identifies 95 countries as providing a right to a quality environment, including provisions that impose duties on state actors to uphold a quality environment.[5] Moreover, Ginsburg reports that about three-quarters of constitutions in force promote environmental protection in some fashion. He observes that constitutionally embedded environmental provisions are "almost universal" in Eastern Europe, reflected in about three-quarters of countries in Sub-Saharan Africa and Latin America, but more rare in North Africa, the Middle East and Oceania regions.[6] Ginsburg concludes that 70 countries have provisions that provide a right to a quality environment, with 89 imposing an individual duty and 164 a duty of the state to protect the environment. He also reports that 40 more recognize environmental policies,[7] and that about two-thirds (126) of the constitutions in force address natural resources in some fashion, including water (63), land (62), fauna (59), minerals and mining (45), flora (42), biodiversity or ecosystem services (35), soil/subsoil (34), air (28), nature (27), energy (22), and other (17).[8]

---

that have upgraded or instituted environmental laws since recognizing constitutional environmental rights).

[4] Boyd, David R. *The Right to a Healthy Environment: Revitalizing Canada's Constitution*. UBC Press, 2012: 65.

[5] *Ibid.*, 65–7. See also, Boyd. "The Constitutional Right to a Healthy Environment." *Environment: Science and Policy for Sustainable Development* 54(4) (July–August, 2012), 3–15, available at www.environmentmagazine.org/Archives/Back%20Issues/2012/July-August%202012/constitutional-rights-full.html

[6] Ginsburg, Tom Constitutionmaking.org option reports, environmental provisions (November 6, 2009), available at www.iconnectblog.com/2009/11/new-report-on-constitutional-treatment-of-the-environment

[7] *Ibid.*   [8] *Ibid.*

Thus, environmental constitutionalism is shaping constitutional reformation,[9] intergenerational equity,[10] and legislative responses to environmental challenges[11] worldwide.

We will begin here by considering the factors that might influence the likelihood that a country will instantiate constitutional environmental rights in the first place, and then turn to the extent to which countries expressly recognize substantive constitutional rights to a quality environment, and other forms of constitutional environmental rights. We conclude the chapter by considering textual and structural presumptions about enforceability.

LIKELIHOOD OF CONSTITUTIONAL INSTANTIATION OF ENVIRONMENTAL RIGHTS

Why are some countries more likely to constitute environmental rights than others? Predictors include predilection toward constitutionalization of rights in general, tolerance of other socioeconomic rights, isomorphism, social strife, situational similarities, and degree of environmental degradation.

Debates about environmental constitutionalism are often shaped by three overarching considerations. First is whether human rights, including environmental rights, ought to be constitutionalized at all,[12] and, if so, whether they should be included as a substantive feature in the instrument's "Bill of Rights" or otherwise.[13] On one hand, substantive rights are those that individuals within society might deem most salient, including rights to life, liberty, and dignity.[14] These are preferable to rights' advocates. Entrenched constitutional

---

[9] See, e.g., Turner, *A Substantive Environmental Right*, and Hayward, *Constitutional Environmental Rights*, 12–13 (advocating constitutional incorporation of environmental rights).

[10] See, e.g., Hiskes, *Human Right to a Green Future* (arguing for constitutional consideration of future generations).

[11] See generally, Boyd, *Right to a Healthy Environment* (reporting on the many countries that have upgraded or instituted environmental laws since recognizing constitutional environmental rights).

[12] See Hayward, *Constitutional Environmental Rights*, 63–92 (arguing in favor of constitutionalizing environmental rights).

[13] *Ibid.*, 93–128.

[14] See generally, May, "Constituting Fundamental Environmental Rights Worldwide," 113, citing John Hart Ely, who described the U.S. Constitution as "not one of trying to set forth some governing ideology . . . but rather one of ensuring a durable structure for the ongoing resolution of policy disputes[.]" John Hart Ely, *Democracy and Distrust: A Theory of Judicial Review*. Harvard Paperbacks, 1980: 90.

rights "are strong indicators of national *opinio juris* and represent the highest level of national law operating as a *lex suprema*."[15] They are less destructible "than statements of policy or procedural norms, enjoy the highest level of legal norms, are less subject to political whims, and tend to be better understood by both the polity and citizenry."[16] They can remedy "a public assault upon an individual's substantive right to life and health."[17] They provide explicit positive or negative protections and other advantages.[18] As legal norms they are superior to statutory or regulatory law, and they can promote model character and national pride.[19] Moreover, many countries lack the resources

[15] Pedersen, "European Environmental Human Rights," 111.

> The strongest argument in favor of an environmental fundamental right is that such a right is a mechanism for resolving conflicts … Inclusion of environmental rights in the constitution amounts to a declaration that such rights stand on an equal footing with other fundamental rights and freedoms … [It] indicates that a nation bestows upon environmental protection the same respect it grants the right to life and physical integrity.

[16] May, "Constituting Fundamental Environmental Rights Worldwide," 118.

[17] Brooks, "A Constitutional Right to a Healthful Environment," 1063, 1109. As Professor Brooks explains:

> The fundamental purpose of a constitutional right to a healthful environment is to frame the description of the pollution event in terms of a public assault upon an individual's substantive right to life and health. [These] values … are nationally shared. From this point of view, a federal constitutional right to a healthful environment makes sense.

[18] See, e.g., Abate, "Climate Change," 26 ("[R]ecognition of environmental health as a fundamental right protects citizens from political whims; provides policy guidance to courts, legislatures, corporations, and private citizens; and highlights the growing importance of conserving ecosystems and biodiversity.").

[19] As Brandl and Bungert observed:

> [E]nvironmental protection in a constitution offers several advantages over statutory law. Constitutional implementation enables environmental protection to achieve the highest rank among legal norms, a level at which a given value trumps every statute, administrative rule, or court decision … In addition, addressing environmental concerns at the constitutional level means that environmental protection need not depend on narrow majorities in legislative bodies. Rather, environmental protection is more firmly rooted in the legal order because constitutional provisions ordinarily may be altered only pursuant to elaborate procedures by a special majority, if at all.
>
> In addition, as the supreme law of the land, constitutional provisions promote a model character for the citizenry to follow, and they influence and guide public discourse and behavior. On a practical level, the public tends to be more familiar with constitutional provisions than specific statutory laws. Citizens tend to identify with, and in turn are identified by, the form of their national constitution. Thus, establishing some form of environmental protection in a national constitution results in the identification of environmental protection with expressions of national pride and character. The establishment process itself further informs the nation's consciousness.

and statutory and regulatory architectures to provide a quality environment.[20] When these mechanisms fail, constitutional substantive environmental rights provide a safety net for addressing environmental issues.[21]

On the other hand, skeptics argue that constitutionalizing a human right trivializes it,[22] has unacceptable counter-anti-majoritarian effects,[23] dilutes other fundamental rights, creates "spillover" effects that curtail rights associated with the ownership of private property,[24] undermines executive mandates,[25] and invites political and societal backlash.[26] Others maintain that a specific environmental right is redundant in those constitutional systems that already guarantee a right to life, which some courts have construed as including a right to a quality environment.[27]

> Thus, constitutional enactment of environmental goals offers an opportunity to promote environmental concerns at the highest and most visible level of a legal order, where the impact on laws and the public could prove to be quite dramatic.
>
> Brandl and Bungert, "Constitutional Entrenchment," 4–5.

[20] Bruch *et al.*, "Constitutional Environmental Law," 134 ("Even countries with advanced environmental protection systems find that their laws do not address all environmental concerns; this problem is more pronounced in nations that are still developing environmental laws and regulations.").

[21] Bruch *et al.*, "Constitutional Environmental Law," 134. For an interesting argument in favor of amending the South African Constitution to include fundamental environmental rights, see Glazewski, Jan. "The Environment, Human Rights and a New South African Constitution." *South African Journal for Human Rights* 7 (1991): 177, 177–98.

[22] See May, "Constituting Fundamental Environmental Rights Worldwide," 127.

[23] See *ibid*. [24] See *ibid.*, 128.

[25] See Onzivu, "International Environmental Law," 673–4 ("Constitutional provisions offer a strong tool for health and environmental protection in developing countries and courts are instrumental in ensuring their application. However, some commentators have stated that excessive environmental activism by courts has undermined executive mandates to protect the environment.").

[26] Professor Lazarus makes the following observation about rights-based political theory:

> [T]here are individuals on both sides of the environmental protection debate who summarily reject any characterization of environmental lawmaking as the attempt to balance competing economic interests.
>
> Each camp views their position as being supported by absolute, not relative, rights. The right to human health. The right to a healthy environment. The rights of nature itself. The right to private property. The right to individual liberty and freedom from the will of the majority ... Each side tends to view the other as beginning from an unacceptable moral premise.
>
> Lazarus, *Making of Environmental Law*, 28.

[27] Onzivu, "International Environmental Law," 672 ("The right to life is an important basis to promote health and the environment. Courts have positively ruled on concerns such as pollution, environmental health, and related health concerns."). Hayward says that this proposition "is ultimately ... not very credible, since environmental protection is not a primary aim." Hayward, *Constitutional Environmental Rights*, 13.

In light of these countervailing concerns, a country's predilection toward constitutional acceptance of social, economic, and cultural rights (SECs) may be the most significant predictor of potential acceptance of environmental rights. SECs are designed to protect human well-being and quality of life, aiming to foster minimum standards of or access to economic and social well-being. They include rights to work, to form or join a trade union, to strike, to social security, to child protection, to food and housing, to health care, and to education. While some might consider environmental rights to be third generation (i.e., solidarity) human rights, thus placing them in a category related to, but distinct from, SECs, for the reasons described throughout this book, rights to a quality environment, to a sustainable environment, to water, and to process in environmental matters are replete with social, economic, and cultural implications.[28]

Once standing in constitutional line behind traditional liberal civil and political rights particularly in the west, SECs now stand astride them in many nations. In a sweeping report, the Toronto Initiative for Economic and Social Rights (TIESR) dataset measures the presence, absence, and justiciability of 17 SECs[29] including a right to a healthy environment among constitutions worldwide.[30] The dataset compiles information about where economic and social rights are constitutionally enshrined, and whether they are expressly subject to judicial remedy. Evaluating these data, Jung and Rosevear conclude: "In the last 30 years, economic and social rights have gained widespread currency and legitimacy."[31]

Timing matters, too. Most environmental constitutionalism has occurred concurrently with the last time a country has undergone constitutional reform to adopt SECs, or a type of SEC. While there are wide temporal, geographic, and other variations in the distribution of SECs, most of the constitutions currently in effect on the planet have them. They are now nearly as commonplace as the panoply of civil and political rights. However, they belie predictive certainty. They were relatively uncommon in those constitutions that were enacted from the end of World War II to about 1974. The peak occurrence of SECs was from 1974 to 1989, then waned from 1990 to about 2004, and has grown steadily since.[32] Not surprisingly, then, as discussed in Chapter 1, most environmental constitutionalism has occurred in the past 40 years.

---

[28] Courtney Jung and Evan Rosevear, "Economic and Social Rights Across Time, Regions, and Legal Traditions: A Preliminary Analysis of the TIESR Dataset." *Nordic Journal of Human Rights* 30 (2012): 372, 376.

[29] The TIESR report refers to these as "Economic and Social Rights," or "ESRs."

[30] The TIESR dataset is available online at www.tiesr.org

[31] Jung and Rosevear, "Economic and Social Rights," 382.   [32] *Ibid.*, 383.

SECs also display tendencies based on geography, legal and economic systems, and especially Cold War ideology. They are found in constitutions in Latin America and the former Soviet Bloc to such an extent as to reflect a regional model or norm. They are least common in the Arab States and parts of Asia. The instance of SECs in the constitutions of Asia and Sub-Saharan Africa is so varied as to evade generalization.

Legal systems are somewhat predictive of the acceptance of SECs. SECs are far more common in constitutions in civil law countries than those that operate under other legal traditions, as is constitutionalism generally. This is significant considering that most of the world operates under a civil law tradition, long trailed by customary, common, and Muslim-based systems.[33] Common law systems are less likely to include SECs than civil law systems. Constitutions that include some aspect of Muslim or customary law are least likely to include SECs.[34]

Importantly, the TIESR study shows a strong correlation between SECs in general and environmental rights in particular. It shows that countries with multiple SECs are more apt to enshrine a right to a quality environment. The TIESR study determined that 73 of all countries with SECs (about 53.7 percent of the survey field) also constitutionally enshrine a right to a quality environment.[35] It also shows that countries with SECs are more likely to address environmental protection constitutionally in other ways as well. It concludes that constitutions from 86 nations, or about 63.2 percent of the survey field, address environmental protection in some other fashion, including as duty or directive principle.[36] On the other hand, others, including Gellers, conclude that no paradigmatic legal system best accommodates individual rights to an adequate environment.[37]

Yet the tendency to consider the adoption of social and economic rights, including environmental rights, may have much more to do with external normative pressures than an internal economic and social rights agenda. Gellers performed a statistical analysis of the likelihood that a country adopts constitutional environmental rights based on five factors – gross domestic produce (GDP) per capita, international civil society influence, level of democracy, population density, and protection of civil liberties. He concludes

---

[33] The TIESR study distinguished constitutions as follows: Civil Law, n=112; Common Law, n=35; Customary Law, n=57; Muslim Law, n=34; Jung and Rosevear, "Economic and Social Rights," 388.

[34] Jung and Rosevear, "Economic and Social Rights," 394. [35] *Ibid.*, 381. [36] *Ibid.*

[37] Joshua Gellers, "Righting Environmental Wrongs: Assessing the Role of Legal Systems in Redressing Environmental Grievances," *Journal of Environmental Law and Literature* 26(2) (2011): 461.

that the propensity of constitutional instantiation of environmental rights correlates most significantly with peer pressure asserted by the external influence of international civil society, and with internal regime characteristics. He argues that "norm socialization and transnational activism offer more explanatory purchase than domestic politics and rationalist-materialist considerations in understanding the trend toward constitutionalization of environmental rights."[38]

Gellers examined outcomes in Nepal – which adopted an environmental rights amendment in 2006 – and Sri Lanka – which hasn't. Based on his research, he determined that whether a country enshrines environmental rights constitutionally is predicated on three factors: (1) civil society activism, often influenced by international norms and influences, (2) the existing environmental regulatory framework, and (3) government responsiveness to popular concerns during constitutional drafting. Gellers found that the most consequential of these factors was the influence of civil society organizations, especially those that operate internationally. Interestingly, local communities were less enthusiastic about the constitution's right to a quality environment, considering it to be a "consolation prize for not having secured the right of local communities to manage their own natural resources."[39] For the sake of comparison, Ecuador's constitutional right of nature would appear both to advance environmental rights and protect autonomy over natural resources. We will return to the Ecuadorian provision in Chapter 9.

Several other factors may be somewhat predictive of whether a country is likely to have constitutionalized environmental rights. One is isomorphism – that is, the tendency to copy or converge around certain constitutional features of an adjacent country. Indeed, some countries that have been most active in this arena share borders, including India, Pakistan, and Nepal, as well as several nations in the former Soviet Bloc and others in Latin America. Yet Gellers concludes that a country's decision to embed environmental constitutionalism appears to have little if anything to do with developments in nearby nations.[40] In fact, many countries that have eschewed environmental constitutionalism share borders with countries that have embraced it.

---

[38] Joshua Gellers, "Survival of the Greenest: A Statistical Analysis of Constitutional Environmental Rights" (2012), available at http://papers.ssrn.com/sol3/papers.cfm?abstract_id=2103960

[39] Joshua Gellers, "Expecting the Elephant but Getting the Mouse: Analyzing the Adoption of a Constitutional Environmental Right in Nepal" (2013), available at http://papers.ssrn.com/sol3/papers.cfm?abstract_id=2238073

[40] Joshua Gellers, "Greening Constitutions with Environmental Rights: Testing the Isomorphism Thesis" (2011), available at http://papers.ssrn.com/sol3/papers.cfm?abstract_id=1902346

Situational similarities may be another predictor: say, democratizing following a period of conflict against autocratic rule. Egypt and Tunisia (in its draft constitution) both chose to instantiate environmental rights constitutionally following transition toward democratic rule in what came to be known as the "Arab Spring." Many conflict-prone countries in both Africa and the former Soviet Bloc have opted to instantiate environmental rights constitutionally, including, most recently, Zimbabwe.[41]

Internal conditions may also contribute to constitutionalization of environmental rights. Some countries that have included environmental rights in their constitutions have modeled those rights not on comparable provisions in foreign constitutions but on their own substantial environmental legislation. In considering a constitutional environmental rights provision, for instance, the government of Scotland cited its "world-leading climate change legislation" from 2009 as well as the world's first Climate Justice Fund as reasons to "enshrine environmental protection in the constitution."[42]

Desperation with current environmental conditions may be another predictor. In the case of Nepal, citizens turned to constitutional reform after they had exhausted other means for advancing social goals, including environmental protection.[43] Gellers concludes that in Nepal, "the main contextual factor that served as the impetus to enact substantial environmental policy reform at the constitutional level was environmental degradation, mainly due to deforestation. Thus, poor environmental quality, the result of increasing industrialization, precipitated the need for enhanced legal protections."[44] Though different in form, a similar degree of despair produced the environmental rights included in Zimbabwe's constitution of 2013. Chirisa and Muzenda write that upon the failure of service delivery in 2008 and 2009, "There is no doubt, that the eventualities of outbreaks of cholera and related diarrhoeal diseases created a serious awareness among citizens for inclusion of the agenda in the constitution-making."[45]

Ultimately, it is often these factors on the ground that will have the most salience in the decision whether or not to include environmental rights in a new or newly amended constitution.

---

[41] Chirisa and Muzenda, "Environmental Rights."

[42] The Scottish Government. *Scotland's Future* (2013), Chapter 8, available at www.scotland.gov.uk/Publications/2013/11/9348

[43] Narayan Belbase, *Environmental Rights in the New Constitution*. IUCN Policy Brief (2009), available at http://cmsdata.iucn.org/downloads/environmental_rights_in_the_new_constitution.pdf

[44] Gellers, "Elephant," 282.   [45] Chirisa and Muzenda, "Environmental Rights," 104–21.

SUBSTANTIVE INDIVIDUAL ENVIRONMENTAL RIGHTS
TO A QUALITY ENVIRONMENT

Substantive environmental rights are those that recognize a right to some degree of environmental quality, such as a right to an "adequate," "clean," "healthy," "productive," "harmonious," "sustainable" environment. Moreover, environmental rights have been recognized as an exponent of non-environmental substantive rights, such as the right to life.[46] See Appendix A.

The common adjectival denominator to substantive environmental rights is that they embody basic human rights to a quality environment, a concept Johnston describes this way:

> Human environmental rights are those rights that insure basic human survival. They include those universal rights pertaining to minimum biological requirements necessities such as access to food, water, and shelter, as well as those rights that support and sustain life over months, years, and generations – those relative rights that allow the production and reproduction of sociocultural, political, and economic systems that define critical resources and manage access and use in ways that insure social and ecosystemic viability. They include both the rights of the individual and the rights of groups to survive and thrive.[47]

Recognizing substantive environmental rights has been a popular notion. Boyd calculates that 177 of the 193 UN-recognized nations on the planet recognize environmental rights by way of their constitutions, environmental legislation, court decisions, or ratification of an international agreement, with the holdouts being the United States, Canada, Japan, Australia, New Zealand, China, Oman, Kuwait, Brunei Darussalam, Lebanon, Laos, Myanmar, North Korea, Malaysia, and Cambodia.[48] More than two-fifths of countries worldwide have constitutions that include substantive environmental rights. See Appendix A. This is more than any other single form of environmental

---

[46] See, e.g., Sumudu Atapattu, "The Right to a Healthy Life or the Right to Die Polluted? The Emergence of a Human Right to a Healthy Environment Under International Law." *Tulane Environmental Law Journal* 16 (2002): 65.

[47] Johnston, Barbara Rose (ed.). *Life and Death Matters: Human Rights, Environment and Social Justice.* Left Coast Press, 2011: 11.

[48] Boyd, "Constitutional Right to a Healthy Environment," 3–15. See also, Binod Prasad Sharma. "Constitutional Provisions Related to Environmental Conservation: A Study." IUCN Policy Brief (September 2010), available at http://cmsdata.iucn.org/downloads/constitutional_provisions_related_to_environment_conservation___final.pdf

constitutionalism.[49] Indeed, since the turn of the millennium about two dozen countries have adopted new or newly amended substantive environmental rights provisions in their constitutions, including Armenia, Bolivia, Dominican Republic, Ecuador, France, Guinea, Hungary, Jamaica, Kenya, Madagascar, Maldives, Montenegro, Myanmar, Nepal, Rwanda, Serbia, South Sudan, Sudan, and Turkmenistan. At this writing, environmental constitutionalism is under consideration in several other countries, including Egypt, Fiji, Iceland, New Zealand, Sri Lanka, and Tunisia, and is bound to find new national homes into the future.

There is good reason that substantive environmental rights are the most common brand of environmental constitutionalism. As a general matter, substantive rights also provide "repose" because they are often viewed as being self-executing and enforceable.[50] They are also "less susceptible to ... political airs,"[51] and more likely to endure because of resistance to constitutional reform.[52] Substantive environmental rights, therefore, aim to afford the most durable and enforceable means for environmental protection.

Despite the relative commendations of substantive environmental rights, few countries had even considered amending or adopting constitutions to recognize an express substantive right to a quality environment before 1972. In those days, the United States was at the vanguard of environmental constitutionalism. In the late 1960s, the US Congress considered several measures to amend the US Constitution to provide an express right to a quality environment. While these measures failed, their consideration contributed to the adoption of express substantive environmental rights at the subnational level in several states.[53] These developments show that embracing substantive environmental rights constitutionally was an idea whose time had come and was ripe for export.

---

[49] See generally, May, "Constituting Fundamental Environmental Rights Worldwide," 113 (60 countries affording fundamental environmental rights since early 2005); Boyd, *Right to a Healthy Environment*, 74 (reporting 94 countries with constitutional recognition of rights to a quality environment as of early 2013).

[50] Kay, Richard S. "American Constitutionalism." In *Constitutionalism: Philosophical Foundations*, by Larry Alexander (ed.), 16, 27. Cambridge University Press, 1998 ("Central to constitutionalism, as I have defined it, is security. Effective liberty requires assurance as to its duration and extent. Put another way, constitutionalism aims to invest at least some aspects of life with a promise of psychological repose."). See, e.g., Finer *et al.*, *Comparing Constitutions*, 1 (questioning value of comparative constitutionalism).

[51] Kay, "American Constitutionalism," 134.   [52] *Ibid.*

[53] See, e.g., Brooks, "A Constitutional Right," 1063, 1068 (1992) (detailing efforts to amend US Constitution to include environmental rights provision).

Yet it wasn't for a few more years that countries began to amend their constitutions to afford environmental rights, first idiosyncratically, and then nearly routinely. The Stockholm Conference in 1972 seems to have been the sentinel spark of environmental constitutionalism worldwide, if originally under an unorthodox set of circumstances. In the days leading up to that venerated meeting, a group of contrarians led by Jacques Cousteau – who did not think much was afoot – set off to hold a "counter" summit to apply pressure against those attending the official event.[54] The alternate summit helped convince those at the principal conference to recognize a right to a healthy environment.[55] The alternate summit also cajoled the Stockholm Conference to issue a resolution that continues to resonate: it encouraged nations to have their domestic constitutions entrench a fundamental right to an adequate environment.[56] Of all the resolutions at Stockholm, this one was thought to be the "most innocuous."[57]

Astonishingly, though, that innocuous resolution morphed into an elegant forerunner of constitutional embodiment of substantive environmental rights worldwide. Stockholm is widely viewed as the high point of international accord that human beings have a fundamental human right to a quality environment. International enthusiasm for creating a mechanism to recognize such a right thereafter diminished, creating a vacuum that domestic environmental constitutionalism has been filling. To be sure, since Stockholm, dozens of countries have adopted provisions specifically guaranteeing an individual right to a quality environment.[58] The list of those nations that have adopted substantive environmental rights includes nations that are developing

---

[54] Houck, Oliver A. "A Case of Sustainable Development: The River God and the Forest at the End of the World." *Tulsa Law Review* 44 (2008): 305.

> However, a group of dissidents led by Jacques Cousteau, who had quit the French delegation to take a more proactive role, held a counter-summit with their own agenda, paralleling the official one, but treating each issue on the agenda the day before it would be taken up by the official event. Quickly seized on by the press, their proposals became, in effect, the agenda to which the government delegations had to respond. One of the more dramatic proposals was a declaration of a right to a healthy environment. Who could oppose that? Who even knew what it meant? And so, emerging from Stockholm was an official resolution that nations should declare a constitutional right to a clean and healthy environment. Most nations in attendance did just that, and little more. Of all the resolutions adopted, this one seemed the most innocuous.

Ibid. (footnotes omitted).

[55] *Ibid.*   [56] *Ibid.*   [57] *Ibid.*

[58] See Appendix A. See also, May, "Constituting Fundamental Environmental Rights Worldwide," 129; EarthJustice. *Environmental Rights Report 2008*, available at http://earthjustice.org/sites/default/files/library/reports/2008-environmental-rights-report.pdf; for another compilation, see Boyd, *Right to a Healthy Environment*, 67.

and developed, north and south, east and west: Africa, the Middle East, Western Europe, the Former Soviet Bloc, Latin America, and Oceania and archipelago, as well as those with civil, common law, Islamic, indigenous, and other traditions.

Provisions that recognize some sort of substantive right to a quality environment run the gamut from spare to spectacular and much in between. Straightforward provisions are reflected in the constitutions of Bénin ("Every person has the right to a healthy, satisfactory and sustainable environment and has the duty to defend it"), Rwanda (entitling "every citizen ... to a healthy and satisfying environment"), Afghanistan ("[Ensuring] a prosperous life and a sound environment for all those residing in this land"), and France ("[e]veryone has the right to live in a balanced and health-friendly environment"). Other examples of this spare approach are found in the constitutions of Angola ("All citizens shall have the right to live in a healthy and unpolluted environment"), Azerbaijan ("Everyone has the right to live in a healthy environment"), Bulgaria ("Citizens have the right to a healthy and favorable environment"), Chad ("Every person has the right to a healthy environment"), Chile ("All have ... [t]he right to live in an environment free from contamination"), Colombia ("Every individual has the right to enjoy a healthy environment"), Congo ("All persons have the right to a healthy environment that is favorable to their development"), Costa Rica ("Every person has the right to a healthy and ecologically balanced environment"), Ethiopia ("All persons have the right to a clean and healthy environment"), Iraq ("Every individual has the right to live in a correct environmental atmosphere"), Jamaica ("Citizens have the right to enjoy a healthy and productive environment free from the threat of injury or damage from environmental abuse and degradation of the ecological heritage"), Macedonia ("Everyone has the right to a healthy environment to live in"), Mali ("Every person has the right to a healthy environment"), Mongolia ("The citizens of Mongolia shall enjoy ... the right to a healthy and safe environment and to be protected against environmental pollution and ecological imbalance"), Montenegro ("Everyone shall have the right to a sound environment"), Mozambique ("All citizens shall have the right to live in ... a balanced natural environment"), Nepal ("Every person shall have the right to live in clean environment"), Nicaragua ("Nicaraguans have the right to live in a healthy environment"), Niger ("Each person has the right to a healthy environment"), Paraguay ("Everyone has the right to live in a healthy, ecologically balanced environment"), Portugal ("Everyone has the right to a healthy and ecologically balanced human environment"), Serbia ("Everyone shall have the right to healthy environment"), Slovak Republic ("Every person has the right to a favorable environment"), South Korea ("All citizens have the right to a healthy and pleasant environment"), South Sudan ("Every person or community shall have the right to a clean and healthy environment"), Spain ("Everyone has the right to enjoy an environment suitable for the development of the person"), Sudan ("The people of the Sudan shall have the right to a clean and diverse environment"), Togo ("Anyone has the right to a healthy environment"), Turkey ("Everyone has the right to live in a healthy, balanced environment"), Turkmenistan ("Everyone has the right to a healthy environment"), and Venezuela ("Every person has a right to individually and collectively enjoy a life and a safe, healthy and ecologically balanced environment").

Provisions in some countries are very specific, recognizing environmental constitutionalism for a select cohort. For example, countries that reserve substantive environmental rights for residents, women, children, indigenous populations, or future generations include Argentina ("All residents enjoy the right to a healthy, balanced environment which is fit for human development and by which productive activities satisfy current necessities without compromising those of future generations"), El Salvador ("Every child has the right to live in familial and environmental conditions that permit his integral development, for which he shall have the protection of the State"), and Madagascar ("The Fokonolona can take the appropriate measures tending to oppose acts susceptible to destroy their environment, dispossess them of their land, claim the traditional spaces allocated to their herds of cattle or claim their ceremonial heritage, unless these measures may undermine the general interest or public order").

Some countries connect substantive environmental rights to other national norms or rights. For example, countries that combine substantive rights to national norms such as sustainable development or cultural advancement include Bolivia ("Everyone has the right to a healthy, protected, and balanced environment. The exercise of this right must be granted to individuals and collectives of present and future generations, as well as to other living things, so they may develop in a normal and permanent way"), Ecuador ("The right of the population to live in a healthy and ecologically balanced environment that guarantees sustainability and the good way of living (*sumak kawsay*), is recognized"), Georgia ("Everyone shall have the right to live in a healthy environment and enjoy natural and cultural surroundings"), and Greece ("The protection of the natural and cultural environment constitutes ... a right of every person"). Moreover, some constitutions connect environmental to other constitutionally protected human rights, such as rights to dignity, health, life, or shelter. Countries to have done so include Afghanistan ("ensuring a prosperous life and a sound environment for all those residing in this land"), Belgium ("Everyone has the right to lead a life worthy of human dignity ... [including] the right to enjoy the protection of a healthy environment"), Brazil ("All persons are entitled to an ecologically balanced environment, which is an asset for the people's common use and is essential to a healthy life"), Guinea-Bissau ("The object of public health shall be to ... encourage [the people's] balanced integration into the social ecological sphere in which they live"), Moldova ("Every person (*om*) has the right to an environment that is ecologically safe for life and health"), Norway ("Every person has a right to an environment that is conducive to health and to natural surroundings whose productivity and diversity are preserved") and Sao Tomé and Príncipe ("All have the right to housing and to an environment of human life").

Other constitutions place environmental rights near separate but related rights, such as a right to health. These include Croatia ("Everyone shall have the right to a healthy life"), Guatemala ("The right to health is a fundamental right of the human being without any discrimination"), and Honduras ("The right to the protection of one's health is hereby recognized"). Such co-constitutionalism has a synergistic effect, fortifying substantive environmental rights.

Last, a few countries seem to grant expansive environmental rights that arguably combine many if not most of the foregoing features. For example, South Africa provides an example of more sophisticated substantive environmental rights that are widely shared and recognize sustainable development and future generations. Its constitution reads:

Everyone has the right[:]

a. to an environment that is not harmful to their health or well-being; and
b. to have the environment protected, for the benefit of present and future generations, through reasonable legislative and other measures that –
   i. prevent pollution and ecological degradation;
   ii. promote conservation; and
   iii. secure ecologically sustainable development and use of natural resources while promoting justifiable economic and social development.[59]

---

[59] South Africa constitution, ch. 2, art. 24. Even in South Africa, where volumes have been written about the writing of the constitution, relatively little attention has been paid to this provision. See Ebrahim, Hassen. *The Soul of a Nation: Constitution-making in South Africa.* Oxford University Press, 1998. See also Argentina constitution, pt. I, ch. 2, art. 41.

Other countries adopting this more integrative approach include the Dominican Republic ("Every person has the right, both individually and collectively, to the sustainable use and enjoyment of the natural resources; to live in a healthy, ecologically balanced [*equilibrado*] and suitable environment for the development and preservation of the various forms of life, of the landscape and of nature"), East Timor ("All have the right to a humane, healthy, and ecologically balanced environment and the duty to protect it and improve it for the benefit of the future generations"), Kenya ("Every person has the right to a clean and healthy environment, which includes the right – (a) to have the environment protected for the benefit of present and future generations through legislative and other measures . . .; and (b) to have obligations relating to the environment fulfilled"), and South Sudan ("Every person shall have the right to have the environment protected for the benefit of present and future generations, through appropriate legislative action and other measures that: (a) prevent pollution and ecological degradation; (b) promote conservation; and (c) secure ecologically sustainable development and use of natural resources while promoting rational economic and social development so as to protect genetic stability and bio-diversity").

Substantive environmental rights have found their way into some countries that have not as yet adopted an express right to a quality environment. Constitutional and apex courts in some countries have derived substantive environmental rights from other constitutional guarantees, such as a right to life.[60] Courts in India have most commonly enlisted a "right to life" as implying rights to a quality environment, as well as other socioeconomic rights.[61] On the other hand, attempts to infer environmental rights in some other countries have failed, including in the United States.[62] Because implicit constitutional substantive rights are largely a judicial invention, we will return to them in Chapter 3 in our examination of juridical environmental constitutionalism.

Embedding substantive environmental rights is on the rise in common law countries, including former British colonies, as well as in Europe. Pedersen

---

[60] Bruch *et al.* "Constitutional Environmental Law", 166–76 (discussing constitutional interpretation in Tanzania, India, Pakistan, Bangladesh, Nepal, Colombia, Ecuador, Costa Rica, and some countries in Africa).

[61] Bruch *et al.* "Constitutional Environmental Law," 167–70. See generally, Vijayashri Sripati, "Human Rights in India – Fifty Years after Independence," *Denver Journal of International Law and Policy* 26, (1997): 100.

[62] See, e.g., Pettigrew, Harry W. "A Constitutional Right of Freedom from Ecocide." *Environmental Law* 2 (1971): 1–41; Klipsch, Ronald E. "Aspects of a Constitutional Right to a Habitable Environment: Towards an Environmental Due Process." *Indiana Law Journal* 49 (1974): 203.

observes: "Although the approach to a substantive right to the environment is perhaps one of caution on a regional level in Europe, a number of national constitutions recognize rights to a healthy environment. These constitutional provisions, while effective only on a national level, indicate that the issue is one of increasing importance throughout Europe."[63]

Other countries seem to have closed the door to constitutionalizing substantive environmental rights, including Austria,[64] Canada,[65] Germany,[66] the United States,[67] and some countries in the Caribbean.[68] Yet, remarkably, the constitutions of political subdivisions in some of these countries expressly provide a substantive right to a quality environment,[69] including five explicitly and eleven implicitly in the United States,[70] as well as some subnational units in Brazil, Canada, and Germany. On rare occasions, even nations that have

[63] See Pedersen, "European Environmental Human Rights," 108.

[64] See, e.g., Brandl and Bungert, "Constitutional Entrenchment," 23–52 (discussing proposed environmental rights amendments in Germany and Austria).

[65] See generally, Boyd, *Right to a Healthy Environment*, 61–6.   [66] *Ibid.*

[67] See Cramer, "Human Right to Information," 90 ("In America, protection of the environment has not yet become an inalienable constitutional right for citizens, though there are statutory protections for obtaining information *about* protection of the environment.") (emphasis in original); "[T]o capture a normative statement about the environment and plug it into the United States Constitution is simply a bad idea." Ruhl, "Metrics of Constitutional Amendments," 245, 252. He also notes that of "over ten thousand proposed amendments to the Constitution . . . [o]nly a handful have [succeeded,] and hence . . . there is little chance that an [environmental quality amendment] will ever find its way into the Constitution." Ruhl, "Metrics of Constitutional Amendments," 250–1.

> The U.S. Congress, which has enacted what are arguably the strongest environmental laws yet conceived, has, however, allowed each attempt to create an express individual right in environmental quality to languish. Congress' reluctance, in some significant part, may have to do with the structure of the federal-state government relationship, more than any specific objection to creation of an environmental right . . . Commentators have, therefore, pointed out that creation of a constitutional-environmental right would create structural questions with respect to basic notions of federalism, namely the establishment of federal plenary authority.
>
> Hill *et al.*, "Human Rights and the Environment," 389–90 (footnotes omitted).

See generally, Brooks, "A Constitutional Right," 1083; Craig, Robin Kundis. "Should There Be a Constitutional Right to a Clean/Healthy Environment?" *Environmental Law Report* 34(12) (2004): 11013.

[68] See Hill *et al.*, "Human Rights and the Environment," 381, n. 84 ("Caribbean constitutions generally have not addressed a right to a healthy environment.").

[69] For a discussion of the interconnectedness between human rights and the environment at the subdivision level, see generally Deimann and Dyssli, *Environmental Rights*.

[70] See Weiss, *International Environmental Law and Policy*, 416 (identifying Illinois, Hawaii, California, Florida, Massachusetts, Montana, Pennsylvania, Rhode Island, and Virginia). For a discussion of judicial application of fundamental environmental rights in state constitutions in the United States, see Tucker, "Constitutional Codification of an Environmental Ethic,"

adopted national environmental constitutionalism have subnational components that do so, too, such as Brazil. We will return to developments at the
subnational level in Chapter 7.

OTHER SUBSTANTIVE ENVIRONMENTAL RIGHTS

While express guarantees to a quality environment are the most common
exponent of national environmental constitutionalism, other approaches to
advancing substantive rights are fairly common as well. For example, about
30 constitutions provide for rights to water as a human or environmental right,
including at least one dozen countries that instantiate a human right to a fair
distribution of clean, safe, or potable water.[71] See Appendix G. South Africa's
constitution makes a strong commitment to acknowledging water as a fundamental human right by asserting an enforceable individual right to drinking
water.[72] Kenya's 2010 constitution follows this course.[73] Somalia's interim
constitution, which was adopted by a parliamentary majority in 2012, also
includes the human right to water and, Zimbabwe's amended constitution
includes a right to safe and potable drinking water. But in most other countries, the right to water must be inferred from other rights – such as the right to
life, to dignity, or to health – if it is to be recognized at all. Constitutional
engagement with water rights warrants further examination and is discussed as
an emerging issue in environmental constitutionalism in Chapter 6.

Less common are constitutionally recognized rights of nature that are
adopted for biocentric – rather than anthropocentric – ends. See Appendix F.
Thus far, Ecuador is the sole example of this approach. In 2008, it amended its
constitution to recognize that *nature itself* has enforceable rights. In four
extensive sections, the constitution spells out that "Nature, or Pachamama,
where life is reproduced and created, has the right to integral respect for her
existence, her maintenance, and for the regeneration of her vital cycles,

---

315–24. For an argument for devolving fundamental environmental rights to the states, see
Brooks, "A Constitutional Right", 1063.

[71] These are: Bolivia (Art. 16[I]), Colombia (Art. 366), the Democratic Republic of Congo
(Art. 48), Ecuador (Art. 12), Ethiopia (Art. 90[1]), Gambia (Art. 216[4]), the Maldives (Art. 23),
Panama (Arts. 110 and 118), Swaziland (Art. 215), Switzerland (Art. 76), Uganda (Arts. XIV[b]
and XXI), Uruguay (Art. 47), Venezuela (Arts. 127 and 304), and Zambia (Art. 112[d]). See Boyd,
Right to a Healthy Environment, 85.

[72] South Africa constitution, ch. 2, art. 27(1)(b): "Everyone has the right to have access to –
(b) sufficient food and water..."

[73] Constitution of Kenya, ch. 4, pt. 2, art. 43(1)(d): ("43. (1) Every person has the right – ... to
clean and safe water in adequate quantities.").

structure, functions, and evolutionary processes."[74] The section further confirms that this right is not merely hortatory in that it empowers each "person, community, people, or nationality"[75] to exercise public authority to enforce the right, according to normal constitutional processes.[76] Constitutional rights *of* – and not just *to* – nature is an emerging component of environmental constitutionalism, to which we return in Chapter 9.

ENVIRONMENTAL DUTIES AND RESPONSIBILITIES

A common variant couples substantive environmental rights with a corresponding individual duty to protect or defend the environment.[77] See Appendix B. Countries following this path include Armenia ("Everyone shall have the right to live in an environment favorable to his/her health and well-being and shall be obliged to protect and improve it in person or jointly with others."), Bénin ("Every person has the right to a healthy, satisfying and lasting environment and has the duty to defend it."), Cape Verde ("Everyone shall have the right to a healthy, ecologically balanced environment, and the duty to defend and conserve it."), and Guinea ("Every person has the right to a healthy and lasting environment and the duty to defend it. The State sees to the protection of the environment.").

Just what the legal significance is of constitutional provisions that impart environmental duties and/or responsibilities is hard to discern. In general, such provisions are not enforceable. Boyd observes: "It is unclear what legal purpose is served by the constitutionalization of individual environmental duties. These provisions appear to be symbolic, hortatory, and educational, confirming that everyone has a part to play protecting the environment from human-imposed damage and degradation."[78] And as detailed in Chapter 3, constitutional and apex courts have so far failed to engage these sorts of provisions.

STATE ENVIRONMENTAL DUTIES AND POLICIES

Several constitutions expressly advance environmental policy or impose duties upon the state or state actors. See Appendices C & D. Policy directives are intended to influence governmental decision making but are generally not

---

[74] Constitución Política de la República del Ecuador, title II, ch. 7, art. 71 and arts. 72–4.
[75] *Ibid.*, art. 71.   [76] *Ibid.*
[77] Boyd reports that "[i]ndividual responsibility for protecting the environment is provided in eighty-four constitutions." Boyd, *Right to a Healthy Environment*, 80.
[78] *Ibid.*

judicially enforceable. For example, Uruguay's constitution contains a policy directive that "[t]he protection of the environment is of common interest."[79] The Constitution of Qatar provides that "[t]he State endeavors to protect the environment and its natural balance, to achieve comprehensive and sustainable development for all generations."[80] The Constitution of the Philippines provides in part that "[t]he State shall protect and advance the right of the people to a balanced and healthful ecology in accord with the rhythm and harmony of nature."[81] The Chilean Constitution states that it is "the duty of the State to see to it that [environmental rights are] not affected and to control the preservation of nature."[82] Such constitutional policy directives can be instrumental in establishing environmental norms that loomed large, for example, in saving Greece's famed Acheloos River from being dammed beyond recognition.[83]

Environmental constitutionalism is also in play with constitutions under consideration in the aftermath of the Arab spring. For example, Egypt's draft constitution provides that: "Every person has the right to a healthy, undamaged environment. The state commits itself to the inviolability of the environment and its protection against pollution. It also commits itself to using natural resources in a way that will not harm the environment and to preserving the rights of all generations to it."[84] Even the constitutions of countries in waiting advert to the environment: Palestine's draft constitution commits the country to "striv[ing] to achieve a clean, balanced environment."[85] And Scotland's government, arguing for a change in status to a constitutional monarchy, has argued that "a constitutional convention should examine how principles on

---

[79] Constitución Política de la República Oriental del Uruguay de 1967 con las Modificaciones Hasta 1996, sec. II, ch. II, art. 47. In 2004, the constitution was amended to state that "water is a natural resource essential to life," and that access to piped water and sanitation services are "fundamental human rights." *Ibid.*

[80] Permanent Constitution of the State of Qatar, pt. II, art. 33.

[81] Constitution (1987), art. 16 (Philippines).

[82] Constitución Política de la República de Chile de 1980, ch. III, art. 19(8).

[83] See Houck, "Case of Sustainable Development," 286–7. See also, Houck, *Taking Back Eden*, 131–50 (Archeloos story, with pictures).

> In the absence of legislation, all the court had to work with was Article 24 of the Greek constitution, which stated opaquely that environmental protection was an "obligation of the state" and that the government should take "special measures" to conserve it. There was nothing about citizen lawsuits, impact assessment, or sustainability … The court took Article 24 and within a few years created a roadmap for environmental impact review, and strong protections for coastal areas, urban ecology, and other sensitive parts of the landscape – and the right of all Greek citizens to enforce them.

[84] Constitution of Egypt, art. 63 (draft).

[85] Third draft constitution for a Palestinian State, ch. 1 art. 15 (2003), available at www.mideastweb.org/palconstitution.htm

climate change, the environment and the sustainable use of Scotland's natural resources should be constitutionally protected to embed Scotland's commitment to sustainable development and responsible and sustained economic growth" and believes further that "a written constitution should include a constitutional ban on nuclear weapons being based in Scotland."[86]

Some environmental provisions specifically address certain types of activities that may be harmful to the environment. For example, several countries prohibit the disposal of nuclear or hazardous wastes or substances that are imported from another country, including the Dominican Republic ("The introduction, development, production, possession [*tenencia*], commercialization, transport, storage and use of chemical, biological and nuclear and agrochemical weapons [that are] internationally forbidden, is prohibited, as well as of nuclear residues [and] toxic and hazardous wastes."), Ecuador (similar), Haiti ("No one may introduce into the country wastes or residues of any kind from foreign sources."), Hungary ("No pollutant waste shall be brought into Hungary for the purpose of dumping."), Namibia ("The Government shall provide measures against the dumping or recycling of foreign nuclear and toxic waste on Namibian territory."), and Niger ("The transit, importation, storage, landfill, [and] dumping on the national territory of foreign pollutants or toxic wastes, as well as any agreement relating [to it] constitute a crime against the Nation, punished by the law.").

Other provisions combine miscellaneous policies and duties. See Appendix F. Some constitutions identify governmental responsibilities toward specific objects of the environment, including nature, animals, future generations, and the climate. These include those from Dominican Republic ("The formulation and execution, through the law, of a plan of territorial ordering that assures the efficient and sustainable use of the natural resources or the Nation, in accordance with the need of adaption to climate change, is [a] priority of the State."), Germany ("Mindful also of its responsibility toward future generations, the State protects also the natural bases of life and the animals within the framework of the constitutional order by legislation, and in accordance with law and justice, by executive and judicial power."), Lithuania ("The State shall concern itself with the protection of the natural environment, its fauna and flora, separate objects of nature and particularly valuable districts, and shall supervise the moderate utilization of natural resources as well as their restoration and augmentation."), and the Sudan ("The State shall not pursue any policy, or take or permit any action, which may adversely affect the

---

[86] The Scottish Government, *Scotland's Future*, 1.10.

existence of any species of animal or vegetative life, their natural or adopted habitat.").

The constitutions of other countries expressly restrain or restrict energy-related activities that could adversely affect the environment. See Appendix F. These include Brazil ("Power plants with nuclear reactors shall be located as defined in federal law and may not be installed otherwise."), the Dominican Republic ("The State shall promote, in the public and private sectors, the use of alternative and clean [*no contaminantes*] technologies and energy."), and Ecuador ("The State shall promote, in the public and private sectors, the use of environmentally clean technologies and nonpolluting and low-impact alternative sources of energy. Energy sovereignty shall not be achieved to the detriment of food sovereignty nor shall it affect the right to water.").

Some constitutions allow the government to elevate environmental values over others. Some allow the government to restrict private property rights in favor of environmental policies. These include Mauritius (making exceptions to the constitution's prohibition against the compulsory taking of property when: "(v) by reason of its being in a dangerous state or injurious to the health of human beings, animals, trees or plants"), and Mongolia ("The State shall have the right to . . . confiscate the land if it is used in a manner adverse to the health of the population, the interests of environmental protection and national security."). See Appendix E. Others elevate environmental values over the right to travel and engage in commerce, including Estonia ("The right to freedom of movement may be restricted only in the cases and in accordance with procedures established by law . . . to protect the environment."), and Madagascar ("The State guarantees the freedom of enterprise within the limits of respect for the general interest, the public order and the environment."). France's constitution requires environmental education and training ("Education and training on the environment shall contribute to the exercise of the rights and obligations defined by this Charter."). Chile's constitution even contains a "trump" card over all other rights in favor of the environment: "The law can establish specific restrictions on the exercise of certain rights or freedoms in order to protect the environment."

Most constitutions link environmental duties and rights. Boyd reports that all but six nations that guarantee substantive environmental rights constitutionally contain concomitant putative obligations for individuals and/or the government to protect the environment.[87] This suggests that rights and duties provisions enjoy a symbiotic relationship.

---

[87] Boyd, *Right to a Healthy Environment*, 80.

PROCEDURAL CONSTITUTIONAL ENVIRONMENTAL RIGHTS

The constitutions of about three dozen countries specifically recognize procedural rights in environmental matters, primarily to advance a human right to a quality environment, including Brazil, Bolivia, France, and the Ukraine, to name a few. See Appendix I. Such rights to information, participation, and access to justice in environmental matters are a modern constitutional innovation. These sorts of provisions appear to serve both human and environmental interests, and can advance democratic values.[88] For example, Kosovo's constitution provides that: "Recognizing the importance of creating a free, open and safe environment which facilitates the participation of all persons including all members of Communities in the process of establishing democratic institutions of self-government."[89]

Most of these constitutional procedural environmental rights provisions seem to be designed to help implement substantive environmental rights. Boyd maintains that with one exception every country to guarantee procedural environmental rights constitutionally contains a companion provision that guarantees a substantive right to a quality environment.[90] This suggests that procedural environmental rights in those countries are designed to complement substantive environmental rights. Brazil's constitution, for instance, protects the substantive right "to an ecologically balanced environment" but also imposes obligations on the government to "ensure the effectiveness of this right," including the obligation to demand and make public environmental impact studies.[91] The French constitutional bloc incorporates the 2004 Charter of the Environment, which guarantees that "every person has the right, under conditions and limits defined by law, to access information relative to the environment that is held by government authorities and to participate in the development of public

---

[88] See Onzivu, "International Environmental Law," 672 ("International human rights law and national constitutions provide for procedural rights that are instrumental in the protection of human health and the environment. These rights include freedom of association, freedom of information, public participation in decision-making processes, and access to justice and judicial review."); Cramer, "Human Right to Information," 74 ("The push for a fundamental human right to environmental protection is in turn inspiring demands for access to government documents and meetings that deal with environmental matters."); Bandi, Gyula. "The Right to Environment in Theory and Practice: The Hungarian Experience." *Connecticut Journal of International Law* 8 (1993): 450–65 (discussing the Hungarian constitution's public participation provisions); Hayward, *Constitutional Environmental Rights*, 200–03 (discussing procedural environmental rights in Africa and elsewhere).

[89] Constitution of Republic of Kosovo. Preamble available at www.kushtetutakosoves.info/?cid=2,246

[90] See Boyd, *Right to a Healthy Environment*, 65–7.

[91] Constitution of Brazil, title VII , ch. 6, art. 225.

decisions having an impact on the environment."[92] Procedural environmental rights are a fast-growing area of environmental constitutionalism warranting isolated examination, and are the subject of Chapter 8.

PRESUMPTIONS ABOUT ENFORCING CONSTITUTIONAL ENVIRONMENTAL RIGHTS

The most effective substantive environmental rights are those that are self-executing. Self-executing provisions may be enforced without the need for interceding legislative action. As Bruckerhoff says: "It is important for fundamental rights to be self-executing because enforcement of such rights should not depend on the legislative machinery. It can be particularly important for environmental rights to be self-executing because legislatures often do not provide sufficient implementing legislation."[93] Indeed, the whole point of entrenching a right is to ensure that the value remains protected even if (and especially when) a political majority does not support it.

Self-execution can be exhibited either structurally or syntactically. Substantive environmental rights provisions that appear structurally in a constitution alongside first generation constitutional rights are those most likely to be self-executing.[94] Some nations place substantive environmental rights among other first generation civil and political rights by designating them as an express "Right," or as a "Major," "Human," "Fundamental," "Basic," or "Guaranteed" right.

The constitutions of the majority of nations that have adopted substantive environmental rights seem to classify them as first order, self-executing rights. Countries in Central and Eastern Europe have led the way in this regard, including Albania,[95] Azerbaijan,[96] Belarus,[97]

---

[92] Chartre de l'environment (2004), art. 7, incorporated into the French constitution (1958) by the Préambule.

[93] Bruckerhoff, "Giving Nature Constitutional Protection," 627–8.

[94] See Hayward, *Constitutional Environmental Rights*, 93–128 (examining challenges of judicial enforcement of fundamental environmental rights); Bruckerhoff, "Giving Nature Constitutional Protection," 627–8.

[95] Albania constitution, pt. II ("The Fundamental Human Rights and Freedoms"), ch. IV ("Economic, Social and Cultural Rights and Freedoms"), art. 56 ("Everyone has the right to be informed about the status of the environment and its protection.").

[96] Azrbaycan Konstitusiya [Azer. Konst.] [Constitution], second part ("Major Rights, Freedoms, and Responsibilities") sec. 3 ("Principal Human Rights and Civil Liberties"), art. 39 ("[R]ight to live in a Healthy Environment.") (Azer.).

[97] Kanstytucyja Rèspubliki Belarus' [Kanst. Belarus.] [Constitution], sec. 2 ("The Individual, Society and the State"), art. 46 ("Everyone is entitled to a wholesome environment and to compensation for loss or damage caused by violation of this right.").

Bulgaria,[98] Chechnya,[99] Croatia,[100] Estonia,[101] Georgia,[102] Hungary,[103] Moldova,[104] Montenegro,[105] Romania,[106] Russia,[107] Serbia,[108] Slovakia,[109] Slovenia,[110] and Ukraine.[111] Most countries with constitutional substantive environmental rights in Africa also place them among first generation

[98] Konstitutsiya na Balgariya [Konst. Bulg.] [Constitution], ch. 2 ("Fundamental Rights and Duties of Citizens"), art. 55 ("Citizens have the right to a healthy and favorable environment . . .").

[99] Konstituciia Chechenskoj Respubliki [Konst. Chech. Ich.] [Constitution of Chechen Republic of Ichkeria], § 1, ch. 2, art. 39 ("Everyone has the right to a decent environment, reliable information about its condition and compensation for damage caused to their health or property as a result of ecological violations of the law.").

[100] Const. Ustav Republike Hrvatske [Constitution], ch. III ("Protection of Human Rights and Fundamental Freedoms"), pt. 3 ("Economic, Social, and Cultural Rights") art. 69 (Croat.) ("Everyone has the right to a healthy life.").

[101] Eesti Vabariigi põhiseadus [Constitution of the Republic of Estonia], ch. 2, § 53 ("Everyone shall be obligated to preserve the human and natural environment . . .").

[102] Constitution of Georgia, ch. 2, art. 37(3) ("Everyone shall have the right to live in a healthy environment . . .").

[103] A Magyar Köztársaság Alkotmánya [Constitution of Hungary], ch. I, art. 18 ("The Republic of Hungary recognizes and shall implement the individual's right to a healthy environment."); ch. XII, art. 70/D(1) ("Everyone living within the territories of the Republic of Hungary has the right to the highest possible level of physical and mental health."); ch. XII, art. 70/D(2) ("The State shall implement this right . . . through the protection of the . . . natural environment.").

[104] Moldova constitution, title II ("Fundamental Rights, Freedoms, and Duties"), ch. II ('Fundamental Rights and Freedoms'), art. 37(1) ("Every person has the right to an environment that is ecologically safe for life and health as well as to safe food products and household goods.").

[105] Const. (Mont.) sec. 2, art. 23 ("Everyone shall have the right to a sound environment. Everyone shall have the right to receive timely and full information about the status of the environment, to influence the decision-making regarding the issues of importance for the environment, and to legal protection of these rights."); art. 65 ("The state shall protect environment.").

[106] Constitutia României (Rom.) title II, ch. II, art. 35(1) ("The State recognizes the right of every person to a healthy, well-preserved and balanced environment.").

[107] Konstitutsiia Rossiikoi Federatsii [Konst. RF] [Constitution], ch. II ("Rights and Freedoms of Man and Citizen"), art. 42 ("Everyone shall have the right to a favorable environment . . .").

[108] Serbia constitution, pt. 2, art. 74 ("Everyone shall have the right to healthy environment and the right to timely and full information about the state of environment. Everyone, especially the Republic of Serbia and autonomous provinces, shall be accountable for the protection of environment. Everyone shall be obliged to preserve and improve the environment.").

[109] Ústava Slovenskej Republiky [Constitution] (Slovk.) pt. 2, ch. 6, art. 44(1) ("Every person has the right to a favorable environment.").

[110] Ústava Republike Slovenije [Constitution] (Slovenia) pt. 3, art. 72 ("Everyone has the right . . . to a healthy living environment.").

[111] Konstitutsiya Ukraini [Constitution] (Ukr.), ch. II ("Human and Citizens' Rights, Freedoms and Duties"), art. 50 ("Everyone has the right to an environment that is safe for life and health . . .").

rights, including Angola,[112] Bénin,[113] Burkina Faso,[114] Chad,[115] Congo,[116] Ethiopia,[117] Mali,[118] Niger,[119] South Africa,[120] Sudan,[121] Togo,[122] and the island nations of Cape Verde,[123] and Seychelles.[124] Countries in Central and South America[125] to do so include Argentina,[126]

---

[112] Angola constitution, pt. II, art. 24(1) ("All citizens shall have the right to live in a healthy and unpolluted environment.").

[113] La Constitution de la République du Bénin, title II ("Rights and Duties of the Individual"), art. 27 ("Every person has the right to a healthy, satisfying and lasting environment . . .").

[114] La Constitution du Burkina Faso, title I, ch. 4, art. 29 ("The right to a healthy environment is recognized.").

[115] Constitution de la République du Tchad (Chad), title II, ch. I, art. 47 ("Every person has the right to a healthy environment.").

[116] Constitution de la République Démocratique du Congo (Congo), title II, art. 35 ("Every citizen has the right to a healthy satisfying and durable environment and the duty to defend it. The State watches over the protection and conservation of the environment."). See also Constitution de la République Démocratique du Congo (Dem. Rep. Congo), title III, art. 53 ("All persons have the right to a healthy environment that is favorable to their development.").

[117] Federal Negarit Gazeta of the Federal Democratic Republic of Ethiopia [Constitution], ch. III ("Fundamental Rights and Freedoms"), pt. II ("Democratic Rights"), art. 44(1) ("All persons have the right to a clean and healthy environment.").

[118] La Constitution de la République du Mali, title I ("The Rights and Duties of the Human Person"), art. 15 ("Every person has the right to a healthy environment.").

[119] Constitution de la République du Niger du 18 Juillet 1999, title II ("On Rights and Duties of the Human Person"), art. 27 ("Each person has the right to a healthy environment.").

[120] South Africa constitution, ch. 2 ("Bill of Rights"), art. 24 ("Everyone has the right to an environment that is not harmful to their health or well-being; and to have the environment protected, for the benefit of present and future generations . . .").

[121] The Transitional Constitution of South Sudan, adopted in 2011, provides that "41. Every person or community shall have the right to a clean and healthy environment, . . . the obligation to protect the environment for the benefit of present and future generations, . . . [and] the right to have the environment protected for the benefit of present and future generations, through appropriate legislative action and other measures that: (a) prevent pollution and ecological degradation; (b) promote conservation; and (c) secure ecologically sustainable development and use of natural resources while promoting rational economic and social development so as to protect genetic stability and bio-diversity." It further provides that "All levels of government shall promote energy policies that will ensure that the basic needs of the people are met while protecting and preserving the environment."

[122] La Constitution de la IVe Republique Togolaise (Togo), title II, sec. 1, art. 41 ("Anyone has the right to a healthy environment.").

[123] Constituição da República Cabo Verde [Constitution] (Cape Verde), pt. II, title III, art. 72(1) ("Everyone shall have the right to a healthy, ecologically balanced environment . . .").

[124] La Constitution du République des Seychelles (Sey.), ch. III, pt. I ("Seychellois Charter of Fundamental Human Rights and Freedoms"), art. 38 ("[R]ecognises the right of every person to live in and enjoy a clean, healthy and ecologically balanced environment . . .").

[125] Ankersen, "Shared Knowledge," 820.

[126] Argentina constitution, pt. 1, ch. 2 ("New Rights and Guarantees"), art. 41 ("All residents enjoy the right to a healthy, balanced environment fit for human development, and by which productive activities satisfy current necessities without compromising those of future generations . . .").

Brazil,[127] Ecuador,[128] El Salvador,[129] Guatemala,[130] Honduras,[131] and Venezuela.[132] Western European countries that appear to recognize substantive environmental rights as rights of the first order include Belgium and France.[133,134] Countries in Asia to have done so include Kyrgyzstan and Mongolia.[135,136] Such structural placement makes it more likely that such provisions are self-executing and enforceable.

Other provisions are written in such a way as to leave little doubt that they are self-executing, enforceable, and subject to redress without the need for intervening state action. Notably, constitutions from the former Soviet Bloc make it clear that affected parties can recover compensation for violations of environmental rights, including Belarus ("Everyone is entitled to a wholesome environment and to compensation for loss or damage caused by violation of this right."), Chechnya ("Everyone has the right to favorable environmental surroundings . . . and to compensation for damage caused to his/her health or property through ecological violations of the law."), the Kyrgyz Republic ("Citizens of the Kyrgyz

---

[127] Constituição Federal [C.F.] [Constitution] (Brazil), title II ("Fundamental Rights and Guarantees"), ch. I, art. 5, para. LXXIII ("[A]ny citizen has standing to bring a popular action to annul an act injurious to the public patrimony or to the patrimony of an entity in which the State participates . . . to the environment . . ."). For a discussion of the extensive reach of Brazil's constitutional environmental provisions, see Tucker, "Constitutional Codification," 312–14.

[128] Constitución Política de la República del Ecuador, title III, ch. 5, sec. 1, art. 86 ("The State shall protect the right of the population to live in a healthy and ecologically balanced environment, that guarantees sustainable development.").

[129] Constitución de 1983, Reformas hasta 2003 incluídas de República de El Salvador, title II, ch. 2, sec. 1, art. 34 ("Every child has the right to live in familial and environmental conditions that permit his integral development, for which he shall have the protection of the State.").

[130] Constitucion de 1985 con las Reformas de 1993 (Guatemala.), title II, ch. 2, sec. 7, art. 93 ("The right to health is a fundamental right of the human being without any discrimination.").

[131] Constitucion Política de la République de Honduras 1982, title III, ch. 7, art. 145 ("The State shall maintain a satisfactory environment for the protection of everyone's health.").

[132] Constitución de 1999 República Bolivariana de Venezuela, title III, ch. IX, art. 127 ("Every person has a right to individually and collectively enjoy a life and a safe, healthy and ecologically balanced environment.").

[133] De Belgische Grondwet/La Constitution Belge/Die Verfassung Belgiens [Constitution] (Belg.) title II ("Belgians and Their Rights"), art. 23(4) ("Everyone has the right to lead a life worthy of human dignity . . . [including] the right to enjoy the protection of a healthy environment.").

[134] French constitution. 1958, title XVII ("Charter of the Environment"), art. 1 ("Everyone has the right to live in a balanced and health-friendly environment.").

[135] Constitution of Kyrgyzstan, sec. 1, ch. II, ("Citizens") sec. 3, ("Rights and Duties of a Citizen") art. 35(1) ("Citizens of the Kyrgyz Republic have the right to a favorable and healthy natural environment . . .").

[136] Mongol Ulsyn Ündsen Khuuli [Ündsen Khuuli] [Constitution] (Mong.) ch. II ("Human Rights and Freedom"), art. 16(1) ("The citizens of Mongolia shall enjoy . . . [t]he right to healthy and safe environment, and to be protected against environmental pollution and ecological imbalance.").

Republic have the right to a favorable and healthy natural environment and to compensation for the damage caused to health or property by the activity in the area of nature exploitation."), the Russian Federation ("Everyone shall have the right to a favorable environment . . . and to compensation for the damage caused to his or her health or property by ecological violations."), and Ukraine ("Everyone has the right to an environment that is safe for life and health, and to compensation for damages inflicted through the violation of this right.").

Structural placement or syntax can also suggest that some substantive environmental rights provisions may not be self-executing and enforceable. Rights that fall outside of the first order orbit are often described as second generation socioeconomic rights that are presumptively not self-executing. Such second order rights include education, food, health, shelter, and water. Constitutions that appear to relegate substantive environmental rights to this category include Chile,[137] Colombia,[138] Costa Rica,[139] East Timor,[140] Macedonia,[141] Mozambique,[142] Nicaragua,[143] Paraguay,[144] Poland,[145]

---

[137] Constitución Política de la República de Chile de 1980, ch. III ("Constitutional Rights and Duties"), art. 19(8) ("The right to live in an environment free from contamination.").

[138] Constitución Política de la República de Colombia de 1991, title II ("Rights, Guarantees, and Duties"), ch. III ("Collective Rights and the Environment"), art. 79 ("Every individual has the right to enjoy a healthy environment.").

[139] Constitución Política de la República Costa Rica, title V ("Social Rights and Guarantees"), art. 50 ("Every person has the right to a healthy and ecologically balanced environment . . .").

[140] Konstitusaun Du Timor-Leste [Constitution] (E. Timor), pt. II ("Rights, Duties, Liberties and Fundamental Guarantees"), title III ("Economic, Social and Cultural Rights and Duties"), art. 61(1) ("All have the right to a humane, healthy, and ecologically balanced environment and the duty to protect it and improve it for the benefit of the future generations.").

[141] Macedonia constitution, ch. 2 ("Fundamental Freedoms and Rights of the Individual and Citizen"), pt. 2 ("Economic, Social and Cultural Rights"), art. 43 ("Everyone has the right to a healthy environment to live in.").

[142] Mozambique constitution, pt. 1, ch. 4, art. 37 ("The State shall promote efforts to guarantee the ecological balance and the conservation and preservation of the environment for the betterment of the quality of life of its citizens."), pt. 2 ("Fundamental Rights, Duties and Freedoms"), ch. 1, art. 72 ("All citizens shall have the right to live in, and the duty to defend, a balanced natural environment.").

[143] Constitución Política de la República de Nicaragua [Cn.] [Constitution] title IV, ch. 3 ("Social Rights"), art. 60, La Gaceta [L.G.] January 9, 1987, as amended by Ley No. 330, Reforma Parcial a la Constitución Política de la Republica de Nicaragua, January 18, 2000, L.G. January 19, 2000 ("Nicaraguans have the right to live in a healthy environment.").

[144] Constitucion Politica del Paraguay de 1992, pt. I ("About Basic Principles, Rights, Duties, and Guarantees"), title II ("Rights, Duties, and Guarantees"), ch. I ("About Life and Environment"), sec. 2 ("About the Environment"), art. 7 ("Everyone has the right to live in a healthy, ecologically balanced environment.").

[145] Konstytucja Rzeczpospolitej Polskiej [Constitution] (Poland) ch. II ("Freedoms, Rights and Duties of Man and Citizens"), art. 71 ("The Republic of Poland . . . ensures the protection of the natural environment . . .").

Portugal,[146] Sao Tomé,[147] South Korea,[148] Spain,[149] and Turkey.[150] Such second order constitutional rights tend not to enjoy the same presumption of enforceability as do first order civil and political rights, particularly insofar as they are conceived as social or collective rather than individual rights.

Moreover, placing substantive environmental rights within preambles, among general provisions, or in statements of general policy may suggest something other than a self-executing right. Nations that recognize substantive environmental rights in this fashion include Afghanistan,[151] Algeria,[152] Comoros,[153] and Norway.[154] Even though such provisions are usually not justiciable, they can still wield tremendous influence over legislative, policy, and judicial interpretation.[155] For instance, while Cameroon's constitution recognizes environmental rights in its Preamble, it also states that the provision is "part and parcel" of the remainder of the constitution.[156]

But the constitutions of some countries are explicit that the right to a quality environment is not self-executing. The two most common variants require interceding state action, or are written so turgidly as to burden enforcement. First, enforceability in some countries seems to be conditioned on state action or implementation, rendering such rights unenforceable until executed by the state. Constitutions written in this vein include Finland ("The public authorities shall endeavor to guarantee for everyone the right to a healthy environment."),

---

[146] Constituição da República Portuguesa [Constitution] (Portugal) pt. 1 ("Fundamental Rights and Duties"), sec. 3 ("Economic, Social, and Cultural Rights and Duties"), ch. II ("Social Rights and Duties"), art. 66(1) ("Everyone has the right to a healthy and ecologically balanced human environment and the duty to defend it.").

[147] São Tomé and Príncipe constitution, pt. II, title III, art. 49(1) ("All have the right to housing and to an environment of human life ...").

[148] South Korea constitution, ch. II ("Rights and Duties of Citizens"), art. 35(1) ("All citizens shall have the right to a healthy and pleasant environment.").

[149] Constitución [C.E.] (Spain) title I, ch. III, art. 45(1) ("Everyone has the right to enjoy an environment suitable for the development of the person, as well as the duty to preserve it.").

[150] Türkiye Cumhuriyeti Anayasas' [Turkey Republic Constitution], pt. II, ch. III, art. 56 ("Everyone has the right to live in a healthy, balanced environment.").

[151] Constitution of Afghanistan, preamble. ("[E]nsuring a prosperous life and a sound environment for all those residing in this land ...").

[152] Constitution, title I, ch. V, art. 66 (Algeria) ("Every citizen has the duty to protect public property and the interests of the national collectivity and to respect the property of others.").

[153] Constitution of Comoros, preamble. ("[There is] the right ... to health ...").

[154] Kongeriget Norges Grundlov (Norway), pt. E ("General Provisions"), art. 110b ("Every person has a right to an environment that is conducive to health and to natural surroundings whose productivity and diversity are preserved.").

[155] Hill *et al.*, "Human Rights and the Environment," 382.

[156] Constitution of Cameroon, preamble. ("[E]very person shall have a right to a healthy environment.") and art. 65 ("The Preamble shall be part and parcel of this Constitution.").

Hungary ("Hungary shall recognise and enforce the right of every person to a healthy environment."), Maldives ("Every citizen [has] the following rights pursuant to this Constitution, and the State undertakes to achieve the progressive realisation of these rights by reasonable measures within its ability and resources: . . . (d) a healthy and ecologically balanced environment."), Morocco ("The State, the public establishments and the territorial collectivities work for the mobilization of all the means available [*disponibles*] to facilitate the equal access of the citizens to conditions that permit their enjoyment of the right . . . to the access to water and to a healthy environment."), Seychelles ("The State recognises the right of every person to live in and enjoy a clean, healthy and ecologically balanced environment."), and Slovenia ("Everyone has the right in accordance with the law to a healthy living environment."). Such wording likely dilutes the efficacy of these rights at inception.

Second, the wording of some provisions makes them inscrutable. For example, Burkina Faso's constitution employs the passive voice ("The right to a healthy environment is recognized.") rather than the more impactful active voice (e.g., "Everyone has the right to a healthy environment."). And the Central African Republic's provision seems to suggest that substantive rights exist only to the extent that they are subsequently recognized ("The Republic guarantees to every citizen the right . . . to a healthy environment."). Syntactical imprecision can thwart effective implementation and exacerbate built-in reluctance to enforce substantive environmental rights provisions because "countervailing economic and social factors, such as lack of political will or resource constraints, are likely to affect nations' decisions to enforce environmental rights provisions."[57] Conversely, "the constitutional provision itself can, if properly written, help resolve some of the principal questions surrounding the enforcement of environmental rights by directing the judiciary to construe the environmental provision as an individually enforceable right."[58]

The variety of constitutional provisions, aiming to protect different aspects of the environment with a range of scaffolding and enforcement mechanisms, attests to the growth of environmental constitutionalism throughout the world in the past four decades. But the value of constitutional guarantees is measured not only by their textual manifestations but perhaps even more importantly by the extent to which the rights are vindicable by the nation's courts. In Part II, we turn our attention to the question of judicial acceptance of these rights, examining whether, to what extent, and why (or why not) courts are taking environmental constitutional rights seriously.

[57] Abate, "Climate Change," 27.
[58] Bruckerhoff, "Giving Nature Constitutional Protection," 637.

PART II

VINDICATION AND PRACTICES IN ENVIRONMENTAL CONSTITUTIONALISM

3

Adjudicating environmental constitutionalism

It is possible that the globalization of constitutional and environmental law will provoke a race to the top, with different countries adopting, adapting and building on the precedents established elsewhere.

David R. Boyd[1]

[I]t has fallen frequently to the judiciary to protect environmental interests, due to sketchy input from the legislature, and laxity on the part of the administration.

Chief Justice B.N. Kirpal, Supreme Court of India[2]

As we have seen, environmental constitutionalism has evolved from an inchoate notion rooted in philosophical conceptions of human rights into a vibrant norm rooted textually in constitutions throughout the globe. This chapter addresses the extent to which courts have engaged constitutional guarantees to a quality environment.

Courts are a valuable if not a necessary exponent of preserving essential fairness in the political process, which cannot be accomplished by the political process itself. Courts are necessary because they can help draw attention to interests that are otherwise likely to go unprotected either because they are diffuse, such as environmental rights, or because they lack effective and powerful constituencies, such as the rights of poor or marginalized communities, which are often environmental in nature. Judicial attention to such rights can contribute to ways of thinking and talking about them so that they

[1] Boyd, David R. "The Implicit Constitutional Right to Live in a Healthy Environment," *Review of European Community and International Environmental Law* 20(2) (July, 2011): 171–9.

[2] Kirpal, B.N., Chief Justice, Supreme Court of India, M.C. Bhandari Memorial Lecture: Environmental Justice in India (2002), *in* (2002) 7 SCC 1, available at www.ebc-india.com/lawyer/articles/2002v7a1.htm

resonate within the political community, not only tapping into the values that are already held, but helping to foster awareness of important new values. An engaged judiciary is fundamental to environmental constitutionalism reaching its potential: judges are the ultimate vanguards of the rights discussed throughout this book. Yet convincing a court to animate a constitutional provision – especially one rooted in environmental constitutionalism – is no mean feat. Constitutional adjudication is complex. It invariably involves orbiting issues of text, costs, equities, and political fallout. While these issues arise in most forms of constitutional litigation, they are magnified in cases involving environmental constitutionalism because environmental claims are conceptually distant from the traditional form of constitutional litigation, which is typically specific to a discrete set of facts that indicate injury to a particular claimant and can be supported by clear evidence. Environmental rights, by contrast, can be broad and their contours vague because environmental problems can creep into so many different areas of life: a single leak may pollute the water and the air, prevent farming, poison the water, cause disease, and produce social insecurity. When the injuries can be so wide-ranging, it can be challenging to find the nugget of a violation of a particular right and to define a particular remedy.

As we explain, judicial receptivity of environmental constitutionalism belies predictable juridical patterns. There is wide variability in constitutional structure and traditions, judicial systems, sophistication of parties, acceptance of judicial outcomes, funding, cultural customs, timing of enactment, and societal norms. Each of these affects judicial outcomes. This variability makes it infeasible to provide unitary predictions about judicial receptivity at the national, state, and local levels. Rather than prognosticate, this book strikes a descriptive chord.

What we see is that environmental constitutional jurisprudence is gaining salience around the globe. In India and neighboring countries, and throughout Latin America, for instance, courts are increasingly vindicating rights in a wide variety of settings, from mining to water and air pollution. And new rights are continually being recognized. In Ecuador, in the few years since the constitution recognized the rights of nature, judicial recognition of the idea of rights pertaining to and for the benefit of nature itself has begun to take root in society, so that invocations of the rights of nature by both politicians and the public are gaining salience within the culture. This helps to spread knowledge and understanding throughout the population about issues relating to environmental protection in its many manifestations, as it affects people's lives, health, dignity, and culture. This in turn makes public officials and private actors more likely to comply with environmental norms, ultimately even without the threat of litigation.

This chapter examines judicial engagement of constitutionally embedded environmental rights provisions. It first examines the myriad challenges presented by adjudicating claims rooted in environmental constitutionalism, including textual interpretation, costs, balancing, and judicial boundaries. It then bores into just how constitutional and other apex courts have received such claims. We conclude that, while some courts have avoided engaging environmental constitutionalism, there is noticeable and steady progress toward recognition of environmental rights as independent, dependent, derivative, or dormant rights in courts throughout the world. Moreover, even when courts have not accepted that a constitutional environmental right has been contravened, the mere fact that such arguments are being made and considered augments the attention that constitutional environmental rights receive in public discourse. And this, in itself, can meaningfully contribute to the success of environmental claims in the future. The result is that, collectively, courts will continue to play a necessary role in the vindication of environmental constitutionalism worldwide.

We also conclude that there is utility in comparing judicial engagement of substantive rights to a quality environment across the globe. As courts become more aware of what their peers are doing, this momentum toward receptivity of environmental constitutionalism is likely to increase.[3]

CHALLENGES IN ADJUDICATING ENVIRONMENTAL RIGHTS

Claims seeking to vindicate individual rights to a quality environment engender unavoidable challenges. We identify some of these problems here in order to foreground the challenges that courts face when they confront constitutional environmental claims; in later chapters, we explore how courts have responded to these challenges. First, courts need to develop or interpret new concepts and vocabulary. Does the noun "environment" mean human environment, natural environment, or both? And what environmental outcome does the qualifier – "quality," "healthful," "sound," "clean," "beneficial," "adequate," etc. – demand? Is a "quality" environment better than a "sound" environment? What does a fundamental right to a quality environment entail? And how might a judge recognize an infraction, identify who is responsible, and impart remedies? The applications of these provisions seem limitless, ranging from whether a fundamental environmental right

---

[3] See generally, Slaughter, "Judicial Globalization" and "A Typology of Transjudicial Communication."

engenders a right to potable water to whether they can protect a population from the effects of climate change.

Second, even the usual hurdles of litigation are often exacerbated in constitutional environmental cases. Foremost is that constitutional litigation is expensive, even in a prevailing effort. And losing a case can result in economic catastrophe, especially under systems that use the "loser pays" approach that requires the unsuccessful party to pay the prevailing party's litigation expenses. Yet, those most affected by environmental degradation tend to be the least able to pay for defending it. Constitutional environmental rights, therefore, can be out of reach to the vast majority of individuals who might otherwise seek to vindicate them. Moreover, litigating constitutional environmental rights requires a high degree of competence due to technical complexities and the difficulty of demonstrating causation. These issues are made all the more acute when considering that those resisting such claims often enjoy superior funding, familiarity with the judicial process, and access to power.

Third, vindicating environmental rights typically presents fundamental questions of policy choices. In some ways, environmental rights are similar to other social and economic rights that are routinely vindicated in the world's courts in that remedying their violation often entails expenditure of significant resources. But environmental rights are different in that they often pit human rights claims against each other, such as when an industry closure improves water quality at the expense of jobs, or when the cost of expensive equipment to alleviate air pollution is borne by consumers or employees. Protecting the environment can help preserve the way of life for some, but it can impair the way of life for others.

Interpreting constitutional text

Constitutional provisions are often enacted with little if any guidance on threshold questions. They typically have little or no drafting history, and they tend to leave much unsaid in the text itself. Save some exceptions, there is little evidence of the intent of the drafters of these provisions that would provide guidance to their interpreters.[4] Rarely is it clear, for instance, whether the right is meant to be self-executing or requires implementing legislation,

---

[4] The lower court in the Ecuadorian rights of nature case constitutes one exception, because it quotes at length from the speech of Alberto Acosta, President of the Constituent Assembly, to understand more fully the purpose of constitutionalizing the rights of nature. See *Wheeler c. Director de la Procuraduria General Del Estado de Loja Juicio*, No. 11121-2011-0010 [hereinafter *Wheeler*], available at http://blogs.law.widener.edu/envirolawblog/2011/07/12/ecuadorian-court-recognizes-constitutional-right-to-nature

whether it imposes horizontal obligations on private entities or just on state actors, whether it is intended to justify the imposition of damages (including punitive damages) or solely equitable relief, whether it is meant to operate retroactively or not, and many other issues that invariably arise in constitutional litigation. Any of these interpretations is possible under most constitutional environmental provisions, but they obviously involve dramatically different types of inquiries, and they place courts in the vortex of very different types of constitutional controversies. At bottom, environmental constitutionalism requires judges to be grammarians, deconstructing nouns, verbs, predicates, subjects and objects, deciding what a "right" to a "quality" "environment" means, to whom it applies, and what to do about it. Each of these choices can have wide-ranging consequences that can affect the health and dignity of individuals, the lives of communities, the health of ecosystems, and potentially national economies and political outcomes.

Noun: environment

There is inherent lack of certainty about what the "environment" entails and how a meaningful conception of the environment can be incorporated into the structure of constitutional adjudication. Unlike specific interests like housing or medical care, the "environment" may encompass everything, and almost everything that happens in society can implicate the environment. The Chilean Supreme Court has recognized the potential reach of the term:

> [T]he environment ... is everything which naturally surrounds us and that permits the development of life, and it refers to the atmosphere as it does to the land and its waters, to the flora and fauna, all of which comprise nature, with its ecological systems of balance between organisms and the environment in which they live.[5]

Other courts have also construed "environment" broadly, invoking it in disparate circumstances. The Kenyan High Court held that the environment is the physical landscape of a people's history and future.[6] The Nepal Supreme Court required environmental protection for an object of religious, cultural, and historical importance.[7] Other courts have found the environment is not

---

[5] *Pedro Flores et al. v. Codelco, División Salvador.* No. Rol. 2.052, at 259 (Copiaco Court of Appeals, June 23, 1988); *Pedro Flores y Otros v. Corporacion Del Cobre, Codelco, División Salvador.* No. Rol. 12.753 FS. 641, at 259 (Supreme Court of Chile, July 28, 1988).

[6] *Ogiek People v. District Commissioner.* Case No. 238/1999 (Kenya High Court, March 23, 2000) (Indigenous Rights to Tinet Forest).

[7] *Advocate Prakash Mani Sharma for Pro Public v. His Majesty Government Cabinet Secretariat and Others.* WP 2991/1995 (Nepal Supreme Court, Joint Bench, 1997.06.09).

the physical space itself but the animals that live in forests and oceans.[8,9] "Environment" may include not only what is natural and pristine, but what has been built into the environment over time or uses in some way the air, water, and soil, including pipelines, dams, electrical transmission wires, bore-holes, and so on.

If the environment is everything around us, the constitutional environmental injuries that plaintiffs may claim are correspondingly expansive and diverse. In *Minors Oposa*, the Philippine Supreme Court recognized the difficulty of giving meaningful boundaries to the constitutional mandate of "a balanced and healthful ecology":

> The list of particular claims which can be subsumed under this rubric appears to be entirely open ended: prevention and control of emission of toxic fumes and smoke from factories and motor vehicles; of discharge of oil, chemical effluents, garbage and raw sewage into rivers, inland and coastal waters by vessels, oil rigs, factories, mines and whole communities; of dumping of organic and inorganic wastes on open land, streets and thorough-fares; failure to rehabilitate land after strip-mining or open-pit mining; kain-gin or slash-and-burn farming; destruction of fisheries, coral reefs and other living sea resources through the use of dynamite or cyanide and other chemicals; contamination of ground water resources; loss of certain species of fauna and flora; and so on.[10]

A degraded environment may affect people's lives, dignity, health, housing, access to food and water, and livelihood, or it may affect no human interest but the environment itself. Or, at the other extreme, cases may arise in which there is little effect on the environment at all, such as when a court determines questions of access to water where it is limited not by environmental conditions but by political and business interests, such as in a South African case involving the provision of free water to those who could not afford to pay. In general, the cases do not readily distinguish between environmental and human harms. This doctrinal fluidity may be due in part to the underdevelopment of the law, or it may be due to the interlinked nature of the harms themselves. Access to drinking water is a human right unrelated to environmental dimensions as long

---

[8] *Greenwatch v. Uganda Wildlife Authority*. Miscellaneous Application No. 92 of 2004 (High Court of Uganda in Kampala, 2004) (arising from Miscellaneous Cause No. 15 of 2004).

[9] *Pedro Flores y Otros v. Corporacion Del Cobre* (Chile).

[10] *Minors Oposa*, 175 (Philippines, 1993; Feliciano, J., concurring). By contrast, the concurring justice in the *Oposa* case expressed significant reservations about the lawsuit as it went forward on remand: "My suggestion is simply that petitioners must, before the trial court, show a more specific legal right – a right cast in language of a significantly lower order of generality than Article II (15) of the Constitution …" *Ibid.*, 203.

as there is sufficient supply; it devolves into an environmental right when it becomes scarce (perhaps due to desertification) or polluted (perhaps in violation of environmental laws).

With this broad conception of the environment in mind, it is easy to see why admitting, or rather denying, particular claims is challenging. With some exceptions – including subnational constitutions in Brazil, for example – constitutions seldom if ever delimit the scope of environmental protection or the types of actions that may be pursued in courts. Hence, courts are left to define for themselves the boundaries of their own authority, an exercise that tends to hinder judicial activation of environmental constitutionalism.

Adjective: healthy, balanced or quality (environment)

The adjectives that drafters around the globe have used to qualify the meaning of the "environment" seldom elucidate it or mitigate the interpretive challenges: more often, they exacerbate the problem by adding a level of vagueness. What satisfies the constitutional requirement of a "quality," "safe," "healthy," "productive," or "balanced" environment? How does a court decide when that standard has been achieved? Constitutional provisions that contain compound adjectives add to the confusion. The Philippine constitution, for example, requires the State to "protect and advance the right of the people to a balanced and healthful ecology."[11] Does "healthful" entail balanced or does it impose an independent requirement? The challenges mount when one considers that human activity has already inexorably altered virtually all aspects of the "environment." In the industrialized or industrializing world, how "clean" must the environment be to meet the constitutional standard? And should a court determine what to weigh to determine whether an environment is "balanced"?

Beyond the problem of measurement is the question of attribution. If "healthy" modifies the environment, then the right would extend to cases involving environmental degradation *per se*, regardless of its effect on humans. This would include cases requiring the clean-up of beaches of Chañaral, Chile, for instance, where copper tailing wastes had been deposited for 50 years, destroying marine life.[12] In *Pedro Flores*, the Chilean Supreme Court observed:

> [T]he daily accumulation of thousands of tons of contaminants by whose fast and silent chemical action the ecology, along the coast, is destroyed, producing the ecological destruction of all forms of marine life in hundreds of

[11] Philippine constitution, art. II, sec. 16.
[12] *Pedro Flores y Otros v. Corporacion Del Cobre* (Chile).

square kilometers ... a devastation that blossoms over the whole coastal area of the National Park Pan de Azúcar, with which dies a piece of Chile.[13]

When this is the standard, the case would center on whether the environment itself is healthy, not on whether the environmental degradation induced any harm to human beings.

But in most cases, the courts consider a "healthy environment" in the opposite way – as relating to the health of the local population, not of the environment. Sometimes the anthropocentric nature of the right is justified or even demanded by the constitutional text itself. For instance, it is clear in the Turkish constitution that the purpose of protecting the environment is to benefit people, not ecology: "Each individual has the right to live in a healthy and balanced environment ... The State must provide centralised health institutions and organise related services, so that people's lives are protected, people can continue to live in a physical and mental health, saving human and material energy, increasing efficiency and developing cooperation."[14] Likewise, the Peruvian constitution creates the right "to peace, tranquility, enjoyment of leisure time and to rest, as well as to a balanced and appropriate environment for the development of his life." Thus, in a Peruvian case against an American corporation operating a lead smelter, it was sufficient to show evidence that the health of the children in the local community was severely impacted, regardless of any attendant degradation to the environment itself.[15]

More often, courts blend human and ecological impacts because the text itself is ambiguous. The Argentinian constitution, for instance, states that "[a]ll inhabitants are entitled to the right to a healthy and balanced environment fit for human development in order that productive activities shall meet present needs without endangering those of future generations; and shall have the duty to preserve it."[16] "Healthy" may relate to human health but "balanced" surely qualifies the environment, so in the landmark case requiring the clean-up of the Matanza-Riachuelo river basin, for example, the evidence and

---

[13] *Pedro Flores et al. v. Codelco* (Chile), translated in *Georgetown International Law Review* 2 (1989): 251, 253 (Claudia C. Bohorquez trans.).

[14] Türkiye Cumhuriyeti Anayasas' [Turkey Republic Constitution] pt. II, ch. III, art. 56, quoted in *Senih Özay v. Ministry of the Environment, Ankara and Eurogold Madencilik AS*. Ref. No. 1996/5477; Ruling No. 1997/2311 (Sixth Chamber, Higher Administrative Court, Turkey, May 13, 1997) [hereinafter *Senih Özay* (Turkey, 1997)], translated in *International Environmental Law Report* 4 (1997): 452, reprinted in Kravchenko and Bonine, *Human Rights*, 90–1.

[15] *Sentencia De Pablo Miguel Fabián Martínez Y Otros*, EXP. N.º 2002–2006-PC/TC (Peru Constitutional Tribunal).

[16] Argentine constitution, pt. I, ch. II, art. 41.

discussion of harm to the water itself and harm to the people who live near it were inextricable. The lines between human and environmental health may be imperceptible and incremental, but real nonetheless – lending credence to the charge that the boundaries of the environment are virtually impossible to discern.

Object: right

Provided a court can discern just what it means to have a "quality environment," how is it to determine whether one has a right to have it? How can one have a "right" to something that *is*, and that is all-encompassing, eternal, and yet ever-changing? Rights are not interests that an individual holds, but ways to structure relationships – among people within a legal community and between people and the state, as Nedelsky argues. It is apt, then, to constitutionalize environmental rights to help structure those relationships insofar as the environment is concerned. Environmental rights, as we have seen, structure the relationships between present and future generations, by limiting what the former can do to the latter, as well as the contemporaneous relationship among people. Environmental rights also structure the relationship between neighbors, for instance, as they regulate how a property owner might use his land, or between upstream and downstream users of water. Courts, then, have an important role to play in mediating the relationships that are described and structured by constitutional environmental rights.

In particular, what does it mean to have a "right" to a particular quality environment, the way one might have a right to equal treatment or due process? There are no generally accepted standards for identifying or vindicating these interests *as rights* in part because, in straddling every familiar category of rights, environmental constitutionalism defies easy classification.[17]

Environmental rights hybridize human rights and environmental protection, as Chapter 1 explains. Environmental rights partake of human rights as well as non-human rights, protecting such values as biodiversity and nature itself. As a human right, the environment can be protected through civil and political rights of participation and access to information, but it can also be protected as a social, economic, and even cultural right. Environmental rights

[17] See Hayward, *Constitutional Environmental Rights*, 25–58 (making a case for a human right to an "adequate environment"); Hill *et al.*, "Human Rights and the Environment, 361 "([W]hile there appears to be a growing trend favoring a human right to a clean and healthy environment – involving the balancing of social, economic, health, and environmental factors – international bodies, nations, and states have yet to articulate a sufficiently clear legal test or framework so as to ensure consistent, protective application and enforcement of such a right.").

can be collective or individual and they can apply to the majority or to a discrete, insular, and politically powerless minority. They can be treated as immediately enforceable or realized progressively over time, according to a legislative plan and limited by the availability of fiscal resources. They can be implicit or explicit, procedural or substantive, and they can be amenable to judicial review or immune to it. They can be positive or negative or both (sometimes in the same case). They can be remedied injunctively or through compensation or declaration, for violations occurring in the past, as well as for harms as yet unknown and to people as yet unborn. In some ways, remedying environmental harms is long overdue, and yet the primary beneficiaries of environmental rights are those in the next generations. Environmental rights define the relationship between people and the world we live in, though invariably in broad and amorphous terms without clear foci or boundaries.

So how do courts give content to the concept of environmental rights without allowing them to swallow up every other right? One approach, which borrows from the discourse at the international level, is to limit the reach of environmental rights to already accepted human rights.[18] Environmental constitutionalism has pushed the conventional limits of this approach in two directions. First, national courts are recognizing an ever-increasing number of constitutional human rights claims, and many of these have been held to touch on environmental phenomena. The Constitutional Court of South Africa, for instance, has held that the right to housing, which may be more readily amenable to enforcement than environmental rights *per se*, may be violated by inattention to environmental problems.[19] Even when constitutions do not specifically enumerate particular rights, courts have expanded the scope of interests that constitute violations of familiar human rights by recognizing, for instance, that environmental degradation can constitute a violation of privacy and family life or that esthetic and recreational environmental interests are essential to enjoying a dignified existence. As the Supreme Court of Pakistan has said: "The Constitution guarantees dignity of man and also right to life . . .

---

[18] Abate, "Climate Change", 10, on environmental constitutional rights ("Existing sources of domestic and international law embrace a human-centered approach to environmental protection and recognize the connection between human rights and environmental protection. These mechanisms can serve as a viable foundation upon which to build a new system to recognize and protect international environmental human rights."); Onzivu, "International Environmental Law," 667 ("An emerging right to a healthy environment favors the protection of public health. This is because such a right is viewed as anthropocentric and ecocentric, supporting environmental protection for both public health and intrinsic or aesthetic reasons.").

[19] *Pheko v. Ekurhuleni Metropolitan Municipality*. Case CCT 19/11 [2011] ZACC 34 (recognizing that the right to housing and to dignity protect against forced eviction of a community notwithstanding the naturally occurring sinkhole in the area).

and if both are read together, question will arise whether a person can be said to have dignity of man if his right to life is below bare necessity like without proper food, clothing, shelter, education, health care, clean atmosphere and unpolluted environment."[20] Second, courts have expanded the range of putative beneficiaries by including not only property owners but also non-traditional rights holders, including neighbors, communities, and future generations. As this body of law expands, there are very few interests of any consequence that remain outside the framework of constitutional human rights. Still, the environmental interest would have to be seen as an incident of an already recognized human right.

A slightly less anthropocentric option is explicitly to recognize environmental rights *as* a human right, so that environmental harms do not have to fit neatly into the other human rights boxes.[21] This view reflects an international environmental law approach and has been incorporated into constitutions throughout the world. This also ensures that environmental values are given at least as much weight as other constitutional values, and perhaps more than some,[22] and more than non-constitutional values such as development or some property interests.

An even less anthropocentric approach involves a class of rights somewhere between human rights and rights of nature that permit humans to commence constitutional environmental claims to protect nature or wildlife. A final approach would entirely reject anthropocentrism and recognize instead the rights of nature, as Ecuador and Bolivia have recently done and as may be spreading to other regions of the world. To vindicate these rights, it is not necessary to refer at all to human interests or rights; rather, the harm to be vindicated is the violation to nature itself.

---

[20] *Shelhla Zia* v. WAPDA (Pakistan, February 12, 1994) (finding that "a person is entitled to protection of law from being exposed to hazards of electromagnetic fields or any other such hazards which may be due to installation and construction of any grid station, any factory, power station or such like installations" (at para. 12). See also *Francis Coralie* v. *Administrator, Union Territory of Delhi and Others*. Writ. Pet. No. 3042 of 1980 (Supreme Court of India, January 13, 1981).

[21] Shelton, "Human Rights and the Environment," 163 [hereinafter Shelton II] ("Moreover, recognizing a right to environment could encompass elements of nature protection and ecological balance, substantive areas not generally protected under human rights law because of its anthropocentric focus."); Bruckerhoff, "Giving Nature Constitutional Protection," 646 ("A less anthropocentric interpretation of constitutional environmental rights could be one, albeit small, component of national and international efforts to protect the wonders of nature for us and for the benefit of our children.").

[22] See the *Wheeler* case noting that environmental rights should prevail over other constitutional rights.

All four models are viable and all present conceptual and practical challenges. These are outlined here and explored in detail in later chapters.

Subject: proper litigants

Few constitutional texts identify the intended beneficiaries of the environmental right, which presents courts with yet another open-ended challenge. Conventional provisions relating to both civil and political rights and socioeconomic rights are designed to protect the population of the nation or some cohort thereof (e.g., ethnic minorities, criminal defendants). These individuals or groups are the bearers of the rights and the putative litigants who would enforce those rights. The putative beneficiaries of environmental constitutionalism, however, are often not obvious. For example, under a directive principle of state policy, the Indian Constitution requires the state to "endeavour to protect and improve the environment and to safeguard the forests and wild life of the country."[23] This protection seems to be as much for the benefit of the citizens as for the wildlife and even the forests themselves. But who can sue if the wildlife is not safeguarded? This is not only a question of standing (which is addressed in more detail in Chapter 4) but of the nature of the right and purpose of judicial intervention into the policy-making authority of the state. Is the court empowered to protect the flora and fauna or only to protect the people of the nation? Is a government constitutionally obligated to legislate for the benefit of the rivers, or may it limit its portfolio to helping the citizens directly? Can a constitution protect non-human interests?

If vindicating environmental rights does not require harm to humans, it is hard to square with the concept of a constitutional right. A plaintiff would be complaining about a bad state of affairs, like suing over the global financial crisis or the prevalence of cancer. If it does require harm to humans, then it starts to look more like a constitutional (or indeed any kind of common law) claim, but the difficulty of proof increases with each additional required showing. While it may not require significant litigation resources to prove that dumping toxic waste has occurred, it may be very difficult to prove that such dumping has increased or will increase the incidence of cancer in the local community, or that it caused a particular plaintiff's illness. The problem is magnified when litigation seeks to vindicate the rights of future generations; how can future generations be "made whole" to use the common legal remedial standard? Constitutional texts typically shed little light on these questions respecting beneficiaries.

---

[23] India constitution, art. 48A. 1976. Forty-second Amendment.

These difficult questions of public policy may, in some instances, even require recalibrating the boundaries between the public and private spheres. While some governments are held responsible for the environmental degradation caused by their licensees, some corporations are required to take on public goods like environmental clean-up. Environmental litigation may often in fact invert the normal expectations relating to the roles of public and private parties. Whereas traditional constitutional rights litigation pits the private individual against the public authority, environmental litigation often pits members of the public against a private entity (thus invoking the principle of the horizontal application of constitutional rights and obligations). Moreover, in many of these cases, private individuals are asserting public rights, whereas the government is facilitating private gain.[24] As a result, environmental litigation is increasingly forcing courts to adjust long-held views about the proper allocation of public and private power.

Identifying breaches

Typically, a constitutional violation exists when a government actor has impaired a person's ability to exercise the full scope of his or her rights – when, for instance, a person is unable to speak freely or where he or she is treated unequally to those who are similarly situated. But identifying the nature of the violation in environmental rights is a quixotic task. First, some environmental degradation is inevitable, so the baseline is not maximal enjoyment of the right but something less than that. No defendant can be held liable for air that is not pure or for the use of some non-renewable resources the way it can be held liable for even a small infringement of a traditional constitutional right. Indeed, most environmental law (including the principles underlying the public trust doctrine and sustainable development) is premised on the principle that some nature is to be consumed by humans – just not too much nor too selfishly. As a result, constitutional environmental claims, unlike other human rights, are necessarily limited by other important interests: whereas courts typically are not concerned about overprotecting speech or demanding too much equality, excessive environmental protection is often seen as derogating from economic development, the rights of property owners, or other significant social values.

---

[24] See, e.g., *ibid.*; *Minors Oposa*, 173 (Philippines 1993) (involving government-issued timber licenses); Kravchenko and Bonine, *Human Rights*, 79 (referring to Hungary helping to sell off forests to private interests).

Another challenge in implementing environmental constitutionalism is to identify the actual harm that has been done. Establishing causation can be problematic. Sometimes, this problem can be operationalized as a choice between human rights and environmental rights, although in the concrete context of litigation even these classifications do not answer all questions. In all too many cases, divining the line between a problem and a cognizable injury – identifying when the proper use of river water becomes an abuse, or when the release of toxins becomes injurious to public health – requires courts to balance equities with little if any prescriptive guidance. This problem is magnified with the growing number of claims relating to climate change, of which there is abundant evidence, but the evidence tying it to specific harms suffered by specific humans within a specific nation is much more tenuous. Usually, something more is needed to turn a misfortune into a claim.

Costs and benefits

Costs also exacerbate judicial recognition of environmental constitutionalism. Civil and political rights, like the right to free speech, typically cost little to enforce. For example, rights like the right to vote or due process can implicate structural costs that are not usually significant in the context of a national budget, particularly when considered as simply part of the cost of democracy, and essential parts at that. And, although there are occasional exceptions to this, social and economic rights are usually seen as well worth the costs: providing a health benefit to a class of patients or improving educational opportunities for a group of students produces palpable and indispensable benefits.

Environmental protection, by contrast, is problematic on both sides of the cost-benefit ledger. It can be far more costly than the vindication of other rights both in terms of outlays, including the cost of cleaning up toxic sites or large bodies of water, and in terms of lost revenues, when, for instance, a mining or timber license is canceled or tax revenues from industrial development are forgone. At the same time, environmental constitutionalism can be less palpably beneficial: saving a virgin forest may produce psychic benefits for the population as a whole or for future generations, but it is unlikely to benefit any particular individual or group of individuals enough to be appreciated, particularly at reelection time. As hard as it is to prove illness from the fact of environmental violations, it is much harder to attribute good health to environmental protection. The Supreme Court of Nepal has acknowledged this challenge: "It is beyond doubt that industry is the foundation of development of the country. Both the country and society need development; however it is essential to maintain an environmental balance along with industry."[25]

And, as we discussed earlier, there is the potential that judicial vindication of environmental constitutionalism can contribute to adverse societal outcomes. If protecting against soil or water pollution means closing down a factory or increasing regulation of a whole industry, environmentalists may applaud the result, but poor residents may be less sanguine about it if they lose the jobs and benefits associated with private enterprise investing in the community. And increased poverty can produce environmental degradation of a different but often equally pernicious sort. For instance, in India, when the Supreme Court ordered the closure of the tanneries that were causing massive pollution in the Ganges River, it noted that "closure of tanneries may bring unemployment [and] loss of revenue, but," the Court reasoned, "life, health and ecology have greater importance to the people." While the court should be applauded for appreciating the enormous environmental values at stake, it is not at all obvious whether the displaced workers would balance competing interests in the same way.[26] Moreover, widespread poverty itself can be detrimental to the environment.[27]

Those courts that have engaged these provisions have varied in where they draw the line: some would allow environmental degradation in the name of private rights unless it seems neglectful or vindictive,[28,29] others have privileged development over almost other interests, while still others have done the opposite, taking a strong stand in favor of the ecological interests of present and future generations. For instance, in invalidating a gold mining and processing license, the highest administrative court in Turkey found it "obvious that the public interest is to be interpreted in favour of human life, if one compares the economic gains attainable upon completion of the activities with the damage that will be caused by the risk to the environment and directly or indirectly to human life."[30] But it is not, in fact, obvious how the

[25] *Dhungel v. Godawari Marble Indus.* Writ Pet. 35/1992 (Supreme Court of Nepal, October 31, 1995) (en banc), reprinted in Kravchenko and Bonine, *Human Rights*, 96, 97.

[26] *M.C. Mehta v. Union of India.* 4 SCC 463 (Supreme Court of India, 1987).

[27] See, e.g., www.globalissues.org/article/425/poverty-and-the-environment#TheImpactof PovertyontheEnvironment

[28] See, e.g., *Defensoria de Menores Nro 3 v. Poder Ejecutivo Municipal, Agreement 5* (Argentina Superior Court of Justice. Neuguen, March 2, 1999). Court required State Government to provide 100 liters of drinkable water per day to each individual member of the families living in rural colony of Valentina Norte who were drinking water polluted with hydrocarbons.

[29] See, e.g., *Social and Economic Rights Action Center v. Nigeria* 155/96 (African Commission on Human and Peoples' Rights, October 27, 2001), available at www.escr-net.org/docs/i/404115

[30] *Senih Özay* (Turkey, 1997).

court reached this conclusion, appealing though it may be. The court provided no rubric and referred to no controlling authority. But courts that engage environmental constitutionalism have to draw lines somewhere. And the drafters of constitutional environmental provisions tend to offer little help to courts about what to balance or how much. Thus, what starts out as a constitutional right built on aspirations and high principles often becomes, in the hands of courts, a distinctly pragmatic evaluation of costs and benefits, constrained by limited judicial power considered in the face of towering political, economic, and social pressures. While most of these concerns resonate in all constitutional litigation, they are inescapable and particularly salient in constitutional environmental rights cases.

JUSTICIABILITY IN ENVIRONMENTAL CONSTITUTIONALISM

In light of these challenges, to what extent are constitutionally enshrined environmental rights justiciable? Constitutional rights are "justiciable" when particular rights appear to be formally enforceable through the domestic court system, as manifest in the relevant constitutional text.[31] The Toronto Initiative for Economic and Social Rights (TIESR) dataset first described in Chapter 2 is helpful insofar as it captures the constitutional status (or "strength") of such rights – as justiciable, aspirational, or absent.[32] Based on text, structural placement, and other factors, the TIESR dataset shows that in the 73 countries with constitutional guarantees to a quality environment, 45 are justiciable – that is, about 33 percent of the survey field. The TIESR dataset also indicates that, in the 86 nations with some other form of constitutionally embedded environmental protection, only 39 of these are justiciable, or about 28.7 percent of the survey field.[33]

Predictions about justiciability tend to follow the same patterns as those pertaining to constitutionalizing environmental rights in the first place. Foremost is that courts tend to tolerate constitutional environmental rights to the extent that they do other social, economic, and cultural rights (SECs). The challenge for vindicating constitutional environmental rights is that courts have historically accorded SECs secondary status to political and civil rights. Older constitutions that included SECs, such as the Indian constitution, identified them as directive principles of state policy. The trend, however, is that many constitutional texts identify SECs as justiciable and accord them equal status with traditional civil and political rights.[34] Indeed, as

---

[31] Jung and Rosevear, "Economic and Social Rights," 372, 380.
[32] *Ibid.*, 376.   [33] *Ibid.*, 381.   [34] *Ibid.*, 377.

we will see, constitutional and apex courts in India, South Africa, and a handful of Latin American countries are "leading the way in using courts and SECs to alleviate the effects of poverty and improve human well-being."[35]

Again, as with predicting adoption of SECs, other factors such as timing and isomorphism are somewhat predictive of justiciability. For example, constitutions written between 1974 and 1989 are more likely to include SECs, and significantly more likely to identify them as justiciable, than constitutions written after 1990.[36] And some countries that share borders are those wherein SECs are most likely justiciable, including India, Bangladesh, Pakistan, and Nepal.

The proof about justiciability, however, is revealed by examining judicial outcomes themselves.[37] Even when rights have strong textual and structural footing, justiciability is still a "judgment call," especially interpreting provisions that are presumably vague by design.[38] Some courts are more prone to address constitutional environmental rights than others. Thus far, constitutional and apex courts in South America have been the most receptive to constitutional rights to a quality environment. For example, as of this writing, the Constitutional Court of Colombia has rendered at least 135 decisions in which the constitutional right to a quality environment is addressed.[39] The Federal Supreme Tribunal of Brazil has addressed its corresponding constitutional environmental rights provision at least 26 times.[40] The Supreme Court of India has addressed environmental protection in a constitutional context more than 80 times since 1975.[41]

Judicial borrowing in the emerging socioeconomic context of environmental constitutionalism can be especially useful due to the relative newness and lack of juridical pronouncements about SECs compared with other civil and political rights.[42] Of course, judicial borrowing can also be limiting due either to parochialism in decision making or a dearth of available well-reasoned decisions.[43] Borrowing can also be problematic because SECs invariably involve courts in complex questions of policy and social justice. For example, litigating constitutionally guaranteed environmental rights raises questions beyond the normal legal line drawing to which common and civil law courts

---

[35] *Ibid.*, 374.   [36] *Ibid.*, 282.   [37] *Ibid.*, 373.   [38] *Ibid.*, 377.
[39] See www.corteconstitucional.gov.co (searching "derecho al ambiente sano").
[40] See www.stf.jus.br/portal/principal/principal.asp (searching "225 and ambiente").
[41] See http://judis.nic.in (searching "48A and environment").
[42] Ran Hirschl. "From comparative constitutional law to comparative constitutional studies." *International Journal of Constitutional Law* 11(1) (2013).
[43] Wiktor Osiatynski, "Paradoxes of constitutional borrowing," *International Journal of Constitutional Law* 1(2) (2003): 244.

are accustomed. Thus, in this area, courts can seem to be constrained only by their own unfettered sense of equity. The Kenyan Supreme Court explained the challenge of balancing this way: "We do not want a situation where our constitutional terrain on which human and property rights systems are rooted, cultivated and exploited for short term political, economic or cultural gains and satisfaction for a mere maximization of temporary economic returns, based on development strategies and legal arrangements for land ownership use and exploitation without taking account of ecological principles and the centrality of long term natural resources conservation rooted in a conservation national ethic."[44] Expecting courts to weigh these competing short- and long-term political, economic, and cultural interests raises the serious concern that they have too much discretion, at the expense of democratic discourse. The problem exists, in different guises, as to whether the rights are thought of as independent, dependent, or derivative of other rights (as discussed later), and it becomes even more compelling as the emerging needs of sustainable development and mitigation of climate change find their ways into constitutional discourse.

Line drawing without the benefit of legal rules or even general principles to guide them imposes on judges a task that they are typically under-equipped and reluctant to embark on. For some courts, this is enough to conclude that managing the environment is a job for the executive branch, not the judiciary, as one Hong Kong court decided, for instance.[45] Environmental constitutionalism presents even deeper challenges than other constitutional claims because the particular type of balancing that it demands, some argue, is political and therefore especially unsuited to judicial resolution. Should the coastline be saved for the local public to enjoy or developed to bring in tourists and economic development? Is 25 liters per household per day enough water, and how much of it should be made available free of charge? What kinds of regulatory protections are necessary to ensure safe mining practices or the development of natural gas reserves while maintaining the viability of the industry? These are not only problems of interpretation (What is a "healthy environment"? What does it mean to live "in harmony with nature"?); rather, they raise fundamental policy questions that are often best left to politically accountable branches to decide.

Indeed, judicial discretion in the context of environmental constitutionalism often raises several of the concerns that actually define what is known as the political question doctrine in American law. As the US Supreme Court

---

[44] *Ogiek People* v. *District Commissioner* (Kenya) (Indigenous Rights to Tinet Forest).
[45] *Ng Ngau Chai* v. *Town Planning Board*. No. 64 of 2007 (Hong Kong).

explained in *Baker* v. *Carr*, the political question doctrine precludes judicial cognizance of an issue when there is "a lack of judicially discoverable and manageable standards for resolving it; or the impossibility of deciding without an initial policy determination of a kind clearly for nonjudicial discretion; or the impossibility of a court's undertaking independent resolution without expressing lack of the respect due coordinate branches of government" among other things.[46] How can a court discern the legal standard embedded in the right "to live in an environment free of pollution?"[47] How could it manage the standard to ensure continuing compliance with its order over time? And how, as a practical matter of judicial politics, could it enforce that judgment against public and private actors who have different views and who are beholden to a public that may be equally divided?[48] Although courts around the world do not typically expressly invoke the American political question doctrine, their reluctance to engage with fundamental environmental rights may be attributable to the same concerns: institutional bodies with frail historical legitimacy and with neither police power nor economic muscle to back up their orders are reluctant to try to force coordinate branches to make radical policy changes.

This argument rests in part on the view that courts are not institutionally competent to make such decisions: judges are experts in legal interpretation but not in the scientific, sociologic, or economic fields in which these decisions must be rooted, and they are not institutionally capable of gaining such expertise. It is perhaps no answer that much of modern constitutional law raises similar questions: what medical treatments should be covered by constitutional guarantees to a right to "health"? What reproductive rights does "liberty" entail? What level of pension benefit is necessary to ensure that everyone can live in "dignity"? These questions, too, one might argue, require the kind of policy judgment that should not be arrogated to courts.

For these constitutional skeptics, constitutionalization has costs, particularly felt in the impoverishment of the political community. The view is reflected in the traditional way of thinking about the constitutionalization of rights as a zero-sum game: if rights are enshrined in constitutions, they are removed from the political sphere of negotiation and compromise. In excoriating the American Supreme Court's pre-Civil War *Dred Scott* decision, Abraham Lincoln said that, when the people allow the Supreme Court to decide matters of

---

[46] *Baker v. Carr*, 369 U.S. 186, 217 (Supreme Court of the United States, 1962).
[47] *Pedro Flores et al. v. Codelco* (Chile), 251, 260.
[48] For a discussion on similar issues in the context of climate change litigation, see May, James R. "Climate Change, Constitutional Consignment, and the Political Question Doctrine." *Denver U. L. Rev.* 85 (2008): 919.

public importance, they cease to be their own rulers.[49] And this view of courts as derogating from the political process has continued to hold sway.

In fact, though, courts in many parts of the world have moved beyond this particularly limited way of thinking: throughout Latin America, in Europe, in parts of Africa, and in the Indian sub-continent, courts have engaged not only with environmental constitutionalism but also with other socioeconomic rights, including the right to health care, to housing, and to education, in ways that were previously thought of as within the exclusive sphere of political authorities. Equally interesting, these courts have engaged with no less enthusiasm constitutional provisions such as those protecting the right to dignity and the right to life, which are as amorphous and ill-defined as environmental provisions, if not more so.[50] (It is worth noting, however, that, while there is significant overlap between the countries whose courts protect environmental rights and those whose courts protect other socioeconomic rights, European countries are outliers: the constitutional courts of Europe have tended to protect environmental interests anemically if at all, while giving robust protection to most other socioeconomic rights and values.)

To be sure, countries with democratic deficits are likely to be those that lack judicial review as well. But constitutional activity does not thwart democratic discourse or the ability of the people to mark their own paths: democracy is hardly moribund in countries such as South Africa, India, Israel, Canada, and Germany, all of which have courts that energetically enforce a wide range of constitutional norms. The experiences in these countries suggest the opposite. In part, this is because constitutionalization and its partner, judicialization, do not remove issues from the political process, but rather help to galvanize public discourse by setting the terms of debate.

At most, rights in constitutions provide a sort of ballast or counterweight to other constitutional rights to ensure that particular values get counted in the political calculation. For example, when no countervailing values are at issue, environmental rights will often prevail. But when, as is often the case, other constitutional values such as property are in play, environmental rights must be balanced against those. As courts construct and reconfigure their roles within developing systems of democratic constitutionalism, the rights they protect become the subject of ongoing political negotiation, rather than falling outside of it. When it is done by constitutional courts, rather than by international or regional tribunals, the kind of balancing that environmental

---

[49] Lincoln, First inaugural address, March 4, 1861.
[50] See Erin Daly. *Dignity Rights: Courts, Constitutions and the Worth of the Human Person.* University of Pennsylvania Press, 2012.

constitutionalism entails is likely to be more in line with the political community's values and expectations. If, as Nedelsky argues, judges inevitably "justify their decisions on the basis of some form of collective choice, though that language is not used,"[51] then judges will root their application of equity in the choices not of the global community but of their national collective. Each court will define its own "conservation national ethic" according to the nation's own traditions and needs. It will give meaning to a "clean" or "healthy" environment in a way that is consistent with the country's own cultural values, or will weigh the value of development against the protection of nature in a way that is tolerable to the competing claimants within the society. As a result, adjudication at the domestic constitutional level can have resonance within the political and legal culture of a country.

Moreover, judicial discretion can diminish over time, as legal principles become settled, just as case law on what constitutes "due" process or a "humane" treatment of detainees gives substance to those amorphous terms. With each case, these skeletal provisions begin to develop meaning that has content and boundaries. When courts implement environmental rights in particular, they tend to import many of the principles and values of environmental law that have become widely accepted throughout the world in similar cases, such as the precautionary principle, the principle that the polluter should pay for the damage, principles of sustainable development and intergenerational equity, and sometimes procedural principles that are unique to environmental litigation including the reversal of the burden of proof and probabilistic evidence. The incremental growth of a body of law through case-by-case application can ensure that the law develops progressively and relatively smoothly over time. This can help to increase its acceptance in the local society.

But even if there is consensus in the nation about the importance of environmental protection, how does any court possess the wherewithal to effectively enforce constitutional fundamental environmental rights? While constitutions are often criticized for being aspirational if not downright unrealistic, environmental constitutionalism epitomizes this problem: in what society are policies promulgated "in accord with the rhythm and harmony of nature," as the Philippine constitution requires?[52] How can a country promote industry, create jobs, provide housing, and secure other things people need without throwing nature – "the created world in its entirety"[53] – out of balance? While the aspirational attributes of constitutionalism are not without value, they may

---

[51] Nedelsky, *Law's Relations*, 240.   [52] Constitution (1987), art. 2, sec. 16 (Philippines).
[53] *Minors Oposa*, 185 (Philippines, 1993).

be inconsistent with the idea of judicial enforcement, which entails the expectation of realization: one sues not because one hopes someday to change something but because one is entitled to vindication at the present moment. It is therefore quite possible that substantive environmental rights are included in constitutions not with the expectation that they will be realized or judicially enforced but with the hope that they will, at most, influence the attitudes of policymakers, maybe the public, and perhaps, in the long term, encourage people within the nation to take environmental concerns into account.

And yet, despite the myriad conceptual and practical challenges both to the articulation of constitutional environmental rights, and to the development of legal rules and their enforcement, courts throughout the world have accepted these challenges by adopting, interpreting, and implementing constitutionally entrenched provisions that provide substantive rights to a quality environment. Shelton writes:

> The constitutional rights granted are increasingly being enforced by courts. In India, for example, a series of judgments between 1996 and 2000 responded to health concerns caused by industrial pollution in Delhi … South African courts also have deemed the right to environment to be justiciable. In Argentina, the right is deemed a subjective right entitling any person to initiate an action for environmental protection. Colombia also recognizes the enforceability of the right to environment. In Costa Rica, a court stated that the right to health and to the environment is necessary to ensure that the right to life is fully enjoyed.[54]

Ascertaining the extent of judicial receptivity to environmental constitutionalism is challenging. Domestic constitutional and apex courts are arguably the best indicators of judicial tolerance to constitutionalism in any given country. Their decisions are more likely to engage the definitional, structural, and policy concepts so central to constitutionalism. They are intended and expected to speak with authority, often with the last word that binds lower courts and administrative tribunals. Most importantly to the researcher, they are most likely available and subject to ready interpretation. But as Boyd reports, lower and administrative courts in several countries in Central and South America seem receptive to substantive environmental constitutionalism.[55] For the most part, however, we avoid reaching conclusions based on decisions of lower courts and administrative tribunals. Many lower courts and administrative tribunals do not possess authority to issue binding rulings concerning constitutional claims. Even when they do, decisions from these

---

[54] Shelton II.   [55] Boyd, *Environmental Rights Revolution.*

panels are less indicative of judicial receptivity to environmental constitutionalism nationally. Relying on lower and administrative decisions can be problematic in other ways. Written decisions from these panels may not exist. If they do, they may be difficult to locate or unavailable. And if they can be found, they too can be subject to differences in translation or too spare to offer insight into how environmental constitutionalism shaped the outcome in the case. Thus, we choose to focus on decisions from domestic constitutional and apex courts as the optimal indicators of judicial tolerance to environmental constitutionalism in any given country.

What these decisions reveal is that judicial receptivity to environmental rights cases can be divided into four categories. First, some courts have recognized causes of action to enforce express constitutional rights to a quality environment and of nature. We call these "independent" environmental rights cases because they do not rely upon other constitutional provisions. The leading independent environmental rights cases come from Central Europe and Latin America where many courts have been enthusiastic enforcers of textually explicit environmental provisions. Second, some courts have recognized a right to a quality environment as an adjunct of constitutional provisions that direct the government to protect the environment as a matter of duty or policy. We call these "dependent" environmental rights cases because they depend on the existence of environmental policy provisions that are typically not judicially enforceable. The Supreme Court of the Philippines has been a pioneer in deciding dependent environmental rights cases. Third, some courts recognize environmental rights as being implicitly incorporated into other substantive, enforceable constitutional rights, including a right to life, family, or dignity. We call these "derivative" environmental rights cases because the cause of action derives from another constitutional right. High courts in India, Pakistan, and Nepal have been at the forefront of recognizing dependent environmental rights. Last, constitutional and apex courts in most of the countries to have adopted environmental rights have yet to engage them other than episodically. We call these "dormant" environmental rights. With this framework in mind, we turn to the cases.

Independent environmental rights

Dozens of countries have constitutions that expressly recognize a right to a quality environment, as Chapter 2 details. Only a fraction of these provisions, however, have been tested before domestic constitutional or apex courts. Most cases involving constitutional environmental rights, including some of the earliest, come from courts in South America and Central Europe.

Courts in South America have also been willing to engage environmental constitutionalism. For example and as noted earlier, in 1988, the Supreme Court of Chile in *Pedro Flores y Otros* v. *Corporación del Cobre, Codelco, División Salvador* upheld a constitutional environmental right "to live in an environment free from contamination," to stop the deposition of copper mill tailings onto Chilean beaches, which was adversely affecting protected marine life.[56]

And then in 1997 the Supreme Court issued what may be Chile's most significant constitutional environmental rights decision. The Tierra del Fuego region of Chile contains some of the world's last remaining continuous stands of cold-climate virgin forests, known as "dwarf trees," in the world, stands that were spied upon and written about by Magellan and Darwin. The US-based Trillium Corporation, however, saw the trees as cropland for the global paper market, and asked the Chilean government for permission to log 270,000 hectares of it for $350 million in what was known as the "Rio Condor Project." The Chilean government saw economic opportunity, and approved the application. Controversy ensued. Houck explains it this way:

> Tierra del Fuego remained an isolated dab at the foot of the continent and a dragon at the gate to the Pacific Ocean. One sailed by Tierra del Fuego, God willing, as quickly as one could. The thick and stunted forests also remained untouched and off the radar of a globalizing world until 1993, when an enterprising businessman from Seattle, Washington decided to buy them and cut the timber. Suddenly, Tierra del Fuego mattered, halfway up the chain of the Andes Mountains to Santiago, Chile and back to the boardrooms of corporate North America. The furor was certainly a surprise. Who could possibly care about some dwarf trees at the bottom of the world?[57]

Chilean citizens brought a lawsuit, claiming that the Rio Condor Project violated their constitutional "right to live in an environment free from contamination."[58] The Supreme Court of Chile agreed. In what is known as the *Trillium* decision, the Court enjoined the project, holding that the Chilean

---

[56] The cases include *Pablo Orrego Silva y Otros* v. *Empresa Electrica Pange SA* (Supreme Court of Chile, August 5, 1993), and *Antonio Horvath Kiss y Otros* v. *Nat'l Comm'n for the Env't* (Supreme Court of Chile, March 19, 1997), cited in Kiss and Shelton, *International Environmental Law*, 7.

[57] Houck, "Case of Sustainable Development," 294–5. See also the Center for International Environmental Law (CIEL). *Chilean Supreme Court Rejects Controversial Trillium Logging Project* (March 21, 1997), available at www.ciel.org/Publications/trillium.html (providing case background).

[58] The "Trillium Case," Decision No. 2.732-96, at 8 (Supreme Court of Chile, March 19, 1997), available at www.elaw.org/node/1310 [hereinafter Trillium]. See generally, Houck, *Taking Back Eden*, 151–74 (story behind Trillium, with pictures).

constitution required "the maintenance of the original conditions of natural resources," and that governmental agencies were required to keep "human intervention to a minimum."[59]

In the aftermath of *Trillium*, Chile instituted an environmental review procedure to hear constitutional claims. Houck believes that this has all but relegated the country's constitutional environmental rights to administrative purgatory:

> The constitutional right to protect the environment – the basis of the first Supreme Court opinion – has been lost in the interminable hallways of administrative law. One has the impression that it will be a hot day in Tierra del Fuego before the Chilean judiciary goes this way again. This said, the decision produced one ineludible effect. An intact, virgin, and very unusual forest park at the very bottom of the world.[60]

In the *Trillium* decision, the Court also held that the constitutional right to a healthy environment is owed to all citizens, thus allowing the plaintiffs to pursue the matter as an *acción de amparo* even though none of them had personally suffered any injury.[61] Likewise, in *Proterra v. Ferroaleaciones San Ramon S.A.*, the Supreme Court of Peru permitted citizens to proceed with such open standing to enforce entrenched environmental rights.[62] Moreover, in keeping with the *Minors Oposa v. Factoran* decision, the Philippine Supreme Court in *Metropolitan Manila Development Authority v. Concerned Residents of Manila Bay* recognized broad standing to enforce environmental constitutional rights, allowing for citizen standing in matters that are of

---

[59] Trillium, para 12.   [60] Houck, "Case of Sustainable Development," 314 (footnotes omitted).

[61] An *acción de amparo* is a cause of action to enforce constitutional rights, used widely throughout the Spanish-speaking world. As Professor Houck explains,

> the process is variously called an action of *amparo* or *tutela* and works like a *habeas corpus*. One story goes that a Spanish judge was dining on the veranda one day when a group of soldiers came down the street, kicking and propelling a prisoner ahead of them. The prisoner called out, "Protect me!" (*"Amparo!"*), at which point the judge ordered the soldiers to stop, held a hearing on the matter, and freed the prisoner. Whatever the true origins, Spanish and Latin American jurisprudence have long afforded special adjudication for constitutional rights. When a constitutional violation is alleged, plaintiffs may go directly to a judge, bypassing the labyrinth and delays of civil practice. All of this would be academic but for the fact that, years after they were enacted, enterprising environmental lawyers dug up the forgotten environmental provisions of their country's constitutions and began seeking direct and expedited *amparo* review to determine what the phrase "right to a healthy environment" might mean.

Houck, "Case of Sustainable Development," 306 (footnotes omitted).

[62] *Proterra v. Ferroaleaciones San Ramon S.A.* Judgment No. 1156–90 (Supreme Court of Peru, November 19, 1992), cited in Bruch *et al.*, "Constitutional Environmental Law," 27.

"paramount interest to the public" or of "transcendental significance to the people."[63] (Chapter 4 addresses standing in detail.)

Constitutional and other apex courts in other countries in Latin America have been receptive to environmental constitutionalism. In *Carlos Roberto Garcia Chacon*, the Constitutional Court of Costa Rica upheld a constitutional "right to a healthy and ecologically balanced environment" as being fundamental, self-executing, and enforceable.[64] The Court wrote that "all citizens possess to live in an environment free from contamination. This is the basis of a just and productive society."[65] In another case, the Constitutional Court of Costa Rica invoked the same provision to stop a transnational banana company from clear-cutting approximately 700 hectares near the Tortuguero National Park.[66] The protected area includes nesting habitat for the endangered green macaw.

Courts in Argentina have found enforceable that country's constitutional guarantee that "[a]ll inhabitants enjoy the right to a healthful, balanced environment fit for human development, so that productive activities satisfy current needs without compromising those of future generations . . ."[67] In 1993, the Supreme Court of Argentina observed that "[t]he right to live in a healthy and balanced environment is a fundamental attribute of people. Any aggression to the environment ends up becoming a threat to life itself and to the psychological and physical integrity of the person."[68] In *Alberto Sagarduy*,

---

[63] Velasco, Presbitero J., Jr. "Manila Bay: A Daunting Challenge in Environmental Rehabilitation and Protection." *Oregon Review of International Law* 11 (2009): 445.

[64] See Fabra, Adriana and Eva Arnal, "Review of Jurisprudence on Human Rights and the Environment in Latin America," n.5 (Joint UNEP-OHCHR Expert Seminar on Human Rights and the Environment, Background Paper No. 6, 2002), Office of the United Nations High Commissioner for Human Rights, Geneva, January 14–16, 2002, available at www2.ohchr.org/english/issues/environment/environ/bp6.htm (describing right as a "fundamental human right"). See also *Presidente de law sociedad Marlene S.A.* v. *Municipalidad de Tibas, Sala Constitucional de la courte Supreme de justicia*. Decision No. 6918/94 (Const. Ct. Costa Rica, November 25, 1994), cited in Kiss and Shelton, *International Environmental Law*, 8.

[65] Fabra and Arnal, "Review of Jurisprudence."

[66] See Bruch *et al.*, "Constitutional Environmental Law," 26; Environment Law Alliance Worldwide (ELAW), *Valuing Biodiversity in Costa Rica* (July, 1999), available at www.elaw.org/node/866

[67] Argentina constitution, pt. 1, ch. II, art. 41.

[68] *Irazu Margarita* v. *Copetro S.A.* Camara Civil y Comercial de la Plata, Ruling of May 10, 1993, in Kiss and Shelton, *International Environmental Law*, 7. Accord *Asociación Para la Protección de Medio Ambiente y Educacion Ecologica "18 de Octubre"* v. *Aguas Argentinas S.A. y otros*, Fed. Appellate Tribunal of La Plata (2003); *Kattan, Alberto E. Y. Otro C. Gobierno Nactional-Poder Ejecutivo*. Juzgado Nacional de la Instancia en lo Contencioso administrativo Federal. No. 2 (JNFed Contencioso administrativo, May 10, 1983), La Ley, 1983-D, 576. See also Argentina constitution, pt. 1, ch. II, art. 41.

the Supreme Court of Argentina upheld a citizen's rights to enforce constitutional environmental rights without first having to exhaust administrative remedies.[69] And in *Sociedad de Fomento Barrio* Félix v. *Camet y Otros*, the court even invoked the provision in upholding the right to enjoy an ocean view.[70]

The Constitutional Court of Ecuador has embraced that country's constitutional guarantee of substantive environmental rights. For example, in *Fundación Natura* v. *Petroecuador*, the court upheld a civil verdict against Petroecuador on the basis that the production of leaded fuel violated Ecuador's constitutional guarantee to a "healthy" environment.[71] In *Arco Iris* v. *Instituto Ecuatoriano de Mineria*, using the same right to a healthy environment, the Court concluded that degradation of Podocarpus National Park "is a threat to the environmental human right of the inhabitants of the provinces of Loja and Zamora Chinchipe to have an area which ensures the natural and continuous provision of water, air humidity, oxygenation and recreation."[72] Nonetheless, the temptation of lucrative opportunities to exploit the country's abundant natural resources presents a persistent challenge to responsible stewardship of its globally significant environment.

In the immediate aftermath of the fall of communism, courts in some post-communist countries in Central and Eastern Europe also aimed to implement newly minted constitutional environmental rights provisions. For example, in 1989, Hungary amended its constitution to recognize "the individual's right to a healthy environment."[73] The Constitutional Court of Hungary seems to have been the first in Central and Eastern Europe to give force to this type of provision. In *Alkotmánybróság* (1994), the court held that the Hungarian legislature's efforts to sell for cultivation previously nationalized forested lands under the former communist regime would be unconstitutional, finding that it violated the constitutional environmental rights residing

---

[69] See Fabra and Arnal, "Review of Jurisprudence."
[70] *Ibid.* (citing *Sociedad de Fomento Barrio Félix* v. *Camet y Otros*); see also *Irazu Margarita* v. *Copetro S.A.*, in Kiss and Shelton, *International Environmental Law*, 7.
[71] *Fundación Natura v. Petroecuador*. Case Nos. 377/90, 378/90, 379/90, 380/90 combined. Resolution No. 230-92-CP (Tribunal of Constitutional Guarantees, October 15, 1992).
[72] *Arco Iris v. Instituto Ecuatoriano de Mineria*. Case No. 224/90, Judgment No. 054-93-CP (Constitutional Court of Ecuador), translated in Bruch *et al.*, "Constitutional Environmental Law," 26.
[73] A Magyar Köztársaság Alkotmánya [Constitution of Hungary] ch. I, art. 18 ("The Republic of Hungary recognizes and shall implement the individual's right to a healthy environment."), art. 70/D(2) (requiring State to implement this right "through ... protection of the ... natural environment.").

in the Hungarian constitution.[74] The court rejected the state's justification for the repeal, reasoning that "[t]he right to a healthy environment guarantees the physical conditions necessary to enforce the right to human life ... extraordinary resolve is called for in establishing legislative guarantees for the right."[75] Thus, it held that, once the state created a baseline of environmental protection, it could not thereafter degrade it.[76] The court also held that violation of environmental rights ran afoul of the constitution's "right to life."[77]

The Constitutional Court of Latvia has been particularly active in enforcing that country's constitutionally enshrined environmental rights. Section 115 of the Constitution of Latvia provides: "The State shall protect the right of everyone to live in a benevolent environment by ... promoting the preservation and improvement of the environment." The court has struck several local land use decisions as violative of Article 115, especially in the context of activities that might cause or contribute to flooding. For example, in *Amoliņa v. Garkalne Pagasts Council*, the court held that a local land use development plan that would have permitted development of flood zones was unconstitutional under Article 115.[78] The court held that by allowing development in flood zones the city council had fallen short of its duty to "promote the preservation and improvement of the environment." It also held that that the land use plan violated the affected individuals' "fundamental right to live in a benevolent environment," which, the court wrote, "shall be directly and immediately applied." Likewise, in *Balams v. Ādaži Parish Council*, the court struck a land use plan for largely the same reasons.[79] And in *Gruba v. Jurmala City Council*, the court drew support from the Stockholm Declaration and the Aarhus Convention in striking another land use development plan as violative

[74] *Alkotmánybrróság*. MK. No. 1994/Decision 28. Hungary Constitutional Law Court, 1994, available at http://public.mkab.hu/dev/dontesek.nsf/o/2CA997895285061DC1257ADA005259CE; Kravchenko, Svitlana. "Citizen Enforcement of Environmental Law in Eastern Europe." *Widener Law Review* 10 (2004): 475, 484 (calling it "a remarkable case."); Stec, Stephen. "Ecological Rights Advancing the Rule of Law in Eastern Europe." *Journal of Environmental Law and Litigation* 13 (1998): 275, 320–1.

[75] Alkotmánybíróság (Hungary, 1994).

[76] *Ibid.*, 1–3. Some describe this case as enforcing a "third generation" right. See Dupre, Catherine. *Importing the Law in Post-Communist Transitions: The Hungarian Constitutional Court and the Right to Human Dignity.* Hart Publishing, 2003: 69.

[77] See Dupre, *Importing the Law*, 69, 73–4. As addressed in Chapter 2, Hungary revised the provision, and added policy directives and other provisions addressing the environment.

[78] *Amoliņa v. Garkalne Pagasts Council*, No. 2006-09-03 (Latvia Constitutional Court, 2007) (Latvijas Republikas Satversmes tiesa), available at www.satv.tiesa. gov.lv/upload/judg_2006-09-03.htm

[79] *Balams v. Ādaži Parish Council*, No. 2007-12-03 (Latvia Constitutional Court, 2007) (Latvijas Republikas Satversmes tiesa), available at www.satv.tiesa.gov. lv/upload/judg_2007-12-03.htm

of an individual's right to live in an environment that does not endanger human health and well-being.[80] These decisions were dispositive, meaning that the government decision makers were enjoined from implementing the challenged plans.

Nonetheless, the court had determined that the right to a "benevolent" environment was not absolute, but involved a balancing of costs and the public good.[81] Evidence matters. Accordingly, in *Baldzēns* v. *Cabinet of Ministers*, the court rejected a community's challenge to the Ministry of Environmental Protection and Regional Development's issuance of a permit to operate a hazardous waste incinerator for failure to submit sufficient evidence that environmental harms outweighed ensuing public benefit.[82]

Section 115's right to a benevolent environment can also be outweighed by other constitutional guarantees. For example, *Zandbergs* v. *Kuldīga District* involved a challenge to a water district's plan to condemn a large parcel of property for use as an impoundment to supply water for a hydroelectric station.[83] The affected landowner argued that the plan violated the constitutionally protected use of his private property. The water district countered that the project advanced the use of renewable energy resources, and therefore promoted its constitutional duty to promote a "benevolent environment." The court sided with the landowner, however, finding that the adverse effect on the landowner outweighed the environmental benefits of renewable energy production.

Courts elsewhere in Central and Eastern Europe have shown receptivity to environmental constitutionalism. Most notably, in *Senih Özay* v. *Ministry of the Environment, Ankara and Eurogold Madencilik AS*, the Turkish government agreed to allow the giant French mining conglomerate to use cyanide heap-leaching to mine gold and other metals from a centuries-old

---

[80] *Gruba* v. *Jurmala City Council*, No. 2008-38-03 (Latvia Constitutional Court, 2009) (Ecolex), available at www.ecolex.org/ecolex/ledge/view/RecordDetails; DIDPFDSIjsessionid=BB641885E3AA2968FBE2D79C7AADDA62?id=COU-159872&index=courtdecisions [hereinafter *Gruba*]. See also the case summary, available at http://www.unece.org/fileadmin/DAM/env/pp/compliance/TFon_A_to_J/Latvia_2009_Jurmalas.pdf

[81] *Coalition for Nature and Cultural Heritage Protection* v. *Riga City Council*, No. 2007-11-3 (Latvia Constitutional Court, 2008) (Latvijas Republikas Satversmes tiesa), available at www.satv.tiesa.gov.lv/upload/judg_2007-11-03.htm

[82] *Baldzēns* v. *Cabinet of Ministers*, No. 2002-14-04 (Latvia Constitutional Court, 2003) (Latvijas Republikas Satversmes tiesa), available at www.satv.tiesa.gov.lv/upload/2002-14-04E.rtf

[83] *Zandbergs* v. *Kuldīga District*, No. 2005-10-03 (Latvia Constitutional Court, 2005) (Latvijas Republikas Satversmes tiesa), available at www.satv.tiesa.gov.lv/upload/2005-10-03E.rtf

olive-growing region in Turkey.[84] After government-paid loggers began to remove olive trees, olive farmers brought a suit claiming that the government's license contravened Turkey's new constitutional environmental right "to live in a healthy, balanced environment." Turkey's highest administrative court agreed, stopping the operation in its tracks.[85]

Often inspired by developments elsewhere, courts have upheld independent provisions, including in Portugal, where a court upheld "the right to a healthy and ecologically balanced human environment and the duty to defend it,"[86] and in South Korea, where a court interpreted an independent environmental rights provision as actionable, although it declined to find that the government's failure to regulate the use of loudspeakers used in furtherance of political campaigns to have violated the right.[87]

Dependent environmental rights

Some courts have recognized substantive environmental rights as dependent upon some other constitutional directive that advances good environmental governance. The Supreme Court of the Philippines has led the way in enforcing such dependent environmental rights. In the celebrated case of *Minors Oposa*, attorney, writer, and law professor Tony Oposa filed a lawsuit on behalf of his children, his friends' children, and generations to come to "'prevent the misappropriation or impairment' of Philippine rainforests and 'arrest the unabated hemorrhage of the country's vital life-support systems and continued rape of Mother Earth.'"[88] At one time, the Philippines contained nearly 100 million acres of verdant, ancient forests.[89] By the 1990s, commercial logging had reduced this by about 99 percent.[90] The plaintiffs claimed

---

[84] Sachs, Aaron. "What do Human Rights have to do with Environmental Protection? Everything," *Sierra Magazine* (November–December, 1997), available at www.sierraclub.org/sierra/199711/humanrights.asp

[85] *Ibid.*

[86] Constituição da República Portuguesa pt. I, sec. 3, ch. 2, art. 66(1). See Brandl and Bungert, "Constitutional Entrenchment," 67 (saying provision "is to be seen primarily as a fundamental right" because, inter alia, it is a constitutional "Social right ... and dut[y]" enforceable in the Portuguese Constitutional Court.).

[87] *Case on the Constitutionality of Election Campaign Using Loudspeaker*, 2006 Hun-Ma 711 (July 31, 2008), translated by Professor Jibong Lim, Sogang University College of Law.

[88] *Minors Oposa*, 176 (Philippines, 1993).

[89] *Ibid.*, 179; Houck, Oliver. "Light from the Trees, The Stories of *Minors Oposa* and the Russian Forest Cases." *Georgetown International Environmental Law Review* 19 (2007): 321, 326. See generally, Houck, *Taking Back Eden*, 43–60 (story behind *Minors Oposa* [Philippines, 1993], with pictures).

[90] Houck, *Taking Back Eden*, 326.

that the government's continued issuance of "timber licensing agreements" violated the country's recently minted constitutional directive that, *inter alia*, "[t]he State shall protect and advance the right of the people to a balanced and healthful ecology in accord with the rhythm and harmony of nature."[91]

In reversing the trial court, the Supreme Court upheld Oposa's constitutional claim, and also found that the plaintiffs had standing to represent themselves, their children, and posterity.[92] In a sweeping pronouncement, the Court determined that rights to a quality environment are enforceable notwithstanding whether they are constitutionally expressed, because they "exist from the inception of humankind":

> As a matter of fact, these basic rights need not even be written in the constitution for they are assumed to exist from the inception of humankind. If they are now explicitly mentioned in the fundamental charter it is because of the well-founded fear of its framers that unless the rights to a balanced and healthful ecology and to health are mandated as State policies by the constitution itself, thereby highlighting their continuing importance and imposing upon the State a solemn obligation to preserve the first and protect and advance the second, the day would not be too far when all else would be lost not only for the present generation, but also for those to come – generations which stand to inherit nothing but parched earth incapable of sustaining life.[93]

More recently, in *Manila Bay*, the same court upheld a request for multifaceted injunctive relief by the same lawyer as in *Minors Oposa* to prevent massive pollution discharges from choking Manila Bay, and to clean and protect it for the benefit of future generations.[94]

The *Manila Bay* case is particularly instructive about the potential of environmental constitutionalism. Manila Bay, located in southwest Luzon in the Philippines, is a natural wonder. Its 1,800 square kilometers contain some of the most diverse biodiversity in Southeast Asia. If ever an area could be described as "teeming" with marine and terrestrial life, it is Manila Bay. The area has a rich strategic history. It is where the US Navy, led by Commodore George Dewey, fought and landed in the siege of Manila at the outset of the Spanish American War in 1898.[95] Japanese forces occupied the Philippines after prevailing in a fierce battle with US and Filipino forces at the beginning of World War II. By the end of the war in 1945, nearly all of Manila lay in ruins.[96]

---

[91] *Minors Oposa*, 280–1. See also Constitution (1987), art. 2, secs. 15–16 (Phil.).
[92] *Minors Oposa*, 185.　　[93] *Ibid.*, 187.　　[94] *Manila Bay* (Philippines, 2008).
[95] Velasco, "Manila Bay," 441, 444.　　[96] *Ibid.*

Given its natural beauty, tropical climate, and strategic location, Manila Bay supports a high population density. Twenty million people live in metropolitan Manila. Indeed, Manila City is the most densely populated city in the world, with 43,079 people per square kilometer. Manila Bay's 190 kilometers of coastline also boast significant industrial, commercial, and residential development, and extensive international portage.[97] Not surprisingly, then, Manila Bay is also teeming with pollution from farms, factories, urban runoff, combined sewer overflow, landfills, watercraft, cars, tankers, and trucks, coupled with poor municipal waste planning, poor plumbing, and unlawful or haphazard waste dumping along the bay's tributaries. Most of it ends up in Manila Bay, exceeding the carrying capacity of the ecological system to withstand, rebound, and recover.

In 1999, a group of fourteen young Filipinos – *sub nom. Concerned Residents of Manila Bay* – filed a lawsuit against ten executive departments and agencies for neglecting to protect Manila Bay and to clean and protect the bay for the benefit of future generations. The plaintiffs alleged that they had a constitutional guarantee to a quality environment. In *Manila Bay*, the Philippine Supreme Court upheld the lower court's decisions to grant the citizens' request to enjoin the government from issuing any further permits to pollute Manila Bay.[98]

These cases serve as an important model for other courts to follow, particularly for those construing policy directives that complement substantive rights to a quality environment. What other courts should take away from these cases is that environmental rights provisions provide jurisprudential footing for advancing environmental concerns.

Derivative environmental rights

Some courts have held that other substantive constitutional rights, including a right to life, harbor environmental rights. Most notably, apex courts in India, Pakistan, Bangladesh, and Nepal have each read a constitutional "right to life" in tandem with directive principles aimed at promoting environmental policy to embody a substantive environmental right. Among these countries, India has been particularly active.[99]

---

[97] Velasco, "Manila Bay," 442.   [98] *Manila Bay* (Philippines, 2008).
[99] See Chubai, Sanjay. "Environmental Law of India." In *International Environmental Law and Regulation*, by Schlickman *et al.*, (eds.). Butterworth Legal Publishers, 1995. Vol II; for a helpful discussion of these environmental rights in India, see Anderson, Michael R. "Individual Rights to Environmental Protection in India" in Boyle and Anderson, *Human Rights Approaches*, 199–225. See also Hill *et al.*, "Human Rights and the Environment," 382

In 1984, the Supreme Court of India was one of the first to find that a "right to life" embeds a right to a quality environment.[100] In *Subhash Kumar v. State of Bihar*, the plaintiffs brought an action to stop tanneries from discharging into the Ganges River. While the Court dismissed the action for lack of standing, it observed: the "[r]ight to life is a fundamental right under Article 21 of the Constitution and it includes the right of enjoyment of pollution free water and air for full enjoyment of life."[101] Subsequently in *M.C. Mehta v. Union of India*, the Court ordered the tanneries to shut down unless effluent was first subjected to pretreatment processes approved by the governing environmental agency, privileging, as we have seen, life, health, and ecology over the more tangible benefits of employment and revenue. *Charan Lal Sahu v. Union of India* involved a challenge to the Bhopal Gas Disaster Act, the federal government's response to the Bhopal disaster wherein more than 3,000 people died following exposure to methyl isocyanate from a storage tank operated by Union Carbide (India). The petitioners – some parties adversely affected by the incident – objected to the federal government's exclusive assumption of claims as *parens patriae* on behalf of affected parties, a majority of whom were poor and illiterate. In upholding the Act, the Supreme Court of India interpreted the right to life guaranteed by Article 21 of the Constitution to include the right to a wholesome environment.[102]

Courts in Pakistan have reached the same conclusion.[103] The Supreme Court of Pakistan has held that environmental rights are embedded within that country's constitutional right to life. In *Human Rights Case (Environmental Pollution in Balochistan)*, the Court took judicial notice of a newspaper report that "business tycoons are making attempts to purchase coastal area of Balochistan and convert it into dumping ground" for nuclear and highly hazardous waste.[104] Without much discussion of the scope of the

---

("Perhaps more than in any other country, the judiciary of India has taken a proactive role in developing jurisprudence around environmental and other constitutional provisions to help secure a right to a clean and healthy environment for its citizens.").

[100] *Bandhua Mukti Morcha v. Union of India*. 3 SCC 161 (Supreme Court of India February 21, 1984) and in Shelton, 8; *Charan Lal Sahu v. Union of India*. A.I.R. 1990 S.C. 1480 (Supreme Court of India, December 22, 1989) in Kiss and Shelton, *International Environmental Law*, 8.

[101] *Subhash Kumar v. State of Bihar*. No. 1991 A.I.R. 420, 1991 SCR (1) 5 (Supreme Court of India, January 9, 1991).

[102] *Charan Lal Sahu v. Union of India*. A.I.R. 1990 S.C. 1480 (Supreme Court of India, December 22, 1989).

[103] For discussion of environmental rights in Pakistan, see Lau, Martin. "Islam and Judicial Activism: Public Address Litigation under Environmental Protection in the Islamic Republic of Pakistan." In Boyle and Anderson, *Human Rights Approaches*, 285–302.

[104] *Human Rights Case* No. 31-K/92(Q) (*Environment Pollution in Balochistan*). P.L.D. 1994 S. C. 102 (1992), *in* U.N. *Environment Programme [UNEP], Compendium of Judicial Decisions*

constitutional rights involved, the Court ordered the agency charged with implementing environmental laws in the area to monitor land allocations in the affected area and forbid such use.[105] In *West Pakistan Salt Miners* v. *Industries and Mineral Development, Punjab, Lahore*, the Court upheld a claim that the right to life included a right to water free from contamination from mining activities: "[t]he right to have unpolluted water is the right of every person wherever he lives."[106] And in *Ms. Shehla Zia et al.* v. *WAPDA*, the court held that a constitutional right to life provides a cause of action for electromagnetic hazards associated with the construction of a power plant.[107]

A decision from the Supreme Court of Nepal presents a clear statement of how environmental concerns derive from a constitutionally recognized right to life. In *Godawari Marble*, the Nepalese Supreme Court held "since a clean and healthy environment is an indispensable part of a human life, the right to a clean, healthy environment is undoubtedly embedded within the Right to Life."[108] The Court wrote:

> The works carried out by the respondent Godawari Marble Industries have been disbalanced to the environment. The dust and sand produced during the explosions which is being undertaken in the mining process has polluted the atmosphere and water of the area and caused deforestation. Due to the continuing environmental degradation and pollution created by the said industry, Right to Life of the people has been violated. The absence of appropriate environment caused diminution of human life.[109]

In *Yogi Narahari Nath* v. *Honourable Prime Minister Girija Prasad Koirala and Others*, the Court issued an injunction to stop the government from granting a lease to establish a College of Medical Science on the site of an environmentally and archaeologically significant piece of land.[110] The Court found that the lease would infringe the constitutional "right to life," which it held implicitly includes the right to a pollution-free environment: "the environment is an integral part of human life."[111] Moreover, in *Advocate Kedar Bhakta Shrestha* v. *HMG, Department of Transportation Management*, the

---

in *Matters Related to Environment: National Decisions*, Vol. I, 280 (1998) [hereinafter *UNEP Compendium*]. Also available at www.globalhealthrights.org/asia/in-re-human-rights-case-environmental-pollution-in-balochistan

[105] *Ibid.*, 281.   [106] 1994 S.C.M.R. 2061 (S.C. Pak.), in *UNEP Compendium*, 282.

[107] P.L.D. 1994 S.C. 693, in *UNEP Compendium*, 323.

[108] *Dhungel* v. *Godawari* (Nepal, October 31, 1995), 96, 97.   [109] *Ibid.*

[110] *Yogi Narahari Nath* v. *Honourable Prime Minister Girija Prasad Koirala and Others*, 33 N.L.R. (Supreme Court of Nepal, 1955) in *UNEP, Compendium of Studies of Judicial Decisions In Environment-Related Cases* 134 (2005) [hereinafter *UNEP Summaries*].

[111] *UNEP Summaries*.

court found that the constitutional "right to life" guarantees a right to a quality environment.[112] In a reverse environmental rights action of sorts, petitioners claimed that the government's ban on the use of "tempos," three-wheeled diesel-engine-run vehicles that were a principal source of air pollution in Kathmandu, violated their right to carry on a trade or business.[113] The Court upheld the governmental action, reasoning that personal freedom to carry on business practices yields to environmental rights embodied in the constitution's "right to life": "[e]very individual has an inherent right to live in a healthy environment."[114] These cases suggest a willingness to derive environmental rights from a constitutional right to life in the Nepalese constitution.

In Bangladesh, too, the Supreme Court has held that a right to a quality environment derives from a constitutional guarantee to a "right to life," although in two significant cases, despite sympathetic language, the court dismissed the actions for lack of standing. In *Dr. Mohiuddin Farooque* v. *Bangladesh*, the petitioner alleged that the implementation of a substantial flood control plan would so disrupt the affected community's life, property, and environmental security as to violate a constitutional "right to life."[115] The Supreme Court of Bangladesh held that the constitution's guarantee of a "right to life" included environmental rights, reasoning: "Articles 31 and 32 of our Constitution protect[s] right to life as a fundamental right. It encompasses within its ambit, the protection and preservation of the environment, ecological balance free from pollution of air and water, and sanitation, without which life can hardly be enjoyed. An act or omission contrary thereto will be violative of the said right to life."[116] Nonetheless, the court dismissed the action, reasoning that petitioners did not have standing within the meaning of constitution. And in *Subash Kumar* v. *State of Bihar*, it held that pollutant discharges sufficient to make the Bokaro River in the state of Bihar unfit for drinking and irrigation could abridge a constitutional "right to life."[117] The court held that the "right to life" includes the enjoyment of water and air

---

[112] *Ibid.*
[113] *Advocate Kedar Bhakta Shrestha* v. *HMG, Department of Transportation Management.* Writ No. 3109 of 1999 (Supreme Court of Nepal, 1999) in *UNEP Summaries*, 138.
[114] *Ibid.*
[115] *Dr. Mohiuddin Farooque* v. *Bangladesh.* 48 Dir 1996 (S.C. Bangl. App. Div., Civ.) [hereinafter *Farooque*] in *UNEP Summaries*, 90.
[116] *Ibid.* Quoted in Hassan, Parvez and Azim Azfar, "Securing Environmental Rights Through Public Interest Litigation in South Asia." *Virginia Environmental Law Journal* 22 (2004): 215, 242.
[117] *Subash Kumar* v. *State of Bihar.* A.I.R. 1991 S.C. 420, in *UNEP Summaries*, 104. See also *Dr. Mohiuddin Farooque* v. *Sec'y, Ministry of Commc'n, Gov't of the People's Republic of Bangl. and Twelve Others*, in Kiss and Shelton, *International Environmental Law*, 8.

free of pollution. Nonetheless, the Court dismissed the action, holding that the petitioner was motivated by self-interest and thus did not have standing to file a petition on behalf of the public interest.

A court in Hong Kong recently accepted that a *prima facie* case could be made that a deteriorated environment infringed upon constitutionally guaranteed rights to health and life. In *Clean Air Foundation Ltd. and Another* v. *Government of HKSAR*, plaintiffs alleged that the provincial government of Hong Kong's failure to adequately protect air quality in Hong Kong amounted to a violation of constitutional rights to health and life.[118] Here, while the government prohibited the sale of diesel fuel, it did not prohibit its use or importation. The plaintiffs alleged that this contributed to soot levels nearly three times higher than that of New York City. The Court of First Instance found "that it is at least *prima facie* arguable that the constitutional right to life may apply."[119] Yet it found the matter to be essentially one of policy consigned to the political process, observing: "[h]ow possibly can this court decide that this decision fails to reach a fair balance between the duty Government has to protect the right to life and the duty it has to protect the social and economic well-being of the Territory? It cannot do so . . ."[120]

Apex courts in South America have also been willing to construe environmental rights from other constitutional prerogatives, although in many of these countries the constitutions also create substantive environmental rights, which would seem to suggest even surer interpretive footing. The Constitutional Court of Colombia has read a constitutional "right to life" as encompassing a substantive right to a healthy environment.[121] In *Fundepublico* v. *Mayor of Bugalagrande y otros*, the Constitutional Court of Colombia wrote that "[i]t should be recognized that a healthy environment is a sina qua non condition for life itself and that no right could be exercised in a deeply altered environment."[122] In *María Elena Burgos* v. *Municipality of Campoalegre (Huila)*, the Court upheld a lower court's order to destroy pig stalls that caused neighbors to fall ill with respiratory distress and fever, finding they constituted an actionable violation of the country's fundamental environmental right

---

[118] *Clean Air Foundation Ltd. and Another* v. *Government of HKSAR*, 2007 WL 1824740, para. 5, [2007] HKEC 1356, HCAL 35/2007 (CFI).

[119] *Ibid.*, para. 17.   [120] *Ibid.*, para. 42.

[121] The Colombian constitution now reads: "Every individual has the right to enjoy a healthy environment." Constitución Política de la República de Colombia de 1991, title II, ch. III, art. 79.

[122] *Fundepublico* v. *Mayor of Bugalagrande y otros*, cited in Kiss and Shelton, *International Environmental Law*, 7 (italics omitted).

encompassed in a right to life.[123] And in *Victor Ramon Castrillon Vega v. Federacio National de Algodoneros*, the Court found that emissions of toxic fumes from an open pit contravened a constitutional right to life and ordered a company to remediate the pit and pay medical expenses.[124] In reaching these results, the Court has conceived the right to the environment as "a group of basic conditions surrounding man, which define his life as a member of the community and allow his biological and individual survival[.]"[125] Thus, environmental rights exist "side by side with fundamental rights such as liberty, equality and necessary conditions for people's life ... [W]e can state that the right to the environment is a right fundamental to the existence of humanity."[126] Even in *José Cuesta Novoa v. The Secretary of Public Health of Bogota*, which confirmed on procedural ground a lower court's dismissal of an effort to enforce environment rights, the Court still recognized that a right to life embodies environmental protections.[127] Likewise, as previously mentioned, the Supreme Court in Chile upheld the right of a farmer to bring a constitutional right to life claim to enjoin the drainage of Lake Chungarà in *Comunidad de Chañaral v. Codeco División el Saldor*. These cases demonstrate the potential of vindicating substantive environmental rights derived from other constitutional provisions.

Yet for the most part, apex courts elsewhere have declined to infer that other rights, such as a right to life, include a substantive right to a quality environment. For example, in the United States, while the Supreme Court has never addressed the issue directly and is not likely to do so any time soon, courts have rejected the position that constitutional rights to "liberty" or "life" provide an implied or penumbral right to a clean environment.[128] Even where the duty is clear, courts have sometimes been reluctant to recognize an enforceable environmental constitutional right.

The Federal Supreme Court of Switzerland, for example, declined to read a constitutional passage that the "federal legislature enacts laws concerning the protection of man and his natural environment against detrimental or

---

[123] *María Elena Burgos v. Municipality of Campoalegre (Huila)* (Constitutional Court of Colombia, February 27, 1997) *in UNEP Summaries*, 79.
[124] Hill *et al.*, "Human Rights and the Environment," 386.
[125] Fabra and Arnal (citing *Fundepublico*, cited in Kiss and Shelton, *International Environmental Law*, 7).
[126] *Ibid.* (citing case of *Antonio Mauricio Monroy Cespedes*).
[127] *José Cuesta Novoa v. The Secretary of Public Health of Bogota* (Constitutional Court of Colombia, May 17, 1995) in *UNEP Summaries*, 77.
[128] See, e.g., Pettigrew, "Constitutional Right," 1–41; Klipsch, "Aspects of a Constitutional Right," 203.

burdensome influences" as one that confers a fundamental environmental right.[129] Apex courts in other countries, including the Netherlands ("It shall be the concern of the authorities to keep the country habitable and to protect and improve the environment"),[130] and Greece ("The protection of the natural and cultural environment constitutes a duty of the State"),[131] have declined to infer environmental rights into constitutional provisions requiring sound environmental policy.

Dormant environmental rights

Courts in some countries have yet to engage environmental rights provisions, sometimes for failure to hear such cases at all, sometimes by denying them any force, and sometimes due to the sheer tower of economic, political, and other forces discussed previously, thereby rendering them dormant.

The Constitutional Court of Turkey, for example, has interpreted the constitutional provision that "[e]veryone has the right to live in a healthy, balanced environment"[132] as permitting solely facial challenges to legislation, notwithstanding its orbit with other "Social and Economic Rights and Duties."[133] Courts in Spain have held that the constitutional "right to enjoy an environment suitable for the development of the person"[134] falls outside the actionable private "rights" the constitution otherwise guarantees.[135] Likewise, Namibia's environmental rights provision may only be enforced by an ombudsman,[136] and citizens of Cameroon are not allowed to pursue environmental rights before the country's Constitutional Court.[137] While South Africa's constitution guarantees a fundamental right to a clean environment, functionally open standing, and access to a constitutional court, that court has yet to enforce the right. Brazil's constitution, with its aim to protect the

---

[129] See Brandl and Bungert, "Constitutional Entrenchment," 52–3.   [130] *Ibid.*, 56.

[131] *Ibid.*, 57–60.

[132] Türkiye Cumhuriyeti Anayasası¹ [Turkey Republic Constitution], pt. II, ch. III, art 56.

[133] Brandl and Bungert, "Constitutional Entrenchment," 72.

[134] Constitución [C.E.] title I, ch. III, art. 45.

[135] Brandl and Bungert, "Constitutional Entrenchment," 65 (noting that the provision "is not enforceable through a constitutional complaint brought by an individual," but must be brought by a state-appointed ombudsman); *see also* Herrero de la Fuente, Alberto A. *in Access to Justice In Environmental Matters In the EU*, 421, 442 (Jonas Ebbesson ed., 2002) ("The right to an adequate environment . . . is not understood as a fundamental right, but rather as a leading principle for social and economic politics.").

[136] Weiss, *International Environmental Law and Policy*, 417.

[137] Bruch *et al.*, "Constitutional Environmental Law," 139.

Amazon Rain Forest,[138] has among the most detailed environmental provisions of all national constitutions.[139] Yet, it is doubtful whether its promise that all have "the right to an ecologically balanced environment, which is a public good for the people's use and is essential for a healthy life"[140] will be enforceable.[141] Brazil's environmental constitutional provisions are yielding to high foreign debt and reliance on timber, crop, and cattle farming.[142] Environmental rights provisions in Ecuador have underperformed for similar reasons.[143] Likewise, environmental rights provisions in most of the former Soviet Bloc lie fallow in part because of economic, political, and social challenges.[144]

Sometimes, environmental provisions expressed as directive principles are thought too weak to be worth litigating to advance individual environmental rights. About Cuba's, Ankersen remarks: "Cuba's environmental constitutional language also appears relatively weak and is framed in terms of state duties (*deberes*). It does not appear to confer defensible individual or collective rights."[145] And, as discussed in Chapter 7, constitutionally entrenched provisions in subnational state constitutions in the United States have not fared very well in court, except in Montana and, more recently, in Pennsylvania.[146] Thus many provisions that guarantee environmental rights remain dormant.[147]

---

[138] Bruinsma, James. "Environmental Law: Brazil Enacts New Protections for the Amazon Rain Forest." *Harv. Int'l L. J.* 30 (1989): 503, 503–5.

[139] See Brandl and Bungert, "Constitutional Entrenchment," 77–81 (discussing a panoply of provisions).

[140] Constituição Federal [C.F.] [Constitution] title VIII, ch. VI, art. 225.

[141] Brandl and Bungert, "Constitutional Entrenchment," 78 (describing "[t]he subjective, or individually enforceable, character" of the provision as "very weak."). See also Rosenn, Keith S. "Brazil's New Constitution: An Exercise in Transient Constitutionalism for a Transitional Society." *Am. J. Comp. L.* 38 (1990): 773, 796–7.

[142] Weiss, *International Environmental Law and Policy*, 417. For further discussion of developments in Brazil, see Fernandes, Edesio. "Constitutional Environmental Rights in Brazil." In Boyle and Anderson, *Human Rights Approaches*, 265–84.

[143] For a discussion of environmental rights in Ecuador, see Fabra, Adriana. "Indigenous Peoples, Environmental Degradation and Human Rights: A Case Study." In Boyle and Anderson, *Human Rights Approaches*, 245–64.

[144] See Kravchenko, "Citizen Enforcement"; Shemshuchenko, Y. "Human Rights in the Field of Environmental Protection in the Draft of the New Constitution of the Ukraine." In Deimann and Dyssli, *Environmental Rights*, 33–44 (discussing Ukraine's approach to fundamental environmental rights).

[145] Ankersen, "Shared Knowledge," 826 (footnotes omitted).

[146] Montenegro constitution, art. 2, sec. 3; see generally, Wilson, Bryan P. "State Constitutional Environmental Rights and Judicial Activism: Is the Big Sky Falling?" *Emory Law Journal* 53 (2004): 627.

[147] Abate, "Climate Change," 27. ("Although constitutional statements of environmental rights are increasing, many national courts, such as those in Spain, Hungary, Turkey, Cameroon,

Thus, the majority of constitutional provisions purporting to advance substantive environmental constitutionalism have yet to be engaged meaningfully by domestic courts. Kysar remarks that many if not most constitutional provisions that address the environment have yet to find much traction in domestic constitutional and apex courts: "The provisions tend to be vaguely specified and weakly enforced [and] remain largely symbolic exercises even under the socially and environmentally progressive constitutions that have been adopted during the last half century."[148]

Likewise, Cho and Pedersen conclude that environmental constitutionalism faces challenges similar to those faced by other constitutionally embedded rights:

> The main problems with constitutionalising environmental rights ... relate to the vagueness of such provisions and lack of statutory guidance. As a result, constitutional environmental rights provisions often remain subject to the will of judiciaries and so the extent to which the right is actually protected may be illusory. Indeed, the question remains as to whether these rights are effective in protecting the environment, how people can assert them, especially when the burden of environmental degradation falls disproportionately on the world's poorest and most disenfranchised people, and what strategies will persuade courts to fashion – and enforce – effective remedies for violations of environmental rights. Resistance to entrenched fundamental rights provisions is to some extent a function of the genesis of these rights, and to the haphazard way in which they have been expressed in constitutions. What emerges is that while there may be a trend toward acceptance, the judicial reluctance to enforce fundamental environmental rights is similar to judicial reluctance to enforce certain other constitutionally entrenched provisions.[149]

This reluctance to engage environmental rights provisions is a function of the challenges courts face, including interpretation, equities, and the difficulties of balancing environmental interests against equally important social, political, and economic interests. Countries where environmental constitutionalism is dormant may benefit from comparative considerations. For example, as Bruch has observed, "[T]he near-total absence of African court cases

---

and Namibia, have severely limited the operation of environmental rights provisions, often interpreting them to offer no substantive protections or cause of action."); see Bruch *et al.*, "Constitutional Environmental Law," 138.

[148] Kysar, "Global Environmental Constitutionalism," 83, 87.

[149] H.S. Cho and O.W. Pedersen. "Environmental Rights and Future Generations." In *Routledge Handbook of Constitutional Law*, by M. Tushnet, T. Fleiner and C. Saunders (eds.). Abingdon, Oxon, and New York: Routledge, 2013.

interpreting these provisions suggests that it could be productive to consider how courts in other countries implement fundamental environmental rights."[150]

From a comparative perspective, what is to be observed is that courts across the globe are being called upon to adjudicate constitutional environmental rights with increasing frequency. Concomitant cases show that courts are engaging constitutional environmental rights provisions robustly, and as such are an increasingly potent force in the expansion of environmental constitutionalism globally.

[150] Bruch *et al.*, "Constitutional Environmental Law," 140.

4

Enforcing environmental constitutionalism

[T]he degradation of the environment and its progressive destruction have the capacity to alter the conditions that have permitted the development of man and to condemn us to the loss of the quality of life, for ourselves and our descendents and eventually the disappearance of the human species.

Colombian Constitutional Court, 2010

[T]he harms caused to the environment are the grand theme of the twenty-first century, and it is a duty of all to join together so that these harms are prevented, since, once produced, they are as a practical matter, impossible to repair.

Argentina Supreme Court, 2010

This chapter addresses matters that are central to adjudicating environmental constitutionalism, including standing and rights of action, which, though procedural and threshold in nature, can often be outcome determinative.

STANDING: WHO CAN ENFORCE CONSTITUTIONAL ENVIRONMENTAL RIGHTS?

Before a court reaches the merits of a constitutional claim, it will often consider the preliminary question of standing: whether the party who brought the suit has the right to invoke the court's jurisdiction. Most constitutional traditions have a standing doctrine, although they vary widely from country to country. Some constitutional systems limit who can challenge government action to certain members of the government or to an ombudsman, while others encourage anyone to seek judicial protection. Though sometimes seen as a fringe question, standing rules can have a dramatic effect on a nation's legal culture: where standing rules are broad and inviting, more people are encouraged to bring more cases to enforce more laws not only for their own private benefit but for the public good. Conversely, where courts restrict access to judicial fora, compliance with existing laws, as well as the progressive realization of constitutional promises, may be seen more as a matter of political discretion than of constitutional obligation.

Environmental cases in particular challenge conventional standing practices. Even where constitutional review is open to members of the public, standing has traditionally been limited to those who can assert well-recognized claims, including claims for harms recognized as common law (such as violations of property rights) or interests specifically identified in statutory provisions. In either case, the claims are personal, and standing rules tend to reflect the principle that only individuals who are personally and particularly injured may assert their interests against defendants and lay claim to scarce judicial resources.

Environmental harms, however, tend to affect groups of people generally and similarly. They may affect a whole community or culture or, in the case of climate change, all of humanity. Even where an individual can claim a particular harm – such as, for example, where a toxic leak proves carcinogenic – it is most likely that the plaintiff is not the only person so affected but that a whole community is affected by a greater incidence of cancer; indeed, the plaintiff is more likely to be able to show causation where the defendant's wrongful actions caused a broad-based injury rather than just his or her own illness. In even more difficult cases, the claim is based on the health not of an individual but of the environment in the abstract, and may raise questions about environmental aesthetics or the health of a particular animal population that do not directly affect most people at all.

A court confronting the question of whether a plaintiff who is not uniquely or particularly affected by a defendant's actions can nonetheless sue the defendant must balance competing constitutional values. On the one hand, out of deference to the political process in any constitutional democracy, a court must be wary of allowing too many challenges to legislative and administrative policies which, after all, may be well reasoned or be required by political or economic exigencies that ought not be easily disturbed. This is particularly true in large environmental cases, which often challenge development and other economic activity. Moreover, decisions taken by political actors are in a democracy remediable in political arenas without the necessity of judicial intervention. And courts often feel that they must protect scarce judicial resources against the flood of litigation that would ensue if the courtroom doors were flung open to anyone who had any interest in suing, and for whatever reasons. Such an attitude can have a significant effect on the promotion of environmental interests. In Malaysia, for example, "environmental rights have not received any significant judicial input as non-governmental environmental organisations are shut out from even pursuing court actions."[1] On the other hand, courts have recognized that bending the rules of standing may be the only means available to ensure that governments take environmental factors into account or protect the world's most vulnerable people from environmentally induced injuries.

Some constitutions make the decision for the court, clearly delineating who may sue and who may not, either for all claims or specifically in environmental cases. In Spain, constitutional environmental rights are protected, but they are enforceable only when an ombudsman initiates litigation. This contrasts markedly with the rest of the Spanish-speaking world, which tends to be receptive to constitutional environmental claims. The constitutions of Argentina and Ecuador, for instance, invite any citizen to vindicate such rights, the latter even allowing claims on behalf of nature itself.[2] The Constitution of South Africa, too, adopts an open attitude toward standing, which is buttressed by legislation that reinforces the right of any person to approach the court to assert his or her own interest, the interest of another, or the public interest. The statutory authority to sue extends to suits on behalf of the environment.[3]

Even where the positive law is not as clear, some courts have opened their doors to environmental activists, often seeing these non-traditional stakeholders not only as litigants but as partners in an ongoing campaign in which the courts are equally invested. In one case, the Bangladeshi Supreme Court thanked the Bangladeshi Environmental Lawyers Association (BELA), an environmental NGO, not only for elucidating the issues, but for bringing the case in the first place and particularly for bringing a constitutional claim challenging the government's failure to act: "Before parting with the case, we would like to place on record our deep appreciation for BELA and its members for their tireless, sincere and commendable service in their efforts for maintaining the ecological balance and also for the preservation of the environment in this part of the world."[4]

In the Philippines, the Supreme Court has developed a set of *"Rules of Procedure for Environmental Cases"* that encourages the vindication of

[1] Leng, Ang Hean. "Constitutional Rights Adjudication in Asian Societies." *The Law Review* (Sweet and Maxwell) (2011): 229, 241.
[2] Argentine constitution, pt. I, ch. 2, arts. 41–3; Constitución Política de la República del Ecuador, title II, ch. 7, arts. 71–4.
[3] See Kotzé and du Plessis. "Some Brief Observations," 157, 163–4 (discussing South Africa constitution, art. 20, and the National Environmental Management Act 107 of 1998 (NEMA), art. 32).
[4] *Farooque v. Bangladesh.* 30 CLC (HCD) (Supreme Court of Bangladesh High Court Division, July 15, 2001), 48.

constitutional and other environmental rights in extraordinary ways. Among its provisions are the authorization for citizen suits that can be brought by "[a]ny Filipino citizen in representation of others, including minors or generations yet unborn," (*Rule 2*, sec. 5); the authorization for the issuance of a Temporary Environmental Protection Order (*Rule 2*, sec. 8); the requirement that courts "prioritize the adjudication of environmental cases" and decide them within 1 year from the filing of the complaint (*Rule 4*, sec. 5); and protections against Strategic Lawsuits Against Public Participation, which are designed to thwart vindication of environmental rights (*Rule 6*).[5]

Importantly for environmental rights, the Philippine *Rules* provide for consideration of cases brought on behalf of nature, known as the "writ of Kalikasan." Such a writ can be pursued on behalf "of persons whose constitutional right to a balanced and healthful ecology is violated, or threatened" by a public official or private entity, "involving environmental damage of such magnitude as to prejudice the life, health or property of inhabitants in two or more cities or provinces." (*Rule 7*, sec. 1). The writ petition is filed without docket fees, and within 3 days of filing in the Supreme Court or Court of Appeal the court must decide whether to issue the relief sought, which consists of either an ocular inspection of the relevant place or the production or inspection of documents or things.[6] The writ has already been used in several high-profile cases involving issues ranging from the development of genetically modified foods to metallic ore mining.

Many courts, like the Filipino Court, have expanded standing in environmental suits upon recognizing the monumental challenge of environmental protection. The Indian Supreme Court has put it this way: "Experience of the recent [past] has brought to us the realization of the deadly effects of development on ecosystem. The entire world is facing a serious problem of environmental degradation due to indiscriminate development. Industrialization, burning of fossil fuels and massive deforestation are leading to degradation of environment."[7] The Colombian Constitutional Court has expressed concern about the environment even more starkly: "[T]he degradation of the

---

[5] For a discussion of the potential for environmental courts, including in thwarting strategic lawsuits against public participation ("SLAPP" suits), see George (Rock) Pring, and Catherine (Kitty) Pring, *Greening Justice: Creating and Improving Environmental Courts and Tribunals*, with an Introduction by Lalanath de Silva, The Access Initiative (2009), available at www.law. du.edu/documents/ect-study/greening-justice-book.pdf

[6] A.M. No. 09-6-8-SC, *Rules of Procedure for Environmental Cases*. (Supreme Court of the Philippines, April 13, 2010).

[7] *Karnataka Industrial Areas Development Board v. C. Kenchappa and Others*. AIRSCW 2546, at para. 41 (Supreme Court of India, 2006).

environment and its progressive destruction have the capacity to alter the conditions that have permitted the development of man and to condemn us to the loss of the quality of life, for ourselves and our descendents [sic] and eventually the disappearance of the human species."[8]

In Latin America, constitutional and statutory provisions have encouraged courts to expand standing for environmental cases even to those who cannot show a direct and individual injury; in India and its neighbors, courts have had to infer broad standing from legal and cultural norms. But in both of these regions, as well as in some other countries around the world, the commitment to opening the courthouse doors to environmental claimants is well established.

As far back as 1983, the Argentine courts had recognized "the right of any human being to protect his habitat" in a case seeking to protect the ecological equilibrium with respect to dolphins.[9] The current constitution provides a right to "any person" to "file a prompt and summary proceeding regarding constitutional guarantees … against any act or omission of the public author-ities or individuals which currently or imminently may damage, limit, modify or threaten rights and guarantees recognized by this Constitution" including, expressly "rights protecting the environment." This summary procedure, known as a *tutela* action, may be invoked by "the damaged party, the ombuds-man and the associations which foster such ends registered according to a law determining their requirements and organization forms."[10]

The Argentine Supreme Court has interpreted the provision broadly, invok-ing the diffuse action described by the lower court in the dolphin case. For instance, the Supreme Court of Argentina invalidated a permit that would have allowed mining in a UNESCO Natural Heritage Site on the basis of a diffuse *tutela* action brought under Section 43 of the Argentine Constitution. The Court explained the rationale for giving effect to the provision in these terms:

> The environmental *tutela* reinforces the duties that each citizen has for the care of the rivers, the diversity of the flora and fauna, the nearby soil, the atmosphere. These duties are the correlation that the same citizens have to

[8] *Sentencia C-703/10.* (Colombia Constitutional Court, 2010).
[9] *Kattan* (Argentina), discussed in Allan R. Brewer-Carías. *Constitutional Protection of Human Rights in Latin America: A Comparative Study of Amparo Proceedings.* Cambridge University Press, 2009: 199, cited in Hector A. Mairal. *Collective and Class Actions in Argentina, National Report,* The Globalization of Class Actions Conference Proceedings, December, 2007, available at http://globalclassactions.stanford.edu/sites/default/files/documents/Argentina_National_Report.pdf
[10] Argentine constitution, pt. I, ch. II, art. 43.

enjoy a healthy environment, for themselves and for future generations, because the harm that an individual can cause to the collective good is a harm to himself. The improvement or degradation of the environment benefits or harms the whole population, because it is a good that belongs to the social and trans-individual sphere, and it is from here that the judges derive the particular energy to give effect to these constitutional commands.[11]

The notion that the protection of the environment is a collective good justifies the broad standing rules that permit *any* citizen to sue for a harm done to the whole society. As the Chilean Court said in the landmark Trillium decision:

> The right to live in an environment free of contamination is a human right of Constitutional hierarchy, which presents a double character: public subjective right and public collective right. The first aspect means that its exercise corresponds, as provided in article 19 of the Political Constitution, to all persons, being the duty of the authority through the regular legal suits and through the constitutional protection claim to protect that right. And regarding the second aspect, the right to live in an environment free from contamination is meant to protect social rights of a collective character, whose defense is the interest of the community as a whole, in the local level as well as in the national level, to all the country, because the very basis of the existence as a society and as a nation are comprehended, and due to the fact that in damaging or limiting the environment and natural resources, the possibilities of life and development of the present and future generations are also limited. In this sense, the safekeeping of these rights are in the interest of the whole society, because it affects to a plurality of parties that are placed in the same factual situation, and whose damage, despite the fact that it carries an enormous social harm, does not cause a meaningful damage clearly appreciated in the individual realm.[12]

---

[11] *Expediente:* – 6706–2009 (Argentine Supreme Court, 2010), Libro de Acuerdos N° 53, F° 364/380, N° 118.

> La Corte Suprema de Justicia de la Nación, en el caso "*Mendoza Beatriz S. y otro c/ Estado Nacional y otro*" del 20 de junio de 2006- Cons. 20, ha dicho que "La tutela del ambiente importa el cumplimiento de los deberes que cada uno de los ciudadanos tiene respecto del cuidado de los ríos, de la diversidad de la flora y la fauna, de los suelos colindantes, de la atmósfera. Estos deberes son el correlato que esos mismos ciudadanos tienen a disfrutar de un ambiente sano, para sí y para las generaciones futuras, porque el daño que un individuo causa al bien colectivo se lo está causando a sí mismo. La mejora o degradación del ambiente beneficia o perjudica a toda la población, porque es un bien que pertenece a la esfera social y transindividual, y de allí deriva la particular energía con que los jueces deben actuar para hacer efectivos estos mandatos constitucionales (Cons. 18) ..."

[12] Trillium.

This trend is replicated in courts throughout Latin America, where constitutional texts have already lowered standing barriers by allowing any injured
person to vindicate their constitutional rights in protective or *amparo* or *tutela*
actions; it is not, in these countries, such a large step to extend the right to suit to
persons who seek to vindicate the diffuse rights of a community or of the whole
society. In Peru, the constitution does not explicitly mention the right to bring
collective environmental actions but the Constitutional Procedure Code does.[13]
Likewise, in Ecuador, the *amparo* law permits collective actions to protect the
environment (including that of indigenous communities), though here environmental rights are amplified by the protection of the rights of nature, which by
definition are enforceable by people who are generally affected and who claim
the rights not on behalf of themselves but of nature itself.

In other Latin American countries, courts have read the combination of
substantive protection for the environment and a commitment to ecological
values on the one hand and broad standing provisions on the other to permit
diffuse actions. The Costa Rican Constitutional Chamber, for instance, has
held that "even though a direct and clear suit for the claimant does not
exist ... all inhabitants suffer a prejudice in the same proportion as if it were
a direct harm," such that a claimant may seek to protect the right "to maintain
the natural equilibrium of the ecosystem."[14]

Likewise, the Colombian constitution provides for *tutela* actions, which
dramatically enhance access to justice by providing for broad jurisdiction over
cases by individuals, with or without lawyers, to enforce fundamental rights.[15]
This has become widely used in Colombian courts to vindicate environmental rights, whether under environmental provisions or other provisions relating
to the environment, such as the right to life, to dignity, or to health; most of
the Colombian cases discussed in this book are *tutela* actions, such as those
brought by the recyclers for violation of their environmental and livelihood
rights, cases brought by residents of an apartment bloc that was not connected
to the city's water system for violation of the right to water, the cases brought
by people who lived near an open sewer, and so on.[16] However, where

---

[13] Peru Constitutional Procedure Code, pt. 40, quoted in Brewer-Carías, *Constitutional
Protection of Human Rights*, 198.
[14] *Decision 1700–03* (Costa Rica Constitutional Chamber), quoted in Brewer-Carías,
Constitutional Protection of Human Rights, 200.
[15] Constitución Política de la República de Colombia de 1991. title II, ch. 4, art. 86.
[16] The right to health is particularly well established in Colombia and has been extensively
litigated. "Between 1999 and 2003, the Constitutional Court received almost 145,000 writs of
injunction, 25 percent of them invoking the right to health, with an average of 7.8 tutelage
actions per 10,000 inhabitants during that period. Seventy-one percent of them were based on

plaintiffs assert collective environmental interests that are grounded not on the health of the claimant but on the harm to the environment, courts have accepted the cases under a separate constitutional writ, the *acción popular*, which permits courts to vindicate diffuse interests.[17] The Mexican constitution, for example, permits diffuse rights including in environmental cases.

In Asia, the judicial creativity and commitment to environmental protection and sustainable development has made up for the omissions in the constitutional texts. The principle of broad and diffuse standing was pioneered by the Indian Supreme Court in the 1970s in the form of Public Interest Litigation (PIL), but has since spread to neighboring countries as well as some African nations.

PIL was a deliberate effort by the Indian court to expand the bounds of standing beyond the familiar private right of action that would normally be recognized in a common law court to vindicate a private interest. "Public interest litigation contemplates legal proceeding for vindication or enforcement of fundamental rights of a group of persons or community which are not able to enforce their fundamental rights on account of their incapacity, poverty or ignorance of law."[18] PIL has proven to be extremely important in a wide variety of socioeconomic cases, but it is a particularly useful construct for the vindication of environmental rights because it recognizes not only that environmental harms affect society generally, but that they tend to exert particular pressure on the most vulnerable segments of society. These claims are often based on the environment because it provides access to water, arable land, shelter for the world's poorest people, and to the essentials to sustain a certain quality of life, including individual dignity, a cohesive community, and life itself. They are brought on behalf of the world's poorest people because people with means can often purchase immunity from environmental degradation: they can live in neighborhoods that are not used as landfills, they have sufficient access to medical care to be buffered from the worst health effects of industrial air pollution, they can access food and water from

medical attention rights violations" including the right to a healthy environment and environment-based health claims. Social Watch "National Reports, Colombia: A Resource Allocation that will not meet the MDGs," 2006, 195, n.3, available at www.socialwatch.org/node/10994. Some of these cases involve environmental causes for violations of the right to health.

[17] *Sentencia T-724/11* (Colombia Constitutional Court, 2011) (rejecting a tutela action where the plaintiffs represented the community generally in a case concerning the cleaning of a canal where open sewers had caused illness in the local population).

[18] *Subhash Kumar v. State of Bihar* (India, January 9, 1991).

sophisticated infrastructures in global markets, and they do not depend on the nearby rivers remaining clean for their sustenance.

Litigation that ties environmental harm to deprivation of sustenance can be theoretically easier to maintain because the harm is easily recognizable. However, proving that the complained-of injury resulted from the action of the defendant can be both costly and time-consuming. Most legal services agencies throughout the world are experienced in asserting immediate and direct claims on behalf of their clients (e.g., accessing medical care or social benefits), but environmental litigation entails different and often more complex and more elaborate types of litigation. The Indian Supreme Court and those courts following in its footsteps have recognized the inordinate burdens borne by these groups and have often attempted to alleviate them where they can, starting with standing. "A petition . . . for the prevention of pollution," the Indian court has said, "is maintainable at the instance of affected persons or even by a group of social workers or journalists."[19] The Supreme Court of Nepal has followed suit, recognizing the standing of a non-profit organization to vindicate environmental rights on behalf of the public. In the Nepalese case, the group claimed rights on behalf of residents, as well as on behalf of workers to wear masks.[20] "[A]s the environmental conversation is one of the objectives of the applicant 'Leaders Inc.,' it needs to be accepted that the applicant has the *locus standi* for the prevention of the environmental degradation."[21] In public interest litigation, anyone might entreat the court to vindicate a *public* interest. In such cases, "*Locus standi* has a larger ambit in current legal semantics than the accepted individualistic jurisprudence of old."[22] As the Sri Lankan court has said: "Such action would be for the betterment of the general public and the very reason for the institution of such action may be in the interest of the general public."[23]

In Uganda, the High Court has read a broad standing provision in the constitution to its fullest. The constitutional text reads as follows: "Any person who claims that a fundamental or other right or freedom guaranteed under this constitution has been infringed or threatened, is entitled to apply to a competent Court for redress which may include which compensation." On numerous occasions, the Court has used this language to allow constitutional environmental claims. In one case involving a permit to allow a company to

---

[19] *Ibid.*   [20] *Dhungel* v. *Godawari* (Nepal, October 31, 1995).   [21] *Ibid.*, 97.
[22] *Salley* v. *Colombo Municipal Council and Others*. Application No. 252/2007, 11 (Supreme Court of Sri Lanka, 2007) (quoting *Maharajah Singh* v. *Uttara Pradesh* A.I.R. 1976 S.C. 2602).
[23] *Ibid.*, 17.

grow sugar cane on land that had been set aside as a nature reserve, the Court explained the "importance" of the constitutional language:

> [I]t allows any individual or organization to protect the rights of another even though that individual is not suffering the injury complained of or does not know that he is suffering from the alleged injury. To put it in the biblical sense the Article makes all of us our "brother keeper." In that sense it gives all the power to speak for those who cannot speak for their rights due to their ignorance, poverty or apathy. In that regard I cannot hide any pride to say that our constitution is among the best the world over because it emphasizes the point that violation of any human right or fundamental right of one person is violation of the right of all.[24]

PIL has a strong normative ethos of social justice. It promotes a transformative agenda by encouraging marginalized members of the political community to assert rights embodied even in the constitution's aspirational promises. In one of its landmark PIL cases, the Indian court explained why the matter of standing necessarily must lie within judicial discretion: ". . . in a modern complex society which is seeking to bring about transformation of its social and economic structure and trying to reach social justice to the vulnerable section of the people by creating new social, collective 'diffuse' rights and interests imposing new public duties on the state and other public authorities infinite number of situations are bound to arise which cannot be imprisoned in a rigid mould or a Procrustean formula."[25] Indeed, this was a clear purpose of the Indian court's approach, as described in an early landmark case involving judicial independence: "Where [a person who has been wronged] is by reason of poverty, helplessness or disability or sociality or economically disadvantaged position, unable to approach the Court for relief, any member of the public can maintain an application [in court] in case of breach of any fundamental right to this Court under Article 32."[26]

The normative quality of PIL follows it wherever PIL actions have been recognized, from Tanzania to Sri Lanka, where the court there described its acceptance of PIL "for the purpose of making fundamental rights more meaningful for a majority of the people."[27,28] As one Ugandan court has said,

---

[24] *Advocates Coalition for Development and Environment* v. *Attorney General* Miscellaneous Cause No. 0100 of 2004 (High Court of Uganda, July 13, 2005).

[25] *S.P. Gupta* v. *President of India and Others.* No. AIR 1982 SC 149 (Supreme Court of India, December 30, 1981).

[26] *Ibid.*, 17.

[27] See, e.g., *Felix Joseph Mavika* v. *Dar es Salaam City Commission.* Civil Case No. 316 of 2000 (High Court of Tanzania, October 23, 2000).

[28] *Salley v. Colombo* (Sri Lanka, 2007).

"Public interest litigation usually involves the interest of the poor, ignorant, deprived, ill-informed, desperate and marginalized society where justice is always high horse."[29] The Pakistani Supreme Court has elaborated on this, explaining why standing should be expanded where poor people's rights are especially at stake. In a case about the installation of electrical grids, the Court said that: "Such a danger as depicted . . . is bound to affect a large number of people who may suffer from it unknowingly because of lack of awareness, information and education and also because such sufferance is silent and fatal and most of the people who would be residing near, under or at a dangerous distance of the grid station or such installation do not know that they are facing any risk or are likely to suffer by such risk." In these situations, the rights are most likely to be vindicated only if "some conscientious citizens aware of their rights and the possibility of danger come forward."[30]

Broad standing is also invariably tied to the commitment to rule of law, in that it encourages holding public officials accountable for compliance with constitutional rules and norms. But some courts have seen a deeper, more socially transformative reason for allowing citizens readily to vindicate their constitutional rights. The Bangladeshi Supreme Court, for example, has explained that "[i]f justice is not easily and equally accessible to every citizen there then [can] hardly be a Rule of Law. If access to justice is limited to the rich, the more advantaged and more powerful sections of society, then the poor and the deprived will have no stake in the Rule of Law and they will be more readily available to turn against it. Ready and equal access to justice is a sine qua non for the maintenance of the Rule of Law."[31] The protection of the law, the court has said in another case, "should be available to everyone, rich or poor."[32] In Bangladesh, in fact, the court has been at pains to emphasize that its adoption of public interest litigation is not out of blind deference to the Indian Supreme Court but emanates from Bangladesh's own constitutional history and political culture. It derives, in that country, from the notion of popular sovereignty as the driving force of its revolutionary constitution, as well as from the nation's commitment to socialism:

---

[29] *Advocates Coalition for Development and Environment* v. *Attorney General* (Uganda, July 13, 2005).
[30] *Shelhla Zia* v. *WAPDA* (Pakistan, February 12, 1994).
[31] *Farooque* v. *Government of Bangladesh.* Writ Pet. No. 998 of 1994, Civil Action 24 of 1995 (July 25, 1996) (Supreme Court of Bangladesh High Court Division, August 28, 1997).
[32] *Farooque* v. *Bangladesh* (Bangladesh, 2001), 48 (citing *People's Union for Democratic Rights* v. *Union of India.* 1982 AIR 1473, 1983 SCR (1) 456 (Supreme Court of India, September 18, 1982).

With the power of the people looming large behind the constitution horizon it is difficult to conceive of Article 102 as a vehicle or mechanism for realising exclusively individual rights upon individual complaints. The Supreme Court being a vehicle, a medium or mechanism devised by the Constitution for the exercise of the judicial power on behalf of the people, the people will always remain the focal point of concern of the Supreme court while disposing of justice or propounding any judicial theory or interpreting any provision of the Constitution.[33]

This ethos has practical implications for the problem of standing. "Viewed in this context," the court continued, "interpreting the words 'any person aggrieved' meaning only and exclusively individuals and excluding the consideration of people as a collective and consolidated personality will be a stand taken against the constitution. ... When there is [in the Constitution] a State ownership on behalf of the people of the instruments and means of production and distribution the concept of exclusive personal wrong or injury is hardly appropriate."[34]

Taking public interest and diffuse standing doctrines one step further, a few courts have allowed suits on behalf of people not yet living and on behalf of nature itself. If the purpose of these doctrines is to protect the interests of those who (or that) cannot protect themselves, then extending standing in this way is not illogical. In *Comunidad de Chañaral v. Codeco División el Saldor*, the Chilean Supreme Court held that a farmer had standing to enjoin drainage of Lake Chungarà, recognizing that with environmental damage "future generation[s] would [challenge] the lack of [foresight] of their predecessors if the environment would be polluted and nature destroyed ..."[35] And in *Minors Oposa* the Philippine Supreme Court recognized intergenerational standing – that is, the right of an individual to sue on behalf of future generations – although it did so on the basis of pre-existing norms as much as constitutional right. The Court explained that "even before the ratification of the 1987 Constitution, specific statutes already paid special attention to the 'environmental right'" of the present and future generations, citing two policies that articulate a goal of "fulfil[ling] the social, economic and other requirements of present and future generations of Filipinos." "As its goal," the court said, "it speaks of the 'responsibilities of each generation as trustee and guardian of the environment for succeeding generations.'"[36]

---

[33] *Farooque v. Government of Bangladesh* (Bangladesh, July 25, 1996).   [34] *Ibid.*

[35] Kravchenko and Bonine, *Human Rights*, 70; see also *Pedro Flores et al. v. Codelco* (Chile), 260, or *Pedro Flores y Otros v. Corporacion Del Cobre* (Chile), 260.

[36] *Minors Oposa*, 191 (Philippines, 1993).

Although its actual effectiveness may be debated, intergenerational standing is useful in cases where the environmental damage is long-term and grows over time such that future generations are more threatened by irreversible and irremediable damage than the present one, even for actions taken presently.

Indeed, in certain cases, the problem of intergenerational standing is less challenging than the problem of international standing. While some environmental violations are felt locally, the consequences of others do not stop at national boundaries, which do limit the jurisdictions of constitutions and constitutional courts. This is particularly salient with challenges based on climate change, whose effects are felt not only across time but across space as well, and it is particularly true where, as noted earlier, the harm is felt primarily not only to individuals, but also to other species of flora and fauna and essentially to the environment itself. But international standing, too, makes sense if the purpose of allowing the claim in a judicial forum is to protect those rights that would not be protected politically or in other forums. These international claims may be brought in international tribunals, but only in the rare instance where international law protects the particular type of claim at issue and creates a forum for the enforcement of that protection; in most cases, domestic constitutional tribunals may be the only venues available to environmental litigants, even where the injury transcends national boundaries.

The problem of standing also relates to the definition of a cognizable injury: lowering the threshold for standing almost invariably recognizes broader types of harms. Where a plaintiff's property or health is impaired by reason of the defendant's environmental degradation, standing is clear in large part because the injury is easily recognizable to a common law or civil court. But a court may be less likely to find standing where the claimed injury is that the rivers and forests are no longer as pristine as they once were, or that once-potable water has become contaminated, or that thousands of acres of previously arable land have become desert. These diffuse claims not only open the courthouse doors to more numerous and more different classes of plaintiffs, but require judicial recognition of more diverse types of harms.

WHO IS RESPONSIBLE? IDENTIFYING
THE APPROPRIATE DEFENDANT

In constitutional environmental cases, standing is the most significant hurdle for litigants to surmount as they attempt to invoke a court's jurisdiction, though defendants will often try to dismiss claims on other grounds as well to prevent a court from ever reaching the merits. One common strategy is to assert that the defendant cannot be held liable for the injuries complained of.

In the simplest constitutional cases, defendants are state actors – members of the executive branch or, less frequently, the legislature or even a court – all of whom are normally obligated to comply with constitutional mandates. In most situations, it does not matter whether the government is acting as sovereign, as regulator, as licensor, as a participant in the market, or in any other capacity since its constitutional obligations are the same. In federal systems, the local (state or provincial) government may be liable instead of or in addition to the central authorities; this is particularly common in situations involving water because of the joint responsibility that different levels of government often have for joint management of water resources.

Under the theory of horizontal application that operates in some constitutional systems, private parties may also be held accountable for violation of constitutional norms. The 2008 Kosovo Constitution, for instance, expressly states that "[e]very person and entity in the Republic of Kosovo is subject to the provisions of the constitution."[37] The current Turkish Constitution is more explicit, imposing on "the state and citizens" the duty to "improve the natural environment, to protect environmental health, and to prevent environmental pollution."[38] This means that a private actor may be judicially required to conform to constitutional norms.

In other situations, horizontal application has been inferred mainly from the entrenchment of environmental values in the constitutional culture. In Colombia, the constitutional court found that a private landowner whose commercial pig farm created an environmental nuisance that injured her neighbor was obligated to conform to the constitutional requirements for environmental protection. The court explained that, because each person has a right to not be bothered by environmental intrusions into his or her home, it cannot be said that the exercise of a commercial activity can be exercised to the detriment of a neighbor's rights, given the inactivity of the officials charged with controlling such situations.[39] In that case, the suit was brought against the municipality and the remedy ran against the government officials who were ordered to cease the offending commercial activity, but the

---

[37] Constitution of Republic of Kosovo, art. 16(4).

[38] See Türkiye Cumhuriyeti Anayasas¹ [Turkey Republic Constitution] pt. II, ch. III, art 56 ("Everyone has the right to live in a healthy, balanced environment. It is the duty of the state and citizens to improve the natural environment, to protect environmental health, and to prevent environmental pollution.").

[39] *María Elena Burgos v. Municipality of Campoalegre. Sentencia T-095/97* (Colombia Constitutional Court, February 27, 1997).

burden was directly felt by the private entrepreneur whose actions caused the environmental violation. In another case, the Colombian court ordered the water and sewage company to conduct a study which, in conjunction with governmental authorities, would help determine the most effective ways of cleaning up a canal that had caused illness among members of the adjacent community.[40] For several years in the 1980s, the Indian Supreme Court sought to expand the reach of the constitution "primarily to inject respect for human-rights and social conscience in our corporate structure. The purpose of expansion has not been to destroy the raison d'[être] of creating corporations but to advance the human rights jurisprudence."[41]

Horizontal application of constitutional obligations is useful in environmental litigation because a court may be more likely to find liability against a private party than against the government, both because separation of powers principles tend to protect government actors, and because in most cases the private party's action (e.g., the cutting down of the forests or the mining) is more likely to be the direct cause of the environmental degradation than is the government's decision to authorize the private party's action or its failure to protect against it. Aside from liability, a court may be more likely to award damages against a private defendant than against a government defendant, because the latter is likely to be protected against damage awards by sovereign immunity and, in any event, may be less likely to comply with a court order.

TIMING: WHEN IS THE RIGHT TIME TO FILE A CLAIM?

Typically, a constitutional violation occurs *after* a defendant's actions have caused a cognizable harm to a defined cohort of individuals who are the intended beneficiaries of the constitutional right. But the precise timing of an environmental injury often makes it difficult to determine when a claim may be brought. This is perhaps a question of the definition of the right: is the constitutional right to a healthy environment violated any time a governmental policy throws out of balance the "rhythm and harmony" of nature? Or is the triggering action when there is a showing of harm to the environment – that is, when the river is polluted or the forest is cut? Or perhaps before the harm occurs, when the government issues the permit or allows the development project? Or perhaps after the injury has become evident and can be quantified?

---

[40] *Sentencia T-724/11* (Colombia Constitutional Court, 2011).
[41] *M.C. Mehta v. Union of India* (India, 1987) (rejecting American state action doctrine, but not confirming liability against corporation, in that case due to lack of time and information, in a case involving a leak of oleum).

Or all of the above? Most courts would require at least some action on the part of the defendant to have taken place, and many courts will require more.

These questions may be closely linked to standing. Standing normally requires that the plaintiff prove that the injury is actual or imminently threatened; courts will typically not recognize a cause of action if the harm is speculative or conjectural because there is no basis for holding a defendant liable for harm that he or she has not yet caused. At that point, there is nothing for the defendant to be responsible for and predicting the harm is far too speculative: will the plaintiff actually become ill, how severely, how much will treatment cost, how long will it last, and so on? Even where diffuse standing is accepted, it can be challenging for plaintiffs' groups to prove *in advance*, even by a preponderance of the evidence, how widespread an adverse health effect will be or how devastating to the community it will be when it strikes. Thus, a court may be less likely to accept a suit where the plaintiff's physical condition is not at present compromised. Similar problems arise where the plaintiff's claim of *future harm* is based on the right to life, dignity, property, or some other human right.

In cases claiming harm to the environment – as opposed to claims of harm to individuals or communities – courts have recognized the need to act *before* the damage occurs and many have shown particular solicitude to claims of *threatened* environmental damage. In the Argentine case that sought to protect against threats to a UNESCO world heritage site, the court reiterated (from a previous case) the conviction that "the harms caused to the environment are the grand theme of the twenty-first century, and it is a duty of all to join together so that these harms are prevented, since, once produced, they are as a practical matter, impossible to repair." As a result, the court continued, no one can have a right to compromise public health and bring death and harms to neighbouring residents by the use of their property or, specifically, by the practice of a profession or industry.[42] In a Turkish administrative case, the court cancelled a license for gold processing before it even went into effect, upon finding that it "would operate at a risk which, if materialised, would certainly directly or indirectly impair human life due to the resulting damage to the environment."[43] Implicitly or explicitly, many courts entertaining constitutional environmental claims have adopted the precautionary principle, which permits the vindication of rights before harm has been done on the assumption that if it were to occur, the harm might be devastating to humans or nature and would likely be irreversible.

---

[42] *Expediente: – 6706–2009* (Argentina, 2010).   [43] *Senih Özay* (Turkey, 1997).

At the other end of the timeline, environmental claims may sometimes be brought too late. This could occur where the harm caused by the environmental violation is not known, such as where, for instance, dumping or mining contributes to increased cancer rates in a community. In these cases, courts may be leery of accepting such claims if the evidence of the violation has disappeared or dissipated, if corporate control over the defendant has changed making assessment of liability difficult, or if the applicable statute of limitations has run.

OTHER UNIQUE PROCEDURAL RULES CHALLENGES

Many constitutional and other apex courts have also varied some other procedural requirements for the purpose of facilitating the vindication of environmental rights. Most of these variations apply in environmental rights cases generally, regardless of whether the source of the right asserted lies in the constitution or elsewhere.

For example, the Philippine *Rules of Procedure in Environmental Cases* explicitly adopts the precautionary principle as a matter of evidence, explaining that: "When there is a lack of full scientific certainty in establishing a causal link between human activity and environmental effect, the court shall apply the precautionary principle in resolving the case before it. The constitutional right of the people to a balanced and healthful ecology shall be given the benefit of the doubt."[44] The *Rules* also broadly define the types of evidence that may be admissible in environmental cases: "Photographs, videos and similar evidence of events, acts, transactions of wildlife, wildlife by-products or derivatives, forest products or mineral resources subject of a case shall be admissible when authenticated by the person who took the same, by some other person present when said evidence was taken, or by any other person competent to testify on the accuracy thereof."[45] As a result, the absence of proof of particular harm does not typically preclude a cause of action or the finding of a violation, given the consequences of failing to protect the environment. The Colombian court has been emphatic on this point as well: it has upheld a set of reforms that permit the pre-emptive confiscation of property that would be used to harm the environment, even in the absence of scientific certainty of the damage, noting that the ill effects, harms, risks, and dangers that the environment faces guide the interpretation of constitutional environmental rights. In that case, upholding the regulations ensured

---

[44] Philippine Rules, pt. V., rule 20, sec. 1.   [45] *Ibid.*, rule 21.

that the respective authorities had the necessary means to protect the environment.[46] In south Asia, the principle has also been broadly recognized: in one case from Sri Lanka, the court ordered an environmental impact statement for a mining enterprise, noting that "if ever pollution is discerned, uncertainty as to whether the assimilative capacity has been reached should not prevent measures being insisted upon to reduce such pollution from reaching the environment."[47]

This concern for the environment sometimes leads to the suspension of other procedural rules. The Argentine court, for instance, put to one side "the ancient concepts of the burden of proof," ordering the mining companies seeking a permit to prove that their activities would not cause environmental damage. The court also noted that, because environmental harms often elude certitude, it would accept probabilistic evidence of harm to allow the case to proceed. Indeed, it has been noted that throughout Argentina "a theory developed in the last decades [that] has changed the traditional rule that plaintiff bears the main burden of proof. According to it, the party required to prove or disprove a given fact is the one that is in a better situation to do so. On these grounds, important companies who are defendants are often placed in the need to prove their defenses, while individual plaintiffs may offer little or no evidence (and are not subject to perjury sanctions when they lie)," according to a report on Argentine diffuse and collective rights.[48]

Such probabilistic elasticity seems to apply in a broad array of situations but when invoked in environmental cases it can be particularly helpful in two ways. Leaving the burden of production with the plaintiff deters litigation, increases the cost on plaintiffs of maintaining litigation, and makes success less likely simply because of the difficulty of amassing sufficient evidence to prove the existence of or potential for harm to humans or nature. Shifting the burden may in some cases dramatically reduce these obstacles. In addition, shifting the burden of persuasion to the defendant also makes it substantially easier for the plaintiff because the defendant's obligation to persuade a court that no harm will ensue from its activities may be much more onerous than showing the potential for some harm. This can be seen, for instance, in the Ecuadorian case vindicating the rights of nature, where the court imposed on

---

[46] *Expediente D-8019* (Colombia Constitutional Court, 2010).
[47] *Bulankulama and Six Others* v. *Ministry of Industrial Development and Seven Others*. S.C. Application No 884/99 (F.R) (Supreme Court of the Democratic Socialist Republica of Sri Lanka); see also e.g., *Vellore Citizens' Welfare Forum* v. *Union of India*. Writ. Pet. No. 914 of 1991 (Supreme Court of India, April 26, 1996); *Shelhla Zia* v. *WAPDA* (Pakistan, February 12, 1994).
[48] Mairal, "Collective and Class Actions in Argentina," 21.

the defendant the obligation to prove that road construction did not harm the environment, an obligation that the government could not satisfy.[49]

In other cases, courts have removed even more specific barriers that could impede the vindication of environmental rights. The Ugandan High Court has inferred from the constitution's broad standing the dilution of certain procedural requirements in order to permit a suit to proceed. The court inferred that the ordinary rule that defendants have 45 days in which to respond to a constitutional complaint "cannot apply to a matter where the rights and freedoms of the people are being or are about to be infringed." The right at issue in that case was the environmental right "to a clean and healthy environment" that would be violated if the government allowed chimpanzees to be exported to China.[50] Despite these concessions, though, the costs of litigation can still be a significant deterrent for many putative plaintiffs.[51]

DEFENSES AND LIMITATIONS

Jurisdictional limitations, as between federal and subnational courts, like rules governing venue may frustrate efforts to pursue claims. Even if jurisdiction is accepted, most constitutional defenses and limitations apply similarly in substantive environmental rights litigation. State and non-state defendants may assert the usual factual defenses (e.g., that they did not do the complained-of action, or that their actions or omissions did not cause the complained-of injury) and legal defenses (e.g., that their actions or omissions did not violate any legal duty imposed by the constitution). Legal objections may be particularly pertinent where the fundamental environmental right falls under a directive principle of state policy and is therefore formally judicially unenforceable. As we have seen, however, even in these situations, some courts have overcome this objection by finding that the unenforceable environmental right appertains derivatively to another enforceable right, such as the right to life or to health.

---

[49] *Wheeler.*
[50] *Greenwatch v. Uganda Wildlife Authority* (Uganda, 2004) (arising from Miscellaneous Cause No. 15 of 2004).
[51] In some countries, procedural rules are adjusted for environmental cases in statutory rather than constitutional provisions. The Tort Law in China, for instance, places the burden of proof on the polluter. Tort Liability Law of the People's Republic of China, December 26, 2009, available at www.gov.cn/flfg/2009-12/26/content_1497435.htm, discussed in Tseming Yang and Adam Moser, *Environmental Tort Litigation in China* (2011), available at http://digitalcommons.law.scu.edu/facpubs/434

In most constitutional systems, environmental rights are not absolute and may be limited or overcome in at least three situations, all of which pertain equally to the enforcement of other constitutional rights. First, the right may be limited if it conflicts with another right, such as the right to life or a non-derogable right like the right to dignity. As we have seen, however, in some cases, the court's concern for the environment overrides even seemingly compelling human interests, as happened, for instance, when a Colombian court held that the health of a disabled man, which improved through animal therapy with a parrot, had to yield to the environmental interest in protecting wild birds.[52] In an Israeli case involving the provision of water to residents of illegal desert settlement, the court tried to "find the balance between the demand for keeping the law and its appropriate enforcement and the concern for a person's basic and existential need for water, even if he does not abide by the law."[53] As noted in the previous chapter, however, the positive law that controls judicial discretion rarely identifies how competing interests should be balanced.

Second, the environmental right, like other rights, is almost always subject to a limitations clause or a proportionality test.[54] The South African consti-tution, for instance, states that: "The rights in the Bill of Rights may be limited only in terms of law of general application to the extent that the limitation is reasonable and justifiable in an open and democratic society based on human dignity, equality and freedom, taking into account all relevant factors ..."[55] Thus, Parliament could restrict environmental rights if necessary to protect human dignity or equality such as, for instance, where the government develops electrical or water infrastructure that benefits the ability of people to live in dignity though at the same time impairing the natural environ-ment.[56] This could happen, too, where the right to work is pitted against environmental interests. Likewise, even where a constitution is not explicit on the topic, most constitutional rights are subject to a proportionality test, so that an environmental right may be limited in proportion to a particularly strong need. The requirement of proportionality is especially relevant in environ-mental litigation where balancing is almost intrinsic: a timber permit that harms the environment may nonetheless be permitted if its scope is appropri-ate to the need. In South Africa, for example, the court has limited vindication

---

[52] *Sentencia T-608/11* (Colombia Constitutional Court, 2011).
[53] See also *Abu Masad v. Water Commissioner* (Israel Supreme Court, 2011) (considering the proportionality and reasonableness of the Water Authority's manner of providing water).
[54] On proportionality, see generally, Barak, A. *Proportionality: Constitutional Rights and their Limitations*. Cambridge Studies in Constitutional Law, 2012.
[55] South Africa constitution, ch. 2, art. 36.　　[56] See Daly, *Dignity Rights*, 119, 156–7.

of some socioeconomic rights where the infringement is "reasonable" in light of all the relevant factors.[57]

Third, courts may decline to vindicate environmental interests if they are deemed to be not an individual right but an obligation on the state, such as is often the case with SECs. Thus, a court may order the government to develop a plan for environmental protection, but will not find that a government or private actor has violated a particular plaintiff's right to a healthy environment. Sometimes, this precludes the cause of action; other times, as will be discussed in the next chapter, it dictates the form of remedy.

In each of these situations, environmental rights are limited and subject to being "trumped" by other considerations. A counterexample is found in a rule of decision used in some courts of *"in dubio pro natura,"* which means that when in doubt or when equities are balanced evenly, a court must defer to the decision that upholds environmental rights.

Plaintiffs seeking to enforce constitutional rights face a number of hurdles just getting and staying in court. Defendants have many opportunities to petition courts to dismiss cases for reasons having to do with the identity of the parties, the timing, or simply because the plaintiffs lack adequate proof of the injury they seek to remedy. While adhering to the general principles that govern litigation throughout the world, many courts have nonetheless found ways to encourage plaintiffs to bring constitutional environmental claims by shifting, bending, or outright ignoring certain rules out of an appreciation for the important values at stake in such litigation – the potential cost to humans and to the environment itself of doing nothing and the likely irreversibility of environmental damage. In many cases, the authority for doing so comes not from the constitution itself but from common law principles relating to environmental law. Even so, once plaintiffs have effectively invoked judicial authority, the challenges to obtaining a remedy and having it enforced are enormous. We consider these challenges in the next chapter.

---

[57] *Lindiwe Mazibuko and Others v. City of Johannesburg and Others.* CCT 39/09 2009 ZAC 28 (Constitutional Court of South Africa).

5

Identifying remedies and practices in environmental constitutionalism

[The Constitution lays an] obligation on this Court to protect the fundamental rights of the people and for that purpose this Court has all incidental and ancillary powers including the power to forge new remedies and fashion new strategies designed to enforce the fundamental rights. It is in realization of this constitutional obligation that this Court has in the past innovated new methods and strategies for the purpose of securing enforcement of the fundamental rights, particularly in the case of the poor and the disadvantaged who are denied their basic human rights and to whom freedom and liberty have no meaning.

Indian Supreme Court, *Shriram Foods Case* (1987)[1]

Environmental cases are among constitutional law's most complicated to remedy because the injuries, as we have seen, can be multifaceted with many interdependent and often moving parts, and with both short- and long-term consequences for the environment and for the humans who live, or will live, in it. And most courts are keenly aware of the limitations of their own power – of the fact, namely, that courts have no particular resource other than their own legitimacy to ensure respect for or compliance with judicial orders. And yet, courts have chosen to engage because they realize that, through coordination with other parts of government and in dialogue with both the public and private sectors, they can play a pivotal role in securing environmental rights.

This chapter surveys the types of remedies courts have developed in the environmental cases where they have found liability for violation of constitutional rights. Despite the challenges, courts have been extraordinarily creative in designing remedies that are ambitious enough to be effective in remedying the environmental damage, yet defined and limited enough that

---

[1] *M.C. Mehta v. Union of India and Others (Oleum Gas Case 3)*

1987 AIR 1086; 1987 SCR (1) 819; 1987 SCC (1) 395; JT 1987 (1) 1; 1986 SCALE (2) 1188, available at www.globalhealthrights.org/asia/m-c-mehta-v-union-of-india-and-ors-oleum-gas-case-3

defendants can implement them. Still, defendants – both official and private – can be recalcitrant, and we consider in the second part of the chapter the challenges that courts face in enforcing the remedies they have ordered.[2]

STATE OBLIGATIONS UNDER THE INTERNATIONAL LAW FRAMEWORK

Internationally accepted ideas of the various obligations engendered by human rights indicate that all rights – both civil and political rights and social and economic – generate at least four levels of duties for a state that undertakes to adhere to a rights regime: namely, the duty to respect, protect, promote, and fulfill these rights.[3] This approach has been incorporated into many countries' environmental constitutionalism. The Philippine Court, for instance, has made clear that the state owes different levels of obligation: rights to "a balanced and healthful ecology and to health are mandated as state policies by the Constitution itself, thereby highlighting their continuing importance and imposing upon the state a solemn obligation to preserve the first and protect and advance the second . . ."[4] The Dutch constitution uses mandatory language. It states that "[i]t shall be the concern of the authorities to keep the country habitable and to protect and improve the environment,"[5] although, as we've seen, this provision has not been judicially enforced. Similarly, but more emphatically, the constitution of Bhutan devotes an entire article to the protection of the environment, which, in addition to imposing duties on citizens to safeguard the environment, also imposes these obligations on the government: "The Royal Government shall (a) protect, conserve and improve the pristine environment and safeguard the biodiversity of the country; (b) prevent pollution and ecological degradation; (c) secure ecologically balanced sustainable development while promoting justifiable economic and social development; and (d) ensure a safe and healthy environment."[6] As previously noted, the Chilean Court has already used the affirmative obligation in that country's constitution to hold the government liable for failure to protect,[7] as has the Turkish administrative court.[8] This echoes the

---

[2] Some arguments in this chapter have also been published as Daly, Erin and May, James. "Constitutional Environmental Rights and Liabilities." *Environmental Liability* 3: 75 (2012); available at Social Science Research Network (SSRN): http://ssrn.com/abstract=2221561.

[3] The Social and Economic Rights Action Center and the Center for Economic and Social Rights/Nigeria (African Commission, 2001).

[4] *Minors Oposa* (Philippines, 1993).   [5] Netherlands constitution, ch. 1, art. 21.

[6] Bhutan constitution, art. 5.   [7] Trillium.   [8] *Senih Özay* (Turkey, 1997).

levels of obligation that have been identified by some courts even in the absence of textual adumbration.

These levels of obligation require progressively greater commitment on the part of the government (and sometimes private parties). Yet, even the most moderate level may, in the hands of the right court, significantly constrain the government and obligate it to change its policies. For instance, licensing a company to clear-cut a forest may violate even the obligation to "respect" the environment.

Beyond that, under a constitution that requires the government to "protect" the environment, a court might require the government to take affirmative steps to create an environmental protection agency or to incorporate environmental concerns into its energy or economic development program. "Protection" could also require the government to take measures to ensure sustainability, since unsustainable development, by definition, fails to protect the environment.

A constitutional obligation to "promote" may authorize judicial orders not only to preserve but also to improve the environment, including, for instance, cleaning up a long-standing toxic waste site, reducing air or water pollution below current levels, and so on.

And finally, where the obligation to "fulfill" the right to a clean environment exists, a court may order the government to provide the means by which a clean and healthful environment can be enjoyed. For example, a government might be required to set aside land or waters as a nature reserve, or may be required to include green spaces within development plans for enjoyment by present and future generations.

Each of these levels requires not only increasing action from the state, but increasing resources as well. This is, of course, where the obstacles to judicial enforcement creep in. Plaintiffs are unlikely to sue where the payback is not worth the cost of litigation: if the most that can be gained under a "respect" case is the cancellation of one license, a putative litigant may not bother suing if it is likely that the government will simply issue another license to a different timber company the next year. Even if a plaintiff is successful in securing a judicial order mandating the development of an environmental plan, he or she may not have the resources to sue the following year to ensure that the plan is implemented. In some countries where environmental protection is most needed, it is least likely to be enforced for reasons of cost, if not also political will. Where millions live in deprived conditions with inadequate access to shelter and clean water, even a sympathetic court may not have enough muscle to force the government to "protect and improve the environment." In any of these situations, the remedy may run against private or public

entities if the constitutional rules permit horizontal application of constitutional norms, as discussed previously.

THE RANGE OF REMEDIES

Preventing further environmental harm

In the narrowest cases where the environmental right is vindicated, the court
denies the remedy on environmental grounds. In these cases, the claimant
typically seeks to vindicate a property interest of some kind, and the environmental issue arises by way of defense; to vindicate the environmental interest,
the court denies the remedy sought by the claimant. Under its prior constitution, the Hungarian Constitutional Court once rejected a proposed amendment that would have converted a protected forest into private land because it
would have violated the constitutional right to a healthy environment to "the
highest level of physical and spiritual health."[9] For cases like this to be
successful, environmental advocates within and outside the government must
be vigilant in identifying property, business, and development-oriented litigation that nonetheless raises environmental concerns. In Venezuela, in the
1990s, the Supreme Court of Justice invalidated a mining lease on some forest
lands that had been previously granted by the Mining and Energy Ministry
because it had ignored environmental consequences. In that case, the forest
sectoral service of the Mining Ministry had challenged the government's
previous action.[10]

Injunctions

By far the most common remedy in environmental cases is injunctive relief
aimed at stopping – and then remediating – the environmental degradation.
Injunctions come in an almost infinite variety of shapes and sizes; a few of the
most significant types are discussed here.

The most direct injunctions order the defendant to stop the activity that
is producing the environmental harm. In one of the first cases brought by
M.C. Mehta, the Indian environmental activist and lawyer, the Indian
Supreme Court ordered the closure of the tanneries along a section of the

---

[9] *Magyar Közlöny.* Case No. 1994/No. 55 (Hungarian Constitutional Court, 1994).
[10] *Jesús Manuel Vera Rivera v. Ministry of Environment and Renewable Natural Resources*
(Supreme Court of Justice, September 21, 1999), available at www.unep.org/delc/Portals/119/
UNEPCompendiumSummariesJudgementsEnvironment-relatedCases.pdf

Ganges because "life, health, and ecology have greater importance to the people" than the tannery work.[11] In another case, the court enjoined mining activity on forest land, even though the land came under the protection of the Conservation Act, only after the mining license had been granted. The court explained that "the mining activities being a user of the forest land for non-forest purpose has to be stopped," and further required the defendant to obtain additional authorization from the central government under the Act if it intended to continue similar activities.[12] Similarly, the Supreme Court of Nepal prohibited the use of diesel trucks in the city of Kathmandu,[13] and courts in Bangladesh have at times been particularly active in this regard. Parvez Hassan and Azim Azfar describe one series of cases:

> In a public interest litigation concerning air and noise pollution, the Dhaka High Court ordered the Government to convert petrol and diesel engines in government-owned vehicles to gas-fueled engines; the same order also calls for the withdrawal of hydraulic horns in buses and trucks by 28 April 2002. Another far reaching decision of the Dhaka High Court has called for the withdrawal of two-stroke engine vehicles from Dhaka City by December 2003, the cancellation of licenses for nine-year-old three-wheelers, the provision of adequate numbers of compressed natural gas stations, and the establishment of a system for issuing fitness certificates for cars through computer checks.[14]

Courts in Latin America have been willing not only to remedy existing problems but to intervene in proposed projects and development programs in order to vindicate environmental interests. The Chilean Supreme Court enjoined the construction of six hydroelectric dams on Bio Bio River because the project failed to comply with environmental standards, threatening both environmental and human rights.[15] And in *CODEFF v. Ministry of Public Works*, the Court stopped the extraction of water of Lake Chungará for an irrigation project because it would have raised salinity levels in a UNESCO biosphere reserve.[16]

---

[11] *M.C. Mehta v. Union of India* (India, 1987).

[12] *Samatha v. State of Andhra Pradesh and Others.* No. AIF 1997 SC 3297 (Supreme Court of India, July 11, 1997), following *T.N. Godavarman Thintmulkpad v. Union of India and Others.* Writ. Pet. No. 202 of 1995 (Supreme Court of India, September 26, 2008).

[13] *Advocate Kedar Bhakta Shrestha v. HMG, Department of Transportation Management* (Nepal, 1999).

[14] Hassan and Azfar, "Securing Environmental Rights," 215, 244.

[15] *Pablo Orrego Silva y Otros v. Empresa Electrica Pange SA.* (Chile, August 5, 1993).

[16] *CODEFF v. Ministro de Obras Públicas y otros Corte de Apelaciones* (Court of Appeals of Arica and Supreme Court of Arica, 1985).

In other Latin American cases, courts have authorized the destruction of private property if necessary to stop the despoliation of the environment. In *Donato Furio Giordano v. Ministry of Environment and Renewable Natural Resources*, the Supreme Court of Justice of Venezuela ruled that the destruction of private property (where some septic tanks had been polluting marine water) was not only authorized, it was not subject to restitution or compensation as government destruction of property normally would be because of the environmental hazard that such property posed.[17] And in a case brought by the Ecuadorian government to enjoin illegal gold mining in rivers, a provincial court held that given the failure of previous governmental efforts to stop the mining and based on the rights of nature, the government was authorized to destroy the mining machinery – an order that the government carried out with explosives a few days after the ruling.[18]

Courts may also design injunctions not only to stop the threatened or ongoing degradation of the environment but to clean up or remedy damage that has already occurred. This may involve removal of debris, as it did in *Rural Litigation and Entitlement Kendra (RLEK) v. State of Uttar Pradesh*, where the Indian Supreme Court ordered lessees of limestone quarries to "remove whatever minerals found lying at the site or its vicinity, if such minerals were covered by their respective leases and/or quarry permits."[19] The Court mandated the removal be completed by the lessees within 4 weeks.

Courts seem to be more likely to require immediate action when not only environmental rights are at stake but human rights as well. In the lime quarry case, the court held that "Article 21 of the Constitution guaranteeing the right to life must be interpreted to include the right to live in a healthy environment with minimum disturbances of ecological balance and without avoidable hazard to [the people] and to their cattle, homes and agricultural land and undue affection of air, water and environment."[20] It was likely the harm to the local residents that prompted the court's order of immediate action.[21] Likewise, in *Aurelio Vargas v. Municipality of Santiago*, the Supreme Court of Chile ordered the clean-up of a garbage dump within 120 days because of health considerations to neighboring residents.[22] Where the harm to humans can be documented, defendants may be required not only to remediate but

---

[17] *Donato Furio Giodano v. Ministry of Environment and Renewable Natural Resources* (Supreme Court of Justice, Venezuela, November 25, 1999).

[18] *Wheeler.*

[19] *Rural Litigation and Entitlement Kendra (RLEK) v. State of Uttar Pradesh.* AIR 1987, SC 359.

[20] *Ibid.*, 179–80.   [21] *Ibid.*

[22] *Aurelio Vargas y otros v. Municipalidad de Santiago y otros* (The Lo Errazuriz Case) (Chile Supreme Court, May 27, 1987).

also to compensate the individuals for injuries incurred or likely to be incurred. In one Colombian case, where toxic fumes emanated from an open pit, defendants were required "to remediate the site and to pay past and future medical expenses to those who became sick." The court said it violated the right to life of local residents, even though the evidence concerned threats to their health, but not to their lives.[23]

Some injunctions raise more complex separation of powers questions because they require not only a change of practice but also a change of policy. In some cases, courts have required governments to reorganize their bureaucracies with jurisdiction over the environment. The *Manila Bay* court ordered the creation of a Manila Bay Advisory Committee to receive and evaluate the quarterly progressive reports submitted by the various agencies.[24] In one case involving the adverse environmental effects of an electrical grid, the Supreme Court of Pakistan – instead of balancing the claims of competing stakeholders itself – ordered a *private* engineering consultant company, NESPAK, to manage the process. "In the problem at hand the likelihood of any hazard to life by magnetic field effect cannot be ignored. At the same time the need for constructing grid stations which are necessary for industrial and economic development cannot be lost sight of," the Court explained. Because the government had proceeded without any attention to the hazards the grid might cause to human health, the Court appointed "NESPAK as Commissioner to examine and study the scheme, planning, device and technique employed by [the government] and report whether there is any likelihood of any hazard or adverse effect on health of the residents of the locality."[25] The government was then ordered to submit all the relevant information to NESPAK.[26] The Court required the government in future cases to issue public notices and invite objections (orally or in writing) prior to installing or constructing any grid station or transmission line; this was to continue until such time as "the Government constitutes any commission or authority as suggested above."[27]

Courts have also ordered governments to create environmental plans where none previously existed. In fact, it has been argued that one of the principal benefits of constitutionalizing environmental rights is to create the political pressure necessary to compel governments to adopt statutory frameworks to

[23] Kravchenko and Bonine, *Human Rights*, 70 (discussing Corte [Constitucional, Chamber of Civil and Agrarian Appeals], *Castrillon Vega v. Federación Nacional de Algodoneros y Corporacion Autonoma Regional del Cesar. Acción de Tutela Case No. 4577* [Colombia Constitutional Court, November 19, 1997]).

[24] *Manila Bay* (Philippines, 2008).

[25] *Shelhla Zia v. WAPDA* (Pakistan, February 12, 1994), para. 16.   [26] *Ibid.*   [27] *Ibid.*

protect the environment.[28] In Nepal, the Supreme Court ordered the government to formulate national policies to protect objects of religious, cultural, and historical importance in keeping with environmental standards.[29]

In other cases, a court limits itself to compelling further study of an environmental problem, as has happened in Sri Lanka and elsewhere.[30] Some of these orders designate the timing, process, format, or contents of the study being ordered in order to minimize the government's tendency to avoid the obligation or delay its execution. In the Sri Lankan case, the court ordered that the mining interest was not permitted to enter into any contract relating to a particular phosphate deposit until the government conducted "a comprehensive exploration and study."[31] The court prescribed in detail some of the contents of the study, insisting that the study be done in consultation with the National Academy of Sciences of Sri Lanka and the National Science Foundation, and further requiring that the results of the study be published. As usual, the Indian Supreme Court has been painstaking in directing the process of public participation, ordering committees of experts to investigate the environmental implications of projects.[32] In at least one case, requiring the clean-up of a mining site, the Indian court identified the particular individuals who should or should not be involved: "Such removal will be carried out and completed by the lessees within four weeks from the date of this Order and it shall be done in the presence of an officer not below the rank of Deputy Collector to be nominated by the District Magistrate, Dehradun, a gazetted officer from the Mines Department nominated by the Director of Mines and a public spirit[ed] individual in Dehradun . . ."[33] In a Colombian case involving

[28] Boyd, *Environmental Rights Revolution*; Boyd, "Implicit Constitutional Right."
[29] "Therefore, taking into account the necessity of concrete and effective measures, a directive order issued to His Majesty's Government Cabinet Secretariat to monitor whether the concerned authorities are complying with commitments expressed in the Convention Concerning the Protection of World Cultural and Natural Heritage, 1972, as well as Nepalese laws, and then to take actions for maintaining uniformity in protecting all areas by formulating national policies regarding objects of religious, cultural and historical importance." *Advocate Prakash Mani Sharma for Pro Public v. His Majesty Government Cabinet Secretariat and Others* (Nepal, 1997).
[30] *Bulankulama and Six Others v. Ministry of Industrial Development and Seven Others.* S.C. Application No 884/99 (F.R) (Supreme Court of the Democratic Socialist Republica of Sri Lanka), published in *South Asian Environmental Reporter* 7(2) (June, 2000).
[31] *Ibid.*
[32] See *T.N. Godavarman Thintmulkpad v. Union of India and Others.* Writ. Pet. No. 202 of 1995. (Supreme Court of India, September 26, 2008) (establishing committee of experts to conduct a valuation of forests).
[33] *Rural Litigation and Entitlement Kendra (RLEK) v. State of Uttar Pradesh.* No. 1985 AIR 652, 181 (Supreme Court of India, March 12, 1985).

the rights of marginalized people who earned their living by searching through trash to find recycled items to sell, the court ordered the formation of a committee within 2 weeks of the judgment to determine how best to integrate the recyclers into the formal economy, identifying the groups and interests who would be represented on the committee, including, unsurprisingly, representatives of the recyclers' organizations. The committee, the court said, would participate in the design and implementation of a plan to include the recyclers in the local waste management economy and would design affirmative steps that must be taken to ensure their effective participation. The court further ordered the committee to submit a report to the constitutional court within seven months detailing not only its progress on the implementation of the plan, but the metrics it would use to determine the plan's effectiveness in "the process of inclusion and in the effective enjoyment of rights by the recyclers and their families."[34] And in a land use planning case from Austria, the administrative court insisted on the need to obtain an expert opinion about the environmental impact of a revision of the land use plan.[35] Some of these remedial orders are related to or based on constitutionally entrenched procedural environmental rights, as discussed in Chapter 8.

Depending on the nature of federal–state relations in each country, judicial injunctions may issue against or in favor of subnational units. In one case involving marine life, the Philippine Supreme Court upheld the power of local governments to promote the constitution's environmental values by capturing certain aquatic life in order to protect fish and corals.[36]

Courts that are especially engaged in the vindication of constitutional environmental rights may issue elaborate injunctive orders that not only reflect real knowledge of the local conditions but deep empathy with the individuals affected by the balance of human and environmental interests. In an early Indian Supreme Court's environmental case, the court ordered the temporary closure of limestone quarries and further study to determine whether they should be reopened and on what conditions. But, recognizing that the workmen employed at these quarries would be either temporarily or permanently "thrown out of work," the court insisted that "as far as practicable

---

[34] *Sentencia T-291/06*, 96 (Colombia Constitutional Court, April 23, 2009).
[35] Judgment of March 1, 1989, Verwaltungsgerichtshof [VGH] V 25/88 (Administrative Court).
[36] *Tano v. Socrates*. G.R. No. 110249, 278 S.C.R.A. 154 (Supreme Court of the Philippines, August 21, 1997); see also *Social Justice Society v. Atienza*. G.R. No. 156052, 517 S.C.R.A. 657 (Supreme Court of the Philippines, March 7, 2007), reconsidered 545 S.C.R.A. 92 (Supreme Court of the Philippines, February 13, 2008) (regarding authority of local legislatures and executives to fulfill constitutional environmental obligations).

and in the shortest possible time, [they] be provided employment in the afforestation and soil conservation programme to be taken up in this area."[37]

In another Indian case, the Supreme Court ordered the closure of stone-crushing businesses because of the environmental harm and damage to human life and health to nearby residents (as well as workers); but as stone crushing was already starting up in areas further from where people lived, the court ordered that additional lands be made available and distributed by lots to those whose businesses had closed. As is common in the Indian Supreme Court, the court required reports by the responsible authorities and calen-dared a follow-up hearing.[38]

But by far the most far-reaching environmental case of the Indian Supreme Court was the *Godavarman* case. In 1995, T.N. Godavarman Thirumulpad filed a writ petition to protect the Nilgiris forest from deforestation from illegal timber operations.[39] Rather than limiting itself to ordering relief for the claim asserted, the court used the case to develop and manage a new national forest policy, maintaining continuing mandamus for more than 10 years, and hear-ing over 800 interlocutory applications in the process. Initially, the court "ordered all non-forestry activities, such as saw mills and mining operations, which had not received explicit approval from the central government to cease operating immediately," and it temporarily but immediately suspended all tree felling in almost all the nation's forests. But the court did not stop there: it also established a new forest policy, thereby arguably usurping the legislative role, and it "ordered investigations into various complaints of illegal mining oper-ations," thereby exercising executive authority. According to one group of critics, "the Court made itself a director and an overseer of forest issues, involving itself in national and local forest protection, timber pricing, timber transport, licensing of timber industries, management of forest revenue, and enforcement of its own orders concerning forest law, all independent of the central and state governments."[40] While the court may be praised for recog-nizing the dire necessity of developing and enforcing a serious forest policy, it is criticized for taking on the responsibility itself rather than ordering the central and local governments to act, even according to constitutional prin-ciples. As Rosencranz *et al.* explain, "In the *Godavarman* case, the Court

---

[37] M.C. Mehta v. *Union of India and Others.* 1991 SCR (1) 866 1991 SCC (2) 353 JT 1991 (1) 620 1991 SCALE (1) 427 at 4.
[38] *Ibid.*
[39] Rosencranz, Armin, Edward Boenig, and Brinda Dutta. "The *Godavarman* Case: The Indian Supreme Court's Breach of Constitutional Boundaries in Managing India's Forests." *Environmental Law Reporter* 37 (2007): 10032.
[40] *Ibid.*, 10033.

impinged upon the power of the legislature by banning the transport and felling of timber and by creating the [Central Empowered Committee]. It assumed the role of the executive in administering its own interpretation of the law in addition to its specific orders." The result of this, they say, is that "the Supreme Court has restricted the growth of a responsible and independent bureaucracy" in matters relating to national forestry policy.[41]

This is particularly problematic in the context of an issue as broad and complex as forest policy, where the conditions vary from region to region around the country, and where the implications are significant not only for purposes of economic growth and development but for the human rights of those who live near, within, and in reliance on the nation's forests.

Another landmark constitutional environmental case, producing one of the most elaborate remedial orders ever, involved Argentina's Matanza-Riachuelo river basin. In 2008, the Supreme Court of Argentina ruled in favor of a group of residents who had sued 44 companies as well as governmental authorities at the local, provincial, and national levels to demand clean-up of the river basin, which had been the most contaminated in the country (*Mendoza Beatriz Silva et al. v. State of Argentina et al.*).

According to one assessment:

> The Matanza-Riachuelo river basin represents both an environmental and a social catastrophe. It has an estimated population of 4.9 million people, of which many live in squatter settlements lacking basic services such as potable water, sewage services, satisfactory health care services, and decent housing. The environmental pollution is caused by different sources of contamination, such as waste-fills in open air, sewage from illegal sewage pipes and toxic spills from the industries. Many of the squatter settlements are flooded with polluted water from the river. Many of the industrial establishments have outdated technology and lack commitment or means to comply with current standards. Dangerous levels of arsenic, chrome, mercury and lead are found in the river basin. People suffer from diarrhea, respiratory problems, skin-diseases, cancer, allergies and anemia. Blood samples from some of the inhabitants show alarmingly high levels of lead.[42]

The Supreme Court's order was directed at all levels of government and at certain private parties who were deemed to have contributed to the disastrous condition of the river basin. The court fully understood that remediation

---

[41] *Ibid.*, 10038.
[42] Staveland-Saeter, Kristi. "Can Litigation Clean Rivers? Assessing the Policy Impact of 'the Mendoza Case' in Argentina." CHR Michelsen Institute. *CMI Brief* 11(3) (May, 2012), available at www.cmi.no/publications/file/4467-can-litigation-clean-rivers.pdf

would take years and require the commitment and cooperation of many different entities, and, in fact, it was only in response to the judicial reprimand that the Argentine Congress developed a plan to coordinate the clean-up and allocated funds for its effectuation. Still, the pace of clean-up has been slow. According to one report, "There is an environmental management plan, but not much has been done, and the river is still contaminated. The Supreme Court has issued several follow-up judgements as a response to the lack of compliance. Judicial control of the implementation of the judgement seems to have been important to ensure compliance with the judgement."[43] Nonetheless, judicial involvement has had a galvanizing effect: the influential Chr. Michelsen Institute maintains that the case has had substantial positive impact in a variety of ways: in order to comply with the judgment, the government has been forced to develop public policies and set up a special interjurisdictional river basin authority; NGOs are developing capacity to monitor compliance and are insisting on higher quality compliance and inspections; and all of this is putting environmental justice on the government's agenda and in the public's consciousness, widening the public debate and providing a model to others, within and outside Argentina, to pursue.[44]

In *Manila Bay*, the Philippine Supreme Court issued a comprehensive twelve-point injunctive order, which directed not only the results to be accomplished but the process to be used to ensure their accomplishment.

The court's order specified the meetings that government agencies must organize, studies to determine the adequacy of sewage facilities, that violators of environmental laws and regulations be apprehended, that licensing requirements be enforced, and so on. The court also ordered the Education Department to "integrate lessons on pollution prevention, waste management, environmental protection, and like subjects in the school curricula of all levels to inculcate in the minds and hearts of students and, through them, their parents and friends, the importance of their duty toward achieving and maintaining a balanced and healthful ecosystem in the Manila Bay and the entire Philippine archipelago."[45] Most of these requirements flowed from the statutory and regulatory framework, but they were enacted, and enforced in this case, to vindicate the constitutional environmental right to a clean environment.

The Philippine Supreme Court is not the only court to require public information about environmentalism as part of a remedial plan. In a landmark case involving noise and air pollution caused by vehicles in the city of Dhaka, the Bangladeshi Supreme Court directed the government to publicize

---

[43] *Ibid.*   [44] *Ibid.*   [45] *Manila Bay* (Philippines, 2008).

"through print and electronic media" the extant legal requirements and to "proceed against the vehicle operators by taking penal action if they fail to remove such types of prohibited horns after the expiry of the period of 30 days."[46] In the judicial orders regarding the replacement of diesel engines in government and other transport vehicles, the court ordered the government to "give publicity to the directions of this Court in print and electronic media on consecutive two days twice in a week for one month."[47] In *Karnataka Industries*, the Indian Supreme Court articulated the importance not only of environmental improvement but of what might be thought of as environmental acculturation: "The importance and awareness of environment and ecology is becoming so vital and important that we, in our judgment, want the appellant to insist on the conditions emanating from the principle of 'Sustainable Development.'"[48] To implement these principles, the court directed that "in future, before acquisition of lands for development, the consequence and adverse impact of development on environment must be properly comprehended and the lands be acquired for development that they do not gravely impair the ecology and environment."[49] Such comprehension on the part of all the stakeholders requires that information be made available to all in advance of any decision that would adversely affect the natural environment.

As with the Indian Supreme Court's continuing mandamus, the Bangladeshi court also required the government to "submit reports every six months of actions and results of the ... above directions to this court."

Despite the range and variety of judicial orders and the extraordinary efforts that some courts have made to ensure compliance with their orders, courts do realize that environmental rights are usually considered socioeconomic rights, which, in many systems, are not subject to individual demand or amenable to immediate implementation. In *Mazibuko* v. *City of Johannesburg*, the South African Constitutional Court explained that the constitutional right to water "does not require the state upon demand to provide every person with sufficient water without more." Rather, the court said, "it requires the state to take reasonable legislative and other measures progressively to realise the achievement of the right of access to sufficient water, within available resources."[50]

---

[46] *Farooque* v. *Bangladesh*. Writ. Pet. 300 of 1995 (2002.02) (Supreme Court of Bangladesh High Court Division, February 2002).

[47] *Ibid.*

[48] *Karnataka Industrial Areas Development Board* v. *C. Kenchappa and Others*. AIRSCW 2546, 104 (Supreme Court of India, 2006).

[49] *Ibid.*

[50] *Lindiwe Mazibuko and Others* v. *City of Johannesburg and Others*, para. 55 (South Africa, 2009).

Indeed, the constitution itself requires that "[t]he state must take reasonable legislative and other measures, within its available resources, to achieve the progressive realisation of each of these rights." The *Mazibuko* court explained that a state's compliance with this requirement would be measured by the reasonableness of its efforts, not by their success. While this disappointed many South African activists, the court maintained that courts "[A]re ill-suited to adjudicate upon issues where Court orders could have multiple social and economic consequences for the community. The Constitution contemplates rather a restrained and focused role for the Courts, namely, to require the State to take measures to meet its constitutional obligations and to subject the reasonableness of these measures to evaluation."[51]

Thus, a litigant may always argue that the state has failed to develop a policy concerning the right – namely, environmental protection – or that the policy has not been adequately revised and updated, and has been allowed to lie dormant. However, the court emphatically rejected the notion that socio-economic rights contain a particular "minimum core" that must be respected or provided in the legislative plan.[52] The Colombian Constitutional Court has also adopted the principle of progressive realization, noting that it requires, at a minimum, for the state to provide a plan for the effective enjoyment of the right.[53] (The idea of progressive realization derives from the International Covenant on Economic, Social and Cultural Rights, which provides that: "Each State Party to the present Covenant undertakes to take steps, individually and through international assistance and cooperation, especially economic and technical, to the maximum of its available resources, with a view to achieving progressively the full realisation of the rights recognised in the present Covenant by all appropriate means, including particularly the adoption of legislative measures."[54] While sourced in international law, it has been incorporated into the constitutional jurisprudence of many countries. In the South African *Mazibuko* case, for instance, the court explained that: "The concept of progressive realisation recognises that policies formulated by the state will need to be reviewed and revised to ensure that the realisation of social and economic rights is progressively achieved.")[55]

Progressive realization – though not named as such – may also be seen in the continuing injunctions that many courts have issued in environmental

---

[51] *Ibid.*   [52] *Ibid.*; see also *ibid.*, paras. 40, 53, 56.
[53] *Sentencia T-291/09* (Colombia Constitutional Court, 2010).
[54] Article 2(1) of the International Covenant on Economic, Social and Cultural Rights GA Res 2200A (XXI), 21 UN GAOR Supp. (No 16), 1966, UN Doc A/6316.
[55] *Lindiwe Mazibuko and Others v. City of Johannesburg and Others* (South Africa, 2009).

cases. In the Bangladeshi industrial pollution case, the court ordered some existing industrial units and factories to adopt "adequate and sufficient measures to control pollution" within 1 year and others within 2 years, and in every case to report back to the court; it further ordered that no new industrial units and factories be, at any time in the future, "set up in Bangladesh without first arranging adequate and sufficient measures to control pollution."[56] This process instantiates and adapts to local conditions the principles of progressive realization.

In some cases involving future development, the Supreme Court of India has insisted that certain specified conditions be satisfied before land can be acquired or plants can be reopened.[57] And in one notable case from Pakistan – initiated when a member of the court saw a newspaper notice about dumping of nuclear waste along a coastal area, which turned out to be unfounded – the court ordered not only that a list of all persons to whom coastal land had been allotted be submitted to the court but also that the state government submit the particulars of any application for future allotment of coastal lands. The court took these actions because "[t]o dump waste materials including nuclear waste from the developed countries would not only be [a] hazard to the health of the people but also to the environment and the marine life in the region."[58]

Perhaps recognizing the limits of the judicial power, some of these courts have included in their mandatory orders provisions that are merely hortatory. In the Pakistani case, the court also suggested that the responsible authorities "should insert a condition in the allotment letter/license/lease that the allottee/tenant shall not use the land for dumping, treating, burying or destroying by any device waste of any nature including industrial or nuclear waste in any form."[59] In the Lahore pollution case, the court went further and included a list of "suggestions . . . for formulating the policy and relevant rules and law."[60] In *Manila Bay*, the Philippine court required the budget department to "consider incorporating an adequate budget in the General Appropriations Act of 2010 and succeeding years to cover the expenses relating to the cleanup, restoration, and preservation of the water quality of the Manila Bay."[61] And in the groundwater pollution case, the Indian Supreme Court asked the

---

[56] *Farooque v. Bangladesh.* Writ. Pet. No. 891 of 1994 (2007.07.15) (Supreme Court of Bangladesh High Court Division, July 15, 2007).

[57] *See Karnataka Industrial Areas Development Board v. C. Kenchappa and Others.* AIRSCW 2546 (Supreme Court of India, 2006); *M.C. Mehta v. Union of India* (India, 1987).

[58] *UNEP Compendium.*   [59] *Ibid.*

[60] *Anjum Irfan v. Lahore Development Authority.* Writ Petition No. 25084 of 1997, P L D 2002 Lahore 555 (Ch. Ijaz Ahmad, J, June 14, 2002).

[61] *Manila Bay* (Philippines, 2008).

government to consider whether "chemical industries should be regulated separately and whether the siting of both new and existing plants should be revisited, given the water-intensive nature of the activities."[62] While the language was hortatory, the court insisted that the government's quarterly reports include reference to these considerations.[63] The extent to which these admonitions are in effect is a function of the relationship between the political authorities and the court.

Hortatory or suggestive orders may be particularly appealing to courts when enforcing directive principles of state policy that may be explicitly exempt from judicial review. In one such case, the Supreme Court of Nepal issued "a directive order ... to His Majesty's Government ... to monitor whether the concerned authorities are complying with [both international and domestic laws], and then to take actions for maintaining uniformity in protecting all areas by formulating national policies regarding objects of religious, cultural and historical importance."[64] But, reflecting some impatience, the court demanded to see not only the efforts but the results: "It is not sufficient to state, in its written statement, that the government is alert about protection. Commitment should also be reflected by action and creation of public awareness. Plans adopted since 1954 should be evaluated for how successful they have been."[65]

Most injunctive remedial orders reflect well-recognized environmental law principles and values, including especially the precautionary principle and the norm that polluters pay for the costs of remediating the environmental harms they have caused. Some of these obligations are imposed as a matter of international law; the Treaty for the Functioning of the European Union, for instance, states that "Union policy on the environment ... shall be based on the precautionary principle and on the principles that preventive action should be taken, that environmental damage should as a priority be rectified at source and that the polluter should pay."[66] Many governments have incorporated these principles into their framework laws,[67] and courts that are sensitive to the peculiarities of environmental damages have been quite willing to adopt

---

[62] *ICELA v. Union of India* 1996 AIR 1446 1996 SCC (3) 212, JT 1996 (2) 196 1996 SCALE (2) 44, 35.

[63] *Ibid.*

[64] *Advocate Prakash Mani Sharma for Pro Public v. His Majesty Government Cabinet Secretariat and others* (Nepal, 1997).

[65] *Ibid.*

[66] European Union, *Consolidated Version of the Treaty on the Functioning of the European Union*, art. 191.

[67] See, e.g., Ecuador Environmental Law 99 of 1993.

them as a matter of their own domestic constitutional law. In seeking to protect the Taj Mahal, for instance, the Indian Supreme Court said, "the 'primary duty' of the government and its Ministry of Environment was to 'safeguard' the monument."[68] That court has further explained the policy underlying the polluter pays principle in this way:

> The Polluter Pays principle demands that the financial costs of preventing or remedying damage caused by pollution should lie with the undertakings which cause the pollution, or produce the goods which cause the pollution. Under the principle it is not the role of Government to meet the costs involved in their prevention of such damage, or in carrying out remedial action, because the effect of this would be to shift the financial burden of the pollution incident to the taxpayer.[69]

Another option, which has not been sufficiently developed, would be to require those whose activities may have an impact on the environment to take out ecological insurance.[70]

Damages

In Colombia, as in other jurisdictions, the framework environmental laws permit damages to compensate for the misuse of natural resources, as well as punitive damages in some cases. A 1993 law, which the Constitutional Court upheld in 1996, also permits the application of retributive taxes on those whose activities contribute to environmental deterioration or unsustainability, such as in the case of waste dumping, as well as compensatory taxes and taxes for the usage of water. The court explained that a retributive tax is an obligatory payment imposed not for services provided but for the damage caused to the environment; it has, in that sense, the character of an indemnity.[71]

Colombian law creates a more elaborate set of sanctions including preventative, compensatory, and punitive damages than is available in most other countries; this statutory scheme was upheld against charges that the damage awards were ill-defined and that the law subjected defendants to liability

---

[68] *M.C. Mehta v. Union of India.* A.I.R. 1997 SC 723 (India), as discussed in Dannenmaier, "Environmental Law," 463, 474.

[69] *Indian Council for Enviro-Legal Action v. Union of India.* No. 3 SCC 212 (Supreme Court of India, 1996), quoted in *Karnataka Industrial Areas Development Board v. C. Kenchappa and Others.* AIRSCW 2546 (Supreme Court of India, 2006).

[70] Trillium. See also Dannenmaier, "Environmental Law," 463, 478.

[71] *Marlene Beatriz Duran Comacho v. Republic of Colombia* (Colombia Constitutional Court, September 26, 1996).

multiple times for the same infraction. In an extraordinary opinion, which recites at length the obligations that every country has to nature and to future generations, the court explained that "nature is not limited only to the environment surrounding humans, but also is a subject with its own rights which must be protected and guaranteed."[72] Consequently, the court held, a statutory scheme that imposes compensatory damages as well as restitution and that aims to restore nature to its previous condition is fully consistent with both constitutional and international law (including treaties to which Colombia is a party as well as those to which it is not).[73] The defendant is usually in a better position than the plaintiff – particularly where the latter are individuals or non-profit organizations suing on behalf of underserved populations – to remedy the environmental harm because the defendant is likely to have significantly greater resources and means.

But, absent explicit constitutional or statutory authorizations, damages are not typically apt remedies for constitutional environmental violations. Damages shift the cost of engaging in objectionable behavior, but they put the burden of *remedying* the problem on the plaintiff. In environmental cases, however, courts that have been receptive to plaintiffs' complaints are more likely to try to remedy the harm that has been done to the environment than merely make it more costly to harm it; a damage award does not help the broader swath of people who are affected by the environmental degradation, or future generations, or the environment itself. Moreover, where the defendant is the government, as is typically the case in constitutional litigation, courts may be hesitant to exact costs from the national treasury if doing so would result in a windfall to the plaintiffs, particularly where the injuries are widespread and affect more people than those who litigated. Government defendants may also be immune from damage awards under constitutional or statutory authority. Damage awards in environmental cases can also lead to additional and prolonged litigation about the size of the award, particularly when there are significant resources at stake, as, for instance, in the epic litigation in Ecuador against Chevron/Texaco. In such cases, civil suits for damages may be authorized but need to be filed and pursued separately.[74]

---

[72] *Sentencia C-632/11* (Colombia Constitutional Court, 2011).   [73] *Ibid.*

[74] *Indian Council for Enviro-Legal Action v. Union of India.* 3 SCC 212, 34 (Supreme Court of India, 1996). "So far as the claim for damages for the loss suffered by the villagers in the affected area is concerned, it is open to them or any organization on their behalf to institute suits in the appropriate civil court. If they file the suit or suits in forma pauperize, the State of Rajasthan shall not oppose their applications for leave to sue in forma pauperize." (Anton, Donald K. and Dinah L. Shelton, *Environmental Protection and Human Rights.* Cambridge University Press, 2011.)

Even in these jurisdictions, however, costs may be awarded. Finally, there are constitutional cultures, particularly in Asia, in which damage awards are rare in general and no more common in environmental cases.[75]

Where they are permitted, a damage award may be a part of a remedial order, but in few cases does it completely resolve the controversy.

Compliance order

Courts in many countries have available to them something akin to a writ of mandamus – a judicial order that requires the defendant to satisfy a pre-existing duty. Often, plaintiffs seek such a writ in part because compliance is more readily ensured, and in part perhaps because they truly believe that defendants are under a legal obligation to take a particular action. However, courts can be reluctant to use the writ if the legal duty is not "definite and fixed," as the Supreme Court of Nepal said.[76] In one case from the Philippines, the Supreme Court dismissed a petition seeking mandamus because, even though the corporate defendant may have violated the fundamental right to clean air, the legislature had not specifically required the use of natural gas and so the court could not require it by way of mandamus.[77] Indeed, the power of the writ of mandamus may come from the court's inherent authority in certain cases or it may come from the mandatory language of a statute. In the Philippines, the court required all the government entities involved in remedying the pollution in Manila Bay to submit a quarterly progressive report "in line with the principle of 'continuing mandamus.'"[78] In *Ratlam v. Vardhichand*,[79] the Supreme Court of India compelled a municipal council to carry out its duties to the community by constructing sanitation facilities, pursuant to clear and mandatory statutory authority. The Court ordered the municipality – under penalty of imprisonment – to construct the drains and fill up cesspools and other pits of human and industrial waste, notwithstanding the municipality's claimed penury. The court noted that "[t]he Criminal

---

[75] "One other significant aspect of remedies in relation to constitutional rights adjudication is judges making available new remedies such as constitutional compensation for state breaches of constitutional rights. This is an unconventional constitutional remedy." Leng, "Constitutional Rights Adjudication," 268.

[76] *Dhungel* v. *Godawari* (Nepal, October 31, 1995), 98.

[77] *Henares* v. *Land Transportation and Franchising and Regulatory Board.* G.R. No. 158290, 505 SCRA 104 (Philippines, October 23, 2006).

[78] *Manila Bay* (Philippines, 2008).

[79] Municipal Council, *Ratlam* v. *Vardhichand.* No. 1980 AIR 1622, 1981 SCR (1) 97 (Supreme Court of India, July 29, 1980).

Procedure Code operates against statutory bodies and others regardless of the cash in their coffers, even as human rights under Part III of the Constitution have to be respected by the State regardless of budgetary provision."[80] And yet, according to a subsequent report, at least eight agencies are jointly responsible for some aspect of Delhi's drainage and sanitation infrastructure, leading not to overenforcement but to undermanagement and to significant health hazards for the nearly 4 million people who open storm-water drain systems for waste disposal. "These open drains," according to this report, "experience blockage and over-flooding from excessive waste and are a growing safety and health concern throughout populated regions of Delhi/NCR." A number of injuries have resulted when people have accidentally fallen into the open drains.[81]

It may seem odd or unproductive to expend resources to ask a court to order the government to do what it is already obligated to do. But this strategy can produce dividends. In India, for instance, "[t]he main thrust is to substitute the ineffective administrative directives issued by the pollution control boards under the Water Act and the Environment (Protection) Act, with judicial orders, the disobedience of which invites contempt of court action and penalties."[82] Government's nonfeasance in the first place invites judicial review, with the burden usually falling on the party challenging the action and with the typical deference to coequal branches of government; government's failure to comply with a court order, however, shifts the burden to the government to justify its nonfeasance and removes any presumption in favor of the government that might otherwise exist. It also eliminates separation of powers concerns that might otherwise deter judicial involvement.

Imprisonment

Where none of these remedies is sufficient to vindicate environmental rights, repair the damage to the environment, and deter or prevent further abuses, some courts have resorted to the ultimate penalty of imprisonment. In one case, from Antigua and Barbuda, the High Court of Justice ordered sentences of one month each to three government officials for violating a previous

---

[80] *Ibid.*

[81] Leela Khanna. "Open Drainage Throughout Delhi: Who Will Take Responsibility?" New Delhi: Centre for Social Research (July 2, 2012), available at http://csrindia.org/blog/2012/07/02/open-drainage-throughout-delhi-who-will-to-take-responsibility

[82] Shubhankar Dam and Vivek Tewary. "Polluting Environment, Polluting Constitution: Is a 'Polluted' Constitution Worse than a Polluted Environment?" *Journal of Environmental Law* 17 (2005): 383, 389.

interim injunction that sought to forbid a company, Sandco, from mining sand. The Ministry of Mining officials mined the sand instead but then sold it on the spot to Sandco, which the court found to be a clear violation of the interim injunction.[83] Imprisonment under certain circumstances may be statutorily authorized, as in such Indian framework laws as the Water (Prevention and Control of Pollution) Act of 1974, the Environment (Protection) Act of 1986, and the Air (Prevention and Control of Pollution) Act of 1981.

The variety and flexibility of tools in these courts' remedial toolkits facilitate judicial involvement in the vindication of constitutional environmental rights even in situations where courts might otherwise be tempted to yield to principles of comity and to succumb to concerns about their own legitimacy. But in the words of the Indian Supreme Court – certainly the institution with the longest term and deepest commitment to the creative remediation of environmental degradation – "the correct exposition of law in a modern welfare Society" prohibits the court from sitting "idly by" while officials abdicate their legal responsibilities. "The law," the court has said, "will relentlessly be enforced and the plea of poor finance will be poor alibi when people in misery cry for justice . . . The officers in charge and even the elected representatives will have to face the penalty of the law if what the constitution and follow-up legislation direct them to do are denied wrongfully. The wages of violation is punishment, corporate and personal."[84] Clearly, courts have a range of remedies from which to choose in giving effect to environmental constitutionalism.

CHALLENGES TO ENFORCEMENT

Enforcement of judicial orders, particularly in environmental cases, is rarely without its obstacles. In the first Ecuadorian rights of nature case, for instance, the government had taken no steps in the following year to implement the order to clean up the damage done to the river and adjoining property, notwithstanding clear directions from the court, forcing the litigants to pursue follow-up enforcement actions.

Remedial orders in constitutional environmental cases are among the most difficult to enforce for several reasons. First, as we have seen, injunctive orders can be multifaceted and extensive, often requiring multiple entities to coordinate action. Second, they can be time-consuming in both the long and short

---

[83] *The Barbuda Council v. Attorney General.* No. 456 of 1988. (High Court of Justice, Antigua and Barbuda Civil. September 10, 1993).
[84] *Ratlam v. Vardhichand* (India, July 29, 1980).

term. The development of a plan may take months but its full implementation may take years or go on indefinitely. Third, environmental regulation *in general* comes at the expense of other important societal goals such as development and industrialization, which are the primary interests of most defendants, both private and public. And these defendants almost invariably constitute the power and economic elite of the country. In combination, these conditions provide ample incentive to defendants who would prefer to ignore or avoid judicially imposed obligations.

In response, courts have developed certain practices aimed at overcoming these challenges. As we have seen, courts in some countries will regularly require reports and other indications of progress. They also often retain jurisdiction over the cases to facilitate plaintiffs' efforts to hold defendants responsible, often explicitly inviting further litigation to ensure compliance. In one case involving industrial pollution, the Bangladeshi Supreme Court asserted that the environmental advocacy group, BELA, which had brought the suit, was "at liberty to bring incidents of violation of any of the provisions of the Act and the Rules made there under to the notice of this court."[85] In that case, the court also said that "the respondents were at liberty to approach this court for directions as and when necessary so that the objectives of the Act can be achieved effectively and satisfactorily."[86] In some situations, courts have remained alert to persistent controversies resulting from their decisions and have had to issue increasingly emphatic follow-up judgments to compel compliance, as has happened in the Colombian cases involving the livelihood of recyclers and the Pakistani case involving pollution in the city of Lahore.[87,88]

Where courts have maintained their vigilance, there have in some cases been notable successes. As a result of the landmark *Minors Oposa* decision, it has been claimed, "Logging concessions were withdrawn and abandoned at such a pace that the one hundred and forty-two concessions that existed when Oposa first took up the issue had shrunk to three by 2006."[89] The cleanup of

---

[85] *Farooque* v. *Bangladesh* (Bangladesh, July 15, 2007).
[86] *Ibid*. See also *Mehta* v. *Union of India* (India, 1987).
[87] Solicitud de cumplimiento de la *Sentencia T-724* de 2003 y del Auto 268 de 2010 (Colombia Constitutional Court, 2011).
[88] *Anjum Irfan* v. *Lahore Development Authority* (Pakistan, 1997, 2002).
[89] Dannenmaier, "Environmental Law," 463, 472. This has been challenged by Dante Gatmaytan-Mango. See generally, Gatmaytan-Mango, Dante. "Judicial Restraint and the Enforcement of Environmental Rights in the Philippines." *Oregon Review of International Law* 12 (2010).

Manila Bay after the Supreme Court's decision in that case provides another example of effective litigation.

Ensuring enforcement of court orders is difficult, though not impossible to do.[90] The history of environmental litigation, constitutional and otherwise, is littered with examples of abandoned litigation. Indeed, one commentator contends that the *Minors Oposa* litigation was never fulfilled because the original plaintiffs did not pursue the matter after the Philippine Supreme Court's remand.[91] In Chile, where indigenous and other groups were able to stop construction of dams on the Bio Bio River in the early 1990s because of failures to comply with regulations, the government was able, within 10 years, to pursue construction of other dams when the additional hurdles were overcome.[92] The moderate victory is the increased participation of the affected communities and increased sensitivity to environmental concerns as new and ongoing hydroelectric projects are pursued. In Nepal, the NGO Pro Public has been forced to adopt "a comprehensive strategy for obtaining compliance" with court orders.

Litigating claims borne in environmental constitutionalism requires a continued commitment not only on the court's part but also on the part of the plaintiffs who originally brought the suit or their successors. And this is problematic as well: continued vigilance on the part of plaintiffs privatizes the burden for securing what is clearly a public good, and it requires the plaintiffs to ensure, on an ongoing basis, that the government takes responsibility for the environmental violation and that the government complies with the rule of law as mandated by the judicial branch. Enforcing even favorable judgments thus requires significant resources on the part of the original litigants and their lawyers. As the Bangladeshi organization, BELA, has said: "winning a court case is only the first step."

---

[90] Kravchenko and Bonine, *Human Rights*, 99.

[91] See Gatmaytan-Mango, "Judicial Restraint," 459: "The Supreme Court did not order the cancellation of the TLAs, but ordered the case to be remanded for trial. Because the petitioners did not pursue the case after it was remanded, no TLA was cancelled."

[92] Jose Aylwin. *The Ralco Dam and the Pehuenche People in Chile: Lessons from an Ethno-Environmental Conflict.* Institute of Indigenous Studies, University of la Frontera, 2002 (describing the cultural and environmental significance of the Bio Bio River).

PART III

EMERGENCE AND FUTURE OF ENVIRONMENTAL CONSTITUTIONALISM

6

Water and environmental constitutionalism

Water is life. Without it, nothing organic grows. Human beings need water to drink, to cook, to wash and to grow our food. Without it, we will die. It is not surprising then that our Constitution entrenches the right of access to water.
Mazibuko et al. v. City of Johannesburg[1]

The constitutions of nearly three-quarters of the world's countries address environmental matters in some way, either by guaranteeing substantive or procedural environmental rights, by imposing duties and responsibilities, by promoting specific policy objectives such as sustainable development, or by addressing competing demands over specific resources. This chapter addresses the most prominent of the last listed variant – rights to water.

Water is becoming a critical issue for nations in every part of the world. At any given moment in the early twenty-first century, somewhere in the world water is the subject of protests, theft, litigation, warfare, and, increasingly, constitutional reform and adjudication. Water's significance is recognized by all those who need it or who would exploit it, including individuals, industry, state governments, and non-state actors with good, as well as nefarious, intents. One recent assessment from the US intelligence community concluded that stresses on the supply of clean water in many countries "will risk instability and state failure" and will "hinder the ability of key countries to produce food and generate energy, posing a risk to global food markets and hobbling economic growth."[2] There is, as a result, growing concern that water can be used as a justification for war, as a weapon of war by states against neighboring states, and for terrorist purposes by non-state actors. Indeed, what have come to be

[1] *Lindiwe Mazibuko and Others v. City of Johannesburg and Others* (South Africa, 2009).
[2] Global Water Security. *Intelligence Community Assessment.* ICA 2012–08, at iii. 2012.

called "water wars" have already broken out in Bolivia and elsewhere, spurred by the failure of the state to provide adequate, affordable, and clean water.

Population growth is increasing the demand for clean water, while climate change, pollution, and the impact of floods are decreasing its supply. The combination is threatening access to clean water for billions of people world-wide.[3] Some nations have responded by recognizing some type of right to water in their constitutions. For example, Somalia's interim constitution, which was adopted by a parliamentary majority in 2012, includes the human right to water. Zimbabwe's 2013 constitution includes the right to safe and potable drinking water. In the drought-prone countries of East Africa, includ-ing Tanzania and Sudan, where persistent and bloody conflicts erupt between herders and farmers over the allocation of scarce water resources on disputed lands, constitutional reformation is emerging as a preferable construct for resolving competing claims to water.

Accordingly, as more constitutions recognize the importance of water, domestic courts are increasingly being called upon to adjudicate water issues arising under constitutional law. For instance, in Malaysia, citizens have turned to the courts to apply constitutional provisions concerning a private water company's threats to ration water in response to governmental failure to approve a rate hike. In South Africa, people who have little or no access to drinking water have asserted constitutional rights to water to force government action to protect water resources from mining pollution. In India, questions about which level of government should manage water resources – the states, as is stipulated by the constitution, the central government, or local commu-nities – are continually simmering, as groundwater levels decline in the service of development and industrialization. In all of these situations, the discourse of complaint and remedy adopts constitutional language: whether the govern-ment has the constitutional responsibility or the constitutional authority to manage the distribution of water, its price, and its use and availability now and for future generations.

Constitutional water rights raise issues of both quantity and quality. Some constitutional provisions guarantee a right to a quantity of water for drinking or irrigation, for example. Generally, these provisions can be thought of as providing a human right to water. Other provisions are qualitative – for instance, guaranteeing rights to unpolluted water. These types of provisions can be thought of as guaranteeing rights akin to the environmental rights discussed elsewhere in this book.

---

[3] *Ibid.*, 2.

Constitutional courts do not tend to distinguish between claims relating to human and environmental rights. Nor do they treat water-based claims any differently from any other human or environmental claims. In water-related human rights cases, the courts proceed as they ordinarily would, considering whether the plaintiffs have standing, whether the remedy is immediately or progressively realizable, and so on. And when the cases concern environmental rights, courts routinely apply general principles of environmental law, such as the public trust doctrine and the polluter pays principle. Where courts are inclined to grant open standing or shift the burden of proof from the claimant to the party in the best position to assert the evidence, they will do so without regard to whether the cases concern land or water.

But water is different in both contexts. It is more likely than other rights considered here to straddle the environmental right–human right divide. And rights to water are more likely in the coming years to be the subject of contestation in almost all nations of the world – contests that will be resolved through violence, if not as a matter of constitutional law. And while a constitutional right to water will not always prevent violence, it may galvanize and inform public debate, shape legal rights and responsibilities, and put the onus on government to ensure adequate access to clean water for all.

This chapter proceeds in four parts. First, it discusses water's unique features that warrant constitutional recognition. Second, it assesses the various ways in which constitutions recognize the importance of water, either as a marker of jurisdiction and authority or as an enforceable human or environmental right. Third, it surveys the cases that have vindicated water rights either as a human or environmental right, or both. Fourth, it considers the challenges of fashioning and enforcing remedies in cases involving water.

THE UNIQUENESS OF WATER

Although all elements of the environment may have an impact on the human right to health or, in some circumstances, even life, the human rights dimensions of water are far more pronounced. Water is essential for life in a way that healthy forests or pristine mountains are not. Water must be accessible in certain amounts and at certain levels of quality for consumption and sanitation, as well as for other uses. As a result, clean water must be made available to people to ensure that neither quantity nor quality fall below a certain minimum level.

Because it is necessary not only to maintain clean water but also to provide it, water requires management in a way that air and soil do not. It is not enough to leave water alone in its natural state; those in control of water resources must take affirmative steps to ensure its protection, its equitable distribution, and its appropriate use for personal, communal, and industrial purposes. This is just as true in drought-prone countries like South Africa and Mozambique as in water-rich environments like Brazil; water must be managed everywhere. As a result, the regulation of water, more than of other parts of the environment, is interlaced in regulatory, statutory, and constitutional arenas.

The need to manage water resources imposes a positive obligation on states, which means that governments can be sued for failure to act much more readily in this area of law than in others. And this obligation, whether voluntarily undertaken or judicially imposed, usually requires ongoing administration and coordination with multiple parts of government – including legislative and executive authorities at both the central and subnational levels – and often with the private sector as well. This contrasts with the constitutional mandate to protect the environment, which may often be satisfied by the negative responsibility to avoid endangerment. And this difference has an impact on the role that courts play in vindicating these constitutional rights: imposing a positive obligation to manage water resources effectively and equitably can be far more challenging for courts than ordering the cancellation of a timber license or even overseeing the remedial clean-up of a bay.

The need to manage water resources also differs from most environmental regulation because it requires significant infrastructure. To satisfy these capital and operational demands, governments often find themselves turning to nongovernmental actors, increasingly including multinational enterprises and international financing organizations that have more fiscal resources than over-extended or debt-ridden nations; in fact, tax, licensing, and other revenues derived from the privatization of water can be a significant source of income for nations. Moreover, the global financing system often prefers privatization, both because it produces a better return on investment and because it meshes with western concepts of marketization.

And yet, water privatization is enormously controversial politically. Privatization also raises important constitutional questions, particularly insofar as the state retains a constitutional obligation to manage water or to hold it in the public trust. For some, the privatization of water raises conceptual questions of a political nature because it may be seen to commoditize a public or social good, often to the detriment of those who lack the resources to enter the market. Indeed, in many countries, the poor pay substantially more for water than those who are well-to-do. As Fitzmaurice writes, "Poor people living in slums often pay 5–10 times more per litre of water than wealthy people in the same place, since water passes through intermediaries and each adds transport and marketing fees."[4] This is so even though most people recognize that water has positive externalities in that safe and adequate water for drinking and sanitation improves health, enables education (particularly for girls, which has still other follow-on benefits), increases productivity, and is indispensable to human dignity.

But the concern about privatization may be overstated. The worst form of privatization, from the standpoint of constitutional accountability, is foreign and global investment, but "about 90 percent of investment comes from domestic sources."[5] Moreover, there is no clear consensus on whether public or private distribution of water is better in terms of cost and availability: there are shining examples, as well as disasters, in both columns. But the critical point is that "the crucial factor of successful privatization is good governance and the right institutional framework (i.e. an effective regulation)."[6] And if governance is effective enough to regulate the private water distribution system, it may be effective enough to provide the water in the first place – and with greater public input, public oversight, and compliance with constitutional norms.

Part of the reason that water management is so costly is that it requires a comprehensive and integrated approach. Managing water at its source may not take into account the complexities of transport or result in appropriate distribution to all those who need it; managing its distribution may not take into account the limits of the source. Unlike other parts of the environment, water management must be integrated across an entire ecosystem and throughout a social system. Water flows, varies in form, and changes functions as it moves from glacier to river and groundwater to ocean. It moves through space and time, in a way that is unique in the natural world. One Indian case, for example, examines how pumping groundwater near the Arabian Sea could produce seepage of the ocean water, which would contaminate the residents' drinking water.[7]

This difference between water cases and other environmental cases may be more of degree than of character. Water cases involving boreholes or rights of dumping in a local bay can be localized, while climate change poses global environmental challenges to all environments. But the difference is noticeable in the run of cases. Water cases pose significant new challenges to judicial tribunals seeking to adjudicate and remedy rights relating to water in all its forms. In fact, in the majority of cases, water must be regarded not

---

[4] Fitzmaurice, Malgosia. "The Human Right to Water." *Fordham Environmental Law Review* 18 (2007): 537.

[5] *Ibid.*, 522. [6] *Ibid.*, 507.

[7] *Thangal* v. *Union of India*. COU-144405 (Kerala High Court, September 17, 2002).

only as part of an ecosystem, but as an ecosystem in and of itself, because the changes that water undergoes in one place will affect it in other places: melting glaciers will affect the river flow of water for miles, just as pollution in a water catchment area can diminish the availability of clean drinking water for scores of communities near and far.

Water also provides different kinds of value to those who interact with it. In many cultures throughout the world – both indigenous and not – it has enormous and unique religious and spiritual significance. It has economic value to those who would use the resources it harbors, from marine life to natural gas, and to those who would use it as a means of transportation, a basis for tourism, a source of energy production, or for other industrial purposes. And it has value to a nation's sovereignty, as a marker of its boundaries and a defining value of its patrimony.

But perhaps the most significant difference between water and other parts of the environment is that water is fast becoming scarce, both economically and in fact.[8] Indeed, as water becomes scarce, environmental harms almost invariably devolve into human rights harms because pollution or other forms of degradation in the quality of water reduce the quantity of water to which people have access, resulting in deprivations that threaten health and life. Because people *need* water to survive, the severe degradation in the quality of water will implicate basic human rights, including first generation human rights. This can happen as well in particular cases involving other environmental elements, such as when a forest is cut down, resulting in loss of home or diminution in access to food for local inhabitants; the difference with water is that scarcity on a global scale is inevitable, life-threatening, and invariably affects far more people than those living adjacent to the locality of the problem. And distribution and use of water are more likely than other environmental issues to adversely affect vulnerable populations, including those displaced by war or natural calamities, women, the poor, small-scale farmers, and others who depend on an effective infrastructure to ensure water security.[9] In many countries, where the most vulnerable populations are racial or ethnic minorities, there is an additional overlay of injustice. These problems exist

---

[8] Fitzmaurice, Malgosia. "The Human Right to Water." In Anton and Shelton, *Environmental Protection.*

[9] "The crisis in water and sanitation is – above all – a crisis for the poor. Almost two in three people lacking access to clean water survive on less than $2 a day, with one in three living on less than $1 a day. More than 660 million people without sanitation live on less than $2 a day, and more than 385 million on less than $1 a day." *Human Development Report 2006, Beyond Scarcity: Power, Poverty, and the Global Water Crisis.* United Nations Development Programme, 2006, reprinted in Anton and Shelton, *Environmental Protection*, 465.

in some form whether the government controls the allocation of water or whether it relegates it to private hands. As a result, the constitutional dimensions of water quality and access are unavoidable.

MANIFESTING CONSTITUTIONAL RECOGNITION OF RIGHTS TO WATER

The term "water" or "waters" appears in the constitutions of almost half the countries of the world, cumulatively more than 300 times. While most of these references are concerned with governmental authority to control and allocate water resources, about thirty constitutions provide for a human right to water or an environmental right to clean water. See Appendix G. We focus on these rights provisions first because they are more likely to support constitutional claims for vindication.

Human and environmental rights to water

The constitutions of at least fourteen countries instantiate a human right to a fair distribution of clean, safe, or potable water.[10] For example, South Africa's constitution makes a strong commitment to acknowledging water as a fundamental human right by asserting an enforceable individual right to drinking water.[11] Kenya's 2010 constitution follows this course with a provision that gives "[e]very person []the right – ... to clean and safe water in adequate quantities."[12] But in most other countries, the right to water must be inferred from other rights – such as the right to life, to dignity, or to health – if it is to be recognized at all.

Other constitutions extend the environmental-rights perspective to protection of water. In Andorra, for instance, "The State has the task of ensuring the rational use of the soil and of all the natural resources, so as to guarantee a befitting quality of life for all and, for the sake of the coming generations, to restore and maintain a reasonable ecological balance in the atmosphere, water

---

[10] These are: BOLIVIA CONST. art. 16, COLOMBIA CONST. art. 366, THE DEMOCRACTIC REPUBLIC OF CONGO CONST. art. 48, ECUADOR CONST. art. 12, ETHIOPIA CONST. art. 90(1), GAMBIA CONST. art. 216(4), THE MALDIVES CONST. art. 23), PANAMA CONST. arts. 110 and 118, SWAZILAND CONST. art. 215, SWITZERLAND CONST. art. 76, UGANDA CONST. arts. XIV(b) and XXI, URUGUAY CONST. art. 47, VENEZUELA CONST. arts. 127 and 304, and ZAMBIA CONST. art. 112(d); see BOYD, *Environmental Rights Revolution*, 85.

[11] SOUTH AFRICA CONST. art. 27 (1)(b): "Everyone has the right to have access to— (b) sufficient food and water ..."

[12] KENYA CONST. art. 43(1)(d).

and land, as well as to protect the autochthonous flora and fauna."[13] [i]n Guyana, the environment, including water, is protected "In the interests of the present and future generations"[14] and, likewise, in Tajikistan, the constitutional provisions strongly imply fundamental environmental law principles like the public trust doctrine, guaranteeing that the state will guarantee the "effective utilization" of "the earth, its resources, water, the atmosphere, flora, fauna, and other natural resources ... in the interests of the people."[15] By contrast, the constitution of Laos imposes on the people the duty to protect the environment: "All organisations and citizens must protect the environment and natural resources: land, underground, forests, fauna, water sources and atmosphere."[16]

In general, these provisions track the twin paths for managing water resources at the international level. As an international human right, water is recognized as a basic necessity for life to be allocated for adequate access to maximum numbers of people. In 2002, the Committee on Economic, Social, and Cultural Rights issued General Comment 15, which confirmed a "human right to water" as "indispensable for leading a life in human dignity" and a "prerequisite for the realization of other human rights."[17] This is probably the strongest statement to date at the international level of the human right to water and has been reinforced by a 2009 Human Rights Council Resolution (adopted by the General Assembly in 2010) on access to safe drinking water and sanitation. This Resolution calls on states to, among other things, "develop appropriate tools and mechanisms, which may encompass legislation, comprehensive plans and strategies for the sector, including financial ones, to achieve progressively the full realization of human rights obligations related to access to safe drinking water and sanitation, including in currently unserved and underserved areas" and to "ensure effective remedies for human rights violations by

---

[13] ANDORRA CONST. art. 31.

[14] GUYANA CONST. art. 25: "the State will protect and make rational use of its land, mineral and water resources, as well as its fauna and flora, and will take all appropriate measures to conserve and improve the environment." See also LITHUANIA CONST. art. 54: "The State shall take care of the protection of the natural environment, wildlife and plants, individual objects of nature and areas of particular value and shall supervise a sustainable use of natural resources, their restoration and increase. The destruction of land and the underground, the pollution of water and air, radioactive impact on the environment as well as depletion of wildlife and plants shall be prohibited by law."

[15] TAJIKISTAN CONST. art. 13; see also UGANDA CONST. art. XIII: "Protection of natural resources. The State shall protect important natural resources, including land, water, wetlands, minerals, oil, fauna and flora on behalf of the people of Uganda."

[16] LAOS CONST. art. 17.

[17] United Nations Economic and Social Council (ECOSCO). "General Comment no. 15: The Right to Water." E/C.12/2002/11, para. 1, January 20, 2003.

putting in place accessible accountability mechanisms at the appropriate level."[18] The United Nations Development Programme's Millennium Development Goals also include the need to improve access to drinking water and sanitation although, like many constitutions and cases, they conflate the importance of water as a human right and as an environmental right, by including this target in the goal on environmental sustainability.[19]

As a purely environmental issue, water has been recognized at the international level as a natural resource to be used in accordance with environmental values for its preservation for future generations at, for instance, the 2002 World Summit on Sustainable Development in South Africa. Regional international law has also recognized the importance of water: it is the subject of a 2000 European Framework Directive under which the European Commission can bring a state to the European Court of Justice for violation or failure of implementation.[20] The European approach depends on management by geographic, rather than administrative or political boundaries; since many river basins straddle national boundaries, this may implicate how nations interpret and implement their obligations under their national constitutions. At the same time, Latin America has gone one step further by establishing a "Water Court" to hear both interstate and intrastate disputes. This tribunal "follows a model of exigent ethics and alternative justice"[21] and, according to the Organisation for Economic Co-operation and Development (OECD):

> it is indeed an autonomous, independent and international organization of environmental justice created to contribute in the solution of water related conflicts in Latin America. It is not only an ethical institution committed to preserving the water and to guaranteeing its access as a human right for current and future generations, but also a justice setting for searching solutions to the water conflicts, in addition to those efforts made by Latin-American citizens before other judicial and administrative institutions for the preservation of the environment and the water protection.[22]

---

[18] United Nations Human Rights Council. "Human Rights and Access to Safe Drinking Water and Sanitation." A/HRC/RES/15/8, paras. 9(a) and (f), September 30, 2010.

[19] United Nations. "Millennium Development Goals, Goal 7, Target 3." 2000. ("Reduce by half the proportion of people without sustainable access to safe drinking water and basic sanitation.").

[20] European Parliament and of the Council. "Directive 2000/60/EC." October 23, 2000. OJ L 327, 22.12.2000 (establishing a framework for the Community action in the field of water policy).

[21] Tribunal Latinoamerica del Agua, available at http://tragua.com/quienes-somos/historia

[22] Akhmouch, A. "Water Governance in Latin America and the Caribbean: A Multi-Level Approach.' OECD *Regional Development Working Papers*, 2012/04. OECD Publishing, 2012: 31", available at http://dx.doi.org/10.1787/5k9crzqk3ttj-en

The principles developed through these regional and international systems to protect water resources as both a human and environmental right are often seamlessly and implicitly integrated into domestic constitutional law. Still, constitutional water cases tend to rely less on international law than other constitutional environmental cases simply because the international body of law relating to the human and environmental rights to water is less developed than it is for environmental rights generally.

Through these various constitutional provisions, we can begin to see the complexity of protecting water at a constitutional level. One aspect of that complexity is that water *is* so many different things and its value changes with its form, whether in the ground, as freshwater or saltwater, and whether it is to be used for personal, industrial, political, or ecological purposes. Nonetheless, environmental constitutionalism is commonly used to address how water is or should be used to advance human rights and/or protect the environment.

Governmental control over water resources

Because water is inherently valuable, and because it is, in and of itself, a natural resource capable of being managed, exploited, used, or abused by anyone who can assert control over it, it has political significance as well as personal value. Nations recognize the need to protect waterways from harms both internal and external, and have vested interests in asserting control over water within their territory.

Accordingly, the vast majority of constitutional water provisions relate to the control and use of a nation's waters. Sometimes, waters are included in general environmental provisions, such as when the Indian constitution protects " ... forests, lakes, rivers, wild life ..."[23] but more often constitutions contain separate provisions relating to how water should be classified and how its exploitation should be managed. Typically, they refer to some specific form of water: oceans, rivers, and reservoirs, including underground aquifers, ice, glaciers, ports, and so on.

The most common reference to water in constitutions is as a limit on the nation's territory. The Mexican constitution, for instance, defines "the national territory" as comprising, among other things, "[t]he continental shelf and the submarine shelf of the islands' keys, and reefs; [and] the waters of the territorial seas."[24]

---

[23] INDIA CONST. arts. 48A and 51A.   [24] MEXICO CONST. art. 42.

Beyond establishing the sovereign territory, many constitutions also assert the right to control and govern the waters within the territories. For example, the Slovak constitution asserts that "[n]atural wealth, caves, underground water, natural medicinal springs, and waterways are in the ownership of the Slovak Republic."[25] Likewise, "[i]n Mongolia the land, its subsoil, forests, water, fauna and flora and other natural resources shall be subject to people's power and State protection."[26] Some constitutions assert public control over waters and their associated resources subject to private ownership ("Land, water and natural resources below and above the surface of the land and in the continental shelf and within the territorial waters and the exclusive economic zone of Namibia shall belong to the State if they are not otherwise lawfully owned"),[27] while others, such as Haiti's, limit private ownership over waters ("The right to own property does not extend to the coasts, springs, rivers, water courses, mines and quarries. They are part of the State's public domain.")[28] Still others seek to develop a cooperative model of public–private control.[29]

These simple assertions of control often mask deeply contentious tensions in the allocation of power over important and often scarce water resources. In particular, constitutional language reflects a balance of power as between the public and private sectors, and within the government itself as between the central authority and the subnational or regional authorities. Both of these aspects of the allocation of control can be fractious and highly politicized. With respect to the first – the allocation of control between public and private authorities – many constitutions assert public control over water, and yet, scarce economic resources, as well as pressure from international banks and donor nations especially since the end of the Cold War, have resulted in the ceding of that control to private national and foreign concerns. This leaves open important political and constitutional questions about the degree of control that a government needs to assert to comply with its constitutional obligations to control water and in what forms that control needs to be asserted. For instance, must the government regulate the cost of water to consumers and the level of subsidy for those who can't pay, even if a private enterprise controls the distribution of water? Questions like these are significant in many countries, particularly where the government is not able to exert exclusive control over water resources. In Chile, for instance, what has been

---

[25] SLOVAKIA CONST. art. 4.   [26] MONGOLIA CONST. art. 6.
[27] NAMIBIA CONST. art. 100.   [28] HAITI CONST. art. 36.
[29] BRAZIL CONST. title III, art. 43: "the Republic shall grant incentives for the recovery of arid lands and shall cooperate with small and medium sized rural owners in implementing water sources and small scale irrigation in their tracts of land."

called "extreme privatization" resulted in foreign companies owning rivers for purposes of developing hydro-electric dams, especially in Patagonia. In Indonesia, the treatment and distribution of piped water in Jakarta "has been run by two foreign companies since the final years of then-President Suharto regime,"[30] although efforts continue to try to ensure that at least the price of water is regulated by the government. There is an inevitable tension between public and private control over water and there are good and bad examples of each,[31] although the IUCN insists that, at a minimum, "the stewardship function of water management can not be privatized."[32] The inextricability of the tension between public and private authority in the management of water is one reason constitutional water cases can sometimes be more complex than cases involving other elements of the environment.

With respect to the second aspect of control – as between the central government and the subnational entities – there is also a range across the globe. In many countries, control over water resources is a matter of exclusive federal or national control (whether as an incident of sovereignty or otherwise),[33] though in some countries it is listed as a concurrent power shared between the center and the states,[34] while a very few countries allocate water management to local authorities. In Paraguay, for instance, "[a] departmental government will have jurisdiction: to coordinate activities among the various municipalities within the department, to organize joint departmental services such as public works, power supply, potable water, and others that would serve more than one municipality; as well as to promote associations to promote

---

[30] Jacobson, Philip. "In Jakarta, a Fight Over Money and Water." *Jakarta Globe* (December 27, 2011), available at www.thejakartaglobe.com/jakarta/in-jakarta-a-fight-over-money-and-water/487216

[31] Mohamad Mova Al'Afghani, Mohamad. "Constitutional Court's Review and the Future of Water Law in Indonesia." *Law, Environment and Development Journal* 2(1) (2006), available at www.lead-journal.org/content/06001.pdf (noting that examples of well-managed public water systems include some in the United States, the Dutch Water Companies, Australian State Water Authorities, and the Singapore Water Board, while well-run private water utilities include those in France and the United Kingdom as well as ones in La Paz, Bolivia; Macao, China; and Argentina, citing Gary H. Wolff, P.E and Meena Palaniappan, "Public or Private Water Management? Cutting the Guardian Knot," *Journal of Water Resources Planning and Management*, ASCE, January/February 2004).

[32] IUCN (2009), 9.

[33] NIGERIA CONST. art. 29 (exclusive federal legislative list): "Fishing and fisheries other than fishing and fisheries in rivers, lakes, waterways, ponds and other inland waters within Nigeria; ... Maritime shipping and navigation ..."

[34] SRI LANKA CONST. art. 17:1 and art. 19: "Water storage and management, drainage and embankments, flood protection, planning of water resource; ... Fisheries – Other than fishing beyond territorial water."

cooperation among them."[35] In several countries, the question of the allocation of control over waters is a recurring source of tension. Collectively, these provisions evince a paradoxical attitude toward water-related resources. Their ubiquity in constitutions throughout the world indicates the critical importance of water in its various forms to national sovereignty and governance. On the other hand, the fact that most of these provisions simply assert authority over water, without indicating *how* it will be managed or how the competing claims on water will be negotiated and resolved, indicates a reluctance to make difficult decisions about water management and a willingness to leave the details to others in the near or distant future. While the failure to resolve water management issues in the constitutional text makes sense in that constitutions are not appropriate vehicles for specifying the details of a water management plan, excessive vagueness can thwart the aims of protecting water resources if they are left to vagaries of economic and political jockeying; these provisions all but guarantee that questions about the quality of and access to water will be resolved, if at all, in the political and judicial realms and offer little or no guidance about how the decisions should be made in the context of a particular nation's needs and resources. In the aggregate, constitutions contain virtually no indication of how political and judicial actors ought to balance competing claims on water – whether using water for agricultural, industrial, or personal purposes should be privileged over other uses, or over leaving water in its pristine state – nor do these mere assertions of jurisdictional authority identify the appropriate institutional actors who should be making the decisions, nor the institutional or individual competences that these actors should have. Malaysia's constitution presents an extreme example of this. While it refers to water thirty-one times, all references are associated with jurisdiction and none with the substance or values associated with the management of water. This suggests that water, in this peninsular and island nation, is viewed as an economic and political resource whose control must be rigorously managed, rather than as an integral part of an ecosystem, or an essential element of life. Many other constitutions protect the interest as a directive of social policy rather than as a judicially enforceable right.[36] While

---

[35] PARAGUAY CONST. art. 163.

[36] See, e.g., MALDIVES CONST. art. 23: "Every citizen [has] the following rights pursuant to this Constitution, and the State undertakes to achieve the progressive realisation of these rights by reasonable measures within its ability and resources: (a) adequate and nutritious food and clean water[.]" COLOMBIA CONST. art. 366: "The general welfare and improvement of the population quality of life are social purposes of the state. A basic objective of the state's activity will be to address unsatisfied public health, educational, environmental, and potable water needs[.]" ETHIOPIA CONST. art. 90 ("Social objectives"): "Every Ethiopian shall be entitled,

some of these provisions recognize water as a basic human need, they more often value it as a lucrative economic asset. In Cambodia, for example, water is protected solely for its economic value. Under the constitution's section on "The Economy," the state is required to "protect the environment and balance of abundant natural resources and establish a precise plan of management of land, water, air, wind, geology, ecological systems, mines, energy, petrol and gas, rocks and sand, gems, forests and forestrial products, wildlife, fish and aquatic resources."[37] Likewise, Eritrea's strong protection for the environment is nonetheless found in a section on social and economic development: "The State shall have the responsibility to regulate all land, water and natural resources and to ensure their management in a balanced and sustainable manner and in the interest of the present and future generations; and to create the right conditions for securing the participation of the people to safeguard the environment."[38] The Philippine constitution also integrates economic and environmental protection: "The State shall protect the nation's marine wealth in its archipelagic waters, territorial sea, and exclusive economic zone, and reserve its use and enjoyment exclusively to Filipino citizens."[39] In South Korea, the commodification of water is explicit: "Licenses to exploit, develop, or utilize minerals and all other important underground resources, marine resources, water power, and natural powers are available for economic use,"[40] although in the next paragraph, the Constitution affirms that "[t]he land and natural resources are protected by the State and the State establishes a plan necessary for their balanced development and utilization."[41] Some constitutions recognize the importance of water both as a right and as a social policy priority.[42] The December 2013 draft constitution

within the limits of the country's resources, to food, clean water, shelter, health, education and security of pension." GAMBIA CONST. Social objective 216: "The State shall endeavour to facilitate equal access to clean and safe water, adequate health and medical services, habitable shelter, sufficient food and security to all persons." UGANDA CONST. art. XIV: "The State shall endeavour to fulfill the fundamental rights of all Ugandans to social justice and economic development and shall, in particular, ensure that – ... (b) all Ugandans enjoy rights and opportunities and access to education, health services, clean and safe water, work, decent shelter, adequate clothing, food security and pension and retirement benefits[.]" UGANDA CONST. art. XXI: "Clean and safe water. The State shall take all practical measures to promote a good water management system at all levels."

[37] CAMBODIA CONST. art. 59.   [38] ERITREA CONST. art. 10
[39] PHILIPPINE CONST. art. XII, sec. 2.   [40] SOUTH KOREA CONST. art. 120.   [41] *Ibid.*
[42] Compare KENYA CONST. art. 43 ("Every person has the right— ... (d) to clean and safe water in adequate quantities") with KENYA CONST. art. 56 ("The State shall put in place affirmative action programmes designed to ensure that minorities and marginalised groups— ... (e) have reasonable access to water, health services and infrastructure").

of Egypt protects the environment, the Nile, and the Suez Canal as elements of the "economic component" of society (as opposed to the social or cultural components). The Nile features prominently if symbolically throughout the constitution; in Article 44, the state commits to protecting it but also recognizes the human right that every citizen has to "enjoy the Nile River" as well as the need to protect "the river environment" itself by prohibiting encroachments upon it. In addition, the draft requires the state to commit to "protecting its seas, beaches, lakes, waterways, mineral water, and natural reserves" and prohibits encroachments upon or pollution or use of them "in a manner that contradicts their nature." The state also "commits to the protection and development of green space in urban areas; the protection of plants, livestock, and fishers; the protection of endangered species; and the prevention of cruelty to animals ... as regulated by law."[43] Textual provisions like these go beyond merely asserting sovereignty or control and begin to suggest the values that should undergird decisions about water management.

ADJUDICATING CONSTITUTIONAL RIGHTS TO WATER

As a result of water's unique but critically important attributes and the growing competition over limited resources, domestic constitutional and apex courts are increasingly being called upon to settle disputes over who has rights to water and who has responsibility to ensure that it is available in adequate quantities and in a clean condition to all those who need it. This trend is likely to accelerate in the coming years because these courts are uniquely situated to help mediate these complex and controversial disputes.

Relying on constitutional rights and principles, courts can help to limit the influence that money and politics play in the distribution of water; they can help protect unrepresented interests – including those of poor people, women, minority populations, children, and even future generations, as well as the rights of nature itself – because they are less beholden to majoritarian politics; they can help to ensure that equitable water distribution remains atop the nation's political agenda; they can help to ensure the availability of public information and the participation of the public in policy decisions affecting the management of water resources; and they can make justice more accessible than is possible under international and regional regimes. Indeed, many

---

[43] The Arab Republic of Egypt, Draft Constitution 2013 (New Constitutional Document After Amending the Suspended 2012 Constitution), prepared by International IDEA, available at www.atlanticcouncil.org/images/publications/20131206EgyptConstitution_Dec.pdf.pdf

of the purported benefits of international law – among them, in the words of Francis, to translate the right to water into specific legal obligations and responsibilities, to renew national governments' efforts to meet the basic water needs of their populations, and financially to prioritize meeting basic human water requirements over other investment and management decisions – are more likely to be more effective at the domestic constitutional level because the pressure on national governments may be far more direct.[44] At the same time, constitutional courts often have more political and moral authority than local courts and may, as a result, be more effective.

Overall, constitutional and other apex courts have been responsive to claims based on access to and quality of water and have recognized the need for comprehensive and sensible water management plans to protect both environmental and human rights. But they have not effectively provided guidance as to when water should be treated as an environmental right, when it should be treated as a human right, and when it should be treated as presenting a unique set of problems warranting a unique jurisprudential approach, as the following sections explain.

Vindicating human rights to water

Many constitutional and other apex domestic courts have vindicated the constitutional human right to water by following principles similar to those that have developed in the context of other environmental human rights. Principles of justiciability, including those relating to standing, apply identically whether the case involves water or some other part of the environment. For instance, when the environmental activist M.C. Mehta sought enforcement of environmental laws protecting the River Ganges from excessive pollution, the Indian Supreme Court recognized that:

> The petitioner in the case before us is no doubt not a riparian owner. He is a person interested in protecting the lives of the people who make use of the water flowing in the river Ganga and his right to maintain the petition cannot be disputed. The nuisance caused by the pollution of the river Ganga is a public nuisance, which is wide spread in range and indiscriminate in its effect and it would not be reasonable to expect any particular person to take proceedings to stop it as distinct from the community at large."

---

[44] Francis, Rose. "Water Justice in South Africa: Natural Resources Policy at the Intersection of Human Rights, Economics, and Political Power." *Georgetown International Environmental Law Review* 18 (2005): 149, 186.

Given these facts, the court said, the plaintiff had standing to pursue the action as public interest litigation.[45]

The Colombian Constitutional Court has given content to the right to water by defining it as involving "availability, quality, access, and non-discrimination in distribution, consistent with the obligation to use maximum available resources to effectuate the right to water for all."[46] Three of these requirements are necessarily and exclusively for the benefit of humans; the requirement of quality may be to ensure that the access people have is to water of a certain quality so that it is in fact potable and available for use for washing and other purposes, but ensuring the quality of water may also promote the environmental interest in protecting the quality of an ecosystem. And indeed while Colombia has recognized the interests of nature *per se*, the emphasis in the water cases is on a human right to water. In fact, the constitutional court has recognized that it is a human right on its own merit, as well as being implicit in other fundamental human rights. As a result, the constitutional court has recognized that it can be enforced by any person through the informal mechanisms of the *tutela* action or, when the right is collective, through an *acción de inconstitucionalidad*.[47] In an important case, for instance, the court ordered a water company to supply water to an apartment building, inferring the right to water from the well-recognized rights to life, health, and dignity.[48] The court attempted to encapsulate the various values of the right to water: "to define the content of the fundamental right to water it is necessary to consider that it is an essential prerequisite for the enjoyment of other fundamental rights, such as the right to education, since it is necessary to

---

[45] *M.C. Mehta v. Union of India.* AIR 1988 SC 1115 (Supreme Court of India), cited in *Farooque v. Bangladesh* (Bangladesh, July 15, 2007).

[46] *Sentencia T-616/10,* at 2.3 (Colombia Constitutional Court, 2010): "En cuanto derecho fundamental, la Corte Constitucional ha protegido por vía de tutela diferentes aspectos del derecho al agua relacionados con la garantía mínima de la (i) disponibilidad, (ii) calidad, (iii) acceso y (iv) no discriminación en la distribución, en consonancia con la obligación de emplear el máximo de los recursos que se dispongan para hacer efectivo el derecho al agua a todos sus habitantes."

[47] *Sentencia T-616/10.* (Colombia Constitutional Court, 2010): "Pero, adicionalmente, la Corte ha sostenido que el agua constituye un verdadero derecho fundamental cuando está destinada para el consumo humano. Desde la sentencia T-578 de 1992 se sostuvo que: 'En principio, el agua constituye fuente de vida y la falta de servicio atenta directamente con el derecho fundamental a la vida de las personas. Así pues, el servicio público domiciliario de acueducto y alcantarillado en tanto que afecte la vida de las personas (CP art.11), la salubridad pública (CP arts. 365 y 366), o la salud (CP art. 49), es un derecho constitucional fundamental.' El agua que usan las personas es indispensable para garantizar la vida física y la dignidad humana, entendida esta como la posibilidad de gozar de condiciones materiales de existencia que le permitan desarrollar un papel activo en la sociedad."

[48] *Ibid.*

have functioning water and sewage services in any educational establishment; the right to a healthy environment; and rights to ethnic and cultural diversity, taking into account that some indigenous and afrocolombian communities believe that water has special cosmological significance."[49]

Most constitutional water cases from around the world concern one or more of the four elements of the right to water identified by the Colombian court – availability, quality, access, and non-discrimination – and treat the rights as deriving either from an explicit right to water or from other fundamental human rights typically protected in constitutions. The South African Constitutional Court decided its first right to water case in *Mazibuko* in 2009, recognizing that the claims of the residents of a township to adequate water were based on section 27 of that country's constitution, which, as the court explained, "provides that everyone has the right to have access to sufficient water. Cultures in all parts of the world acknowledge the importance of water. Water is life. Without it, nothing organic grows. Human beings need water to drink, to cook, to wash and to grow our food. Without it, we will die. It is not surprising then that our Constitution entrenches the right of access to water."[50] Notwithstanding water's obvious indispensability to each and every individual, the court ruled that this provision guaranteed not an individual right of each person to sufficient potable water but a social right that the state was obligated to progressively realize. As such, the court upheld Johannesburg's water policy of providing for free only 6 kiloliters per household per month because it was "reasonable," even though it did not consider the number of people in the household; the court also upheld as reasonable the policy of installing pre-paid water meters, which would result in intermittent cessations in water service.[51]

Where there is no explicit right to water, courts have been no less willing to recognize the need for water as a mandate impelled by some other constitutional right, such as a right to dignity or life. For example, in an important case from Israel, neither party disputed that the rights of Bedouins to water was part of their basic right to live in dignity and that this imposed on the state an affirmative obligation to provide them with some amount of water in some way; the application of that principle in the facts of the case, however, raised a socially and politically complex question of the extent of water rights of Bedouins who lived illegally in an unrecognized community in the Negev desert.[52] In India, the Supreme Court has held repeatedly that water is part of

---

[49] *Ibid.*, 2.2.
[50] *Lindiwe Mazibuko and Others* v. *City of Johannesburg and Others* (South Africa, 2009).
[51] *Ibid.*   [52] *Abu Masad* v. *Water Commissioner* (Israel Supreme Court, 2011).

the right to life: "Water is the basic need for the survival of human beings and is part of the right of life and human rights as enshrined in Article 21 of the Constitution of India ... "[53] [t]he court has explained that "The right to live is a fundamental right under Art. 21 of the Constitution and it includes the right of enjoyment of pollution free water and air for full enjoyment of life. If anything endangers or impairs that quality of life in derogation of laws, a citizen has the right to have recourse to Art. 32 of the Constitution for removing the pollution of water or air which may be determined to the quality of life."[54] In Colombia, the Constitutional Court has read the right to water "for human consumption" into the rights to life, to health, and to dignity, which it understands as "the possibility of enjoying the material conditions of existence (of life) that will permit a person to develop an active role in society."[55] Another example comes from Chile, where the Supreme Court in 2009 used a property rights analysis to vindicate the water resources claim of an indigenous community. Over the objections of a private company that sought to bottle and sell the water from the springs, the court recognized the property rights of the Aymara to the land where the springs lay. Although the Aymara's property rights had not been formalized, the court found they were nonetheless ancient and consistent with common and customary law and therefore were valid prior to the company's ownership claims.[56] Whoever controlled the land would control access to the water. But not all human-rights based claims present such critical concerns: some courts have recognized the right of the public to enjoyment of beaches.[57]

In one notable case from Botswana, a group of Basarwa from the Central Kalahari region sought access to boreholes that had originally been installed for mining purposes but were then closed when the mining operations ceased and the Basarwa were evicted from the lands to make way for a game reserve.

---

[53] *Narmada Bahao Andolan v. Union of India*. No. 10 S.C.C. 664 (Supreme Court of India, 2000); *see also Karnataka Industrial Areas Development Board v. C. Kenchappa and Others*. AIRSCW 2546 (Supreme Court of India, 2006).

[54] *Subhash Kumar v. State of Bihar and Others*. Writ. Pet. No. 381/1988 D/-9-1-91 (K.N. Singh, N.D. Ojha JJ, January 9, 1991) (but dismissing petition finding it to be not genuinely in the public interest under Constitution Art. 32 but part the product of a business dispute).

[55] *Sentencia T-616/10*, at 2.2 (Colombia Constitutional Court).

[56] *Alejandro Papic Dominguez Con Comunidad Indigena Aymara Chuzmiza y Usmagama*. No. 2840/2008 (Chile Supreme Court, November 25, 2009).

[57] *Indian Council for Enviro-Legal Action v. Union of India* (Supreme Court of India, April 18, 1996), para. 40: "We, however, direct that fencing should not be raised in such a manner so as to prevent access of the public to public beaches. In other words, the right of way enjoyed by the general public to those areas which they are free to enjoy, should in no way be closed, hampered or curtailed."

When the eviction was found to be illegal, the Basarwa moved back to the area but then had to sue again to gain access to water. Deriving the right to access to water from the constitution's prohibition against inhuman or degrading punishment or treatment, and interpreting the constitution in light of international law, the court ordered the boreholes re-opened, though at the Basarwa's own expense, and upon conditions including limiting access to personal uses.[58] Since the decision in early 2011, the Gem Diamonds Company was granted mining rights on the game reserve, and it has been reported that private capital has contributed to the opening up of the boreholes for drinking water.[59]

The South African *Mazibuko* case and the Botswana case concerning the Basarwa people illustrate the challenges that poor and marginalized people face in gaining access to sufficient amounts of water necessary for their survival. Anticipating that the relevant governments would simply ignore judicial orders to comply with the international recommendations of 50 liters per person per day, the South African court held that a significantly lesser amount is constitutionally permissible, so long as the government's efforts are reasonable and there is indication that the right to more appropriate amounts of water may be progressively realized; with no greater sympathy to Botswana's most vulnerable people, the Botswana court ordered that, while water must be made available, the people themselves must pay for it. In both cases, the value of the right to water though, partially vindicated, was significantly diminished for the impoverished communities.

As a matter of legal analysis, the two African cases also reflect the melting away of legal boundaries in this area: while both cases referred to both domestic and international law, the Botswana case converted a civil and political right (against inhuman treatment) into a right of access to water, while the South African court did the opposite in treating a constitutionally explicit individual right of access to sufficient water as a social right, whose minimum core may be vindicated over time. The conflation of different types

---

[58] *Mosetlhanyane and Others* v. *Attorney General of Botswana.* Civil Appeal No. CACLB-074-10 (Court of Appeal in Lobatse, January 27, 2011) (interpreting Botswana constitution art. 7[1]) 19–20 and relying on a United Nations Report on Substantive Issues Arising in the Implementation of ICESCR, "Water is a limited natural resource and a public good fundamental for life and health. The human right to water is indispensable for leading a life of human dignity. It is a prerequisite for the realization of other human rights" and on a 2010 United Nations call for "full transparency of the planning and implementation process in the provision of safe drinking water and sanitation and the active, free and meaningful participation of the concerned local communities and relevant stakeholders.").

[59] Piet, Bame, "Four boreholes for CKGR Basarwa" (June 21, 2011), Mmegionline, available at www.mmegi.bw (referencing statement from Gem Diamonds Limited).

of human rights claims is characteristic of the judicial treatment of water-related constitutional claims, where practical and economic limitations on political authority often override human needs or the principled vindication of a human right. Where significant political and economic interests are at play, a textual guarantee to water may be less effective.

These cases also reflect the porous boundaries between public and private actors in the provision of water for basic drinking and sanitation needs. In most countries, though public authority alone is responsible for satisfying the constitutional obligations, it lacks the capacity on its own to secure even basic water needs for drinking and sanitation. In South Africa, the water was provided by a municipal corporation, whereas in Botswana the government was responsible for providing the water, but this obligation could only be fulfilled when a large multinational mining corporation stepped in and, for its own economic reasons, reopened the boreholes. Should the company decide in the future not to maintain the water supply for the members of the local Basarwa community, it will be difficult for the government to hold anyone accountable, since the company is under no constitutional obligation to supply water for them, and the government is unable or unwilling to do so.

The disconnect between private control and government responsibility, which is replicated throughout the world, has prompted plaintiffs' groups, particularly in Latin America, to seek to vindicate water rights against both corporate and governmental entities. This happened in *Mendoza*, the Argentinian case discussed in the previous chapter, where plaintiffs sought to hold more than forty public and private entities responsible for the disastrous condition of the river.

In India, however, the success of constitutional litigation against private actors has been less evident. In the most prominent effort to hold corporations accountable, it has taken not only litigation but coordinated and sophisticated public protests lasting years, as well as efforts in administrative, legislative, and judicial arenas in all levels of government to protect access to clean drinking water from overexploitation by Coca-Cola.[60] These cases evidence the complex interplay between public and private authorities that is inherent in all the constitutional litigation but especially pronounced in cases involving the right to water.

Even cases that nominally challenge jurisdictional authority to control water or to assert property rights over land that has water can become human rights cases, particularly as water claims become ever more dire with water's

---

[60] India Resource Center, available at www.indiaresource.org; see *Perumatty Grama Panchayat* v. *State of Kerala*. No. 2004 (1) KLT 731 (Kerala High Court, December 16, 2003).

increasing scarcity. For example, the High Court of South Africa ordered a municipality to restore a discontinued flow of free potable water as necessary for survival.[61] More recently, litigation in South Africa challenged the failure of the government to provide drinking water to residents of Mpumalunga where, after heavy rains, the water became unsafe for drinking and even for washing due to the pollution of the main water supply by acid mine water caused by environmentally irresponsible mining nearby. The national government, which was thought to be responsible both for ensuring compliance with environmental mining laws and for supplying drinking water to all South Africans, quickly argued that it was the responsibility of the local municipalities to provide drinking water for their residents, while the municipalities took the position that they lacked the resources to provide the essential water.

The flood planning controversy in Bangladesh illustrates how flawed water management can have adverse impacts on all aspects of human life. The Supreme Court in *Farooque* v. *Bangladesh* granted standing to an environmental organization to challenge the implementation of a flood action plan that had been years in development and heavily supported by the international community. The plan would have increased the area of arable land by reducing the likelihood of flooding; while this would have benefited those in a position to own land, it would have destroyed the livelihood of those fishers who depended on the waters for their income and for their nutritional needs, including, in particular, women and Hindus who had turned to fishing because they had traditionally been barred from owning land.[62] The Court found that the constitutional right of "any person aggrieved" to bring a claim included an organization whose principal purpose was environmental protection even though the claims were largely framed in terms of human rights.

The question of standing can be particularly important in water rights cases because there is often little opportunity for participation in the decision making. Although "'public participation' has become the new watchword in national water policies," Razzaque concludes that "people rarely participate in decisionmaking," particularly, she notes, in projects involving dams.[63] Indeed, because water management tends to require comprehensive, rather than

---

[61] *Residents of Bon Vista Mansions* v. *Southern Metropolitan Local Council.* 01/12312 (High Court of South Africa, September 2001) (requiring access to free minimum level of water necessary for survival).

[62] Warner, Jeroen. *Flood Planning: The Politics of Water Security.* I.B. Taurus, 2011, 135 (discussing the controversy of the flood action plan, including the litigation); see also *Farooque.*

[63] Razzaque, Jona. "Public Participation in Water Governance." In *The Evolution of the Law and Politics of Water*, by J.W. Dallepenna and J. Gupta (eds.), 355, 364–5. Springer, 2009.

discrete or limited, solutions and because it often involves a complex relationship between government and private (often international) enterprises, procedural water rights can be hard to secure and exercise. And yet, public participation (as discussed in Chapter 8) is as important in preserving rights to water as other environmental rights, and in some ways more so because of its indispensability to human life and the likelihood that poor decisionmaking will adversely affect vulnerable populations.

Throughout these cases, the focus of the court's attention tends to be on fixing the immediate problem of ensuring access to healthful water in adequate quantities to the individual or community plaintiffs. This is as it should be because the plaintiffs are often in desperate need and the courts are their only recourse. But courts should also consider the environmental aspects of these cases: they should understand the environmental causes of the claimed injuries as well as the environmental implications of alternative remedial courses. In order to protect the rights of future generations, courts must keep in mind both human and environmental factors.

Vindicating environmental rights to water

Because water is also an essential element of the broader ecosystem, pollution and misuse or overuse can degrade the *quality* of water as well, giving rise to claims typically thought of as environmental claims asserting the right to clean water.

Most environmental water rights cases arise as a result of pollution, which impairs the local ecology but does not necessarily threaten the health or lives of people living in the local communities.[64] Treating water cases like other environmental rights cases, courts tend to incorporate general substantive principles of environmental law, including the polluter pays principle, the public trust doctrine,[65] the precautionary principle, and principles of

---

[64] United Nations Human Rights Council. "Fact Sheet No. 35." August 2010. 40–1. "A number of courts have adjudicated cases related to the promotion and protection of the right to water, notably in relation to the pollution of water resources and disconnections from water services. Domestic courts have also increasingly heard cases relating to access to safe drinking water and sanitation under the protection of the rights to life, health and adequate housing or the right to a healthy environment."

[65] See, e.g., *M.C. Mehta v. Kamal Nath and Others*, 1 S.C.C. 388 (Supreme Court of India, 1977) ("holding that the government violated the public trust by leasing the environmentally sensitive riparian forest land to a company," thereby diverting the river's flow, as described in John Scanlon, Angela Casar, and Noemi Nemes, "Water as a Human Right?" 9–10 *IUCN Environmental Policy and Law Paper No. 51* (2004); Anton and Shelton, *Environmental Protection*, 477.

sustainable development (including especially the need to balance development and ecology), without making special reference to the water-specific aspects of the case, if any.[66] For instance, the balancing that is required in sustainable development cases is the same whether the places to be developed are terrain or waterways. As the Indian Supreme Court wrote in the context of coastal areas where land development affects the quality of the water, "Both development and environment must go hand in hand, in other words, there should not be development at the cost of environment and vice versa, but there should be development while taking due care and ensuring the protection of environment."[67]

In a landmark decision from Chile, the Supreme Court enjoined a copper mining company from continuing to dump waste onto the beaches of Chile, as it had done for 50 years. The court explained: "Never will it be said that a person or authority has the right to pollute the environment, in which a community of people live and grow, by a voluntary act of its own, as is occurring in this case. Moreover, said act, by affecting nature itself, is violating all civilized norms of cohabitation of man with his environment. The preservation of nature and conservation of the environmental heritage is an obligation of the State, according to our Fundamental Constitution . . ." The claims were asserted in purely environmental terms, and the evidence relied on related to the color of the ocean water, the adverse impact on marine life, the creation of artificial beaches, and other evidence of environmental degradation. Nonetheless, the court found that the harm to nature and to humans was inextricably linked and, however it was categorized, the conduct of the copper company violated the rights of Chileans to live in an environment free

---

[66] See, e.g., L. Krishnan v. *State of Tamil Nadu.* Writ. Pet. No. 20186 of 2000 (Madras High Court, June 27, 2005) (requiring study and other protective actions to protect lands classified as Odai Poromboke for the purpose of storing water); *Indian Council for Enviro-Legal Action v. Union of India* (India, 1996): "Both development and environment must go hand in hand, in other words, there should not be development at the cost of environment and vice versa, but there should be development while taking due care and ensuring the protection of environment." See, e.g., European Union, *Consolidated Version of the Treaty on the Functioning of the European Union,* 13 December 2007, 2008/C 115/01, available at www. unhcr.org/refworld/docid/4b17a07e2.html, art. 191(2): "Union policy on the environment shall aim at a high level of protection taking into account the diversity of situations in the various regions of the Union. It shall be based on the precautionary principle and on the principles that preventive action should be taken, that environmental damage should as a priority be rectified at source and that the polluter should pay." See, e.g., *Intellectuals Forum, Tirupathi v. State of Andhra Pradesh and Others.* Civil Appeal 1251 of 2006 (Supreme Court of India, February 23, 2006).

[67] *Indian Council for Enviro-Legal Action v. Union of India.* Writ Petition (C) No. 664 of 1993 (Supreme Court of India, April 18, 1996), para. 31.

of pollution. And nowhere in the case was particular mention made of the fact that the harm was to water rather than to land.[68]

Likewise, the judicial recognition of the importance of environmental protection for future generations applies equally in water and non-water environmental cases. As the Philippine Supreme Court has said, "Even assuming the absence of a categorical legal provision specifically prodding petitioners to clean up the bay, they and the men and women representing them cannot escape their obligation to future generations of Filipinos to keep the waters of the Manila Bay clean and clear as humanly as possible. Anything less would be a betrayal of the trust reposed in them."[69] Moreover, the adjustments that many courts have made to procedural rules in constitutional environmental cases apply with equal vigor to cases involving water rights. For instance, the tenet that the burden of persuasion is not on the party making the claim as it would ordinarily be, but on the party seeking to prove that *no* damage has been done, applies equally in water and non-water environmental cases.[70]

The two lower court cases vindicating the Ecuadorian rights of nature (discussed further in Chapter 9) both involved damage to rivers, in one case by negligently dumping construction debris into the river, thereby narrowing the channel and causing flooding on adjacent landowners' property, and in the other case by illegal gold mining operations that were polluting the waters. In neither of these cases, however, did the courts treat the claims any differently than they would have done had they been based on the rights of land or soil.

Hybridized human and environmental water rights

In some situations, the human and ecological interests converge, as where a polluter degrades the quality of the water to such an extent that it is neither potable for humans nor environmentally sustainable. In other cases, there are

[68] *Pedro Flores et al. v. Codelco* (Chile) (affirmed), *Pedro Flores y Otros v. Corporacion Del Cobre, Codelco* (Chile), available in translation at 2 *Geo. Int'l Envtl. L. Rev.* 251 (1989).
[69] *Manila Bay* (Philippines, 2008).
[70] *Indian Council for Enviro-Legal Action v. Union of India* (Supreme Court of India, April 18, 1996), at paras. 38–9. "No suitable reason has been given [why the relaxation in environmental standards] was necessary, in the larger public interest, and the exercise of power under the said proviso will not result in large-scale ecological degradation and violation of Article 21 of the citizens living in those areas. ... In the absence of a categorical statement being made in an affidavit that such reduction will not be harmful or result in serious ecological imbalance, we are unable to conclude that the said amendment has been made in the larger public interest and is valid. This amendment is, therefore, contrary to the object of the Environment Act and has not been made for any valid reason and is, therefore, held to be illegal."

competitive interests as where the human rights based demands on access to water derogate from the pristine condition in which environmental interests would seek to protect it.

Most courts do not distinguish between claims based on human rights and those based on environmental rights. This is the situation in Ecuador, for instance, where litigation by indigenous groups and local residents lasting almost 20 years – and ongoing – resulted, at least as of 2012, in an $18 billion judgment against Chevron for the environmental degradation and loss of access to clean water caused by its predecessor's, Texaco, activities in the region.[71] Where the damage to one causes injury to the other, there is little need for the courts to distinguish between the two types of claims.

In India, too, the inextricability of human and environmental interests in water has been repeatedly acknowledged. "Violation of anti-pollution laws," the Supreme Court has said, "not only adversely affects the existing quality of life but the non-enforcement of the legal provisions often results in ecological imbalance and degradation of environment, the adverse effect of which will have to be borne by the future generations."[72] In fact, a plethora of Indian cases reflects the convergence of environmental and human rights strategies, from the cases seeking to clean up the Ganges from toxins from tanneries and other pollutants,[73] to those concerning water storage and use of catchment areas.[74] Typical, too, is the court's statement in *Susetha* v. *State of Tamil Nadu and Others* (concerning the use of storage tanks) that the right to water is envisaged as the part of the quality of life protected under Article 21 of the Constitution, but "also in view of the fact that the same has been recognized in Articles 47 [relating to nutrition, standard of living and public health] and 48-A [relating to protecting and improving the natural environment including forests, lakes, rivers and wild life] of the Constitution of India."[75] Rights to water are protected indistinguishably as human and environmental rights.

In 1996, the Indian Supreme Court decided a case that challenged the national and state governments' failure to develop and implement a policy that

[71] Keefe, Radden Patrick. "Reversal of Fortune: A crusading lawyer helped Ecuadorans secure a huge environmental judgment against Chevron. But did he go too far?" *The New Yorker.* January 9, 2012. 38.

[72] *Indian Council for Enviro-Legal Action* v. *Union of India* (Supreme Court of India, April 18, 1996), at para. 26.

[73] *M.C. Mehta* v. *Union of India.* Writ Petition No. 3727 of 1985 (Supreme Court of India, January 12, 1988).

[74] See, e.g., *Intellectuals Forum, Tirupathi* v. *State of Andhra Pradesh and Others* (Supreme Court of India, February 23, 2006).

[75] *Susetha* v. *State of Tamil Nadu And Others.* Civil Appeal No. 3418 of 2006 (Supreme Court of India August 8, 2006).

would protect or sustainably develop India's 6,000 kilometers of coastline. Although there was *some* regulation and *some* implementation in *some* places, the plaintiff – an environmental NGO called the Indian Council For Enviro-Legal Action (ICELA) – argued, and the court agreed, that there needed to be a comprehensive coastal zone plan that the government was bound to implement and enforce.[76] The court was sympathetic, recognizing the complex web of interests that were at play in the case.

The court accepted the plaintiff's claim that the high level of pollution in the coastal waters was caused by "the stresses and pressure of high population growth, non-restrained development, [and] lack of adequate infrastructure facilities for the resident population." In particular, the harms were caused by "indiscriminate industrialisation and urbanisation, without the requisite pollution control systems."[77] But the waters were affected differently in different places. Tidal waves and cyclones were destroying the mangrove forests, while anthropogenic but ecologically unsound development was threatening the major fishing areas in some of the coastal areas, and overexploitation of groundwater in certain coastal areas was "stated to have resulted in growing intrusion of salt water from the sea to inland areas and fresh water aquifers previously used for drinking, agriculture and horticulture." At the same time, "unplanned urbanisation and industrialisation in the coastal belts is stated to be causing fast disappearance of fertile agricultural lands, fruit gardens and energy plantations like casuarina trees," and this can have devastating consequences for the human and natural environment because these areas "serve as windbreakers and protect inland habitations from the cyclonic damages."[78] These causes of the damage run the gamut from intentional human causes to human causes for which no one could really be held responsible, such as population growth to entirely natural causes such as cyclones. While it is difficult to lay a claim against a public or private entity for the damage caused by extreme weather phenomena, courts are increasingly holding governments accountable for failing to protect against such harms, particularly when they are cyclical or foreseeable.

In *Manila Bay*, the Philippine Supreme Court went further and held the government accountable for being neglectful in failing to protect the bay. It described the bay as "a dirty and slowly dying expanse mainly because of the abject official indifference of people and institutions that could have otherwise made a difference" and chastised the government for "[t]heir cavalier attitude

---

[76] *Indian Council for Enviro-Legal Action v. Union of India* (Supreme Court of India, April 18, 1996).
[77] *Ibid.*, para. 3.   [78] *Ibid.*, para. 4.

towards solving, if not mitigating, the environmental pollution problem," which, it said, "is a sad commentary on bureaucratic efficiency and commitment."[79] The court ordered the rehabilitation and restoration of the waters in Manila Bay "to make them fit for swimming, skin-diving, and other forms of contact recreation."[80]

In the ICELA case, the Indian Supreme Court's description of the actual injuries is also impressive in its breadth and sophistication. It described the injuries as being both short- and long-term, and "physical, chemical and biological" in nature. They were both anthropocentric and ecocentric, because they included "damage to flora and fauna, public health and environment." The resources that were at stake included "extensive groundwater resources and sometimes mineral resources, while in other areas, there are iron ore, oil and gas resources and mangrove forests."[81] The court was able to see that the water at issue in this case included coastal waters, groundwater, aquifers, and, in their most menacing forms, tidal waves and cyclones. But the court recognized that, in any of these forms, water is part of a larger ecosystem that includes flora and fauna, mangrove forests, fishing areas, cities and towns, fruit gardens, energy plantations, and fertile agricultural lands, which, in turn, protect population centers from cyclonic damage. The use to which water is put and for which it is valued was also understood to be varied and included mineral resources, fishing, drinking, agriculture, and horticulture.[82] Water, the court was ready to appreciate, is clearly not a *single* thing that merits protection but a complex of elements and interests whose competing values need to be carefully assessed and managed.

The case also illustrates the types of claims that are typically seen in constitutional water cases because they include – and conflate – questions of access and quality. Questions of access are typically deemed to raise human rights claims because the human use of water is so critical to life, dignity, health, and other commonly recognized human rights. Many parts of Africa, where water shortages are already evident and likely to intensify in the coming decades, have already seen a number of constitutional cases aimed at assuring adequate access to water. These urgent and competing demands for water create a tension for the vindication of constitutional water rights: courts that are asked to vindicate the immediate human rights to water may well sacrifice

---

[79] *Manila Bay* (Philippines, 2008).   [80] *Ibid.*, 36.
[81] *Indian Council for Enviro-Legal Action* v. *Union of India* (Supreme Court of India, April 18, 1996), paras. 3–4.
[82] *Ibid.*, para. 4.

the environmental interests in protecting water resources for future generations and for the benefit of the world's ecosystems.

The effect of constitutional provisions on these cases seems indirect. Courts tend to see through the text and focus instead on the actual interests at play, assessing whether the human claims to adequate access outweigh the competing corporate or political pressures. The text never determines the result of the balancing process, and, given the complexity of the cases, courts often ignore the text altogether, reading environmental provisions to protect human rights and sometimes vice versa. Nonetheless, the existence in the constitution of a provision relating to water seems to encourage courts to pay more attention than they otherwise might to its importance to human life and to nature itself.

REMEDIES, IMPLEMENTATION, AND ENFORCEMENT

Like constitutional environmental adjudication generally, constitutional water cases often result in a multipronged remedial approach. Certainly, monetary damages and fines for harm already done are common. In *Tirupur* v. *Noyyal*,[83] the Indian Supreme Court allowed substantial fines against a tannery even though it had already installed remedial pollution measures such as pretreatment plants to minimize water pollution from dyeing. In the Coca-Cola case in the Indian state of Kerala, the state legislature set up a claims court allowing claims against Coca-Cola up to $47 million. And, as noted, in the Ecuadorian case against Texaco, damages were assessed at $18 billion.[84] In *Mendoza*, the Argentine case involving the clean-up of the polluted river basin near Buenos Aires, fines against the companies were also available. However, the *amparo* nature of the cases required plaintiffs to obtain compensation only through separate civil litigation. Unfortunately, it is often the case that payments to marginalized populations may not be forthcoming, and, when they are, they are often inadequate to compensate for the many kinds of harms caused when clean water is unavailable or insufficient.

Other common remedial forms are also available, sometimes but not always in conjunction with damages. In *Manila Bay*, the court ordered mandamus against the government because, in its view, cleaning the bay was a non-discretionary duty.[85] "In the light of the ongoing environmental degradation,"

---

[83] *Tirupur Dyeing Factory Owners* v. *Noyyal River A. Protection Association* (Supreme Court of India, 2009) (basing its judgment that the fine was appropriate on the precautionary principle and polluter pays principle deriving from art. 21 [citing *Vellore Citizens Welfare Forum* v. *Union of India* AIR 1996 SC 2715. Supreme Court of India, August 28, 1996.]).

[84] Keefe, "Reversal of Fortune."   [85] *Manila Bay* (Philippines, 2008).

the court said, it "wishes to emphasize the extreme necessity for all concerned executive departments and agencies to immediately act and discharge their respective official duties and obligations. Indeed, time is of the essence; hence, there is a need to set timetables for the performance and completion of the tasks, some of them as defined for them by law and the nature of their respective offices and mandates."[86] But the court went much further and ordered a wide-ranging set of remedies, including education, inspection of commercial buildings, and reviewing licenses. In particular, the court said that the Department of Education "shall integrate lessons on pollution prevention, waste management, environmental protection, and like subjects in the school curricula of all levels to inculcate in the minds and hearts of students and, through them, their parents and friends, the importance of their duty toward achieving and maintaining a balanced and healthful ecosystem in the Manila Bay and the entire Philippine archipelago." And, as is becoming typical in these cases, the court retained jurisdiction over the case and, "in line with the principle of 'continuing mandamus,'" it required the government to submit quarterly reports showing the progress it had made in complying with the decision.

In the *Mendoza* river basin case from Argentina, the court "established an action plan requiring the government agency responsible for the Matanza-Riachuelo basin ... to fulfill specific measures, including: a) producing and disseminating public information; b) controlling industrial pollution; c) cleaning up waste dumps; d) expanding water supply, sewer and drainage works; e) developing an emergency sanitation plan; f) adopting an international measurement system to assess compliance with the plans goals."[87] Moreover, "In order to ensure adequate enforcement, the Court delegated the enforcement process to a federal court, ... to monitor enforcement of the decision [and it] created a working group formed by the national Ombudsman and the NGOs that had been involved in the case as non-litigant parties, seeking to strengthen and enable citizen participation in monitoring enforcement of the decision."[88] Indeed, a major part of the decision was to encourage public awareness and discussion about the effects of decades of environmental degradation.

Ordering the creation of boards or commissions to monitor not only the parties' compliance with the court's order, but other ongoing issues relating to

---

[86] *Ibid.*

[87] *Mendoza Beatriz Silva et al. v. State of Argentina et al.* M.1569.XL (Supreme Court of Argentina, July 8, 2008) [hereinafter *Mendoza*].

[88] *Mendoza* on damages (damages resulting from environmental pollution of Matanza-Riachuelo river). File M. 1569.XL, available at www.escr-net.org/docs/i/1469150

the particular water in controversy, is not uncommon, though it necessarily raises difficult theoretical and practical questions about political accountability and the balance of power between the courts and the other limbs of government, as well as questions about the allocation of fiscal resources. The Indian Supreme Court in the ICELA case strongly encouraged but did not require the central government to set up State Coastal Management Authorities in each state as well as a National Coastal Management Authority. The court urged this course in light of the fact that the existing Pollution Control Boards had limited jurisdiction over the important issues in question and, the court noted, "are ... overworked."[89]

Ensuring compliance of remedial orders can be the most challenging part of any constitutional environmental case, and cases about water are no different. It cannot be assumed that a private party or governmental authority will automatically comply with a judicial order, particularly if it seeks to do anything more than impose a moderate fine or require the fulfillment of a non-discretionary duty with minimal political consequences. Rather, the expectation should be that restoration of access to water and repair of degradation to the environment requires an integrated response on behalf of courts, legislators, and executive actors at all levels of government. In the ICELA case, the court emphasized, moreover, the important role that state courts have in ensuring compliance with environmental norms, particularly where they are more likely to be familiar with local conditions.[90] It is also worth remembering that those conditions, which vary from place to place as the environment itself changes, are bound to change over time. In the ICELA case, for instance, the government issued one directive in 1991, but 3 years later, and apparently due to political pressure particularly from developers and the tourism industry, significantly relaxed the environmental standards.[91] Plaintiffs should be mindful to frame their claims precisely, unless they are confident that the court is committed to engaging with political actors to compel the development and ongoing implementation of a comprehensive water management plan.

In fact, many cases reflect the reality that good laws have been enacted and, in some cases, environmentally friendly administrations seek to enforce

---

[89] *Indian Council for Enviro-Legal Action v. Union of India* (Supreme Court of India, April 18, 1996).

[90] *Ibid.*, para. 42.

[91] *Ibid.*, para. 37: "The Central Government has, thus, retained the absolute power of relaxation of the entire 6000 kms long coastline and this, in effect, may lead to the causing of serious ecological damage as the said provision gives unbridled power and does not contain any guidelines as to how or when the power is to be exercised ... Far in excess of what was demanded by the Hotel and Tourism Industry."

them; yet, the lure of investment and development, combined with limited fiscal and human resources thwart their best intentions, so that judicial action is required to impel action on an ongoing basis. As the ICELA court recognized:

> If the mere enactment of the laws relating to the protection of [the] environment was to ensure a clean and pollution-free environment, then India would, perhaps, be the least polluted country in the world. But, this is not so. There are stated to be over 200 Central and State Statutes which have at least some concern with environment protection, either directly or indirectly. The plethora of such enactments has, unfortunately, not resulted in preventing environmental degradation which, on the contrary, has increased over the years.[92]

The situation in Brazil is similar:

> Despite an impressive set of laws and policies, the pace of implementing the modern water regime remains a challenge ... Brazilian water law – like all of Brazilian environmental law – must address the problem that its statutes are strong, but enforcement is weak. This situation is partially due to a lack of resources and an accompanying lack of political will in the face of competing development priorities. In addition, although there is no way to measure it precisely, corruption remains a factor undermining the enforcement of environmental laws in Brazil.[93]

The Indian court went on to say, "If the people were to voluntarily respect such a law, and abide by it, then it would result in law being able to achieve the object for which it was enacted. Where, however, there is a conflict between the provision of law and personal interest, then it often happens that self-discipline and respect for law disappears."[94]

The question then is what a court can do in these situations to compel respect for the law. One option is for it to require the development of a water management plan that balances constitutional human rights with environmental protection and with the practical necessities of development and economic growth. Such a plan should normally be developed at the national or central level, so that water remains protected equally throughout the nation and to avoid the competitive race to the bottom that decentralization often

---

[92] *Ibid.*
[93] Cassuto, David N. and Rômulo S.R. Sampaio. "Water Law in the United States and Brazil – Climate Change and Two Approaches To Emerging Water Poverty." *William and Mary Environmental Law and Policy Review* 35 (2011): 371, 400.
[94] *Indian Council for Enviro-Legal Action* v. *Union of India* (India, April 18, 1996), para. 25.

fosters, particularly in stressed economic times. A national policy would also ensure that a national tax base is available to subsidize equitable water distribution throughout the nation. This course is essentially what courts are doing when they monitor the progressive realization of a social right, as the South African Constitutional Court in particular is wont to do.

Another solution, where a legislative framework already exists, is for a court to build up the administrative machinery to monitor and implement the policies already chosen either by ordering the establishment of a new administrative office or, if a relevant one exists, by expanding it to include the responsibility for water. The Nepali Supreme Court did this, for example, in the face of corporate recalcitrance. Noting that the Drinking Water Corporation "seems reluctant to perform its duties to protect public health," the court "decided to alert the Ministry of Housing and Physical Development to be the contact ministry for providing necessary directions to the Drinking Water Corporation in order to make the Corporation accountable and responsible and to make proper arrangements for providing pure drinking water as per its legal obligations under the Act."[95] If a court believes that constitutional challenges are likely to continue, then another solution is the development of specialized courts, as is happening with environmental courts in general and as has already happened in Latin America at a regional level specifically for water. Indeed, George and Catherine Pring report that water courts have existed in Europe since the early twentieth century and that "water issues have been the catalyst for broader-based [environmental courts] in a number of countries."[96]

By highlighting the importance of water, constitutional provisions can invite litigation to protect water. And the value of the litigation may extend beyond the judgment. In Argentina, the highly publicized litigation over the pollution in the Matanza-Riachuelo river basin contributed to a World Bank program to support its clean-up. Even in the South African *Mazibuko* case, where the plaintiffs' claims were rejected, and where the ruling has been roundly criticized by human rights groups and those representing poor and disenfranchised populations, one United Nations publication has indicated that there is reason to believe that "during the litigation, and perhaps because of it, the City has repeatedly reviewed and revised its policies to ensure that they did promote the progressive achievement of the right of access to

[95] *Advocate Prakash Mani Sharma and Others v. Nepal Drinking Water Corporation and Others.* WP 227/1990 (Supreme Court of Nepal, Joint Bench, July 10, 2001).
[96] Pring and Pring, *Greening Justice*, 9.

sufficient water."[97] However, this did nothing to avoid the months-long water deprivation crisis experienced subsequently elsewhere in the country.

With all these fiscal and political complexities and the challenges involved in managing the cases and in developing and enforcing effective remedies, courts might be tempted to avoid adjudicating cases involving rights to water. But, remarkably, courts have not shied away from hearing cases raising claims over water rights. In part, this reflects explicit language in so many of the world's constitutions that seeks to protect and manage water resources as an incident of sovereignty, as a human right, or as an essential element of a healthy ecology. And in part, it reflects the growing muscularity of constitutional courts around the world, especially in regions like Southeast Asia and Latin America, where water resources are both threatened and scarce, along with the growing recognition in both national and international arenas of the importance of water to human life and to the world's ecosystems.

[97] United Nations Human Rights Council. "Fact Sheet No. 35," 41.

7

Subnational environmental constitutionalism

Local governments struggle with the practical realities of how to assess environmental impacts alongside a host of other considerations, including landowner and community interests in using land. These struggles often take place under state enabling legislation that does not expressly address constitutional obligations, or may even undermine those obligations. Yet despite the challenges, the constitutional obligation remains. With these environmental rights[1] approaching their fourth decade of existence, the time is overdue for local governments to heed their constitutional calling.

Mudd (2011), p. 4.

Subnational government – states, provinces, Länder, cantons, or what is sometimes referred to as the meso-level that exists between the national government and local governments – are the final frontier in constitutional environmental rights.[2] Subnational constitutionalism is worldwide, advancing myriad civil, political, and socioeconomic rights, and often filling gaps in federal systems.[3] Many subnational governments have their own constitutions, which can provide the most direct mechanism for advancing local interests, including environmental constitutionalism.[4] Led by states in the Americas in general, and Brazil in

---

[1] The phrase "environmental rights" is used throughout the article to denote the constitutional right to a healthful environment contained in the state constitutions of Illinois, Pennsylvania, Montana, and Hawaii.

[2] Gardner, James A. *In Search of Subnational Constitutionalism.* Prepared for Seventh World Congress, International Association of Constitutional Law, Athens, Greece, June 11–15, 2007, available at http://papers.ssrn.com/sol3/papers.cfm?abstract_id=1017239

[3] Ewald, Sylvia. "State Court Adjudication of Environmental Rights: Lessons from the Adjudication of the Right to Education and the Right to Welfare." *Columbia Journal of Environmental Law* 36 (2011): 413, available at http://columbiaenvironmentallaw.org/assets/pdfs/36.2/Ewald.pdf

[4] Gardner, James A. *Interpreting State Constitutions: A Jurisprudence of Function in a Federal System.* University of Chicago Press, 2005.

particular, subnational governments around the globe have seen fit to constitutionalize substantive and procedural environmental rights, environmental duties, and sustainable development for present and future generations, often with much more specificity and enforceability than provided in national constitutions. See Appendix H. Subnational instantiation of constitutional environmental rights can have special salience in countries that have yet to recognize environmental rights at the federal level, including the USA, Canada, and Australia.

Subnational provisions stand apart from their national counterparts, if any, and warrant independent examination. Subnational developments at the constitutional and judicial levels can be instructive and illustrative. For example, some environmental constitutional provisions are much more elaborate and intricate than national analogs. Developments at the state level can be thought of as "happy incidents" to advance innovations in law, including in constitutional law and in environmental constitutionalism. Brown, for one, contends that experiences in US states with environmental constitutionalism could provide East Europeans with models for making such environmental provisions self-executing and enforceable.[5]

Except for a few notable exceptions, judicial developments at the state level in the USA have not been terribly encouraging, as Thompson has observed: "[s]tate courts have helped ease most of the constitutional provisions into relative obscurity by holding that the provisions are not self-executing, by denying standing to private citizens and groups trying to enforce the provisions, or by establishing relatively easy standards for meeting the constitutional requirements."[6] Nonetheless, subnational constitutions can provide additional proving ground for environmental constitutionalism around the globe because such provisions (if they exist) tend to supply a vital link to the dual objectives of protecting the environment and promoting environmental human rights.

THE NATURE OF SUBNATIONAL ENVIRONMENTAL CONSTITUTIONALISM

Subnational environmental constitutionalism enjoys – or suffers – from many of the same attributes as does its national counterpart. Yet it offers largely untapped opportunities to embed substantive, procedural, and other environmental rights in ways most likely to have the greatest effect at the local level,

---

[5] See Brown, Elizabeth F. *In Defense of Environmental Rights in East European Constitutions.* Vol. 1. University of Chicago Law School Roundtable, 1993: 191, available at http://papers.ssrn.com/sol3/papers.cfm?abstract_id=995326

[6] See generally, Thompson, "Constitutionalizing the Environment," 157, 158.

where environmental degradation is most likely to be sustained and where its effects are most likely to be experienced by people in their communities.

Subnational environmental constitutionalism offers several advantages over national treatment. First, subnational constitutions can reflect local environmental concerns that can be ignored or underserved by the national constitution, even when those concerns may address global challenges. For example, the Dutch provinces of Zeeland, North Holland, Friesland, and Groningen address climate change and sustainable development, problems that the national constitution does not reach.[7]

Second, subnational constitutions can pay attention to minutiae often lacking in national constitutions. Remarkable examples of this are found in Brazil, whose state constitutions delineate extensive governmental functions in the service of substantive environmental rights, including promoting biodiversity and sustainability, protecting species and water quality, advancing conservation and environmental education, and enforcing environmental requirements. The constitution of the Brazilian state of Mato Grosso – which contains agricultural land, part of the Amazon forest, and part of the Pantanal, one of the world's largest wetlands – is typical in this regard. To "ensure the effectiveness" of substantive environmental rights there, it impels the subnational government to:

- "safeguard the rational and sustainable use of natural resources to ensure its perpetuation and minimize environmental impact"
- "preserve the diversity and integrity of the genetic heritage"
- "establish the state policy of sanitation and water resources"
- "require, for the installation of work or activity that may potentially cause significant degradation of the environment, a prior environmental impact study, which shall be made public, guaranteed the community participation through public hearings and their representatives at all stages"
- "fight pollution and erosion"
- "inform, systematic and broadly, the population about pollution levels, the quality of the environment, situations that risk accidents, the presence of substances potentially harmful to health in drinking water and food, as well as the results of audits and monitoring"
- "promote environmental education in all school levels and public awareness for the preservation of the environment"

---

[7] *Ibid.* Comparable provisions at the national level are rare; these are explored further in Chapter 3.

- "stimulate and promote the restoration of native vegetation coverage in degraded areas, aiming at the achievement of minimum standards necessary to maintain the ecological balance"
- "protect the fauna and flora, ensuring the diversity of species and ecosystems, with prohibition, in the manner prescribed by law, to practices that endanger their ecological function and cause the extinction of species or subject animals to cruelty"
- "create, deploy and manage state and local conservation units representative of existing ecosystems in the State, restoring its essential ecological processes, and the alteration and suppression may only allowed by law, with prohibition to any use that compromises the integrity of the attributes that justify its protection"
- "control and regulate, where applicable, the production, sale and use of techniques, methods and substances that represent a risk to life, quality of life and the environment"
- "relate the participation in biddings, access to tax benefits and to official credit lines to environmental compliance, certified by the competent agency"
- "define, create and maintain, in the manner required by law, vital areas for the protection of natural caves, archaeological sites, remarkable natural landscapes, other assets of historical, touristic, scientific and cultural value"
- "define territorial spaces and their components to be specially designed for the creation of environmental protected areas and preserved goods of cultural value as a historical site"
- "promote anthropogenic and environmental zoning of its territory, establishing consistent and differentiated policies for the preservation of natural environments, striking landscapes, water sources, areas of ecological interest within the State, from a physiographic, ecological, water and biological standpoint"
- "promote technical and scientific studies aiming to recycle discarded raw materials, as well as encourage its application in economic activities"
- "stimulate research, development and use of alternative energy sources, clean and energy saving technologies"
- "ensure, in the manner prescribed by law, free access to basic information about the environment."

Most Brazilian states similarly dictate governmental means for implementing substantive environmental rights, including the states of Amazonas, Bahia, Espírito Santo, Goiás, Maranhão, Mato Grosso do Sul, Minas Gerais, Paraíba,

Paraná, Piauí, Rio de Janeiro, Rio Grande do Norte, Rio Grande do Sul, Santa Catarina, Sergipe, and Tocantins, and in the Federal District.

Third, subnational constitutions can combine multiple facets of environmental constitutionalism in a single swath, which can be more challenging at the national level as a result of the challenges outlined earlier in Part I. For example, Article 57 of the proposed Kurdish Regional Constitution of Iraq contains a cavalcade of environmental rights, including individual rights and responsibilities, governmental policies, and sustainability, in a sort of environmental omnibus provision, which provides:

> First: Environmental protection (land, water, air, plants and animals) is a responsibility of all and if anyone causes damage to them, they are responsible to fix it and to be punished by law.
> Second: All citizens have a legitimate right for freedom and equality in an appropriate living status, in a social and economical environment which will provide a prosperous and happy life and has a responsibility for protecting the environment and improving it for the present and future generations.
> Third: The Regional Government shall take action to mitigate and treat the sources of pollution in the environment, and in regard to this it strives to develop forests and protect the fields and protect the green zones inside the cities and their outskirts. The Regional Government shall develop, enlarge and construct public parks, natural parks for protecting animals, plants, and natural resources and prohibit buildings and institutions and the use of machines and instruments in the natural protectorates.[8]

While this draft has not gone into effect, as written, it stands as a model of the potential for environmental constitutionalism; this, despite the fact that control over the land and resources remains in dispute between the regional and national governments.

Fourth, subnational environmental constitutionalism can provide enhanced opportunities for coordinated national-state implementation of national environmental policies. For example, as Kelly describes, the Kurdish Regional Constitution within the framework of the Iraqi Federal Constitution allows for shared responsibility over environmental policy.[9] Jörgensen notes that ten out of the twenty-eight states of India (Tamil Nadu, Karnataka, Andhra Pradesh, Gujarat, Rajasthan, Maharashtra, Madhya Pradesh, West Bengal, Kerala, and Orissa) "are implementing major wind energy

---

[8] See Kelly, Michael J. "The Kurdish Regional Constitution within the Framework of the Iraqi Federal Constitution: A Struggle for Sovereignty, Oil, Ethnic Identity, and the Prospects for a Reverse Supremacy Clause." *Penn State Law Review* 114 (2009–10): 784.
[9] *Ibid.*

programmes" under the aegis of the federal constitution.[10] At times, the allocation of responsibility for the environment between the local and the national can give rise to political tensions and even military activity when the local and national goals are at odds or when the revenues produced by exploitation of natural resources have to be equitably shared; most often, however, constitutional environmental provisions can promote intergovernmental cooperation.

Such national–subnational coordination is fairly common. For example, states that make up the Ethiopian federation (Afar; Amhara; Benishangul-Gumuz; Gambella; Harari; Oromia; Southern Nations, Nationalities, and Peoples' Regional State (SNNPRS); Somali; and Tigray), "share the ... environmental policy objectives" reflected in the national constitution.[11]

Other federal constitutions explicitly delegate environmental protection to subnational entities, including Spains,[12] Germanys, and the Netherlands'.[13] Hudson notes that the federal Canadian constitution "contains explicit language granting *exclusive* regulatory authority over subnational forest policy to the provinces ... [and that] [t]his is a significant state of affairs since the Canadian provinces actually own or otherwise control 84 percent of the nation's forests."[14] Indeed, the constitution of Canada provides in pertinent part:[15]

> In each province, the legislature may exclusively make laws in relation to:
> (a) exploration for non-renewable natural resources in the province;

[10] Jörgensen, Kirsten. *Climate Initiatives at the Subnational Level of the Indian States and their Interplay with Federal Policies.* 2011 ISA Annual Convention, March 16–19, 2011, Montreal, available at www.polsoz.fu-berlin.de/polwiss/forschung/systeme/ffu/publikationen/2011/11_joergensen_montreal/isa11_joergensen_draft.pdf?1367711988

[11] Regassa, Tsegaye. "Sub-national Constitutions in Ethiopia: Towards Entrenching Constitutionalism at State Level." *Mizan Law Review* 2 (2009): 1, available at www.ajol.info/index.php/mlr/article/viewFile/54006/42550

[12] See Kelly, "The Kurdish Regional Constitution," 764.

[13] Bruyninckx, Hans, Sander Happaerts, and Karoline Van Den Brande. *Sustainable Development and Subnational Governments: Policy-Making and Multi-Level Interactions.* Palgrave Macmillan, 2012: 109–15, 121–5, 132–4, available at www.waterstones.com/waterstonesweb/products/hans+bruyninckx/sander+happaerts/karoline+van+den+brande/sustainable+development+and+subnational+governments/8878149 ("As a result of the 2006 federalism reform, the distribution of powers has changed slightly to favor the Bundesländer. This reform provided the Bundesländer the right to deviate from federal law in the areas of nature conservation, landscape planning, and water and flood water management.").

[14] Hudson, Blake. "What Kind of Constitutional Design is Optimal for Environmental Governance?' *Environmental Law Professor Blog*, February 6, 2012, available at http://lawprofessors.typepad.com/environmental_law/2012/02/what-kind-of-constitutional-design-is-optimal-for-environmental-governance.html

[15] See Canada Constitution VI. Distribution of Legislative Powers. 92A(1). English texts of the Constitution Act of 1867 and the Act of 1892 as amended to the Constitution Act 1999.

(b) development, conservation and management of non-renewable natural resources and forestry resources in the province, including laws in relation to the rate of primary production therefrom.

Fifth, even failed attempts to instantiate constitutional environmental rights at the subnational level can contribute to enactment of legislative measures to achieve the same ends. Boyd, for example, reports that negated efforts to advance environmental constitutionalism at the federal and provincial levels in Canada contributed to the enactment of provincial legislation recognizing substantive environmental rights in Nanavut, the Northwest Territories, Ontario, Quebec, and the Yukon.[16] Ontario's legislatively enacted environmental "Bill of Rights," for instance, advances human and environmental rights at the local level.[17]

Sixth, insofar as most citizens are connected to their state government, and state authority is more likely to be responsive to the needs of local communities, subnational constitutionalism affords greater opportunities for both political and legal action to enforce and promote environmental norms. Cusak observes that subnational environmental constitutionalism includes textual provisions "granting citizens the right to a healthful environment; public policy statements concerning preservation of natural resources; financial provisions for environmental programs; and clauses that restrict the environmental prerogatives of state legislatures."[18]

And finally, subnational environmental constitutionalism can provide experience in a country that can normalize environmental constitutionalism and goad activity at the national level. This has happened in Argentina, where, as Hernandez notes, the Province of Córdoba's constitutional environmental rights preceded those that followed at the national level.[19]

---

[16] See Boyd, *Right to a Healthy Environment*, 61–6.

[17] For a discussion of Ontario's approach to environmental constitutionalism, see Walker, Sandra. "The Ontario Environmental Bill of Rights." In Deimann and Dyssli, *Environmental Rights*, 20–32.

[18] Cusack, Mary Ellen. "Judicial Interpretation of State Constitutional Rights to a Healthful Environment." *Boston College Environmental Affairs Law Review* 20(1) (1993): 181; Hill *et al.*, "Human Rights and the Environment" (footnotes omitted): "Environmental constitutional provisions at the state level, however, have fared better than at the federal level. Every state constitution drafted after 1959 explicitly addresses 'modern concerns' regarding pollution control and preservation. Indeed, fully one-third of all state constitutions include: (1) policy statements regarding the importance of environmental quality; (2) environmental enabling language; and/or (3) language creating an individual right to a clean and healthy environment."

[19] Hernandez, Antonio Maria. *Sub-National Constitution Law in Argentina*, 24. Kluwer Law International, 2011.

TEXTUAL SUBNATIONAL ENVIRONMENTAL CONSTITUTIONALISM

Subnational environmental constitutionalism has gained a foothold through-out the globe, including in Argentina, Austria,[20] Brazil, Ethiopia, Germany, India, Iraq, the Netherlands, the Philippines, and the United States (see Appendix H).

The Brazilian brand of subnational environmental constitutionalism is especially striking. Spurred on initially by the Rio Declaration in 1992 (and buffeted by the Rio+20 Conference in 2012), the most ardent examples of subnational environmental constitutionalism occur at the state level in Brazil. The constitutions of all Brazil's twenty-six states – and the Federal District – promote environmental protection, often elaborately and identically so. The Mato Grasso (quoted earlier) constitution is typical, touching all corners of environmental constitutionalism by guaranteeing substantive and procedural rights and imposing duties and responsibilities that apply to all for the benefit of present and future generations.

Notably, the constitutions of most Brazilian states and the Federal District embed a substantive right to a quality environment in some form, most commonly to a "balanced" environment. For example, the constitution of the state of Acre provides that "[a]ll have the right to an ecologically balanced environment." Amapá's provides that "[a]ll have the right to an ecologically balanced environment, which is an asset of common use and essential to a healthy quality of life." Amazonas' says that "[a]ll have the right to a balanced environment, essential to a healthy quality of life." Ceará's constitution refers to a "balanced environment" as an "inalienable right." Goiás' constitution guarantees "an ecologically balanced environment." Mato Grosso's says that: "All have the right to an ecologically balanced environment." Maranhão's calls a balanced environment "an asset of common use and essential to people's quality of life, imposing to all, and especially the State and the Municipalities, the duty to ensure their preservation and restoration for the benefit of present generations and future." Similar provisions recognizing a substantive right to a balanced environment are found in the constitutions of the States of Bahia, Espírito Santo, Goiás, Maranhão, Minas Gerais, Paraíba, Paraná, Piauí, Rio de Janeiro, Rio Grande do Norte, Rio Grande do Sul, Santa Catarina, Sergipe, and Tocantins, and in the Federal District. A couple

---

[20] Marko, Joseph. *Federalism, Sub-national Constitutionalism, and the Protection of Minorities*, available at http://camlaw.rutgers.edu/statecon/subpapers/marko.pdf ("[s]everal land constitutions … contain provisions for the protection of the environment").

of states vary slightly from the "balanced" formulae, including Mato Grosso do Sol, which provides that "[a]ll have the right to enjoy an environment free of physical and social factors harmful to health."

The constitutions of most Brazilian states express environmental rights in terms of duties and responsibilities that are owed by all for the benefit of present and future generations. For example, Espírito Santo's constitution reads that: "All have the right to an ecologically, healthy and balanced environment, and it is incumbent upon them and in particular to the State and the Municipalities, to ensure its preservation, conservation and restoration for the benefit of present and future generations." Likewise, Mato Grasso's constitution imposes a duty on the state, municipalities, and "the community" "to defend and preserve" the environment "for present and future generations," while Acre's says that "both the State and the community shall defend [the environment] and preserve it for present and future generations," and Amapá's that "both the Government and the community shall have the duty to defend and preserve it for present and future generations."

The constitutions of some Brazilian states specifically elevate the interests of nature. For example, Bahia's says that "[i]t is incumbent upon the State, beyond all powers that are not prohibited by the Federal Constitution, to ... protect the environment and fight pollution in any of its forms, preserving the forests, fauna and flora." It remains to be seen whether provisions such as this create a "right" on behalf of nature.

Subnational deployment of environmental rights in the United States is instructive because it underscores both the potential and limitations of environmental constitutionalism.[21] While all efforts to amend the US Constitution to recognize environmental rights have failed,[22] states in the United States have a long tradition of constitutionalizing environmental protection. Indeed, constitutional recognition of natural resources and the environment at the subnational level in the United States harkens back almost two centuries, beginning in 1842 with Rhode Island's protection of "all the rights of fishery, and the

---

[21] See, e.g., Brooks, "A Constitutional Right," 1103–05 (supporting "decentralization" of constitutional provisions that address the environment, observing that "[s]tate judges [would] ... be more sensitive in weighing the state's values."); Thompson, Barton H., Jr. "Environmental Policy and State Constitutions: The Potential Role of Substantive Guidance." *Rutgers Law Journal* 27 (1996): 871; Eurick, Janelle P. "The Constitutional Right to a Healthy Environment: Enforcing Environmental Protection through State and Federal Constitutions." *International Legal Perspectives* 11 (2001): 185; Thompson, "Constitutionalizing the Environment," 174.

[22] See generally, Craig, "Constitutional Right to a Clean/Healthy Environment?" 11013.

privileges of the shore."[23] Among the more notable provisions is the "Wildlands Forever" provision of the New York State Constitution, which provides that: "The lands of the state, now owned or hereafter acquired, constituting the forest preserve as now fixed by law, shall be forever kept as wild forest lands. They shall not be leased, sold or exchanged, or be taken by any corporation, public or private, nor shall the timber thereon be sold, removed or destroyed."[24]

Presently, there are at least 207 natural resource or environment-related provisions in forty-six state constitutions. These provisions reach nineteen different categories of natural resources or the environment, including water, timber and minerals.[25] They also take eleven different forms, including general policy statements, legislative directives, and individual rights to a quality environment.[26] States recognizing environmental protection as an overarching state policy include Louisiana,[27] Michigan,[28] Ohio,[29] South Carolina,[30] and Virginia.[31] Several more address parochial environmental

[23] Rhode Island constitution of 1842, art. I, sec. 17. For a thorough history of the evolution of Rhode Island's constitution, see Leitao, Kevin. "Rhode Island's Forgotten Bill of Rights." *Roger Williams University Law Review* 1 (1996): 58, n.68.

[24] New York constitution, art. 14, sec. 1. See, e.g., *Association for the Protection of the Adirondacks v. MacDonald*, 253 N.Y. 234, 242 (1930) (timber harvesting inconsistent with "Forever Wild" portion of New York State Constitution).

[25] "Environmental and Natural Resources Provisions in State Constitutions." *Journal of Land, Resources, and Environmental Law* 22 (2002): 74. The categories are: (1) public land acquisition, preservation or management, (2) public ownership of land and other resources, (3) sovereignty, (4) the balance of use and development, (5) school trust doctrine, (6) public trust doctrine, (7) takings or eminent domain, (8) access to water, (9) allocation of water, (10) water development and reclamation, (11) water resource protection, (12) mining and mineral rights, (13) fish and wildlife, (14) fishing rights, (15) hunting and fishing restrictions, (16) rights of way, (17) timber and forest management, (18) nuclear power, and (19) agriculture.

[26] *Ibid.*, 75. The other manifestations include provisions respecting (1) legislative protection, (2) agency authority, (3) general financing, (4) taxing authority, (5) bonding authority, (6) funds and trust accounts, (7) educational programs, and (8) private liability.

[27] Louisiana constitution, art. 9, sec. 1 ("The natural resources of the state including air and water, and the healthful, scenic, historic, and esthetic quality of the environment shall be protected, conserved, and replenished insofar as possible and consistent with the health, safety, and welfare of the people. The legislature shall enact laws to implement this policy.").

[28] Michigan constitution, art. 4, sec. 51 ("The legislature shall pass suitable laws for the protection and promotion of the public health.").

[29] Ohio constitution, art. 8, sec. 2 ("environmental and related conservation, preservation, and revitalization purposes ... are proper public purposes of the state and local governmental entities and are necessary and appropriate means to improve the quality of life and the general and economic well-being of the people of this state ...").

[30] South Carolina constitution, art. 12, sec. 1 ("The health, welfare, and safety of the lives and property of the people of this State and the conservation of its natural resources are matters of public concern.").

[31] Virginia constitution, art. 11, sec. 1 ("To the end that the people have clean air, pure water, and the use and enjoyment for recreation of adequate public lands, waters, and other natural

concerns, such as access to water, preservation, re-development, sustainability, pollution abatement, climate change, energy reform, or environmental rights.[32] Dozens more contain provisions fairly characterized as recognizing that the state holds state resources in "public trust."[33]

Currently, five states instantiate a substantive right to a quality environment:[34] Hawaii,[35] Illinois,[36] Massachusetts,[37] Montana,[38] and Pennsylvania.[39] These provisions are independent of state laws that allow citizens to enforce pollution control statutes.[40]

While most provide a "right" to the "environment," the adjectival objective – "clean" or "healthful" or "quality" – differs from state to state. For example, Hawaii's and Montana's constitutions aim to afford a "clean and healthful environment,"[41] Illinois' "a right to a healthful environment,"[42] Massachusetts' a "right to clean air and water, freedom from excessive and unnecessary noise, and the natural, scenic, historic, and esthetic qualities of

---

resources, . . . Further it shall be the Commonwealth's policy to protect the atmosphere, lands, and waters from pollution, impairment, or destruction, for the benefit, enjoyment, and general welfare of the people of the Commonwealth.").

[32] See Appendix H. Of course, whether to categorize a constitutional provision as addressing the environment or resources involves some measure of subjectivity. For example, Eurick, "The Constitutional Right," 201, puts the number at 21.

[33] Craig, "Constitutional Right to a Clean/Healthy Environment?"; "A Comparative Guide to the Eastern Public Trust Doctrine: Classifications of States, Property Rights, and State Summaries," available at http://papers.ssrn.com/sol3/papers.cfm?abstract-id=1008161; "A Comparative Guide to the Western States' Public Trust Doctrines: Public Values, Private Rights, and the Evolution Toward an Ecological Public Trust," available at http://papers.ssrn.com/sol3/papers.cfm?abstract_id=1405822

[34] See Cusack, "Judicial Interpretation," 181 (noting amendments to state constitutions include "those granting citizens the right to a healthful environment; public policy statements concerning preservation of natural resources; financial provisions for environmental programs; and clauses that restrict the environmental prerogatives of state legislatures."). See also, Weiss, *International Environmental Law and Policy* (identifying Illinois, Hawaii, California, Florida, Massachusetts, Montana, Pennsylvania, Rhode Island, and Virginia as embedding environmental rights).

[35] See Appendix H, Hawaii constitution, art. 11, sec. 9.

[36] *Ibid.*, Illinois constitution, art. 11, sec. 2.   [37] *Ibid.*, Massachusetts constitution, art. 97.

[38] *Ibid.*, Montana constitution, art. 2, sec. 3.

[39] *Ibid.*, Pennsylvania constitution, art. 1, sec. 27. See generally, Wilson, "State Constitutional Environmental Rights"; Thompson, "Constitutionalizing the Environment," 158 (discussing Montana's finding of a fundamental right to a "healthful environment.").

[40] See, e.g., Dernbach, John C. "Taking the Pennsylvania Constitution Seriously When it Protects the Environment: Part I – An Interpretive Framework for Article I, Section 27." *Dickinson Law Review* 103 (1999): 693 (explaining purpose of provision).

[41] Hawaii constitution, art. 11, sec. 9 ("Each person has the right to a clean and healthful environment."); Montana constitution, art. 2, sec. 3 (guaranteeing "right to clean and healthful environment."); see generally, Wilson, "State Constitutional Environmental Rights."

[42] Illinois constitution, art. 11, sec. 2 ("Each person has the right to a healthful environment.").

their environment,"[43] and Pennsylvania's "a right to clean air, pure water, and to the preservation of the natural, scenic, historic and esthetic values of the environment."[44]

These provisions have been interpreted to require harm to humans. For example, in *Glisson v. City of Marion*, the Supreme Court of Illinois explained that "the primary concern of the drafters ... was the effect of pollution on the environment and human health. The right to a 'healthful environment' was therefore not intended to include the protection of endangered and threatened species."[45] Yet Montana's constitution suggests biocentric concerns, choosing both "clean and healthful" over "healthful" out of concern that the latter would permit the environmental degradation of Montana's most environmentally pristine areas so long as pollution doesn't harm human health.[46]

Of course, environmental constitutionalism has little traction in subnational governments that either lack a constitution or a Bill of Rights. Accordingly, super-subnational environmental constitutionalism by municipal and other local governmental entities is also trending upward, particularly in subnational governmental entities that operate under constitutional mandates to promote environmental interests. Some of these provisions can be even more protective and expansive than what is typically found at the subnational and national levels, such as, for instance, those American cities whose charters protect rights of nature, including Pittsburgh, Pennsylvania. A recent study reports that many cities in the Philippines, including Puerto Princesa, Naga, Quezon, and Makati, have adopted constitutional local action plans to address various environmental concerns, including climate change.[47] Such super-subnational constitutionalism offers additional and often unexercised potential for achieving environmental objectives. In the United States, for example, as Mudd observes:[48] "The local governments in environmental rights states are poised to become leaders in this

---

[43] Massachusetts constitution, art. 49 ("The people shall have the right to clean air and water.").

[44] Pennsylvania constitution, art. 1, sec. 27 ("The people have a right to clean air, pure water, and the preservation of the natural scenic, historic and esthetic values of the environment.").

[45] *Glisson v. City of Marion*, 720 N.E.2d 1034, 1042 (Illinois, 1999) [hereinafter *Glisson*].

[46] Transcript of Montana Constitutional Convention, Vol. V, 1971–1972, 1243–4 (March 1, 1972), available at http://ia360606.us.archive.org/2/items/montanaconstituto5mont/montanaconstituto5mont.pdf

[47] *Study on Carbon Governance at Sub-national Level in the Philippines*. Ateneo School of Government (November 16, 2011), available at http://pub.iges.or.jp/modules/envirolib/upload/3514/attach/carbon%20governance%20sub-national%20level%20philippines.pdf

[48] Mudd, Michelle Bryan. "A 'Constant and Difficult Task': Making Local Land Use Decisions in States with a Constitutional Right to a Healthful Environment." *Ecology Law Quarterly* 38 (2011): 61, available at www.boalt.org/elq/documents/elq38_1_01_2011_0803.pdf

endeavor by creating and implementing robust environmental land use provisions. Yet that leadership has been lacking to date. Whereas state agencies in Illinois, Pennsylvania, Montana, and Hawaii have integrated environmental review into selected areas of state purview, local governments continue to leave their environmental authority largely unexercised."

JUDICIAL RECEPTIVITY TO SUBNATIONAL CONSTITUTIONAL ENVIRONMENTAL RIGHTS

A constitutionally enshrined right to a quality environment at the subnational level is most effective when it is recognized and enforced judicially.[49] Yet, amid the varied manifestations of constitutionally embedded environmental provisions at the subnational level, one commonality stands out: they are seldom subject to substantive interpretation,[50] leaving them dormant and awaiting clarity through advocacy.[51] This dearth in applicable jurisprudence is likely due to judicial concerns about recognizing and enforcing emerging constitutional features,[52] restraining economic development and property rights, entering what are often seen as political thickets,[53] or providing causes of action that may displace other legislative prerogatives granted to affected persons, such as state citizen suits to enforce state pollution control requirements.[54]

Principally, subnational constitutional environmental rights are underenforced because courts have not found them to be self-executing. A constitutional provision is self-executing if it is "a sufficient rule by means of which the right given may be enjoyed and protected, or the duty imposed

---

[49] For a general discussion of enforcement in this context, see Tucker, "Constitutional Codification," 299.

[50] See, e.g., *Sierra Club v. Department of Transportation.* 167 P.3d 292, 313 n.28 (Supreme Court of Hawaii, 2007) (explaining that "[a]lthough this court has cited this amendment as support for our approach to standing in environmental cases . . . we have not directly interpreted the text of the amendment.").

[51] Constitutional provisions referred to from hereon may be found in the Appendix 4.

[52] McLaren, Robert A. "Environmental Protection Based on State Constitutional Law: A Call for Reinterpretation." *University of Hawaii Law Review* 12 (1990): 149.

[53] See generally, A.E.D. Howard. "The indeterminacy of constitutions." *Wake Forest Law Review,* 31, 383–410, (1996), available at http://heinonline.org/HOL/LandingPage?handle=hein. journals/wflr31&div=21&id=&page=194; McLaren, "Environmental Protection," 132; Thompson, "Constitutionalizing the Environment," 174. The obstacles to enforcing state constitutional environmental rights are strikingly similar to those that afflict enforcement of environmental rights provisions in national constitutions worldwide. See generally, May and Daly, "Vindicating Fundamental Environmental Rights Worldwide."

[54] See generally, May, James R. "The Availability of State Environmental Citizen Suits." *Natural Resources and Environment* 18 (2004): 53.

may be enforced; and it is not self-executing when it merely indicates principles, without laying down rules by means of which those principles may be given the force of law."[55] Thus, a constitutional provision that *is* self-executing requires nothing more from the legislature. A constitutional provision that *is not* self-executing requires implementing legislation to enforce.

In the United States, few state constitutions make clear whether constitutionally embedded fundamental environmental rights are self-executing. Montana's, Pennsylvania's, and Rhode Island's constitutions, for example, are silent about whether their environmental rights are self-executing. Constitutions from other states require subsequent legislative or judicial action. The environmental rights provisions embedded in Hawaii's and Illinois' constitutions, for example, are enforceable by "any person ... through appropriate legal proceedings, subject to reasonable limitations and regulation as provided by law."[56] Massachusetts' environmental rights provision seems to assume judicial action without requiring intervening legislative action.[57]

The constitutions of some states in the US contain a parallel provision that imposes a duty upon the state to enact laws to protect the environment, which suggests to some that corresponding environmental rights provisions are not self-executing.[58] For instance, Rhode Island's constitution provides (with emphasis added) that "it shall be *the duty* of the general assembly to provide for the conservation of the air, land, water, plant, animal, mineral and other natural resources of the state,"[59] and Michigan's that the "legislature *shall provide* for the protection of the air, water and other natural resources of the state from pollution, impairment and destruction."[60] Some see the mandatory "*shall*" as requiring legislative action to effectuate constitutional environmental rights.[61] Others see these provisions as merely invoking "moral force"[62] that does not create a separately enforceable environmental right.[63]

---

[55] *Davis* v. *Burke*, 179 U.S. 399 (Supreme Court of the United States, 1900). See Cusack, "Judicial Interpretation," 182.

[56] Hawaii constitution, art. 11, sec. 9; Illinois Constitution, art. 11, sec. 2. But see Cusack, "Judicial Interpretation," 182 (opining that Hawaii's provision is self-executing).

[57] Massachusetts constitution, art. 97 ("[t]he general court shall have the power to enact legislation necessary or expedient to protect such rights.").

[58] See Howard, "Indeterminacy of Constitutions," 198. See also McLaren, "Environmental Protection," 133.

[59] Rhode Island constitution, art. I, sec. 17 (emphasis added).

[60] Michigan constitution, art. 4, sec. 52 (emphasis added).

[61] Howard, "Indeterminacy of Constitutions," 199.

[62] *Ibid.* (quoting Cooley, T. *Constitutional Limitations*, 165, 8th edn. W. Carrington, 1927).

[63] Howard, "Indeterminacy of Constitutions," 200. See McLaren, "Environmental Protection," 133.

Most state court decisions have found constitutionally embedded provisions in state constitutions *not* to be self-enforcing. For example, in *Enos v. Secretary of Environmental Affairs*,[64] the Supreme Judicial Court of Massachusetts held that the constitutional right to clean air and water does not afford an independent means to challenge an agency's decision to grant a permit to operate a sewage treatment plant under the Massachusetts Environmental Policy Act.[65] And in *Commonwealth v. Blair*,[66] a state court held that the same right to clean air and water does not provide a cognizable cause of action to gain access to water supply in violation of the Commonwealth's Watershed Protection Act: "[t]he judge correctly rejected the argument that the Commonwealth is duty-bound to acquire interests related to the protection of drinking water."[67]

Moreover, state courts in the US have held that state attorneys general could not even enforce environmental rights provisions absent implementing legislation.[68] A leading case is *Commonwealth of Pennsylvania v. National Gettysburg Battlefield Tower, Inc.*, in which the Supreme Court of Pennsylvania held that the state's Attorney General could not enforce the state's environmental rights provision without further grant of authority from the state legislature.[69] The court reasoned that the provision did not grant the Attorney General an unbridled and undefined authority to enforce a vague constitutional mandate to "natural, scenic, historic and esthetic values,"[70] thus exposing individual property owners to enforcement consequences.[71] Likewise, in *State v. General Development Corporation*,[72] a court in Florida held that the state attorney could not enforce Florida's constitutional "policy . . . to

---

[64] *Enos v. Secretary of Environmental Affairs*, 731 N.E.2d 525 (Supreme Judicial Court of Massachusetts, 2000).

[65] *Ibid.*, 532.

[66] *Commonwealth v. Blair*, 805 N.E.2d 1011, 1018 (Massachusetts Appeal Court, 2004).

[67] *Ibid.*, 1018.

[68] Some argue that such judicial reluctance is anathema to the core ideas these provisions were designed to promote. See e.g., McLaren, "Environmental Protection," 135.

[69] *Commonwealth of Pennsylvania v. National Gettysburg Battlefield Tower, Inc.*, 454 Pa. 193, 205, 311 A.2d 588, 594–5 (Supreme Court of Pennsylvania, 1973).

[70] *Ibid.*

[71] *Ibid.* See also *Community College of Delaware County v. Fox*, 342 A.2d 468, 482 (Pennsylvania Commonwealth Court, 1975), in which the court noted that "while [Pennsylvania's environmental rights clause] may impose an obligation upon the Commonwealth to consider the propriety of preserving land as open space, it cannot legally operate to expand the powers of a statutory agency, nor can it expand the statutory powers of the [state agency] as a practical matter here."

[72] *State v. General Development Corporation*, 448 So. 2d 1074 (Florida District Court of Appeal, 1984), *aff'd*; 469 So. 2d 1381 (Florida, 1985). See McLaren, "Environmental Protection," 134.

conserve and protect its natural resources and scenic beauty"[73] to prosecute unauthorized canal construction except under the auspices of "the legislature's enactment of over twenty specific general laws that have explicitly given a state attorney the authority to independently initiate civil suits on behalf of the state in other areas concerning the health, safety, and welfare of Florida's citizens and environment."[74]

The principle outlier at this point is the Supreme Court of Pennsylvania, which recently held that *individuals* may enforce Article I, Section 27 of the Pennsylvania Constitution – which both recognizes an individual right to a quality environment and requires the state to "conserve and maintain" public resources "for the benefit of all the people" – against governmental agencies. In a remarkable decision, the Pennsylvania Supreme Court rejuvenated Article I, Section 27 of Pennsylvania's constitution. In *Robinson Township et al. v. Commonwealth of Pennsylvania*, the Supreme Court struck as unconstitutional major parts of "Act 13" – a state oil and gas law designed to promote "horizontal hydraulic fracturing," or "hydrofracking." The decision has some important implications for environmental constitutionalism.

Section 27 of the state constitution is no accident. Pennsylvania's history includes improvident deforestation, significant loss of biodiversity and wildlife, rampant industrialization, and extensive surface and subsurface coal mining. These activities have taken a significant toll on the quality of the environment in the state. Accordingly, in 1971 by constitutional referendum the people of Pennsylvania adopted the "Environmental Rights Amendment" by a 4–1 margin. Incorporated as Article I, Section 27 of the Pennsylvania Constitution, it provides:

> The people have a right to clean air, pure water, and to the preservation of the natural, scenic, historic and esthetic values of the environment. Pennsylvania's public natural resources are the common property of all the people, including generations yet to come. As trustee of these resources, the Commonwealth shall conserve and maintain them for the benefit of all the people.

The Environmental Rights Amendment affords rights and imposes public trust duties that are commensurate with other constitutional prerogatives: "It is not a historical accident that the Pennsylvania Constitution now places citizens' environmental rights on par with their political rights."[75] Act 27 was

---

[73] Florida constitution, art. 2, sec. 7. See McLaren, "Environmental Protection," 134.

[74] *State v. General Development Corporation* (Florida, 1984), 1080.

[75] *Robinson Township et al. v. Commonwealth of Pennsylvania*, Supreme Court of Pennsylvania, No. J-127A-D-2012 (decided December 19, 2013) (plurality opinion), available at http://blogs.law. widener.edu/envirolawcenter/files/2013/12/J-127A-D-20120ajc1.pdf

enacted based on "the mischief to be remedied and the object to be attained" – namely, to address environmental degradation in the state by promoting individual environmental rights and requiring governmental authorities to hold natural resources in public trust.[76] Horizontal hydrofracking, on the other hand, is a relatively new engineering technique that can be used to gain access to the natural gas and petroleum embedded in deep shale "plays" a mile or deeper under the surface of the earth. The Pennsylvania legislature enacted Act 13 in 2012 to promote the development of the state's extensive "Marcellus Shale" play.

Act 13 constituted a major revision to the state's long-standing Oil and Gas Act in several respects. First, it preempted traditional zoning and planning by local governments to regulate or ban hydrofracking by declaring that state laws "occupy the entire field" of oil and gas regulation, "to the exclusion of" all local ordinances, and thus "preempt[] and supersede[] the local regulation of oil and gas operations." Thus, local governments were not free to reach their own decisions about whether and to what extent to allow hydrofracking, or to impose additional environmental requirements.

Second, Act 13 required local governments to promote hydrofracking, regardless of the wishes of their constituents or concerns about potential adverse environmental effects. It mandated that "all local ordinances regulating oil and gas operations . . . allow for the reasonable development of oil and gas resources," and established strict time periods for local review of proposals, wherein if not kept the project was deemed approved. And while Act 13 prohibited drilling or disturbing area within specific distances of underground sources of drinking water, streams, springs, wetlands, and other water bodies, it required state environmental agencies to waive these restrictions provided the developer submits "additional measures, facilities or practices" to protect these waters. Act 13 also established a system to collect and allocate "impact fees" designed to offset some of hydrofracking's adverse environmental effects. Thus, Act 13 essentially conscripted local governments into the service of promoting state policy prerogatives, which themselves reflected the goals of the oil and gas industry.

Last, Act 13 prevented physicians from obtaining information about the risks of exposure to certain chemicals used in hydrofracking unless they agreed to sign a confidentiality agreement. It then subjected physicians who released information about potential chemical exposure to civil and criminal liability.

[76] *Ibid.*

Seven municipalities, an environmental organization and a physician challenged the constitutionality of Act 13 on a variety of grounds, including as an affront to both Section 27 and federal and state substantive due process.

In response, the state argued that Section 27 was unenforceable. It based its theory on an earlier case, *Payne* v. *Kassab*, which held that Section 27 "recognizes or confers no rights upon citizens and no right or inherent obligation upon municipalities; rather, the constitutional provision exists only to guide the General Assembly, which alone determines what is best for public natural resources, and the environment generally, in Pennsylvania."[77]

While agreeing with the state's interpretation of Act 27, the lower court declared Act 13's statewide zoning provisions to be unconstitutional as a matter of substantive due process, and struck the provisions of the law that required state agencies to grant waivers to setback requirements.[78] It also held that the environmental plaintiffs and the physician lacked constitutional standing. Both sides appealed to the seven-member Pennsylvania Supreme Court.

A four-judge majority of the court found Act 13 to be unconstitutional, although on different theories. A three-judge plurality held that Act 13 is inconsistent with Act 27. A fourth justice joined in the result, but would have struck Act 13 as a violation of substantive due process.[79] Two justices dissented. Another did not participate in the decision.

The plurality determined that Act 13 contravened Section 27's remonstration that the state holds natural resources "as trustee": "we agree with the citizens that, as an exercise of the police power, [Act 13 is] incompatible with the Commonwealth's duty as trustee of Pennsylvania's public natural resources." It observed: "As the citizens illustrate, development of the natural gas industry in the Commonwealth unquestionably has and will have a lasting, and undeniably detrimental, impact on the quality … of Pennsylvania's environment, which are part of the public trust."[80]

---

[77] *Payne* v. *Kassab*, 468 Pa. 226, 245, 361 A.2d 263, 272 (Supreme Court of Pennsylvania, July 6, 1976) [hereinafter *Payne*]. See also *Klink* v. *Department of Transportation*, 29 Pennsylvania Commonwealth Court 106, 370 A.2d 379 (1977) (accord). For an informative discussion on the question of whether Pennsylvania's amendment is self-executing, see Dernbach, John C. "Taking the Pennsylvania Constitution Seriously When it Protects the Environment: Part II – Environmental Rights and Public Trust." *Dickinson Law Review* 104 (1999): 97.

[78] *Robinson Township et al.* v. *Commonwealth of Pennsylvania*, Pennyslvania Commonwealth Court, 52 A.3d 463 (2012), available at http://blogs.law.widener.edu/envirolawcenter/files/2013/12/RobinsonTp-v.-Commonwealth-CommCt2012.pdf

[79] *Ibid.* (Baer, J., concurring), available at http://blogs.law.widener.edu/envirolawcenter/files/2013/12/J-127A-D-2012c01.pdf

[80] *Ibid.*

In particular, the plurality found that preempting local control over hydrofracking "sanctioned a direct and harmful degradation of the environmental quality of life in these communities and zoning districts." It also concluded that Act 13 unconstitutionally shifted the burden to some citizens to bear "heavier environmental and habitability burdens than others" in violation of Section 27's mandate that public trust resources be managed for the benefit of *all* people.

A fourth judge concurred with the outcome, but would have overturned Act 13 as a violation of substantive due process rights of local communities because it would "force municipalities to enact zoning ordinances" despite "Pennsylvania's extreme diversity," noting that Act 13 did not afford adequate "consideration to the character of the municipality," including geology, topography, environmental quality, water supply, and economics.

Two justices dissented, and would have upheld Act 13 and found that the environmental plaintiffs and the physician lacked standing.[81] Another justice did not participate in the decision.

A majority of the court also reversed the lower court's finding that various environmental plaintiffs lacked constitutional standing, ruling that they suffered "a substantial and direct interest in the outcome of the litigation premised upon the serious risk of alteration in the physical nature of their respective political subdivisions and the components of their surrounding environment. This interest is not remote." Likewise, the majority upheld the standing of an affected physician to challenge Act 13's confidentiality requirement, noting that such interests also were "substantial and direct," and that "existing jurisprudence permits pre-enforcement review of statutory provisions in cases in which petitioners must choose between equally unappealing options and where the third option, here refusing to provide medical services to a patient, is equally undesirable." The three justices who dissented would have upheld the lower court's ruling that the environmental plaintiffs and the physician lacked standing.

The plurality's opinion in *Robinson Township* reinforces environmental constitutionalism insofar as it represents an authentic attempt to engage the text of the Environmental Rights Amendment. First, it noted that Article 27 – much like many provisions that provide such rights – vests two rights in the people of the state. The first is a right to clean air, pure water, and to the preservation of the natural, scenic, historic, and esthetic values of the

---

[81] *Ibid.* (Saylor, J. dissenting), available at http://blogs.law.widener.edu/envirolawcenter/files/2013/12/J-127A-D-2012do11.pdf; (Eakin, J. dissenting), available at http://blogs.law.widener.edu/envirolawcenter/files/2013/12/J-127A-D-2012do21.pdf

environment. The second is "a limitation on the state's power to act contrary to this right." Importantly, it held that these rights are equal in status and enforceability to any other rights included in the state constitution, including property rights.

Second, it enforces the "public trust" provisions – that is, the obligations of the state to hold resources in the public trust for all people. Because the state is the trustee of these resources, it has a fiduciary duty to "conserve and maintain" them: "The plain meaning of the terms conserve and maintain implicates a duty to prevent and remedy the degradation, diminution, or depletion of our public natural resources."

Thus, according to the plurality in *Robinson Township*, a constitutional requirement to hold resources in trust involves two separate obligations. The first is "a duty to refrain from permitting or encouraging the degradation, diminution, or depletion of public natural resources." The second takes due regard of present and future generations, and imposes a duty "to act affirmatively to protect the environment, via legislative action." These duties promote "legitimate development tending to improve upon the lot of Pennsylvania's citizenry, with the evident goal of promoting sustainable development."

The plurality's approach also minimized the role of balancing in environmental constitutionalism. Specifically, the plurality rejected the "non-textual" balancing test in *Payne* v. *Kassab* as "inappropriate to determine matters outside the narrowest category of cases, i.e., those cases in which a challenge is premised simply upon an alleged failure to comply with statutory standards enacted to advance Section 27 interests." Accordingly, the General Assembly of Pennsylvania will need to revise or scuttle Act 13.

Last, the plurality in *Robinson Township* made a point to note that the Environmental Rights Amendment serves both present and future generations. Echoing sentiments from the majority opinion in *Minors Oposa*, it observed: "By any responsible account, the exploitation of the Marcellus Shale Formation will produce a detrimental effect on the environment, on the people, their children, and future generations, and potentially on the public purse, perhaps rivaling the environmental effects of coal extraction." In so doing, the plurality opinion in particular advances the purpose of constitutional enshrinement of environmental rights and public trust duties in the first place – to promote environmental protection and advance individual rights to a quality environment.

While an outlier, the Pennsylvania Supreme Court is not alone in engaging constitutional environmental rights. The Supreme Court of Alaska recently read that state's "public interest" constitutional standard for resource development to require that courts take a hard look at whether state agencies adequately considered the cumulative environmental impacts of oil and gas leases.[82] And the Supreme Court of Montana has subjected that state's environmental rights provision to strict scrutiny,[83] although it has since been reluctant to enforce it.[84]

ESTABLISHING STANDING AND IDENTIFYING PARTIES

Another reason that subnational constitutionally embedded environmental rights provisions tend to be underenforced is that they reveal little about who has standing to vindicate the right. As discussed in Chapter 4, federal standing doctrine can impose significant barriers in environmental cases. Thus, it is important for state courts to develop more lenient standing doctrines to ensure that environmental plaintiffs can invoke the state courts' jurisdiction. Examples of more open-ended standing at the subnational level in the United States include Hawaii and Illinois, which provide that "any" (Hawaii) and "each" (Illinois) "person may enforce this right ..."[85] Similarly, Massachusetts's, Pennsylvania's, and Rhode Island's constitutions grant environmental rights to "the people"[86] and Montana's to "all persons."[87]

Those seeking to vindicate constitutionally embedded environmental rights must also demonstrate constitutional standing that may be equal to, or less strict than, federal standing requirements.[88] For example, those seeking to vindicate interests under Pennsylvania's environmental rights provision must satisfy standing akin to federal standing analysis.[89] On the other hand, Hawaii

---

[82] *Sullivan v. Resisting Environmental Destruction on Indigenious Lands*, 311 P.3d 625 (Alaska, 2013).

[83] *Montana Environmental Information Center v. Department of Environmental Quality*, 988 P.2d 1236 (Montana, 1999).

[84] See, e.g., *Northern Plains Resource Council v. Montana Board of Land Commissioners*, 288 P.3d 169 (Montana, 2012).

[85] Hawaii constitution, art. 11, sec. 9; Illinois Constitution, art. 11, sec. 2. See Eurick, "The Constitutional Right," 202.

[86] Massachusetts constitution, art. 49; Pennsylvania constitution, art. 1, sec. 27 Rhode Island constitution, art. 1, secs. 16 and 17.

[87] Montana constitution, art. 2, sec. 3.

[88] Eurick, "The Constitutional Right," 204 (discussing standing to enforce state environmental provisions). See, e.g., *Sierra Club v. Department of Transportation*, 115 Hawaii 299, 320, 167 P.3d 292 (Supreme Court of Hawaii, 2007).

(Hawaii, 2007) (Supreme Court acknowledging that standing in the state had paralleled federal standards in the past, but stated "the appellate courts of this state have generally recognized public interest concerns that warrant the lowering of standing barriers in ... cases ... pertaining to environmental concerns.").

[89] See, e.g., *Community College of Delaware County v. Fox*, 20, 335 (Pennsylvania Commonwealth Court, 1975) (using federal standing analysis in environmental rights case).

and Florida lower the standing bar for individuals and organizations to enforce constitutional environmental rights,[90,91] allowing averment of generalized grievances of environmental injury.[92] In *Life of the Land v. Land Use Commission*,[93] an environmental organization challenged reclassification of land for development in Hawaii. The state court found the group had standing even though its members did not own or use the land at issue. Such a suit would probably have been barred if brought under federal law.

Pursuing subnational environmental rights can be controversial. For example, in *Glisson*, tensions ran high in Marion, Illinois, as city officials sought to build a dam, solving the city's deficient supply of water.[94] The dam would be immense, supplying about 8.9 million gallons per day, easily surpassing the city's required 1.7 million gallons per day. The dam would also create a 1,200-acre lake in place of what was one of Illinois' last wild flowing streams. Building such a large dam would negatively affect the property and nostalgic interests of the town's claim to one of the last wild creeks in the state, as well as two species that the state identified as endangered and threatened – the least brook lamprey and Indiana crayfish. The dam met wide opposition from longtime residents of Marion, by farmers who would lose their property, and by the Illinois Department of Conservation, citing myriad concerns about the unknown environmental ramifications of the dam.[95]

Joseph Glisson – an ardent environmentalist who lived about 15 miles from Marion in neighboring Creal Springs, Illinois – opposed the dam. Glisson argued that the construction of the dam and reservoir on Sugar Creek would infringe Article 11, Section 2 of Illinois' constitution, which grants a constitutional right to a "healthful environment." Glisson reasoned that protection of [the least brook lamprey and Indiana crayfish] was necessary to the maintenance of a "healthful environment."[96] He sought an injunction to stop the

---

[90] See, e.g., *Sierra Club v. Department of Transportation* (Hawaii, 2007) (standing to enforce the state's environmental rights triggers limited inquiry into whether there is a generalized grievance to injury in fact to economic, aesthetic or environmental interests).

[91] Compare *Florida Wildlife Federation v. State Department of Environmental Regulation*, 390 So.2d 64 (Florida, 1980) ("minimum requirements of standing injury" in construing state's constitutionally enshrined environmental provisions) with *State v. General Development Corporation* (Florida, 1984, 1985) (Attorney General of Florida lacked standing to enforce state's environmental rights provisions absent implementing legislation, reasoning that it "made sense" that the state's environmental agencies could seek redress, the Attorney General, responsible for criminal actions, could not).

[92] See Eurick, "The Constitutional Right," 205.

[93] *Life of the Land v. Land Use Commission*, 623 P.2d 431 (Hawaii, 1981).

[94] Davenport, Paula M. "Plan for Dam Sparks Dispute in Marion." *St. Louis Post-Dispatch* (April 15, 1991): 11.

[95] *Glisson*, 1034, 1037 (Illinois, 1999).   [96] *Ibid.*, 1041.

project,[97] concerned about the detrimental effects the dam would have on the continued existence of those species.

Marion city officials were not persuaded to halt the dam or to build it elsewhere, remarking that "[w]e're not worried about a fish or two. There's plenty of 'crawdads.' What kind they are [we] don't know, but we've got enough of them."[98] Following an appeals court ruling that remanded the suit to trial level to consider the merits of the environmental rights claim, Glisson and his attorneys were optimistic about the precedential prospects of enforcing the state's environmental rights provision to save species: "It could very well make a major change in the way environmental law in Illinois works ..."[99]

The Illinois Supreme Court, however, held that the framers of Article II, Section 2 meant for it to protect human health, not wildlife.[100] While recognizing that it is easier to demonstrate standing under the state's environment rights provision than it would be under federal law, the court dismissed the case for lack of standing nonetheless. It held that protecting the least brook lamprey and Indiana crayfish was "not a legally cognizable interest for purposes of standing because it is not included in plaintiff's constitutional right to a 'healthful environment.'"[101] Thus, under the interpretation in *Glisson*, Illinois' "right to a healthy environment" does not protect species or habitat. Not to be outdone by the Illinois Supreme Court, shortly after *Glisson* the Illinois House "approved legislation ... that enable[d] developers to build on the habitats of endangered species under certain conditions." Included was the Marion dam. *Glisson* and the legislative response paralyzed enforcement of Illinois' constitutionally embedded right to a clean environment. There has been little attempt to enforce Article II, Section 2 since then.

Sovereign immunity can sometimes present another obstacle to judicial enforcement, although this has been less of a problem in environmental cases than elsewhere. The constitutions of some states expressly waive sovereign immunity, thereby potentially permitting enforcement against the state itself.[102] Other constitutions have been interpreted to waive sovereign immunity.[103] Most state constitutionally embedded environmental rights provisions,

---

[97] *Ibid.*, 1036.   [98] Davenport, "Plan for Dam," 98.

[99] "Court: Individuals can Sue over Endangered Species." *St. Louis Post-Dispatch* (July 6, 1998): 4.

[100] *Glisson*, 1042 (Illinois, 1999).   [101] *Ibid.*, 1045.

[102] See, e.g., Hawaii constitution, art. 11, sec. 9 ("[a]ny person may enforce this right against any party, public or private, through appropriate legal proceedings."); Illinois constitution, art. 11, sec. 2 ("[e]ach person may enforce this right against any party, governmental or private ...").

[103] Speaking of Pennsylvania's environmental rights provision, Dernbach writes that "the Amendment's drafters contemplated that citizens would also file lawsuits against the

including Hawaii's and Illinois', cast the net wide, allowing for legal action against "any party, public or private, through appropriate legal proceedings."[104] These would appear to preclude the defense of sovereign immunity.

DETERMINING REMEDIES

The third reason subnational environmental rights are underenforced is that none of the constitutions discussed here specify the types of remedies that are available when an environmental right is infringed. As discussed in Chapter 5, traditional remedies include equitable relief, damages, and declaratory relief. Yet courts have been loath to find that constitutionally embedded subnational environmental rights are subject to remedy. For example, in *NBD Bank* v. *Krueger Ringier, Inc.*, an Illinois appellate court held that the state's environmental rights provision "does not create a mechanism by which plaintiffs can recover against [the] defendant for the damages sought in the complaint." In this case, the plaintiffs contended that Illinois' environmental rights provision allowed for a private right for a tort action against a defendant who sold contaminated property.[105] There are not many cases that illustrate the challenges of crafting judicial remedies at the subnational level because few cases even get to that stage.

STANDARDS OF REVIEW

In the United States, one final reason that subnational constitutional environmental rights provisions are undervalued is due to standards of judicial review, an issue that seldom arises elsewhere because of the prevalence of the principle of proportionality in most other countries' constitutional adjudication.[106] But in the United States, most state courts that have engaged their state's environmental rights provision have used a highly deferential rational basis-type standard of review in upholding state action and in finding a lack of constitutional violation; this departs from the traditional rule that alleged violations of constitutional rights are subject to a more searching standard of review, with the burden typically on the government to justify the violation. The leading cases come from Pennsylvania, where courts have imbued the

---

government based on claimed violations of environmental rights." Dernbach, "Part II", 114.
    Accord, Kury, Franklin L. "The Environmental Amendment to the Pennsylvania Constitution: Twenty Years Later and Largely Untested." *Villanova Environmental Law Journal* 1 (1990): 124.
[104] Hawaii constitution, art. 11, sec. 9; Illinois constitution, art. 11, sec. 2.
[105] *NBD Bank* v. *Krueger Ringier, Inc.*, 686 N.E.2d 704, 709–710 (Illinois Appeal Court, 1997).
[106] See generally, Barak, *Proportionality*.

text of the state's constitution with a three-part balancing test such that environmental rights provisions nearly always yield to administrative preroga-tives and economic considerations. Pennsylvania's approach, established in *Payne*, requires courts to consider (1) the extent of compliance with applicable statutes and regulations, (2) efforts to reduce environmental incursions, and (3) whether the unavoidable environmental harm "so clearly outweighs the benefits" that "to proceed further would be an abuse of discretion."[107] In *Payne*, a plurality of the Commonwealth Court held that a street-widening project did not violate constitutionally prescribed environmental rights because "the environmental harm and adverse effect of the River Street project on public natural resources are clearly outweighed by the public benefits to be derived from the project."[108] The court interpreted Article 27's intention to allow "controlled development of resources rather than no devel-opment."[109] Subsequent cases then elevated economic concerns over environ-mental concerns in interpreting Pennsylvania's environmental rights provision under the *Payne* standard.[110]

---

[107] *Payne v. Kassab*, 11 Pennsylvania Commonwealth Court, 14, 29–30, 312 A.2d 86, 94 (1973), affirmed Pennsylvania, 1976. *Cf. Commonwealth v. National Gettysburg Battlefield Tower* (Pennsylvania, 1973):

> To summarize, we believe that, the provisions of section 27 of Article 1 of the Consti-tution merely state the general principle of law that the Commonwealth is trustee of Pennsylvania's public natural resources with power to protect the "natural, scenic, historic, and esthetic values" of its environment. If the amendment was self-executing, action taken under it would pose serious problems of constitutionality, under both the equal protection clause and the due process clause of the Fourteenth Amendment. Accordingly, before the environmental protection amendment can be made effective, supplemental legislation will be required to define the values which the amendment seeks to protect and to establish procedures by which the use of private property can be fairly regulated to protect those values.

[108] *Payne*, 312 A.2d at 96.
[109] *Payne v. Kassab* (Pennsylvania, 1973). See Dernbach, "Part I," 713–14 (Professor Dernbach, in analyzing *Payne*, describes how the *Payne* holding "allows environmental degradation to occur if the state has made a reasonable effort to minimize the environmental incursion ..." while undercutting *Gettysburg's* allowance of the Attorney General to challenge private activities "that interfere with clean air, pure water, and the preservation of certain values.").
[110] See *Borough of Moosic v. Pennsylvania Public Utility Commission*, 429 A.2d 1237, 1239 (Pennsylvania Commonwealth Court, 1981) (applying three-part test from *Payne* in concluding that the Pennsylvania Public Utility Commission's denial of the borough's request to intervene for the purpose of showing environmental harm to be caused by the construction of the Montage Project was not abuse of discretion infringing upon a constitutional environmental right). See also *Butler Township Board of Supervisors v. Commonwealth of Pennsylvania, Department of Environmental Resources*, 99 Pennsylvania Commonwealth Court, 239, 249, 513 A.2d 508, 512–13 (1986) (applying three-part test in upholding order issued by Department of Environmental Resources); *Snelling v. Department of Transportation*, 366 A.2d 1298

John Dernbach argues that *Payne* – as a plurality decision – is not binding in Pennsylvania, is ill-reasoned, and should not be followed elsewhere.[111] Nonetheless, courts in New York and Illinois have used *Payne*-type balancing in determining whether an action comports with their constitutional provisions concerning use and disposition of natural resources, to similar result.[112,113]

Montana's approach is the outlier. Montana courts use an ends-means analysis, echoing strict scrutiny under the Due Process Clause of the US Constitution; this requires the state to demonstrate (1) a compelling state end that is achieved with (2) the "least onerous path."[114] The leading case is *Montana Environmental Information Center* v. *Department of Environmental Quality*,[115] in which the state excluded from water quality non-degradation review a permit to discharge arsenic-laden wastewater from a gold mine into an ecologically sensitive area of the Blackfoot River. The Montana Supreme

(Pennsylvania Commonwealth Court, 1976) (road widening and associated increase in traffic does not violate state's constitutionally protected right to healthy environment). See, e.g., *Blue Mountain Preservation Association* v. *Township of Eldred*, 867 A.2d 692 (Pennsylvania Commonwealth Court, 2005); *Del-AWARE Unlimited, Inc.* v. *Commonwealth of Pennsylvania*, 96 Pennsylvania Commonwealth Court 361, 508 A.2d 348 (1986); *Butler Township Board of Supervisors* v. *Commonwealth of Pennsylvania*, 513 A.2d 508 (Pennsylvania Commonwealth Court, 1986); *Concerned Citizens for Orderly Progress* v. *Commonwealth of Pennsylvania*, 36 Pennsylvania Commonwealth Court 192, 387 A.2d 989 (1978). For a helpful discussion of some of these outcomes, see Cusack, "Judicial Interpretation," 193.

[111] Dernbach, "Part 1."

[112] See, e.g., *Hamilton* v. *Diamond*, 42 A.2d 465, 349 N.Y.S.2d 146, 148–9 (Appellate Division of the Supreme Court of the State of New York, 1973) (upholding New York environmental conservation agency's issuance of a permit to build a new home and sea wall next to Hudson River as consistent with art. 14, sec. 4 of state constitution's policy "to conserve and protect its natural resources and scenic beauty," finding that the agency "require[d], in essence, that a project be in the public interest and minimize any adverse impact on the environment."); *Federated Conservationists of Westchester County, Inc.* v. *Reid*, 377 N.Y.S.2d 380 (Supreme Court of New York, 1975) (applying Hamilton's approach in finding permit to install storm in a school district in the public interest); *Leland* v. *Moran*, 235 F. Supp. 2d 153, 154–5 (New York Northern District Court, 2002) (state's constitutional provisions concerning natural resource protection and pollution abatement do not curb prosecutorial discretion to enforce environmental violations waste management facility). See Cusack, "Judicial Interpretation," 192–4 (discussing the "balancing approach" and its use in other states).

[113] See, e.g., *Illinois Pure Water Committee, Inc.* v. *Director of Public Health*, 104 Ill.2d 243, 470 N.E.2d 988 (Illinois Supreme Court, 1984) (declining to apply strict scrutiny in upholding constitutionality of fluoridating water systems as in the public interest, and not violative of a right to "healthful environment").

[114] Thompson, "Constitutionalizing the Environment," 170 (quoting *Pfost* v. *State*, 219 Montana 206, 216, 713 P.2d 495, 505 [Montana, 1985], overruled by *Meech* v. *Hillhaven W.*, 238 Mont. 21, 776 P.2d 488 [Montana, 1989]).

[115] *Montana Environmental Information Center* v. *Department of Environmental Quality*, 296 Montana 207, 988 P.2d 1236 (Montana, 1999).

Court concluded that Montana's environmental rights provision imparted a fundamental right subject to strict scrutiny analysis,[116] and held that the state's decision was unconstitutional, observing that the Montana "constitution does not require that dead fish float on the surface of our state's rivers and streams before its farsighted environmental protections can be invoked."[117] Likewise in *Cape-France Enterprises v. Estate of Peed*,[118] the court explained that the right to a clean and healthful environment "is a fundamental right that may be infringed only by demonstrating a compelling state interest" that is met by narrowly tailored means.[119] Finding a constitutional violation, the court concluded that "it would be unlawful for Cape-France, a private business entity, to drill a well on its property in the face of substantial evidence that doing so may cause significant degradation of uncontaminated aquifers and pose serious public health risks."[120] Subjecting state actions that infringe environmental rights to strict scrutiny can be unpopular.[121] Even courts in Montana may be applying a watered-down version of strict scrutiny to the state's environmental rights. For example, in *Lohmeier v. Gallatin County*,[122] the court found that the creation of a water and sewer district did not contravene the state's environmental rights provision because it would "actually enhance the environment," thereby dispensing with deliberate ends/means analysis.[123]

Given the variety of subnational constitutional provisions aimed at protecting all facets of the environment in myriad ways, these textual and jurisprudential developments suggest that subnational environmental constitutionalism holds an enormous amount of potential for achieving the dual goals of advancing human rights and environmental protection at a subsidiary level, affords enormous potential for innovation, and should not be overlooked.

---

[116] *Ibid.*, 296 Montana 225, 988 P.2d 1246.   [117] *Ibid.*, 296 Montana 230–1, 988 P.2d 1249.

[118] *Cape-France Enterprises v. Estate of Peed*, 29 P.3d 1011 (Montana, 2001).

[119] *Ibid.*, 1016; see also *Montana Environmental Information Center v. Department of Environmental Quality*, 1236, 1246 (Montana, 1999) ("the right to a clean and healthful environment is a fundamental right ... and that any statute *or rule* which implicates that right must be strictly scrutinized and can only survive scrutiny if the State establishes a compelling state interest and that its action is closely tailored to effectuate that interest ...").

[120] *Ibid.*, 1017 ("Causing a party to go forward with the performance of a contract where there is a very real possibility of substantial environmental degradation and resultant financial liability for clean-up is not in the public interest ... and is, most importantly, not in accord with the guarantees and mandates of Montana's Constitution, Article II, Section 3 and Article IX, Section 1.").

[121] McLaren, "Environmental Protection," 149.

[122] *Lohmeier v. Gallatin County*, 135 P.3d 775, 777 (Montana, 2006).

[123] See also *Clark Fork Coalition v. Montana Department of Environmental Quality*, 347 Montana 197, 197 P.3d 482 (Montana, 2008) (where Montana Supreme Court declined argument extending fundamental right status to anything implicating environment).

8

Procedural environmental constitutionalism

> [T]here are two basic forms or types of constraints, both of which may be described under the constitutional rubric. Procedural constraints ... operate directly on the means through which choices are made, while not directly impinging on the set of options ... Substantive constraints, by comparison, act directly on the set of options around which selections are to be made.
>
> "Why do Constitutions Matter?", p.12.

Without effective information, vigorous participation, and opportunities to seek judicial intervention, substantive environmental constitutionalism can suffocate. Process rights can help to keep substantive rights vital. A constitutional guarantee to a beneficial environment is more likely to take root when stakeholders have the right to receive free and timely information for, participate in deliberations about, and appeal to government agencies granting permission to, for example, dam a wild river, emit mercury-laden air pollutants near an elementary school, clear-cut a forest that provides habitat for endangered megafauna, or inexorably alter scenic landscape.

This chapter addresses constitutionally embedded rights to procedure in environmental matters, or what we term "procedural environmental rights." As explained later, some countries already contain elaborate overlays of constitutional, legislative, and/or regulatory means designed to promote participation, access to information, and access to justice provisions that can be deployed to promote environmental norms. Moreover, some countries have enacted legislation and/or promulgated regulations that specifically promote these pillars in environmental matters. Nonetheless, some countries have made the choice to constitutionalize procedural rights in environmental matters as a means of complementing or supplementing these other constitutional, legislative, and regulatory features. It is also important to note that procedural provisions are among the fewest and youngest in all environmental constitutionalism – three dozen or so in the past three decades.

Procedural rights classically consist of three "pillars," allowing for rights to information, participation, and access to justice.[1] These pillars work in tandem to help ensure better decision making in environmental matters. First, informational rights include access to timely and reliable information from governmental agencies charged with overseeing activities that affect the environment. Second, participatory rights are those that enable stakeholders to shape governmental decisions in environmental matters, including permission to submit comments, ask questions, and attend public meetings. Third, adjudicatory rights are those that allow stakeholders to seek civil mediation and enforce court orders in the face of recalcitrant or improvident government action in environmental matters.[2] Collectively, such process rights can raise awareness, provide opportunities to participate, foster empowerment, strengthen local communities, facilitate government accountability, increase public acceptance of decisions, and contribute to the legitimacy of governmental action.[3] Procedural rights can also promote discourse and democratization through concomitant rights to assemble, speak, and participate in governance.

On the other hand, criticisms of procedural rights include that they unduly reallocate scarce government resources, do not produce optimal results because the public is ill- or under-equipped to make informed decisions, lead to lowest common denominator decision making, hinder agency problem solving, foster decisional paralysis, and invite control by special interest groups and the ruling classes.[4] It may also be argued that procedural rights are weak versions of rights: they do not secure the thing that is of value but only the opportunity to gain the thing of value, and even that opportunity is subject to political manipulation and requires time, effort, and expense to exercise. And even when vindicated, procedural rights produce process, not a desired end, such as a modicum of environmental progress.

---

[1] See generally, Razzaque, Jona. "Information, Public Participation, and Access to Justice." In *Routledge Handbook of International Environmental Law*, by Shawkat Alam, Jahid Hossain Bhuiyan, Tareq M.R. Chowdhury and Erika J. Techera (eds.), Routledge, 2012.

[2] *Taskin and Others* v. *Turkey*. Application no. 46117/99 (European Court of Human Rights, 2004).

[3] *Ibid.*

[4] Zillman, Donald M., Alastair Lucas and George (Rock) Pring. *Human Rights in Natural Resource Development: Public Participation in the Sustainable Development of Mining and Energy Resources*. Oxford University Press, 2002.

This chapter explores the reasons for and extent to which countries have instituted express constitutional protections of process rights in environmental matters, and the extent to which courts have vindicated such rights. We conclude that procedural environmental constitutionalism can fill gaps left by extant international, regional, and domestic laws in promoting procedural rights. We also conclude that procedural environmental rights are important in their own right, and perhaps even more useful than substantive environmental rights because courts might be more inclined to use them to vindicate environmental interests while pushing the actual decision making to the political sphere; all the courts have to do is adjudicate the terms of the conversation without taking the heat for promoting development over the environment or vice versa. As we shall see, as with substantive rights, the arc of procedural rights bends toward constitutionalism.

THE NATURE OF CONSTITUTIONAL PROCEDURAL ENVIRONMENTAL RIGHTS

Similar to its substantive counterpart, procedural environmental constitutionalism originated from and has evolved through a series of international accords and domestic laws. Constitutional instantiation of procedural rights derives from the 1948 UN Declaration of Human Rights,[5] perhaps the first international accord to promote procedural rights, a project further refined by the 1966 International Covenant on Civil and Political Rights.[6]

Procedural rights have gained special salience in environmental matters. Most of the landmark international environmental treaties of the twentieth century promote procedural rights in environmental matters, beginning with the landmark 1972 Stockholm Declaration, which entreats participating countries to advance public involvement as *sine qua non* to "defend and improve the human environment."[7] The 1992 Rio Conference on Environment and Development (known as the "Earth Summit") recognized the paramount importance of procedural rights in environmental matters.[8] The UN Framework Convention on Climate Change maintains that its parties "shall promote and facilitate at the national and, as appropriate, sub-regional and regional levels, and in accordance with national laws and regulations, and within their

---

[5] Universal Declaration of Human Rights (1948), 3rd sess., pt. 1, at 71, arts. 8, 10, 19, 20.
[6] International Covenant on Civil and Political Rights, 999 UNTS 171, arts. 19, 25 (1966).
[7] Declaration of the United Nations Conference, para. 7, Preamble.
[8] UN Declaration on Environment and Development ("Rio Declaration"), UN Doc.A/ CONF.151/5/Rev. 1 (1992).

respective capacities, public access to information and public participation."[9] Numerous regional accords have also promoted procedural rights along continental lines either explicitly or by interpretation, including the 1950 European Convention for the Protection of Human Rights and Fundamental Freedoms (European Convention),[10] the American Convention on Human Rights (American Convention),[11] and the 1981 African Charter on Human and Peoples' Rights (African Charter).[12]

Access to timely and reliable information is perhaps paramount among the three pillars of process rights. The ability of the public to receive information from the government in a timely fashion is a cornerstone of good governance, especially in democratic societies.[13] International law has been particularly supportive of the value and utility of the need for governments to provide timely and reliable access to information.[14] For example, the 1948 UN Declaration of Human Rights promotes the freedom "to seek, receive and impart information and ideas through any media and regardless of frontiers,"[15] notions later refined by the 1966 International Covenant on Civil and Political Rights.[16] Regionally, the European and American Conventions also underscore the importance of access to information, both granting that "[e]veryone has the right to freedom of expression. This right shall include freedom ... to receive and impart information and ideas without interference by public authority and regardless of frontiers." Moreover, the African Charter also declares that "every individual shall have the right to receive information ... [and] to express and disseminate his opinions within the law."[17]

[9] United Nations Framework Convention on Climate Change, Art. 6 (1992).

[10] European Convention for the Protection of Human Rights and Fundamental Freedoms, 213 UNTS 222, arts. 6, 10 (1950).

[11] American Convention on Human Rights, art. 13.

[12] African Charter on Human and Peoples' Rights, 1520 UNTS 217, 21 ILM 59, arts. 3, 7, 9(1), 13, 24 (1981).

[13] See, e.g., Heyer, Eric. "Latin American State Secrecy and Mexico's Transparency Law." *George Washington International Law Review* 38 (2006): 437 ("A fundamental building block of democratic societies is unhindered access to government-held information. Access to such information allows the public to critique government actions and make electoral and economic decisions accordingly, thereby underpinning the notion of a democratic government that derives its authority from the consent of the governed ...").

[14] See generally, Kravchenko and Bonine, *Human Rights*, 219; D. Anton and D. Shelton. "Problems in Environment Protection and Human Rights: A Human Right to the Environment." ANU *College of Law Research Paper* No. 11–17, (June, 2011): 357.

[15] Universal Declaration of Human Rights, GA Res 217 (AIII), UN GAOR, 3rd sess., pt. 1, at 71, art. 19, UN Doc A/810 (1948).

[16] International Covenant on Civil and Political Rights (1966), arts. 19, 25.

[17] African Charter on Human and Peoples' Rights (1981), art. 9.

The import of having access to information in environmental matters is recognized in various multilateral environmental treaties. Notably, Principle 10 of the 1992 Rio Declaration on Environment and Development ("Agenda 21") provides that individuals:

> shall have appropriate access to information concerning the environment that is held by public authorities, including information on hazardous materials and activities in their communities, and the opportunity to participate in decision-making processes. States shall facilitate and encourage public awareness and participation by making information widely available. Effective access to judicial and administrative proceedings, including redress and remedy, shall be provided.[18]

Having access to information on environmental matters can be crucial to advancing substantive environmental objectives. Such access "ensures that members of the public can understand what is happening in the environment around them ... [and] participate in an informed manner."[19] Such transparency "means that the public can clearly follow the path of environmental information, understanding its origin, the criteria that govern its collection, holding and dissemination, and how it can be obtained."[20] Accordingly, Principle 17 of Agenda 21 provides that "[e]nvironmental impact assessment, as a national instrument, shall be undertaken for proposed activities that are likely to have a significant adverse impact on the environment and are subject to a decision of a competent national authority."[21] In general, however, international and regional encomiums about the importance of rights to information are not actionable by affected parties.

The 1998 Convention on Access to Information, Participation in Decision-Making, and Access to Justice in Environmental Matters (the Aarhus Convention) stands apart in this regard.[22] The Aarhus Convention permits individuals and NGOs to petition a "Compliance Committee" to enforce its provisions against member states.[23] The Convention also requires parties, "in response to a request for environmental information," to "make such

---

[18] UN Declaration on Environment and Development (1992).
[19] Stec, Stephen and Susan Casey-Lefkowitz. *The Aarhus Convention: An Implementation Guide*, United Nations, 2000.
[20] *Ibid.*   [21] Rio Declaration, art. 19.
[22] Aarhus Convention on Access to Information, Public Participation in Decision-Making and Access to Justice in Environmental Matters, June 25, 1998, 38 ILM 517 (entered into force October 30, 2001) [hereinafter Aarhus Convention].
[23] See, e.g., "Findings and Recommendations with Regard to Compliance by Kazakhstan" (finding country out of compliance with Convention's provisions regarding access to information), cited in Kravchenko and Bonine, *Human Rights*.

information available to the public, within the framework of national legislation," subject to certain conditions.[24] It provides that environmental information includes the "state of the elements of the environment, factors that affect the environment, decision-making processes, and the state of human health and safety."[25] The Aarhus Convention is widely viewed as the most innovative and important international accord in support of procedural rights in environmental matters.[26]

And yet, most of the work being done to advance procedural rights has been achieved when nations adopt these principles as their own at the domestic level. Many countries have general constitutional, legislative, or other guarantees that promote rights to information, participation, and justice.

The constitutions of more than sixty countries recognize or promote procedural rights. At least fifty, and arguably fifty-seven, of these expressly guarantee a "right" to "information" or "documents" or impose an obligation on the government to make information available to the public. These apply generally, without regard to whether the information relates to environmental matters or not. According to Banisar:

> [T]he 57 countries that constitute a right to information include 11 countries in the Americas (Brazil, Chile, Colombia, Costa Rica, Ecuador, Mexico, Nicaragua, Panama, Paraguay, Peru and Venezuela); 24 in Europe that explicitly (Albania, Bulgaria, Czech Republic, Estonia, Finland, Greece, Hungary, Lithuania, Moldova, Norway, Poland, Portugal, Romania, Serbia, Slovakia, Slovenia, Sweden) or arguably do so (Austria, Azerbaijan, Belgium, Georgia, Macedonia, Russia, Ukraine); 6 in Asia and the Pacific (Nepal, New Zealand, Pakistan, Papua New Guinea, Philippines, Thailand); and 16 in Africa (Burkina Faso, Cameroon, Democratic Republic of Congo, Eritrea, Ghana, Guinea Bissau, Kenya, Madagascar, Malawi, Morocco, Mozambique, Senegal, Seychelles, South Africa, Tanzania, and Uganda).[27]

These include most written constitutions from countries recently in transition, including most of those in Latin America, Central and Eastern Europe, and Central and East Asia.[28] Moreover, the South African constitution guarantees

---

[24] Aarhus Convention, art. 4.   [25] Stec and Casey-Lefkowitz, *The Aarhus Convention*, 36.

[26] See generally, Kravchenko, Svitlana. "The Aarhus Convention and Innovations in Compliance and Multilateral Environmental Agreements." *Colorado Journal of International Environmental Law and Policy* 18(1) (2007).

[27] Open Society Justice Initiative. *Constitutional Rights of the Right to Information*, available at http://right2info.org/constitutional-protections-of-the-right-to (internal citation omitted).

[28] See David Banisar. *Freedom of Information Around the World 2006: A Global Survey of Access to Government Information Laws*, Privacy International, 2006, available at www.freedominfo. org/documents/global_survey2006.pdf

the right to demand information "that is held by another person and that is required for the exercise or protection of any rights."[29] The highest courts in at least six more countries have held that process rights are embedded in other constitutional guarantees, including freedom of speech, assembly, association, and the press.[30]

Many countries have enacted legislation that provides some degree of access to information held by governing bodies. Of these, India's Access to Information Act is among the more comprehensive.[31] It establishes a commission that can order disclosure, impose financial penalties, and award attorney fees for non-compliance.[32] In the United States, the federal Freedom of Information Act has permitted citizens to request disclosure of governmental records since 1967.[33] Furthermore, all fifty states in the United States have enacted laws that permit access to governmental records.[34]

Some countries employ a hybrid approach, with constitutional provisions that specifically permit stakeholders to enforce legislatively granted procedural rights. For example, Sweden's constitution incorporates the Swedish Freedom of Press Act.[35] And freedom of information laws in New Zealand and Canada are viewed as "quasi-constitutional."[36]

Notwithstanding this backdrop of international and regional accords and domestic laws that advance procedural rights generally, constitutionalizing procedural rights in environmental matters can fill gaps. First, with the exception of aspects of the Aarhus Convention, stakeholders generally cannot enforce procedure-advancing provisions in international or regional accords. Yet even the Aarhus Convention has limitations. It applies only to member states. It is not enforceable domestically even in member states, for the most part. And filing a petition can be expensive and time-consuming.

Second, generic constitutional procedural guarantees may not sufficiently fit environmental matters. For example, constitutional guarantees of speech, assembly, and association in the United States have not been viewed as ensuring access to information, participation, or justice in environmental matters.

Third, legislative grants of process often contain huge loopholes saving disclosure of information that might be most important in environmental

---

[29] Constitution of South Africa (1996) section 32(1).   [30] Banisar, *Freedom of Information*, 17.

[31] "The Right to Information Act, 2005," *Gazette of India, Extraordinary*, Part II, section 1 (June 21, 2005), available at www.iitb.ac.in/legal/RTI-Act.pdf

[32] See, e.g., *Satyapal v. CPIO, TCIL*, No. ICPB/A-1CIC/2006 (Central Information Commission, 2006), cited in Kravchenko and Bonine, *Human Rights*, 249.

[33] United States Freedom of Information Act, 5 U.S.C. sec. 552.

[34] Banisar, *Freedom of Information*, 162.   [35] *Ibid.*, 17.   [36] *Ibid.*

matters. For example, while the federal Freedom of Information Act in the United States is widely used to gather information from federal agencies about decision making in environmental matters, it nonetheless exempts wide swaths of information that could prove essential to decisions in environmental matters, including information subject to exemptions due to national security, deliberative process, internal agency rules, business information, inter- and intra-agency memoranda, personal privacy, law enforcement records, financial data, records that would reveal trade secrets, oil and gas wells data, and other privileges.[37] State analogues often have the same or similar exemptions, further limiting process rights in environmental matters.

Last, general process rights granted by international accords and domestic laws can simply fall short in environmental matters. Constitutionally protected speech does not impose a corresponding duty to listen. Governmental information in the hands of entrenched bureaucracies can be lost, hidden, or withheld. Public comments can be overlooked. Access to justice can be thwarted by obstacles concerning standing, justiciability, remedies, and enforcement.[38] A clear mandate of constitutional stature to disclose relevant information in environmental matters is less likely to be avoided or undermined.

Thus, various countries have turned to procedural environmental constitutionalism to fill the gaps left by international, regional, and domestic measures to advance procedural rights in environmental matters.

TEXTUAL PROCEDURAL ENVIRONMENTAL RIGHTS

The constitutions of about three dozen countries specifically recognize procedural rights in environmental matters, primarily to advance human rights to a quality environment. (See Appendix I.) Such rights to information, participation, and access to justice in environmental matters are a modern constitutional innovation. They appear to serve both human and environmental interests, fortifying the advancing democratization of the planet.[39]

---

[37] United States Freedom of Information Act, sec. 552(b).

[38] See, e.g., Ristroph, Elizabeth Barrett and Ilya Fedyaev. "Obstacles to Environmental Litigation in Russia and the Potential for Private Actions." *Environs* 29 (2006): 221 (procedural obstacles to litigating environmental claims in Russia).

[39] See Onzivu, "International Environmental Law," 672 ("International human rights law and national constitutions provide for procedural rights that are instrumental in the protection of human health and the environment. These rights include freedom of association, freedom of information, public participation in decision-making processes, and access to justice and judicial review."); Cramer, "Human Right to Information," 74 ("The push for a fundamental human right to environmental protection is in turn inspiring demands for access to government documents and meetings that deal with environmental matters."); Bandi, "Right to

Procedural and substantive environmental constitutionalism is symbiotic. Understandably, then, all of the roughly three dozen countries that constitutionalize procedural environmental rights also guarantee a substantive right to a quality environment (with the exception of Austria).[40,41] Thus, substantive and procedural environmental rights appear to use similar means – individually vindicable constitutional rights – in pursuit of the same end of environmental protection. On the other hand, only about one-third of the nations with substantive environmental rights guarantee any sort of corresponding procedural rights to information, participation, or access to justice, indicating that while procedural rights seem to be necessary to buttress substantive rights, they are still far less common.

A handful of countries specifically provide for procedural rights to information in environmental matters. Ukraine offers a leading example of a constitutionally recognized right to information. In the wake of the secrecy surrounding the disaster at the Chernobyl nuclear power plant, Ukraine adopted a constitutional mandate that declares: "Everyone is guaranteed the right of free access to information about the environmental situation ... and also the right to disseminate such information."[42] Other countries that have constituted rights to information about environmental matters include Albania ("Everyone has the right to be informed about the status of the environment and its protection"), Argentina ("The authorities shall provide for environmental information and education"), Azerbaijan Republic ("Everyone has the right to collect information on the environmental situation"), Eritrea ("The State shall ... use all available means to enable all citizens to improve their livelihood in a sustainable manner, through their participation"), France ("Everyone has the right, subject to the conditions and within the limits defined by the law, to have access to the information relating to the environment held by the public authorities"), Georgia ("A person shall have the right to receive complete, objective and timely information on the state of his or her working and living environment"), Moldova ("The State guarantees every person the right of free access to truthful information regarding the state of the natural environment, the living and working conditions and the quality

Environment," 450–65 (discussing the Hungarian Constitution's public participation provisions); Hayward, *Constitutional Environmental Rights*, 200–03 (discussing procedural environmental rights in Africa and elsewhere).

[40] See Appendix I; Boyd, *Environmental Rights Revolution*, 47–67.

[41] Boyd concludes: "This suggests that procedural environmental rights are viewed as a complement to, rather than a substitute for, substantive environmental rights." Boyd, *Environmental Rights Revolution*, 66–7.

[42] Konstitutsiya Ukraini [Constitution] (Ukraine), ch. II, art. 50.

of food products and household goods"), Montenegro ("Everyone shall have the right to receive timely and full information about the status of the environment, to influence the decision making regarding the issues of importance for the environment, and to legal protection of these rights"), Norway ("In order to safeguard their right [to a healthy environment] [citizens are] to be informed of the state of the natural environment and of the effects of any encroachments on nature that are planned or commenced"), Poland ("Everyone has the right to be informed of the condition and protection of the environment"), Russian Federation ("Everyone shall have the right to a favorable environment, and reliable information about its condition"), Serbia ("Everyone shall have the right to healthy environment and the right to timely and full information about the state of environment"), and Zambia ("The people shall have access to environmental information to enable them preserve, protect and conserve the environment").

The constitutions of some countries embody the second pillar of procedural environmental rights – public participation in environmental matters. Participatory rights allow the public to shape environmental decision making through comments and other means. Thailand's constitution is a representative example, requiring an environmental assessment and public participation prior to government approval of any project that "may seriously affect the quality of the environment, natural resources and biological diversity . . ."[43] Other countries with constitutions that embed rights to participate in environmental governance – as by requiring a public environmental review process – include Brazil (requiring "a prior environmental impact study, which shall be made public, for installation of works or activities that may cause significant degradation of the environment"), Colombia ("Every individual has the right to enjoy a healthy environment. The law will guarantee the community's participation in the decisions that may affect it"), Ecuador ("All persons, communities, peoples and nations can call upon public authorities to enforce the rights of nature"), Eritrea ("[T]he State shall be responsible . . . for creating the right conditions to secure the participation of the people in safeguarding

---

[43] *Ra tta'tamma noon Ha'eng Raatcha anaaja'k Tai* [Ra tta'tamma noon] [Constitution] (Thailand), pt. 12, sec. 67: "Any project or activity which may seriously affect the quality of the environment, natural resources and biological diversity shall not be permitted, unless its impacts on the quality of the environment and on health of the people in the communities have been studied and evaluated and consultation with the public and interested parties have been organized, and opinions of an independent organization, consisting of representatives from private environmental and health organizations and from higher education institutions providing studies in the field of environment, natural resources or health, have been obtained prior to the operation of such project or activity."

the environment"), Ethiopia ("People have the right to full consultation and to the expression of views in the planning and implementations of environmental policies and projects that affect them directly"), Finland ("The public authorities shall endeavor to guarantee … for everyone the possibility to influence the decisions that concern their own living environment"), France ("Everyone has the right, subject to the conditions and within the limits defined by the law … to participate in the making of public decisions which have an impact on the environment"), Kosovo ("Everyone should be provided an opportunity to be heard by public institutions and have their opinions considered on issues that impact the environment in which they live. The impact on the environment shall be considered by public institutions in their decision making processes"), Poland ("Public authorities shall support the activities of citizens to protect and improve the quality of the environment"), and Zambia ("the people shall be involved and participate in the development of relevant policies, plans and programmes").

The third pillar of procedural rights relates to access to justice. As discussed in Chapter 4, open standing is a key attribute of access to justice. Some constitutions expressly provide for expansive or open standing to the judicial process to pursue environmental rights. A representative example is Brazil, whose constitution declares that: "[A]ny citizen has standing to bring a popular action to annul an act injurious to the public patrimony or the patrimony of an entity in which the State participates … to the environment."[44] Other countries that expressly recognize standing in environmental matters include Bolivia ("Any person, in his own right or on behalf of a collective, is authorized to take legal actions in defense of environmental rights, without prejudice to the obligation of public institutions to act on their own in the face of attacks on the environment"), Burkina Faso ("Every citizen has the right to initiate an action or to join a collective action under the form of a petition against the acts … affecting the environment or the cultural or historic patrimony"), Mozambique ("All citizens shall have the right to … advocate the prevention, termination or judicial prosecution of offences against … environmental conservation"), and Portugal ("To all is conferred – personally or through associations that purport to defend the interests in issue – the right of popular action in the cases and under the conditions specified by law, including the right to advocate on behalf of the aggrieved party or parties … to promote the prevention, the suppression and the prosecution of offenses against … the preservation of the environment").

---

[44] Constitution of Brazil, Title II, Ch. 1, Art. 5, LXXIII.

Relatedly, some constitutions expressly permit individuals to seek redress for violations of substantive environmental rights. A representative example is Angola's, which provides: "Every citizen, either individually or through associations representing specific interests, shall have the right to take legal action in the cases and under the terms established by law, with the aim of annulling acts which are harmful to ... the environment."[45] Other countries to recognize an actionable right to bring substantive claims include Chile ("Anybody who, due to arbitrary or illegal actions or omissions, suffers privation, disturbance or threats in the legitimate exercise of ... the right to live in an environment free from contamination [may seek redress]"), Costa Rica ("Every person has the right to a healthy and ecologically balanced environment. Due to this, the person is justified to denounce those acts which infringe this right and to claim reparation for harm caused"), Kazakhstan ("Officials are held accountable ... for the concealment of facts and circumstances endangering the life and health of the people"), Kenya ("Every person has the right to a clean and healthy environment, which includes the right ... [to apply to a court for redress of damage to the environment]."), and Madagascar ("The Fokonolona can take the appropriate measures tending to oppose acts susceptible to destroy their environment ... unless these measures may undermine the general interest or public order").

The constitutions of some countries expressly provide for compensation to redress violations of substantive environmental rights. A representative example is Chechnya, whose constitution provides that "[e]veryone has the right to a decent environment ... and compensation for damage caused to their health or property as a result of ecological violations of the law."[46] Other constitutions that expressly allow for remedies to redress violations of guaranteed environmental rights include the Azerbaijan Republic ("Everyone has the right ... to get compensation for damage rendered to the health and property due to the violation of ecological rights"), and the Russian Federation ("Everyone shall have the right to ... compensation for the damage caused to his or her health or property by ecological violations"). Of course, where courts are underfunded, lack independence, and struggle to establish and maintain their legitimacy, such provisions are less likely to be effectively invoked.

Some constitutions at the subnational level in the United States provide similar procedural rights to enforce substantive environmental rights, including Hawaii ("Each person has the right to a clean and healthful environment, as defined by laws relating to environmental quality ... Any person may

---

[45] Angola Constitution, pt. 11, art. 24(1).   [46] Constitution of Chechnya.

enforce this right against any party, public or private, through appropriate legal proceedings, subject to reasonable limitations and regulation as provided by law")[47] and Illinois ("Each person has the right to a healthful environment. Each person may enforce this right against any party … through appropriate legal proceedings subject to reasonable limitation and regulation as the General Assembly may provide by law").[48] These provisions advance access to justice in environmental matters.

Iceland's 2011 draft constitution seemed to offer a gold standard of sorts because it embodied all three pillars of constitutional procedural environmental rights:

> The public authorities shall inform the public on the state of the environment and nature and the impact of construction thereon. The public authorities and others shall provide information on an imminent danger to nature, such as environmental pollution. The law shall secure the right of the public to have the opportunity to participate in the preparation of decisions that have an impact on the environment and nature as well as the possibility to seek independent verdicts thereon. In taking decisions regarding Iceland's nature and environment, the public authorities shall base their decisions on the main principles of environmental law.[49]

However, in 2013, the draft failed to win adoption in Iceland's legislature.

Procedural environmental constitutionalism can also be implicit, derived from an express grant to a substantive right to a healthy environment. As Hiskes notes, substantive environmental rights can "include a procedural element aimed at enhancing their positive effect on democratic practice."[50] For example, in *Director: Mineral Development, Gauteng Region and Another v. Save the Vaal Environment and Others*,[51] the Supreme Court of Appeal of South Africa held that constitutional recognition of substantive environmental rights implicitly requires that the government solicit and consider public comments before issuing a mining permit. Ansari et al. conclude that "[b]y this the court recognized the right of the people to be informed and heard in respect of activities likely to damage the environment and violate human rights."[52] This case arises out of a constitutional culture that affirmatively promotes participatory democracy and public participation in decision making.

---

[47] Hawaii constitution, art. 11 sec. 9.   [48] Illinois constitution, art. 11, sec. 2.
[49] Iceland constitution.   [50] Hiskes, *Human Right to a Green Future*.
[51] *Director: Mineral Development, Gauteng Region and Another v. Save the Vaal Environment and Others*, Case No. 133 of 98 (Supreme Court of Appeal of South Africa, March 12, 1999) [hereinafter *Save the Vaal Environment*].
[52] Ansari *et al.*, "Protection of Environmental Rights."

JUDICIAL RECEPTIVITY TO PROCEDURAL ENVIRONMENTAL RIGHTS

In principle, there is no reason procedural environmental rights should be any more or less subject to judicial vindication than substantive environmental rights. If it is difficult for a court to define the outer boundaries of the relevant environment for substantive purposes, the environment becomes no more limited or defined when a court seeks to protect it procedurally, although this challenge may be ameliorated in those countries that have constitutionally established environmental tribunals, chambers, or courts specifically designed to hear environmental claims.[53]

The divergent structures of substantive rights and procedural rights, however, indicate that they perform distinct functions in the development of constitutional law. Substantive environmental rights demand that courts try to answer hard questions about what the environment is and should be to be safe, healthy, or clean. But procedural environmental rights sound in procedure more than in ecology; they demand instead that courts identify specific procedures by which certain decisions are to be made. True, the rights are triggered by the potential for environmental impact, but the rights themselves are commonly recognized rights of access and participation.

Thus, the analytic framework entailed in enforcing procedural rights is narrower, more objectively bounded, and more likely to be within the judicial comfort zone than what substantive rights demand. To determine whether there has been a violation of procedural rights, the court needs to decide that the issue is in some manner environmental, and then needs to determine whether the constitutionally mandated procedures have been followed. The discretion involved in these determinations is minimal and, in nature, is strictly judicial. It raises few of the broad-ranging and policy-based considerations that are inherent in determinations of substantive environmental law. Procedural rights are also easier to enforce than substantive rights. As we've seen, remedial orders in substantive environmental cases can be elaborate and often creative mandates to a variety of public and private defendants to engage in a range of activities over long periods of time, all of which can obligate the court to maintain permanent jurisdiction over the defendants with attendant obligations involving continued monitoring and enforcement proceedings. Remedial orders in procedural cases, by contrast, tend to emanate directly from the constitutional requirements relating to the dissemination of information, the effective means of participation, and access to justice.

---

[53] See generally, Pring and Pring, *Greening Justice*.

The uncertain boundaries of environmental rights force courts onto a tightrope when they seek to enforce substantive rights. If they read the rights too narrowly, they risk damage to the environment that could have deleterious effects on the ecosystem and the lives, dignity, and health of the population for generations to come. Overenforcing substantive environmental rights, however, may unduly limit development and economic progress to the detriment of the local population and perhaps the nation as a whole. In Nepal, the court held that the government's obligation to hold land in the public trust precluded the construction of a medical college on land that had historical, cultural, and archaeological significance, thereby potentially depriving the community of much needed doctors.[54] Another example is the India Supreme Court's closure of tanneries – which had provided jobs and economic opportunities for local residents – because of the resultant pollution to the Ganges.[55] Judges seeking to enforce these rights must constantly balance competing policy claims, and weigh the costs and benefits of each decision: how much sustainability, how much development?

Procedural rights, by contrast, do not raise the same concerns because there is virtually no danger of overenforcement. Casting the net too broadly – that is, subjecting too many policy determinations to constitutional procedural requirements – does not limit economic opportunity or development, but merely opens up too many processes to democratic engagement: more government decisions will be subject to discussion in local communities, their environmental impacts will have to be assessed and the reports disseminated. To be sure, over-democratization has some costs, in terms of the time it takes to come to a final determination and the actual expense of holding meetings, distributing information, developing and modifying initial decisions. But these minimal burdens are simply the costs of a functioning democracy. Moreover, the costs, properly borne, are designed to produce better results that have been more widely debated and more fully considered. Because there are virtually no risks associated with overreading procedural environmental rights, courts need not hesitate to enforce them.

Because the boundaries of procedural environmental rights are more clear and their enforcement more verifiable, more easily managed, and less risky, courts should not have the same separation-of-powers-based reluctance to enforcement as they might have to substantive rights. Whereas vindication of substantive rights requires courts to make policy decisions that either cross

---

[54] *Yogi Narahari Nath v. Honorable Prime Minister Girija Prasad Koirala and Others* (Nepal, 1955).

[55] *M.C. Mehta v. Union of India* (Supreme Court of India, January 12, 1988).

the boundaries of judicial authority or at the very least raise the specter of doing so, vindication of procedural rights not only do not invade the political sphere but, in fact, enhance it by scaffolding political activity.

Much as with substantive rights, the Constitutional Court of Latvia has been receptive to enforcing constitutionally enshrined rights to information in environmental matters. The constitution of Latvia provides: "The State shall protect the right of everyone to live in a benevolent environment by providing information about environmental conditions ..." Accordingly, in *Coalition for Nature and Cultural Heritage Protection* v. *Riga City Council*, the Constitutional Court of Latvia struck a plan to develop the Freeport of Riga because the council had not adequately considered the information that the Coalition had provided concerning the potential impact that the project might have on a bird sanctuary.[56] And in *Gruba*, the court stated that the right to live in a "benevolent environment" entitles an individual not only to the right to obtain information, but also to participate meaningfully in environmental decision making, meaning that government authorities must "duly" consider the public's objections and counter-proposals.[57] Indeed, in *Gruba*, the Court held that the council contravened the constitution by granting a permit over the objections of affected individuals without providing sufficient explanations for doing so.

Courts in other countries have upheld express constitutional rights to information in environmental matters, though not very often. In *Van Huyssteen* v. *Minister of Environmental Affairs and Tourism*,[58] the High Court of South Africa held that the South African constitution granted citizens a constitutional right to information held by governmental agencies respecting the environmental effects of constructing a new steel mill near the West Coast National Park. In *Sociedad Peruana de Derecho Ambiental contra Ministerio de Energia y Minas*,[59] the Peruvian Constitutional Division held that the Peruvian constitution protected an environmental law society's access to information about the environmental effects of mining. And in the *Forests Survey Inspection Request Case*,[60] the Constitutional Court of South Korea

---

[56] *Coalition for Nature and Cultural Heritage Protection* v. *Riga City Council* (Latvia, 2008).

[57] *Gruba* (Latvia Constitutional Court, 2009).

[58] *Van Huyssteen* v. *Minister of Environmental Affairs and Tourism*, 1996 (1) SA 283 (C) (High Court of South Africa, June 28, 1996).

[59] *Sociedad Peruana de Derecho Ambiental contra Ministerio de Energia y Minas* (Habeus Data), Expediente No. 1658–95, Dictamen Fiscal No. 122–96 (Sala de Derecho Constitucional 19 de junio de 1996).

[60] *Forests Survey Inspection Request Case*, 1 KCCR 176 (Constitutional Court of S. Korea, September 4, 1989), available at www.ccourt.go.kr/home/english/decisions/mgr_decision_view. jsp?seq=374&code=1&pg=1&sch_code=&sch_sel=&sch_txt=&nScale=15

upheld a constitutional right to inspect and copy forest title records, private forest use surveys, land surveys, and land tax ledgers kept by governmental authorities: "a person who is denied information could rely on the constitutional provision and sue in Constitutional Court without following procedures required by the country's access to information legislation."

Courts in other countries have found informational rights in environmental matters as an extension of a long line of judicial recognition of constitutional rights to information in general. The Supreme Court of India recognized constitutional rights to information thirty years ago. In *S.P. Gupta* v. *President of India and Others*, the Supreme Court of India found that the public has a constitutional right to correspondence regarding judicial appointments between the Law Minister, the Chief Justice of Delhi, and the Chief Justice of India:[61] "open government is the direct emanation from the right to know which seems to be implicit in the right of free speech and expression guaranteed under Article 19(1)(a)."[62] The Indian Supreme Court has extended this reasoning to recognize constitutional entitlement to information in cases that happen to involve the environment. For example, in *Reliance Petrochemicals Ltd.* v. *Indian Express*,[63] in ordering the disclosure of information regarding development of oil reserves, the court observed that "the right to know is a basic right which citizens of a free country aspire in the broader horizon of the right to live in this age in our land under Article 21 of our Constitution."[64] And in *Bombay Environmental Action Group* v. *Pune Cantonment Board*,[65] the court held that the Indian constitution required a governmental land use planning agency to disclose applications for building permits, stating that "[p]eople's participation in the movement for the protection of the environment cannot be over-emphasized. It is wrong to think that by trying to protect the environment they are opposing the various development projects." Thus, courts in India have once again led the way in promoting environmental constitutionalism by inferring environmental rights – substantive or procedural – from indirect textual provisions.

There is also a growing body of judicial decisions concerning constitutional rights to participate in environmental matters. Some courts have enforced specific constitutional provisions that grant a right to participate in environmental matters. For example, the Constitutional Court of Colombia found

[61] *S.P. Gupta* v. *President of India and Others* (India, December 30, 1981).   [62] *Ibid.*
[63] *Reliance Petrochemicals Ltd.* v. *Indian Express*, No. 1989 AIR 190, 1988 SCT Supl. (3) 212 (Supreme Court of India, September 23, 1988).
[64] *Ibid.*
[65] *Bombay Environmental Action Group* v. *Pune Cantonment Board*, Writ. Pet. No. 2733 (Bombay High Court, 1986).

that the constitution requires that certain indigenous populations be "formally and substantially consulted" about a plan to engage in oil exploration in culturally important lands. In *Federación Independiente del Pueblo Shuar del Ecuador (FIPSE) c. Arco Oriente s/ Amparo [ENG]*,[66] the Ecuador Constitutional Tribunal held that the government's issuance of a license to explore for oil and gas had violated the plaintiffs' constitutional right to be "consulted and ... participate in the design, implementation, and evaluation of national and regional development plans and programs potentially affecting them directly." In *Save the Vaal Environment*,[67] the Supreme Court of Appeal of South Africa decided that a decision to allow mining operations had violated constitutional rights of notification and participation: "since environmental rights are fundamental, this requires that environmental considerations be accorded appropriate recognition and respect in the administrative process of the country. Together with the change in the ideological climate must also come change in our legal and administrative approach to environmental concerns." And in a decision from Slovenia,[68] the Constitutional Court upheld villagers' constitutional rights to participate in decision making in environmental matters. These developments show the potential for constitutionally instantiated procedural environmental rights to help further human rights and environmental protection goals, when invoked.

ENFORCEMENT AND REMEDIES

The principal remedies for breach of constitutionally guaranteed procedural environmental rights include injunctions to gain access to information, participation, or justice. These may be perceived as less efficacious for the protection of the environment because a judicial victory simply earns the claimants a right to more process, which in turns takes more time, more effort, and more resources to exercise. On the other hand, given the difficulty of securing judicial victories of substantive rights in most courts around the world and, perhaps even more significantly, the difficulty of ensuring enforcement of those victories that are gained, it is not obvious that procedural rights are less likely to achieve the ultimate goal of environmental protection than substantive rights. And it is quite possible that the process of pursuing and exercising participatory rights will inure to the benefit not only of the environment but of

---

[66] *Federación Independiente del Pueblo Shuar del Ecuador (FIPSE) c. Arco Oriente s/ Amparo. [ENG]*. Tribunal Constitucional de Ecuador, Sala Primera. April, 2000.
[67] *Save the Vaal Environment* (South Africa, 1999).
[68] *Decision U-I-416/98–38*, Constitutional Court of Slovenia, Ljubljana, March 22, 2001.

civil society as a whole by encouraging the experience and the habit of public participation in the development of consequential policies.

Procedural environmental rights are essential for achieving constitutional environmental ends, including that the public be informed about decisions that affect the environment, have an opportunity to participate, and be given an opportunity to seek judicial review in the event of transgression. Procedural rights can be particularly important in environmental matters, where individual rights can be overwhelmed, collective rights underappreciated, and the rights of present and future generations undervalued. Where a state must determine complex issues of environmental and economic policy, the decision-making process necessarily involves appropriate investigations and studies to allow them to predict and evaluate in advance the effects of those activities that might damage the environment and infringe individuals' rights, and to enable them to strike a fair balance among the various conflicting interests at stake.

The importance of public access to the conclusions of such studies and to information that would enable members of the public to assess the danger to which they are exposed is beyond question. And concerned individuals must also be able to appeal to the courts against any decision, act, or omission where they consider that their interests or their comments have not been given sufficient weight in the decision-making process. By ensuring that more people can participate in more policy decisions, armed with more information and through more types of participatory encounters, judicial protection for procedural environmental rights promotes democratic values and practice. This contrasts starkly with most other forms of judicial activity, where expansion of the judicial sphere derogates from its political counterpart, often to the detriment of principles of democratic authority and accountability. Thus, whereas in most contexts, courts quite rightly exercise their authority cautiously, courts enforcing procedural rights of democratic participation need not be so restrained: the more such rights they vindicate, the richer democratic discourse becomes. And it is likely that as civil society learns to take advantage of increased opportunities to participate with meaningful information in decision making on public policy, it, too, will become more sophisticated and will develop additional tools and fora for engaging in public discourse in this way, not only on issues of environmental protection but quite likely on other issues as well.[69]

---

[69] For a study of the salutary effects of public participation in Zimbabwe, see Chirisa and Muzenda, "Environmental Rights," 104–21.

9

Emerging environmental constitutionalism

Until it can be shown that there is no probability or danger to the environment of the kind of work that is being done in a specific place, it is the duty of constitutional judges to immediately guard and to give effect to the constitutional right of nature, doing what is necessary to avoid contamination or to remedy it.

Wheeler c. Director de la Procuraduria General Del Estado de Loja

As environmental constitutionalism becomes more common, emerging concepts are seeing increasing degrees of attention. This chapter focuses on four of these emerging areas: the right of nature, sustainability, public trust, and climate change. Once again, our aim here is not to make a case *for* the necessity of constitutionalizing these areas. There is perhaps less constitutional and adjudicative evidence in these contexts than any other. As we explain, most of these provisions are either very new or quite limited in expression, and enjoy little if any scholarly or juridical examination. But emerging areas these are, warranting reporting and examination.

RIGHT OF NATURE

Environmental constitutionalism advancing the right of nature is emergent and insistent, but still uncommon. (See Appendix F.) The constitutionalization of the rights of nature is part of a growing global movement highlighting the importance of the natural environment for its own sake and as a whole, rather than as an aggregation of resources to be harnessed by humans for various purposes.[1] Moral philosophers, including Stone, have long proposed that nature

---

[1] Daly, Erin. "The Ecuadorian Exemplar: The First Ever Vindications of Constitutional Rights Of Nature." *RECIEL* 21(1) 2012. ISSN 0962 8797, available at http://celdf.live2.radicaldesigns. org/downloads/The_Ecuadorian_Exemplar_The_First_Ever_Vindications_of_Constitutional_

should have a legally protected right to self-protection.[2] The United Nations has affirmed the importance of such rights in the *Universal Declaration of the Rights of Nature*[3] The rights of nature have also been considered by constitutional and other apex courts, including by one former member of the US Supreme Court who a half-century ago promoted the idea that trees and rivers possess constitutional standing that can be vindicated by interested parties:

> That is why these environmental issues should be tendered by the inanimate object itself. Then there will be assurances that all of the forms of life which it represents will stand before the court – the pileated woodpecker as well as the coyote and bear, the lemmings as well as the trout in the streams. Those inarticulate members of the ecological group cannot speak. But those people who have so frequented the place as to know its values and wonders will be able to speak for the entire ecological community . . .[4]

Nature as a constitutional feature

Environmental constitutionalism addressing nature appears as either governmental duties or substantive rights of nature. First, the constitutions of some countries require all branches of government to protect nature. Germany's constitution, for instance, requires the government to protect "the natural bases of life and the animals within the framework of the constitutional order by legislation, and in accordance with law and justice, by executive and judicial power." Sudan's forbids the government from pursuing "any policy, or take or permit any action, which may adversely affect the existence of any species of animal or vegetative life, their natural or adopted habitat." Kuwait's requires that the government ensure the "preservation and proper exploitation" of natural resources.

Lithuania's constitution is particularly descriptive, requiring the government to "concern itself with the protection of the natural environment, its fauna and flora, separate objects of nature and particularly valuable districts,

Rights_of_Nature.pdf; The Global Alliance for the Rights of Nature, available at rightsofnature. org; the Community Environmental Legal Defense Fund, available at www.celdf.org/rights-of-nature

[2] Stone, Christopher D. *Should Trees Have Standing: Law, Morality, and the Environment*, 3rd edn. Oxford University Press, 2010.

[3] *The Universal Declaration of the Rights of Nature*, available at http://therightsofnature.org/universal-declaration

[4] *Sierra Club v. Morton*, 405 U.S. 727, 741 (Supreme Court of the United States, 1972) (Douglas, J., dissenting).

and shall supervise the moderate utilization of natural resources as well as their restoration and augmentation," and prohibits the "exhaustion of land and entrails of the earth, the pollution of waters and air, the production of radioactive impact, as well as the impoverishment of fauna and flora ..." These are unlikely to be viewed as self-executing and are in any event unlikely to be judicially enforceable.

Second, biocentric environmental constitutionalism – recognizing the *right of nature* – has been pushed most emphatically so far by a couple of countries in South America. Ecuador recently amended its constitution to recognize the right of nature, providing that: "Nature, or Pachamama, where life is reproduced and created, has the right to integral respect for her existence, her maintenance, and for the regeneration of her vital cycles, structure, functions, and evolutionary processes."[5] In a nine-paragraph chapter devoted exclusively to the rights of nature, the Ecuadorian constitution invites implementation of the provision by empowering each "person, community, people, or nationality"[6] to exercise public authority to enforce the right, according to normal constitutional processes.[7] Bolivia has a framework law recognizing the rights of nature,[8] and discussions of constitutional reforms to recognize them have taken place in Turkey.[9] Moreover, rights of nature have recently found traction at the super-subnational level, including in various municipalities in the United States.[10]

Judicial receptivity

Constitutional and other apex courts have yet to engage existing constitutional provisions respecting nature, although as of this writing two provincial and lower courts in Ecuador have shown a willingness to vindicate that country's constitutional rights of nature. In *República del Ecuador Asamblea Nacional, Comisión de la Biodivesidad y Recursos Naturales, Acta de Sesión,*[11] the

---

[5] Constitución Política de la República del Ecuador, title II, ch. 7, arts. 71–4. For an additional review of the judicial progressiveness in securing environmental rights in Ecuador, see Keefe, "Reversal of Fortune."

[6] Constitución Política de la República del Ecuador, title II, ch. 7, art. 71.   [7] *Ibid.*

[8] See Vidal, John. *Bolivia Enshrines Natural World's Rights with Equal Status for Mother Earth,* available at www.guardian.co.uk/environment/2011/apr/10/bolivia-enshrines-natural-worlds-rights

[9] See Global Alliance for the Rights of Nature. *Turkey Calling for Ecological Constitution,* available at http://therightsofnature.org/rights-of-nature-laws/turkey-ecological-constitution

[10] The Community Legal Defense Fund, available at www.celdf.org

[11] *República del Ecuador Asamblea Nacional, Comisión de la Biodiversidad y Recursos Naturales.* Acta de Sesión No. 66 (June 15, 2011), available at http://asambleanacional.gov.ec/blogs/comision6/files/2011/07/acta-66.pdf

Ecuadorian government invoked the constitutional rights of nature to stop illegal gold mining operations. The interior minister argued that the illegal mining that was polluting the Santiago, Bogotá, Ónzole, and Cayapas Rivers violated the rights of nature. The Second Court of Criminal Guarantees of Pichincha issued an injunction ordering the mining operations to cease immediately "for the protection of the rights of nature and of the people."[12] Remarkably, to enforce the prohibition, the court ordered that the "armed forces of Ecuador and the national police should collaborate to control the illegal mining [in the area], including by destroying all of the items, tools, and other utensils [used in the mining activities] that constitute a grave danger to nature and that are found in the site where there is serious harm to the environment."[13] A few days after the order, military forces dropped explosives from helicopters to destroy between 70 and 120 backhoes and other machinery left by the miners.[14]

But this decision was not without controversy: even some supporters of the enforcement of rights of nature questioned whether the judge should have subordinated the miners' property rights to the rights of nature.[15] Importantly, however, following the dramatic events in this case, the government held hearings in which representatives from the region supported the military operation due to the "the dramatic and unhealthy situation that exists because of the mining contamination."[16] Further illustrating the level of support for the rights of nature in all parts of the national government, the president of the National Assembly also testified at the hearings about the importance of "prioritizing the rights of the people to life and to health above the economic interests of the owners of the destroyed machinery."[17]

The other Ecuadorian case vindicating the rights of nature to date – *Wheeler* – is much more typical of constitutional environmental rights. The issue in *Wheeler* was whether the provincial government's construction and expansion of a highway in the mountains of southern Ecuador violated the constitutional rights of nature. Here, the provincial authorities commenced road construction without first completing an environmental impact assessment, securing planning permits for the construction, or planning for the proper disposal of rocks, sand, gravel, trees, and other excavation and construction debris. The debris was then discharged illegally along the banks of

---

[12] *Ibid.*

[13] See *Controversial Injunction for the Rights of Nature*, available at http://pachamama.org.ec

[14] *Ibid.*; *Polémica Medida Cautelar en favor de los Derechos de la Naturaleza*, available at http://mariomelo.wordpress.com/2011/06/28/polemica-medida-cautelar-en-favor-de-los-derechos-de-la-naturaleza

[15] *Ibid.*   [16] See *República del Ecuador Asamblea Nacional.*   [17] *Ibid.*

the Rio Vilcabamba, narrowing its width, quadrupling its rate of flow, and causing significant erosion and flooding in downriver areas, particularly during vernal rains. Affected landowners brought suit, invoking the constitutional rights of nature.

In a ruling unprecedented "in the history of humanity,"[18] the provincial court agreed with the affected landowners, explaining: "[W]e cannot forget that injuries to Nature are 'generational injuries' which are such that, in their magnitude have repercussions not only in the present generation but whose effects will also impact future generations."[19] In support of this strong commitment to protecting the environment, the court quoted Alberto Acosta, who had been the President of the Constituent Assembly and largely responsible for the rights of nature provisions: "The human being is a part of nature, and [we] must prohibit human beings from bringing about the extinction of other species or destroying the functioning of natural ecosystems."[20] Remarkably, the court went so far as to say that rights of nature trump other constitutional rights because in its view a "healthy" environment is more important, and more pervasive, than any other constitutional right.[21] In other words, and consistently with the illegal mining case, the court emphasized the need to protect the environment by all means necessary.

The provincial court in *Wheeler* not only gave substance to the constitutional rights of nature provision but also held that constitutionally prescribed procedural requirements were to be construed so as to ensure the full vindication of the rights of nature. In particular, the court concluded that the *acción de protección* (protective action) is the "only suitable and effective way" to address violations of the rights of nature given the "indisputable, elemental, and irremediable importance of Nature and taking into account how notorious and evident is its process of degradation."[22] The court also allowed the parties to introduce probabilistic evidence of environmental harm to support the action.[23] And consistent with the Ecuadorian Constitution's instruction that "the burden of proof on the inexistence of potential or actual damage rests with the person responsible for the activity (manager) or the defendant,"[24] the court held that the defendant bears the burden of proof of showing lack of harm in cases involving the rights of nature.[25]

Inviting other jurists to vindicate the rights of nature with a stiff spine, the court wrote that: "until it can be shown that there is no probability or danger to the environment of the kind of work that is being done in a specific place, it is

---

[18] *Ibid.*   [19] *Ibid.*   [20] *Ibid.*   [21] *Ibid.*, para. 5.   [22] *Ibid.*, para. 2.   [23] *Ibid.*, para. 3.
[24] Constitución Política de la República del Ecuador, title VII, ch. 2, sec. 1, art. 397(1).
[25] *Wheeler*, para. 4.

the duty of constitutional judges to immediately guard and to give effect to the constitutional right of nature, doing what is necessary to avoid contamination or to remedy it."[26] To date, however, no other court has followed this mandate, despite the clear language in the constitution requiring the state to "apply preventive and restrictive measures on activities that might lead to the extinction of species, the destruction of ecosystems, and the permanent alteration of natural cycles" or to fulfill its obligation in cases of "severe or permanent environmental impact, including those caused by the exploitation of non-renewable natural resources" to "establish the most effective mechanisms to achieve [their] restoration . . ." This would be particularly appropriate in Ecuador, where oil extraction in the Amazon has caused profound environmental degradation and where what would be the world's second largest metals mine is currently under development in the Condor region.

ENVIRONMENTAL SUSTAINABILITY

Environmental sustainability is an amorphous concept that stands for the proposition that present generations should use resources so as to preserve opportunities for future generations. (See Appendix E.) It reflects the Native American proverb that "we do not inherit the Earth from our ancestors: we borrow it from our children."[27] The concept of sustainability has a bearing on many environmental matters, including water and air quality, species conservation, and national environmental policy.[28]

In 1972, the Stockholm Declaration on the Human Environment was the first international instrument to recognize a principle of sustainability.[29] Fifteen years later, the World Commission on Environment and Development released its pioneering study, *Our Common Future*,[30] which defines "sustainable development" as "development . . . that . . . meets the needs of the present without compromising the ability of future generations to meet their own needs."[31] In 1992, the Earth Summit's Rio Declaration then stated that

---

[26] *Ibid.*, para. 3.
[27] This proverb, along with some close variants, is attributed to several sources, including Chief Seattle, Antoine de St. Exupery, Jane Goodall, Ralph Waldo Emerson and David Bower, among others. See Giga Quotes *Earth*, available at www.giga-usa.com/quotes/topics/earth_t001.htm
[28] May, James R. "Of Development, daVinci and Domestic Legislation: The Prospects for Sustainable Development in Asia and its Untapped Potential in the United States." *Widener Law Symposium Journal* 3 (1998): 197.
[29] "Stockholm." 11 ILM 1416. 1972.
[30] World Commission on Environment and Development. *Our Common Future*. New York: Oxford University Press, 1987.
[31] *Ibid.*, para. 8.

sustainable development must "respect the interests of all and protect the integrity of the global environmental and developmental system."[32] The Rio Declaration's blueprint document, Agenda 21, provides that sustainable development must concurrently raise living standards while preserving the environment: "integration of environment and development concerns ... will lead to the fulfillment of basic needs, improved living standards for all, better protected and managed ecosystems and a safer, more prosperous future."[33]

Recognition of the importance of sustainability has grown exponentially since the Earth Summit.[34] Since then, the concept of sustainability has been regularly acknowledged by international accords,[35] by the laws and regulations of nations,[36] in local building codes,[37] and in corporate mission statements and practices worldwide,[38] as well as by some courts,[39] although not in the United States, as examined later.[40] Importantly, sustainability has also found

---

[32] "Rio Declaration on Environment and Development." 31 *ILM* 874. 1992.

[33] UN Conference on Environment and Development, Annex II. "Agenda 21: A Programme for Action for Sustainable Development." UN Doc.A./Conf. 151/26. August 12, 1992 ("Agenda 21").

[34] Dernbach, John C. *Agenda for a Sustainable America*. Washington, DC: ELI Press, Environmental Law Institute, 2009: 2–3.

[35] See, e.g., R.K.L. Panjabi. *The Earth Summit at Rio: Politics, Economics, and the Environment.* New England: Northeastern University Press, 1997: 17 (describing how the Earth Summit in Rio led to a new global consciousness of sustainability in treaty making).

[36] See, e.g., Nelson, Antria. "Steering Sustainability: What, When, and Why," in *Steering Sustainability in an Urbanizing World: Policy, Practice and Performance*, by A. Nelson (ed.), 1, 2–3. Farnham: Ashgate, 2007 (explaining the national policy and reform considerations behind urban sustainability); May, James R. "The North American Symposium on the Judiciary and Environmental Law: Constituting Fundamental Environmental Rights Worldwide." *Pace Environmental Law Review* 23 (2005/2006): 113, Appendix B (listing countries that have constitutionally entrenched environmental policies as governing principles, some including sustainability).

[37] See, e.g., MacLaren, V., A. Morris and S. Labatt. "Engaging Local Communities in Environmental Protection with Competitiveness: Community Advisory Panels in Canada and the United States." In *Sustainability, Civil Society and International Governance*, by J.J. Kirton and Peter Hajnal, 31, 36. Farnham: Ashgate, 2006 (examining examples of community advisory panels in the United States and Canada and how they affect sustainability in the communities).

[38] See, e.g., Biagiotti, Isabelle. "Emerging Corporate Actors in Environment and Trade Governance: New Vision and Challenge for Norm-setting Processes." In *Participation for Sustainability in Trade*, by S. Thoyer and B. Martimort-Asso (eds.), 121, 122. Aldershot: Ashgate, 2007 (describing how global corporations are focusing more on environmental sustainability).

[39] Higgins, Rosalyn. "Natural Resources in the Case Law of the International Court." In *International Law and Sustainable Development: Past Achievements and Future Challenges*, by Alan Boyle and David Freestone (eds.), 87, 111. Oxford: Oxford University Press, 1999 (using the International Court of Justice to highlight environmental sustainability in international courts and other arenas).

[40] May, James R. "Not at All: Environmental Sustainability in the Supreme Court." *Sustainable Development Law and Policy* 10 (2009): 20.

footing in a growing number of national constitutions, either by advancing "sustainable development," "future generations," or some variation of these themes. And of course, Rio+20 in 2012 once again underscored the import of sustainability in context.[41]

"Sustainable development"

Nearly twenty countries expressly recognize a constitutional goal of "sustainability" or "sustainable development," though most of these are in sections of the constitutions or written in language that indicates that they are not amenable to judicial enforcement (see Appendix E). For example, Albania's constitution proclaims that the state "aims to supplement private initiative and responsibility with: Rational exploitation of forests, waters, pastures and other natural resources on the basis of the principle of sustainable development." Belgium's constitution bespeaks a commitment to "pursue the objectives of sustainable development in its social, economic and environmental aspects." Bolivia's constitution states that "the Natural assets are of public importance and of strategic character for the sustainable development of the country." Colombia's constitution requires policy makers to "plan the handling and use of natural resources in order to guarantee their sustainable development . . ." Montenegro's Preamble outlines its "conviction that the state is responsible for the preservation of nature, sound environment, sustainable development, [and] balanced development of all its region." Nepal's constitution provides that "provision shall be made for the protection of the forest, vegetation and biodiversity, its sustainable use and for equitable distribution of the benefit derived from it." The constitution of Seychelles provides that the state will "ensure a sustainable socio-economic development of Seychelles by a judicious use and management of the resources of Seychelles." Somalia's constitution provides that "[l]and shall be held, used and managed in an equitable, efficient, productive, and sustainable manner." Switzerland's constitution contains a specific section entitled "Sustainable Development," which provides that "[t]he Confederation and the Cantons shall endeavor to achieve a balanced and sustainable relationship between nature and its capacity to renew itself and the demands placed on it by the population." The Ugandan constitution states that "Parliament shall, by law, provide for measures intended – to manage the environment for sustainable development." The constitutions of Greece, Mozambique, Poland, Serbia, and Thailand also

---

[41] UN Conference on Sustainable Development, 2012.

expressly require that environmental policy be developed in accordance with "sustainable development."

"Future generations"

Sustainability recognizes responsibilities owed to those who follow. The constitutions from about a dozen countries give at least a passing nod to "future generations." For example, Andorra's constitution directs policy makers to protect natural resources "for the sake of future generations." Argentina's constitution directs the state to manage resources for "a healthy, balanced environment which is fit for human development and by which productive activities satisfy current necessities without compromising those of future generations ..." Armenia's constitution requires that the state "pursue the environmental security policy for present and future generations." Brazil's declares that "[t]he Government and the community have a duty to defend and to preserve the environment for present and future generations." Ethiopia's constitution provides that its natural resources are "a sacred trust for the benefit of present and succeeding generations." Papua New Guinea's constitution requires the state to hold environmental resources "in trust for future generations" and "for the benefit of future generations." The constitutions of both Niger and Vanuatu provide for protection of the environment in the "interests of future generations." Germany's constitution expresses "its responsibility toward future generations." Norway's constitution directs that natural resources be "safeguarded for future generations." The constitution of Iran provides for the "preservation of the environment, in which the present as well as the future generations have a right to flourishing social existence." Lesotho's lists a duty of the state to protect the environment "for the benefit of both present and future generations."

"Sustainable development" and "Future generations"

The strongest embodiment of environmental sustainability would seem to stem from those constitutions that promote sustainable development *for the purpose of* protecting the interests of future generations. The constitutions from about a dozen and a half countries contain this sort of hybrid pronouncement. For example, Albania's constitution bespeaks a "healthy and ecologically adequate environment for the present and future generations." Mozambique's requires the state, "[w]ith a view to guaranteeing the right to the environment within the framework of sustainable development ... shall adopt policies aimed at ... guaranteeing the rational utilisation of natural resources and the safeguarding of their capacity to regenerate, ecological stability and the rights of future generations." France's amended constitution proclaims that "[c]are must be taken to safeguard the environment along with other fundamental interests of the Nation . . . In order to ensure sustainable development, choices designed to meet the needs of the present generation should not jeopardise the ability of future generations and other peoples to meet their own needs . . ." Eritrea's provides for state management of natural resources in a "sustainable manner" for "present and future generations." The constitutions of Namibia and Swaziland provide for the protection of the environment and natural resources "on a sustainable basis" for the benefit of "present and future" citizens and generations. Qatar's provides for protection of the environment "so as to achieve sustainable development for the generations to come." The constitution of South Sudan provides that "[e]very person shall have the right to have the environment protected for the benefit of present and future generations, through appropriate legislative action and other measures that . . . secure ecologically sustainable development and use of natural resources . . ." Uganda's provides that "[t]he State shall promote sustainable development and public awareness of the need to manage land, air and water resources in a balanced and sustainable manner for the present and future generations." In addition, the constitutions of Angola, Bhutan, East Timor, Georgia, Guyana, Malawi, Maldives, Sweden, and Zambia provide for the "sustainable development" of environmental resources in the interests of "future generations."

The constitutions of some countries require that specific resources be developed with future generations in mind. For example, the Dominican Republic provides that "nonrenewable natural resources, can only be explored and exploited by individuals, under sustainable environmental criteria . . ." and provides for the protection of the environment "for the benefit of the present and future generations." The Dominican Republic is the only country on the planet with a constitution to address sustainability, future generations, and climate change.

The incorporation of sustainability into domestic constitutions has great potential to advance both sustainability and constitutionalism. Laxman and Ansari, for example, have examined the relationship among sustainable management, the utilization of the environment, and the constitutional safeguards of environmental rights. They note how constitutional provisions help bridge the gap left by international and domestic laws, even given the array of sustainability provisions already in existence.[42] Even though the vast majority

---

[42] Lekha Laxman and Abdul Haseeb Ansari. "The Interface between TRIPS and CBD: Efforts towards Harmonization." *Journal of International Trade Law and Policy* 11 (2012): 108–132.

of these provisions create no judicially enforceable rights, they nonetheless affirm national values of environmental sustainability to which courts and others may advert.

Constitutionalizing sustainability may contribute to the work that the concept can perform. The principal attraction of "sustainability" is its wide applicability. It can mean so many different things in so many different contexts. But when used appropriately, Dernbach maintains that it can advance passing along an environment that is as suitable for existence as what was inherited; a promise to future generations of opportunity, wealth, satisfaction, or peace; optimal sustained yields of agriculture, animals, or resources; continued employment or employability; and economic development.[43] But because it contains no limiting principle or metrics, its potential application across and even within judicial cultures may be varied and inconsistent.

Judicial receptivity

The elasticity of the concept of sustainability can frustrate implementation and enforcement.

There is very little jurisprudence applying constitutionally embedded provisions regarding sustainability and related provisions. In fact, there is very little jurisprudence explicitly engaging sustainability at all, even where one might expect to find it. For example, while South Africa's constitution embraced sustainable development in 1996, the provision has had little practical effect. Section 24 of its constitution provides that everyone has the right "[t]o have the environment protected, for the benefit of present and future generations, through reasonable legislative and other measures that ... [s]ecure ecologically-sustainable development and use of natural resources while promoting justifiable economic and social development."

Yet, these novel provisions hardly seem to register in everyday decision making in environmental matters. Two decades after the end of apartheid, the provision's constitutional or normative status is unclear. Social striation, economic disparity, and despoliation of natural resources in South Africa accentuate the difficulty of breathing life into the concept of sustainable development. As Kotzé reports, the constitutional court has not engaged the provision so as to define what it means, who can enforce it, to whom it applies, what remedies might redress infractions, or what role sustainable development

---

[43] Dernbach, John. *Stumbling Toward Sustainability*. Washington, DC: Environmental Law Institute, 2002.

could play in the broader environmental constitutionalism paradigm.[44] The passing of President Mandela will serve to place additional strain on the implementation of cultural, social, and economic rights, including environmental constitutionalism, in South Africa.

And while Section 225 of the Brazilian constitution requires that governmental policies promote ecologically sustainable development, apex courts there rarely enforce this provision.[45]

Another leading (by way of lagging) example is the US Supreme Court. More than four decades removed from Stockholm, neither the Supreme Court of the United States nor any Justice on it has yet to recognize or even acknowledge the concept of sustainability.[46] Since Stockholm, the court has decided more than 4,000 cases, including more than 300 involving environmental matters.[47] Yet the word "sustainability" appears not at all before the court in any majority, concurring or dissenting opinion.[48]

Sustainability stands very little chance of being taken seriously by the current US Supreme Court. It is a guiding principle, not a constitutionally enshrined doctrine, and it is not readily shaped into a traditional legal case or controversy. No US law requires or even recognizes sustainability. And, the United States has not ratified an international treaty that does so either. Moreover, no member of the court studied environmental law. None of them has much if any practical experience with environmental law in general, and sustainability in particular. Few Supreme Court justices have held elected political office, and few have regulatory experience that would sensitize them

---

[44] See Kotzé, "Arguing Global Environmental Constitutionalism," 199–233; Louis J. Kotzé, "Sustainable Development and the Rule of Law for Nature: A Constitutional Reading." In *Rule of Law for Nature: New Dimensions and Ideas in Environmental Law*, by C. Voigt (ed.) 130–45. Cambridge University Press, 2013.

[45] E.g., *Associação Nacional do Transporte de Cargas e Logística* v. *Governador do Estado de São Paulo*, S.T.F., ADPF 234 MC/DF, DJe 06.02.12 (Rel. Min. Marco Aurélio) (Brazil) (case brought by asbestos transporters against a state law on constitutional grounds).

[46] See generally, May, James R. "U.S. Supreme Court Environmental Cases 2008–2009: A Year Like No Other." *Environment Reporter* 40 (BNA), No. 36 (September 11, 2009): 2154; May, James R. "U.S. Supreme Court Decisions: Review for 2006–2007 and Outlook." *Environment Reporter* 38 (BNA), No. 34 (August 24, 2007): 1851.

[47] See Lazarus, Richard J. "Restoring What's Environmental about Environmental Law in the Supreme Court." 47 *UCLA Law Review* (2000): 703, 708 (estimating the Court decided more that 240 environmental law cases between 1969 and 2000); see also, May, James R. "The Intersection of Constitutional Law and Environmental Litigation." In *Environmental Litigation: Law and Strategy*, by Cary R. Perlman (ed.), 359. ABA, 2009 (number approaching 300); James R. May and Robert L. Glicksman, "Justice Rehnquist and the Dismantling of Environmental Law," *Environmental Law Reporter* 36 (2006): 10585 (number approaching 300).

[48] May, "Not at All."

to environmental concerns and the complexities and challenges of sustainability. Indeed, most of the current court's legal experience has been predominantly on the business or "development" side of the sustainable development equation. Surprisingly, sustainability – even as a governing principle – has not managed to capture the imagination of litigants, who seldom if ever invoke "sustainability" in pleadings, briefs, and oral arguments.[49]

The experience in the United States is typical: lacking constitutional recognition, sustainability has not yet triggered juridical engagement.

PUBLIC TRUST

Another emerging area of environmental constitutionalism envelops the public trust doctrine. Related to the modern notion of sustainability, this derives from the ancient notion that the sovereign holds certain natural resources and objects of nature in trust for the benefit of current and future generations. The doctrine is "rooted in the precept that some resources are so central to the well-being of the community that they must be protected by distinctive, judge-made principles."[50]

The principle of public ownership underlying the public trust doctrine can be traced from Roman Law through the Magna Carta to present-day constitutionalism and jurisprudence. The Romans codified the right of public ownership of important natural resources: "The things which are naturally everybody's are: air, flowing water, the sea, and the sea-shore."[51] English common law continued the public trust tradition: "There are some few things which, notwithstanding the general introduction and continuance of property, must still unavoidably remain in common ... Such (among others) are the elements of light, air, and water."[52]

Environmental constitutionalism often reflects public trust notions. The constitutions of about six countries reference holding or protecting resources for the "public trust" or some variation of that terminology. These tend to impose a trust responsibility upon policy makers, rulers, or citizens to hold

---

[49] Based on a search of cases, briefs and transcripts of the search terms "sustainability," "sustainable development," "ecologically sustainable development," on Westlaw (last searched March 27, 2013), and on the U.S. Supreme Court database, www.supremecourtus.gov

[50] Wilkinson, Charles F. "The Public Trust Doctrine in Public Land Law." *U.C. Davis Law Review* 14 (1980): 269, 315.

[51] Caesar Flavius Justinian, *The Institutes of Justinian*, Book II, Title I, Of the Different Kind of Things (533).

[52] Blackstone, William. *Commentaries on the Laws of England.* Vols. 2, 4. The Lawbook Exchange, 1766.

resources in trust for current or future generations. Some specify trust responsibilities as a general governing norm. For example, the Ugandan constitution provides that "the Government or a local government as determined by Parliament by law, shall hold in trust for the people and protect, natural lakes, rivers, wetlands, forest reserves, game reserves, national parks and any land to be reserved for ecological and touristic purposes for the common good of all citizens." And the constitution of Ethiopia provides that "[t]he natural resources in the waters, forests, land, air lakes, rivers, and ports of the Empire are a sacred trust for the benefit of present and succeeding generations of the Ethiopian people." The constitution of Papua New Guinea calls for "wise use to be made of our natural resources and the environment in and on the land or seabed, in the sea, under the land, and in the air, in the interests of our development and in trust for future generations." Many of the constitutional provisions that protect water, including those that assert sovereign jurisdictional control, as discussed in Chapter 6, also embody the public trust doctrine.

Reflecting traditional views of sovereignty, some constitutions invest public trust in a supreme leader. The Constitution of Swaziland, for example, provides that "all land (including any existing concessions) in Swaziland, save privately held title-deed land, shall continue to vest in iNgwenyama in trust for the Swazi Nation" and "all minerals and mineral oils in, under or upon any land in Swaziland shall, after the commencement of the Constitution, continue to vest in iNgwenyama in trust for the Swazi Nation." (iNgwenyama is the title of the male ruler or king of Swaziland.) And Ghana's constitution provides that "[a]ll public lands in Ghana shall be vested in the President on behalf of, and in trust for, the people of Ghana," and "every mineral in its natural state in, under or upon any land in Ghana, rivers, streams, water courses throughout Ghana, the exclusive economic zone and any area covered by the territorial sea or continental shelf is the property of the Republic of Ghana and shall be vested in the President on behalf of, and in trust for the people of Ghana."

Some constitutional provisions hold citizens accountable to hold resources in trust for future generations. For example, Tanzania's constitution provides "that all citizens together possess all the natural resources of the country in trust for their descendants." The Bhutanese constitution provides that "[e]very Bhutanese is a trustee of the Kingdom's natural resources and environment for the benefit of the present and future generations and it is the fundamental duty of every citizen to contribute to the protection of the natural environment."

Whether and the extent to which courts engage federal constitutional environmental public trust provisions remains to be seen, although, as we have seen, several courts, including especially those on the Indian sub-continent, have constitutionalized the public trust doctrine despite the absence of any textual basis.[53] In fact, because these textual provisions are largely unenforceable, it seems more likely that a court would import the public trust doctrine from the common law or even from widely accepted principles of international law than enforce one of these provisions in a case for injunctive relief or damages.

CLIMATE CHANGE

Climate change is perhaps the most complex and important environmental challenge of our day. It is at least somewhat attributable to anthropogenic greenhouse gas (GHG) emissions from the use and combustion of fossil fuels.[54] Extracted from underground sources derived from the decomposition of plants and animals that lived and died millions of years ago, fossil fuels (e.g., petroleum, natural gas) have become an indispensable component of life in the modern world. Burning fossil fuels in turn produces copious amounts of GHGs, contributing to global climate change.[55]

The evidence of climate change is exhibited by ice sheet disintegration; regional climate disruptions;[56] changes in precipitation patterns; increasing storm intensity in the Americas, southern Africa, the Mediterranean and southern Asia;[57] warming polar regions;[58] significant species loss due to isotherm displacement that is outpacing adaptation and migration;[59] and more extreme weather events including droughts, floods, and fires.[60] As the United States Supreme Court recently observed, "[t]he harms associated with climate change are serious and well recognized,"[61] potentially including "a

---

[53] See, e.g., *M.C. Mehta v. Kamal Nath and Others* (Supreme Court of India, 1977).

[54] A comprehensive discussion of the evidence surrounding anthropogenic-induced climate change is beyond the scope of this book. For this, the reader is referred to Chapter 1 of the Stern Review from the British government. See generally, Sir Nicholas Stern, *Stern Review on the Economics of Climate Change* (2006), available at http://webarchive.nationalarchives.gov.uk/+/http:/www.hm-treasury.gov.uk/sternreview_index.htm

[55] For contemporaneous impacts, see generally, RealClimate: Climate science from climate scientists (www.realclimate.org).

[56] *Green Mountain Chrysler Plymouth Dodge Jeep v. Crombie*, 508 F. Supp. 2d 295, 340 (D. Vt., 2007) (court decision discussing these effects).

[57] See Gateway to the United Nation's Systems on Climate Change (www.un.org/climatechange/background/ataglance.shtml). This harm also translates into economic costs.

[58] *Ibid.*   [59] *Green Mountain Chrysler Plymouth Dodge Jeep v. Crombie*. (D. Vt., 2007) 340–1.

[60] See, e.g., *ibid.*, 341. Hansen affirmed, *Green Mountain Chrysler Plymouth Dodge Jeep v. Crombie*. Nos. 2:05-CV-302, 2:05-CV-304, 2006 WL 4761053, para. 65 (D. Vt., August 14, 2006).

[61] *Massachusetts v. EPA*, 549 U.S. 497 (2007).

precipitate rise in sea levels by the end of the century, "irreversible changes to natural ecosystems," a "significant reduction in water storage in winter snowpack in mountainous regions," and "an increase in the spread of disease."[62] Coastal states in the United States, for example, have reported rising sea levels, flooding, snowfall reductions, and coastal erosion.[63] And the situation is worsening. GHG emissions are expected to increase at about 2 percent per annum, resulting in a global increase of at least two to three degrees Celsius by 2100,[64] burdening generations to come.[65]

The lack of international response coupled with tepid local action invites consideration of the role of environmental constitutionalism, if any, in addressing climate change. International initiatives have not managed to take hold for the most part, while domestic responses have been uneven, inconsistent, and unreliable. A quarter of a century ago, James Hansen and others alerted the planet about the impending perils of climate change. By 1992, most of the planet joined the UN Framework Convention on Global Climate Change (UNFCC). By 1997, a majority of the world's major GHG emitters signed the Kyoto Protocol on Global Climate Change, agreeing to reduce emissions before the onset of the new century. Many countries, however, neglected to ratify the Protocol, and GHG reductions never happened, except in desultory and piecemeal fashions.[66] Since then, the international community has said much and done relatively little to reduce GHG emissions or address climate change.

Domestic responses to climate change have not fared much better. Just by way of example, political and policy responses to climate change in the United

---

[62] *Ibid.*, 521 (quoting declaration of Michael MacCracken, former Executive Director, U.S. Global Change Research Program).

[63] See, e.g., Franco, Guido. "California Energy Commission, Climate Change Impacts and Adaptation in California." *Integrated Energy Policy Report* 7 (2005), available at www.ccap.org/docs/resources/427/Climate_Change_Impacts_and_Adaptation_in_California.pdf; Washington State, Department of Ecology, "Climate Change: Disrupting our Economy, Environment and Communities," available at www.ecy.wa.gov/climatechange/effects.htm

[64] *Green Mountain Chrysler Plymouth Dodge Jeep v. Crombie* (D. Vt., 2007); see also *Central Valley Chrysler-Jeep, Inc. v. Witherspoon*, 2007 WL 135688 (E.D. Cal., 2007); *Central Valley Chrysler-Jeep v. Witherspoon*, 456 F. Supp. 2d 1160 (E.D. Cal., 2006) (companion case challenging California standards); *Lincoln Dodge, Inc. v. Sullivan*, 558 F. Supp. 2d 224 (D. R.I., 2008) (same for Rhode Island).

[65] Glicksman, Robert L. "Global Climate Change and the Risks to Coastal Areas from Hurricanes and Rising Sea Levels: The Costs of Doing Nothing." *Loyola Law Review* 52 (2006): 1127, 1179.

[66] Abate, Randall S. "Kyoto or Not, Here We Come: The Promise and Perils of the Piecemeal Approach to Climate Change Regulation in the United States." *Cornell Journal of Law and Public Policy* 15 (2006): 369, 372.

States have lacked coordination and cohesion. While most federal representatives lend their name to pending climate legislation, as of this writing Congress has yet to enact any of it, and climate change legislation hardly seems on the horizon. With Australia's late ratification of the Kyoto Protocol in 2007, the United States has the dubious distinction of being the only major industrialized country in the world that has not done so.[67] Moreover, the US Congress has not allocated or appropriated funds to pay for the direct effects of climate change, including loss of shoreline, property damage, crop diminution, and personal health and welfare injuries. While the US administration has taken strides to reduce emissions, domestic responses have overall been sporadic and made little dent in national emissions. Other political and social responses have yet to stem and reverse emissions and are unlikely to do so anytime soon, even if binding and enforceable international accords are placed into effect.[68] Realized reductions are largely due to recessionary economics, not policy. While hardly a model, domestic responses in the United States are fairly representative of those exhibited by much of the industrialized and developing world. Nonetheless, Europe is developing a climate change model, though based more on its structure of regional governance than on environmental constitutionalism.[69]

Shortcomings in international and domestic responses to climate change create opportunities for tactical deployment of environmental constitutionalism. Thus far, however, very few countries have seen fit to address climate change constitutionally. Only the Dominican Republic's constitution is explicit on the point, with a provision under "The Organization of the Territory" that provides for a "plan of territorial ordering that assures the efficient and sustainable use of the natural resources of the Nation, in accordance with the need of adaptation to climate change ..."[70] Other nations, like Scotland, are also considering referencing climate change in their constitutions. Without effective international treaty and domestic legislative responses to climate

[67] *Ibid.*, 370–2.

[68] See Brown, Donald A. "The U.S. Performance in Achieving its 1992 Earth Summit Global Warming Commitments." *Environmental Law Reporter* 32 (2002): 10,741 ("the world's political and economic system cannot respond rapidly enough to make faster changes in some major polluting sources such as gasoline-powered automobiles or coalfired power plants.").

[69] See, e.g., the European Climate Change Programme, available at http://ec.europa.eu/clima/policies/eccp/index_en.htm: "At European level a comprehensive package of policy measures to reduce greenhouse gas emissions has been initiated through the European Climate Change Programme (ECCP). Each of the EU member states has also put in place its own domestic actions that build on the ECCP measures or complement them."

[70] See Appendix F (Miscellaneous constitutional environmental provisions).

change, one might expect to see more countries elect to entrench express constitutional measures.

Some advocate for constitutional primacy over resources affecting climate change, including forests. For example, in a comparative constitutional analysis of Australia, Brazil, Canada, India, Russia, and the United States, which collectively "account for 54 percent of the world's total forest cover,"[71] Blake Hudson concludes that:

> federal systems maintaining three key elements within their constitutional structure are most capable of agreeing to an international climate agreement that incorporates forests in a consequential manner – elements that facilitate successful implementation of a treaty on domestic scales while maintaining the recognized benefits of decentralized forest management at the local level: (1) national constitutional primacy over forest management, (2) national sharing of constitutional forest management authority, and (3) adequate forest policy institutional enforcement capacity.[72]

The causes and consequences of climate change make it a rough fit for domestic constitutional response. Climate change is, of course, a global issue requiring concerted and coordinated global efforts adjunct to mitigation, adaptation, and compensation. Its effects, however, are absorbed locally by nations in response to sea level rise, loss of shoreline, drought, severe weather, and other consequences often attributed to climate change. These local effects are where environmental constitutionalism might play an important if limited role. Constitutions can, for one, direct governments to enact and implement policies to address the effects of climate change in ways not accomplished through existing international and national laws. And once absorbed into constitutional texts, courts can impel action by enforcing these provisions even through progressive realization.

With growing frequency, nations are amending their constitutions not only to protect the environment generally, but to protect in certain kinds of ways (rights of nature and public trust doctrine) and for certain particular purposes (to promote sustainable development and protect against the effects of climate change). It will still take more time for courts in these countries to take these constitutional mandates seriously.

[71] Hudson, Blake. "Federal Constitutions, Global Governance, and the Role of Forests in Regulating Climate Change." *Indiana Law Journal* 87 (2012): 1455–515.
[72] *Ibid.*

10

Conclusion

[R]ather than viewing environmental constitutionalism as a vague or hortatory extension of individual rights into the realm of affirmative entitlements, it instead can be seen to rest comfortably beside more firmly established structural and representative aspects of constitutionalism.

Douglas Kysar[1]

Human suffering attributable to environmental degradation spans the world, from global challenges wrought by climate change, to local issues associated with pollution or access to arable soils and potable water, to every environmental problem in between and intertwined. These problems, of course, have palpable consequences for the planet's inhabitants. Rather than make the case *for* constitutionalizing environmental rights, this book deploys a comparative constitutional framework to examine the role that environmental constitutionalism plays in advancing the human condition. It concludes that environmental constitutionalism can help to ameliorate environmental challenges in meaningful if intersticial ways.

It is a complicated assessment. Environmental constitutionalism is not a silver bullet for all environmental ailments. It does not and cannot do all of the work that is accomplished by existing international, regional and domestic human rights and environmental protection-based domestic laws, principles, customs and regimes, not to mention other legal paradigms, including common and traditional law. That said, environmental constitutionalism is playing an ever more prominent complementary and supplementary role in addressing the sorts of environmental problems felt most acutely by those often

---

[1] Kysar, Douglas A. "Global Environmental Constitutionalism: Getting There from Here." *Transnational Environmental Law* 1 (2012): 83, 87.

ignored or underserved by existing legal structures. And it holds the potential for much more.

Extant international and domestic laws and legal structures do not, in and of themselves, ensure either environmental human rights or environmental protection. International treaties, principles and custom do little to advance environmental rights at the local and subsidiary levels. There is no global environmental rights treaty. Moreover, multilateral and bi-lateral treaties that address environmental concerns are often of limited if any utility to individuals. And while domestic statutory and regulatory law affording environmental protection and resource conservation are quite advanced in many nations, these laws seldom aim to advance environmental rights. In addition, while international human rights regimes most nearly approach the notion that individuals have a fundamental right to a quality environment, they are also often out of reach to individuals who would stand to gain from the recognition of environmental rights at the constitutional level. Environmental constitutionalism can help to bridge the gaps left by these other legal regimes.

Environmental constitutionalism is a global phenomenon. The list of countries to have embraced environmental constitutionalism spans the globe geographically, including countries in Africa, the Middle East, Western Europe, the former Soviet bloc, Latin America, and Oceania. The list is also diverse politically, including jurisdictions steeped in civil, common law, Islamic, Native American, and other traditions. It is also wildly unpredictable. Countries with cultures and histories as diverse as those found in Kenya, Thailand, and Bolivia are among the most generous in according environmental rights.

It is also a recent phenomenon that belies prediction. Over the last four decades nearly three-quarters of the world's countries have adopted constitutional provisions that address environmental matters in some way. Such environmental constitutionalism is variable, manifesting into substantive rights, procedural rights, directive policies, reciprocal duties, or combinations of these and other attributes. For example, at least 75 countries have substantive constitutional provisions that expressly recognise a right to a quality environment. Some substantive provisions are very specific, such as providing a right to potable water. Some are more ephemeral, recognizing trust responsibilities over natural resources or toward future generations, or addressing related subjects like sustainability or climate change. Some have cutting-edge provisions advancing the rights of nature, or sustainability. Some recognize environmental stewardship as a matter of national policy. Some impart a corresponding duty on individuals to protect the environment. Some environmental rights are inferred from other civil or socioeconomic constitutional rights, such as a right to life or health. Constitutions in some countries do all of these things, while others do none of them. Most fall somewhere in between. The variety of provisions, aiming to protect different aspects of the environment with a range of scaffolding and enforcement mechanisms, attests to the growth of environmental constitutionalism throughout the world in number and relevance.

There is also an uptick in provisions that are designed to afford special process rights in environmental matters. Environmental procedural rights normally involve requirements for environmental assessment, access to information, or rights to petition or participate. Such rights help to keep countervailing substantive rights vital. A constitutional guarantee to a beneficial environment is more likely to take root when stakeholders have the right to receive free and timely information, participate in deliberations, and judicially challenge environmental decision making. Procedural environmental constitutionalism is also important in its own right, and can be as or more efficacious than substantive environmental rights because courts are more likely to impart additional process than to impose substantive remedies.

Environmental constitutionalism is growing at the subnational level too, filling gaps in federal systems. Led by states in the Americas in general, and Brazil in particular, subnational governments around the globe have seen fit to constitutionalize substantive and procedural environmental rights, environmental duties, and sustainable development for present and future generations, often with much more specificity and enforceability than provided in national constitutions. Subnational instantiation of constitutional environmental rights can also hold special salience in countries that have yet to recognize environmental rights at the federal level. While underdeveloped, subnational environmental constitutionalism holds enormous potential for achieving the dual goals of advancing human rights and environmental protection at a subsidiary level.

It is one thing to delineate the myriad constitutional provisions that embody environmental rights. It is quite another to discern the work that these provisions accomplish, particularly at the juridical level. National apex and constitutional courts have given real moment to many of these provisions. Some have been willing to find environmental rights implicitly included within the bounds of more traditional civil rights, such as a right to life. Some of the decisions in these cases are breathtaking in breadth and depth.

While courts sometimes provide trenchant encomiums to environmental constitutionalism, many environmental rights provisions are undervalued, underutilized, or virtually ignored. Adjudicating these provisions can be preternaturally complex and ridden with obstacles. The reasons are multifaceted.

These begin with the language of the operative phrase, which invariably triggers orbiting issues of what is protected, who can protect it, what constitutes an offense, and who is responsible for making things better. Most provisions require significant elucidation, the most momentous of which is providing a principled definition of "environment." Indeed, "environment" can be virtually limitless, affecting human lives, dignity, health, housing, access to food and water, and livelihood, and so on. But it can also be biocentric, encompassing flora, fauna, and so on. Yet the term "environment" is rarely if ever explained, so that it is not clear whether it includes air, water, soil, or any combination of these.

The adjectival examination is as daunting. While there may be daylight between an environment that is "beneficial," or "adequate," or "healthful," or "quality," courts are loathe to describe it. Nor is the scope of the right delimited or defined. Consequently it is often up to the courts to determine what it means for the environment to achieve these ends and by whose perspective and how those qualities should be measured.

Identifying appropriate constitutional parties is another challenge. In some countries, the guarantee is for the benefit of people's health or their prosperity, while in others, the right extends to nature itself. Courts have also held private parties accountable for violations of constitutionally embedded environmental rights provisions. The question of identifying proper defendants may turn on the proper definition of the right but it is further complicated because it implicates questions of sovereignty, immunity, extra-territoriality, and the horizontal application of constitutional rights. Most significant environmental claims arise out of a mixture of public and private wrong-doing so that it is often difficult to identify the responsible party. While such issues arise in most forms of constitutional litigation, they are magnified in cases involving environmental constitutionalism. Environmental claims are conceptually distant from the traditional form of constitutional litigation, which is typically specific to a discrete set of facts that indicate injury to a particular claimant and can be supported by clear evidence. Environmental rights, by contrast, are both specific and generalized, with ephemeral contours that impede interpretation, implementation, and enforcement.

Identifying the appropriate constitutional remedy can be problematic, too. In most constitutional litigation, the question of remedies is relatively straight-forward. Even in some environmental cases, where the defendant's action caused the plaintiff's injury, courts have ordered the defendant to cease or to pay damages sufficient to cover the costs of medical care or the loss of employment income, for instance. While this requires careful assessment of damages, experts are usually available to quantify the harm, and the remedy is routinely enforced: if the defendant does not cease its activities or refuses to pay, it can be held in contempt of court. But even these apparently simple orders can be problematic in environmental rights cases, often tempting courts to fashion more elaborate remedial orders. In some environmental cases, fashioning a remedy can be even more complex than ascertaining liability. Environmental cases almost invariably present difficult and far-reaching policy choices that are challenging to judicial resolution. And, when government changes its policy to enhance the environment, it is private individuals who bear the burden even if they indirectly benefit from improved environmental quality.

Moreover, environmental cases are among constitutional law's most complicated to remedy because the injuries, as we have seen, can be multifaceted with many interdependent and often moving parts, and with both short- and long-term consequences for the environment and for the humans who live, or will live, in it. And most courts are keenly aware of the limitations of their own power – of the fact, namely, that courts generally have no particular resource other than their own legitimacy to ensure respect for or compliance with judicial orders. Eloquent exposition alone cannot change a societal structure that does not recognize the rule of law, for example, or that values development and economic progress at least as much as environmental protection. Thus, environmental constitutionalism, with its many commendations, still has vast unrealized potential.

In addition, once plaintiffs have effectively invoked judicial authority, the burdens of enforcement can be enormous. Litigating claims borne in environmental constitutionalism requires a continued commitment not only on the court's part but also on the part of the plaintiffs who originally brought the suit or their successors. And this is problematic as well: continued vigilance on the part of plaintiffs privatizes the burden for securing what is clearly a public good, and it requires the plaintiffs to ensure, on an ongoing basis, that the government takes responsibility for the environmental violation and that the government complies with the rule of law as mandated by the judicial branch. Enforcing even favorable judgments thus requires significant resources on the part of the original litigants and their lawyers.

The breadth of these provisions, which is typical for environmental rights generally, leaves wide berth for judicial abstention, indecision, and discretion. The complexities are not simply matters of definition. Rather, they inhere in the nature of environmental rights, especially at the constitutional level. Vindicating environmental rights presents even more fundamental questions of policy choices. In some ways, environmental rights are similar to other social and economic rights that are routinely vindicated in the world's courts in that remedying their violation often entails expenditure of significant resources, but environmental rights often pit the human rights claims against each other. Protecting the environment can help preserve the way of life for some, but it can impair the way of life for others. The problem is one of proportion requiring careful balancing. The judgment of how to balance the competing claims is one that should typically be done politically and not judicially. But of course, staying out of the fray has substantive consequences that sustain the continued deterioration of the environment: where there is no judicial resolution, the harm may be irremediable.

Adjudicating environmental constitutionalism can also invert the normal expectations relating to the roles of public and private parties. Whereas traditional constitutional rights litigation pits the private individual against the public authority, environmental litigation often pits members of the public against a private entity (thus invoking the principle of the horizontal application of constitutional rights and obligations). Moreover, in many of these cases, private individuals are asserting public rights, whereas the government (through lenient regulation and licensing) is facilitating private gain.

Despite these challenges, the jurisprudence surrounding environmental constitutionalism is gaining salience around the globe. In India and neighboring countries, Central Europe, and throughout Latin America, courts are increasingly vindicating rights in a wide variety of settings, from mining to water and air pollution. And new rights are continually being recognized. In some countries, courts have been willing to expand the universe of possible plaintiffs precisely to enhance the control that the people (via the courts) have over the government. Courts in India, Pakistan, Bangladesh, and Nepal have recognized a form of open standing to vindicate environmental harms on behalf of the public interest. Some courts in Latin America allow amparo actions (or *acciones de inconstitucionalidad*), permitting any citizen to enforce constitutional rights. Cases from around the globe show that courts are an increasingly potent force in the acceptance and expansion of environmental constitutionalism globally.

Courts have also not shied away from hearing cases in novel realms of environmental constitutionalism, such as concerning water rights. In part this reflects explicit language in so many of the world's constitutions that seeks to protect and manage water resources as an incident of sovereignty, as a human right, or as an essential element of a healthy ecology. And in part, it reflects the growing muscularity of constitutional courts around the world, especially in regions like Southeast Asia and Latin America, where water resources are both threatened and scarce, along with the growing recognition in both national and international arenas of the importance of water to human life and to the world's ecosystems.

Courts have chosen to engage environmental constitutionalism perhaps because they appreciate that through coordination with other parts of government and in dialogue with both the public and private sectors, they can play a pivotal role in securing environmental rights. Indeed, some courts have been extraordinarily creative in designing remedies that are ambitious enough to be effective in remedying the environmental damage, yet defined and limited enough that defendants can implement them.

The experience that courts have had in trying to make sense of and take seriously constitutional environmental rights reveals a lesson which, when learned, may significantly enrich the praxis of constitutional law generally. As robust as they are becoming, no judicial orders can unilaterally resolve the problems of environmental degradation or climate change; judicial activity can perhaps at most galvanize the political process and popular movements to take environmental protection seriously.

That some constitutional provisions remain underutilized or dormant judicially is perhaps less consequential than it might seem at first blush. Even where courts have not found a constitutional environmental violation, the mere fact that such arguments are being made and considered augments the attention that environmental constitutionalism receives in public discourse. And this, in itself, can contribute to the success of environmental outcomes in meaningful ways. Given the complexity of the issues involved – the necessary involvement of all branches of government as well as a multiplicity of private and public actors in all facets of public life – the judicial role will be necessary, though not sufficient, to implement the progress and protections promised by environmental constitutionalism.

Robinson Township, for example, is a potentially important corrective to judicial underengagement of environmental constitutionalism. Although only a plurality opinion from the Supreme Court of Pennsylvania, it is nonetheless a powerful vindication of constitutional environmentalism and may represent a significant step forward for American constitutional environmental rights in particular. It is particularly noteworthy that the decision was issued in the context of a hugely significant social, economic, and environmental controversy. While this concerns only one state, its impact may be far-reaching if courts in other states that support hydrofracking take notice. In imposing constitutional impediments to hydrofracking, the Court attended to almost every significant issue that courts around the world are reckoning with, from standing, to questions about self-execution, to interpretation of constitutional provisions, to the public trust doctrine, to enforcement of constitutional environmental provisions. And it has done so in a way that takes seriously the environmental interests of the general public and of future generations. It is likely that other courts within and outside the United States will be encouraged to follow suit, even though these views did not command a majority of the Pennsylvania court.

At bottom, constitutional incorporation of environmental rights, protections and procedures transcends judicial outcomes. Environmental constitutionalism is pervasive and profound: it furthers the possibilities of constitutional reformation, notions of intergenerational equity, legislative responses to environmental challenges, and the need for policy decisions to be made through open and inclusive processes. Environmental constitutionalism also serves as a proxy for social compacts with present and future generations. While imperfect and imprecise, it provides a means for achieving human and ecological rights to a healthy environment, and for advancing the human condition. This alone makes environmental constitutionalism worth the coin.

Appendices

APPENDIX A:

Substantive environmental rights

AFGHANISTAN

Preamble, Paragraph 10: "[E]nsuring a prosperous life and a sound environment for all those residing in this land ..."

ANDORRA

Article 39, Paragraph 1: "Everyone has the right to live in a healthy and unpolluted environment and the duty to defend and preserve it."

ANGOLA

Part II, Article 24(1): "All citizens shall have the right to live in a healthy and unpolluted environment."

ARGENTINA

Part I, Chapter 2, Article 41: "All residents enjoy the right to a healthy, balanced environment which is fit for human development and by which productive activities satisfy current necessities without compromising those of future generations ..."

ARMENIA

Article 33.2: "Everyone shall have the right to live in an environment favorable to his/her health and well-being and shall be obliged to protect and improve it in person or jointly with others."

AZERBAIJAN

Part II, Chapter 3, Article 39(1): "Everyone has the right to live in a healthy environment."

BELARUS

Section 2, Article 46: "Everyone is entitled to a wholesome environment and to compensation for loss or damage caused by violation of this right."

BELGIUM

Title II, Article 23(4): "Everyone has the right to lead a life worthy of human dignity ... [including] the right to enjoy the protection of a healthy environment."

BÉNIN

Title II, Article 27: "Every person has the right to a healthy, satisfying and lasting environment and has the duty to defend it."

BOLIVIA

Article 33: "Everyone has the right to a healthy, protected, and balanced environment. The exercise of this right must be granted to individuals and collectives of present and future generations, as well as to other living things, so they may develop in a normal and permanent way."

BRAZIL

Title VII, Chapter 6, Article 225: "All persons are entitled to an ecologically balanced environment, which is an asset for the people's common use and is essential to a healthy life ..."

BULGARIA

Chapter 2, Article 55: "Citizens have the right to a healthy and favorable environment ..."

BURKINA FASO

Title I, Chapter 4, Article 29: "The right to a healthy environment is recognized."

CAMEROON

Preamble: "[E]very person shall have a right to a healthy environment."
Part 12, Article 65: "The Preamble shall be part and parcel of this Constitution."

CAPE VERDE

Part II, Title III, Article 72(1): "Everyone shall have the right to a healthy, ecologically balanced environment, and the duty to defend and conserve it."

CENTRAL AFRICAN REPUBLIC

Article 9: "The Republic guarantees to every citizen the right ... to a healthy environment."

CHAD, REPUBLIC OF

Title II, Chapter 1, Article 47: "Every person has the right to a healthy environment."

CHECHNYA

Section I, Chapter 2, Article 39: "Everyone has the right to favorable environmental surroundings, reliable information about its condition and to compensation for damage caused to his/her health or property through ecological violations of the law."

CHILE

Chapter 3, Article 19(8): "All have 'The right to live in an environment free from contamination.'"

COLOMBIA

Title II, Chapter 3, Article 79: "Every individual has the right to enjoy a healthy environment."

CONGO-BRAZZAVILLE

Title II, Article 35: "Each citizen shall have the right to a healthy, satisfactory, and sustainable environment and the duty to defend it. The State shall strive for the protection and the conservation of the environment."

CONGO, DEMOCRATIC REPUBLIC OF

Article 53: "All persons have the right to a healthy environment that is favorable to their development."

COSTA RICA

Title V, Article 50: "Every person has the right to a healthy and ecologically balanced environment . . ."

CZECH REPUBLIC

Charter of Fundamental Rights and Basic Freedoms, Article 35(1): "Everybody has the right to a favourable environment."

DOMINICAN REPUBLIC

Article 67(1): "Every person has the right, both individually and collectively, to the sustainable use and enjoyment of the natural resources; to live in a healthy, ecologically balanced [*equilibrado*] and suitable environment for the development and preservation of the various forms of life, of the landscape and of nature."

EAST TIMOR

Part II, Title III, Article 61(1): "All have the right to a humane, healthy, and ecologically balanced environment and the duty to protect it and improve it for the benefit of the future generations."

ECUADOR

Section 2, Article 14: "The right of the population to live in a healthy and ecologically balanced environment that guarantees sustainability and the good way of living (*sumak kawsay*), is recognized ..."

EGYPT

Article 69: "All individuals have the right to a healthy environment."

EL SALVADOR

Title II, Chapter 2, Section 1, Article 34: "Every child has the right to live in familial and environmental conditions that permit his integral development, for which he shall have the protection of the State."

ETHIOPIA

Chapter 3, Part II, Article 44(1): "All persons have the right to a clean and healthy environment."

FRANCE

Charter of the Environment, Article 1: "Everyone has the right to live in a balanced and health-friendly environment."

GABON

Article I: "The Gabonese Republic recognizes and guarantees the inviolable and imprescriptible rights of Man, which obligatorily constrain public powers: [and] shall guarantee to all ... a preserved natural environment."

GEORGIA

Chapter 2, Article 37(3): "Everyone shall have the right to live in a healthy environment and enjoy natural and cultural surroundings."

GREECE

Part II, Article 24(1): "The protection of the natural and cultural environment constitutes . . . a right of every person."

GUINEA

Article 16: "Every person has the right to a healthy and lasting environment and the duty to defend it. The State sees to the protection of the environment."

HUNGARY

Article 21: "Hungary shall recognise and enforce the right of every person to a healthy environment."

INDONESIA

Section 10A, Article 28H(1): "Each person has a right to a life of well-being in body and mind, to a place to dwell, to enjoy a good and healthy environment, and to receive medical care."

IRAQ

Article 33(1): "Every individual has the right to live in a correct environmental atmosphere."

IVORY COAST

Title I, Chapter 2, Article 19: "The right to a healthy environment is recognized to all."

JAMAICA

Chapter 3(l): Citizens have "the right to enjoy a healthy and productive environment free from the threat of injury or damage from environmental abuse and degradation of the ecological heritage."

KENYA

Chapter 42: "Every person has the right to a clean and healthy environment, which includes the right – (a) to have the environment protected for the benefit of present and future generations through legislative and other measures, particularly those contemplated in Article 69; and (b) to have obligations relating to the environment fulfilled under Article 70" (allowing any person to apply to a court for redress of damage to the environment).

KYRGYZSTAN

Section 1, Chapter 2, Section 3, Article 35(1): "[C]itizens of the Kyrgyz Republic have the right to a favorable and healthy natural environment and to compensation for the damage caused to health or property by the activity in the area of nature exploitation."

MACEDONIA

Chapter 2, Part II, Article 43: "Everyone has the right to a healthy environment to live in."

MADAGASCAR

Title II, Sub-title II, Article 35: "The Fokonolona can take the appropriate measures tending to oppose acts susceptible to destroy their environment, dispossess them of their land, claim the traditional spaces allocated to their herds of cattle or claim their ceremonial heritage, unless these measures may undermine the general interest or public order."

MALDIVES

Chapter 2: "Every citizen [has] the following rights pursuant to this Constitution, and the State undertakes to achieve the progressive realisation of these rights by reasonable measures within its ability and resources: ... (d) a healthy and ecologically balanced environment."

MALI

Title I, Article 15: "Every person has the right to a healthy environment."

MOLDOVA

Title II, Chapter 2, Article 37(1): "Every person (*om*) has the right to an environment that is ecologically safe for life and health as well as to safe food products and household goods."

MONGOLIA

Chapter 2, Article 16(1): "The citizens of Mongolia shall enjoy . . . the right to a healthy and safe environment and to be protected against environmental pollution and ecological imbalance."

MONTENEGRO

Environment, Article 23: "Everyone shall have the right to a sound environment."

MOROCCO

Article 31: "The State, the public establishments and the territorial collectivities work for the mobilization of all the means available to facilitate the equal access of the [citizens] to conditions that permit their enjoyment of the right . . . to the access to water and to a healthy environment."

MOZAMBIQUE

Part II, Chapter 1, Article 72: "All citizens shall have the right to live in . . . a balanced natural environment."

NEPAL

Chapter 16(1): "Every person shall have the right to live in clean environment."

NICARAGUA

Title IV, Chapter 3, Article 60: "Nicaraguans have the right to live in a healthy environment."

NIGER

Title II, Article 27: "Each person has the right to a healthy environment."

NORWAY

Section E, Article 110b: "Every person has a right to an environment that is conducive to health and to natural surroundings whose productivity and diversity are preserved."

PARAGUAY

Part I, Title II, Chapter 1, Section 2, Article 7: "Everyone has the right to live in a healthy, ecologically balanced environment."

PORTUGAL

Part I, Section 3, Chapter 2, Article 66(1): "Everyone has the right to a healthy and ecologically balanced human environment ..."

RUSSIAN FEDERATION

Chapter 2, Article 42: "Everyone shall have the right to a favorable environment, reliable information about its condition, and to compensation for the damage caused to his or her health or property by ecological violations."

RWANDA

Article 49: "Every person has a right to a clean and healthy environment."

SAO TOMÉ AND PRÍNCIPE

Part II, Title III, Article 49(1): "All have the right to housing and to an environment of human life and the duty to defend it."

SENEGAL

Title II, Article 8: "The government of Senegal guarantees to all citizens the fundamental individual liberties, economic and social rights, as well as collective rights. These liberties and rights include ... the right to a healthy environment."

SERBIA

Article 74: "Everyone shall have the right to healthy environment and the right to timely and full information about the state of environment."

SEYCHELLES

Chapter 3, Part I, Article 38: "The State recognises the right of every person to live in and enjoy a clean, healthy and ecologically balanced environment . . ."

SLOVAKIA

Part 2, Chapter 6, Article 44(1): "Every person has the right to a favorable environment."

SLOVENIA

Section 3, Article 72: "Everyone has the right in accordance with the law to a healthy living environment."

SOUTH AFRICA

Chapter 2, Article 24:

> Everyone has the right (a) to an environment that is not harmful to their health or well-being; and (b) to have the environment protected, for the benefit of present and future generations, through reasonable legislative and other measures that –
>
> (i)   prevent pollution and ecological degradation,
> (ii) promote conservation; and
> (iii) secure ecologically sustainable development and use of natural resources while promoting justifiable economic and social development.

SOUTH KOREA

Chapter 2, Article 35(1): "All citizens have the right to a healthy and pleasant environment."

SOUTH SUDAN

Article 41(1): "Every person or community shall have the right to a clean and healthy environment."

Article 41(3): "Every person shall have the right to have the environment protected for the benefit of present and future generations, through appropriate legislative action and other measures that: (a) prevent pollution and ecological degradation; (b) promote conservation; and (c) secure ecologically sustainable development and use of natural resources while promoting rational economic and social development so as to protect genetic stability and bio-diversity."

SPAIN

Title I, Chapter 3, Article 45(1): "Everyone has the right to enjoy an environment suitable for the development of the person ..."

SUDAN

Chapter 11(1): "The people of the Sudan shall have the right to a clean and diverse environment."

TOGO

Title II, Subsection I, Article 41: "Anyone has the right to a healthy environment."

TURKEY

Part II, Chapter 3, Section 8, Part A, Article 56: "Everyone has the right to live in a healthy, balanced environment."

TURKMENISTAN

Article 36: "Everyone has the right to a healthy environment."

UKRAINE

Chapter 2, Article 50: "Everyone has the right to an environment that is safe for life and health, and to compensation for damages inflicted through the violation of this right."

VENEZUELA

Title III, Chapter 9, Article 127: "Every person has a right to individually and collectively enjoy a life and a safe, healthy and ecologically balanced environment."

Individual environmental duties and responsibilities

ALGERIA

Title I, Chapter 5, Article 66: "Every citizen has the duty to protect public property and the interests of the national collectivity and to respect the property of others."

ANGOLA

Article 39(1): "Everyone has the right to live in a healthy and unpolluted environment and the duty to defend and preserve it."

ARMENIA

Chapter 1, Article 8: "The right to property may not be exercised so as to cause damage to the environment . . ."

BELARUS

Section 2, Article 44: "The exercise of the right of property must not . . . be harmful to the environment."

Section 2, Article 55: "It is the duty of everyone to protect the environment."

BÉNIN

Title II, Article 27: "Every person has the right to a healthy, satisfying and lasting environment, and has the duty to defend it."

BURKINA FASO

Title I, Chapter 4, Article 29: "[T]he defense and the promotion of the environment are a duty for all."

BURUNDI

Title III, Part II, Article 49: "Public property is sacred and inviolable. Every [person] has the duty to respect it scrupulously and protect it."

CAMEROON

Preamble: "The protection of the environment shall be the duty of every citizen."

Part 12, Paragraph 65: "The Preamble shall be part and parcel of this Constitution."

CAPE VERDE

Part II, Title III, Article 72(1): "Everyone shall have the right to a healthy, ecologically balanced environment, and the duty to defend and conserve it."

CHAD, REPUBLIC OF

Title II, Chapter 2, Article 52: "Every citizen has the duty to respect and protect the environment."

CHECHNYA

Section I, Chapter 2, Article 33:

(1) Citizens and their associations have the right to own land.
(2) The ownership, usage and disposition of land and other natural resources is to be realized freely if it does not inflict damage on the surrounding environment and does not violate the law and legal interests of other people.

Section 1, Chapter 2, Article 55: "Everyone is obliged to preserve nature and prevent damages, as well as to be careful with removing natural riches."

CHILE

Chapter 3, Article 19(24): "The right of property in its different forms in respect of all classes of material and immaterial property. Only the law may establish the manner in which property is acquired, used, enjoyed and disposed of, and the limitations and obligations derived from its social function. This includes, to the extent required by the general interests of the Nation, national security, public utility and public health and the conservation of the environmental patrimony."

CHINA

Chapter 1, Article 9: "The appropriation or damage of natural resources by any organization or individual by whatever means is prohibited."

COLOMBIA

Title V, Chapter 5, Article 95(8): "[Every individual must] protect the country's cultural and natural resources and to keep watch that a healthy environment is being preserved."

CONGO, DEMOCRATIC REPUBLIC OF

Article 53: "All persons have the right to a healthy environment and . . . have the duty to defend it."

CROATIA

Chapter 2, Section 3, Part III, Article 69: "Everyone shall be bound . . . to pay special attention to the protection of human health, nature and the human environment."

CUBA

Chapter 1, Article 27: "It is the duty of the citizens to contribute to the protection of the water and the atmosphere, and to the conservation of the soil, flora, fauna and all the rich potential of nature."

CZECH REPUBLIC

Charter of Fundamental Rights and Freedoms: Article 35(3): "In exercising his or her rights nobody may endanger or cause damage to the environment, natural resources, the wealth of natural species, and cultural monuments beyond limits set by law."

ESTONIA

Chapter 2, Article 53: "Everyone shall be obligated to preserve the human and natural environment and to compensate for damages caused by him or her to the environment."

ETHIOPIA

Chapter 10, Article 92(4): "Government and citizens shall have the duty to protect the environment."

FINLAND

Chapter 2, Section 20: "Nature and its biodiversity, the environment and the national heritage are the responsibility of everyone."

FRANCE

Charter of the Environment, Article 2: "Everyone is obliged to take part in the preservation and improvement of the environment."

Charter of the Environment, Article 3: "Everyone shall, subject to the conditions defined by the law, avoid any disturbance which he or she is likely to cause to the environment or, if that is not possible, limit its consequences."

Charter of the Environment, Article 4: "Everyone shall contribute to the reparation of the damages which he or she caused to the environment, subject to the conditions defined by the law."

GAMBIA, THE

Chapter 20, 218: "The State and all the people of The Gambia shall strive to protect, preserve and foster the ... natural ... heritage of The Gambia."

GHANA

Chapter 6, Article 41(k): "[I]t shall be the duty of every citizen to: ... protect and safeguard the environment."

GUATEMALA

Title II, Chapter 2, Section 7, Article 97: "[T]he inhabitants of the national territory are obliged to promote social, economic, and technological development that would prevent the contamination of the environment and maintain the ecological balance."

GUINEA

Article 16: "Every person has the right to a healthy and lasting environment and the duty to defend it."

HAITI

Title VIII, Chapter 2, Article 253: "[A]ny practices that might disturb the ecological balance are strictly forbidden."

HUNGARY

Article 21(2): "A person who causes any damage to the environment shall be obliged to restore it or to bear all costs of restoration as defined by law."

INDIA

Part IVA, Article 51A(g): "It shall be the duty of every citizen of India ... to protect and improve the natural environment including forests, lakes, rivers and wild life, and to have compassion for living creatures ..."

IRAN

Chapter 4, Article 50: "Economic and other activities that inevitably involve pollution of the environment or cause irreparable damage to it are ... forbidden."

IVORY COAST

Title I, Article 28: "The protection of the environment and the promotion of the quality of life are a duty for the community and for each physical or moral person."

KAZAKHSTAN

Section 2, Article 38: "Citizens . . . are obligated to preserve nature and protect natural resources."

KYRGYZSTAN

Article 48(3): "Everyone should care for the environment, flora and fauna."

LAOS

Chapter 2, Article 17: "All organizations and citizens must protect the environment and natural resources: land, underground, forests, fauna, water sources and atmosphere."

LITHUANIA

Chapter 4, Article 53: "[E]ach individual must protect the environment from harmful influences."

MACEDONIA

Chapter 2, Part II, Article 43: "Everyone is obliged to promote and protect the environment."

MADAGASCAR

Title II, Sub-title II, Article 39: "Everyone shall have the duty to respect the environment."

MALI

Title I, Article 15: "The protection, defense and promotion of the environment are an obligation for all."

MOLDOVA

Title II, Chapter 3, Article 59: "The protection of the environment [and] the preservation and protection of historical and cultural monuments are the duty of every citizen."

Title II, Chapter 2, Article 37(4): "Physical and juridical persons are responsible for damages caused to the health and property of a person as a result of an ecological contravention."

Title II, Chapter 2, Article 46(5): "The right to private property obligates the observance of requirements regarding the protection of the environment and maintenance of good neighborly relations as well as to the observance of other requirements, which are placed upon the owner according to the law."

MONGOLIA

Chapter 2, Article 17(2): "Working, protecting his/her health, bringing up and educating his/her children and protecting nature and the environment shall be a sacred duty for every citizen."

MONTENEGRO

Environment, Article 23: "Everyone, the state in particular, shall be bound to preserve and improve the environment."

MOZAMBIQUE

Article 90(1): "All citizens shall have the right live in a balanced environment and shall have the duty to defend it."

MYANMAR

Chapter 8, Article 390(b): "Every citizen has the duty to assist the Union in carrying out . . . environmental conservation."

NIGER

Article 35: "Each one is required to contribute to the safeguarding and to the improvement of the environment in which he lives."

PANAMA

Title III, Article 115: "[A]ll the inhabitants of the national territory ... have the obligation of promoting economic and social development that prevents environmental contamination, maintains ecological balance, and avoids the destruction of ecosystems."

PAPUA NEW GUINEA

Chapter 1, Preamble, Section 5, Basic Social Obligations (d): "[A]ll persons in [Papua New Guinea] have the ... basic obligations ... to protect Papua New Guinea and to safeguard the national wealth, resources and environment in the interests not only of the present generation but also of future generations ..."

POLAND

Chapter 2, Section 6, Article 86: "Everyone is obligated to care for the quality of the environment and shall be held responsible for causing its degradation."

PORTUGAL

Part I, Section 3, Chapter 2, Article 66(1): "Everyone has the right to a healthy and ecologically balanced human environment and the duty to defend it."

ROMANIA

Title II, Chapter 2, Article 44(6): "The right to own property implies an obligation to comply with duties related to environmental protection ..."

RUSSIAN FEDERATION

Chapter 2, Article 58: "Everyone is obligated to preserve nature and the environment, and care for natural wealth."

RWANDA

Article 49: "Every person has the duty to protect, safeguard and promote the environment."

SERBIA

Article 74: "Everyone shall be obliged to preserve and improve the environment."

SAO TOMÉ AND PRÍNCIPE

Part II, Title III, Article 49(1): "All have the right to housing and to an environment of human life and the duty to defend it."

SEYCHELLES

Chapter 3, Part 2, Article 40(e): "It shall be the duty of every citizen of Seychelles ... to protect, preserve and improve the environment ..."

SLOVAKIA

Part II, Chapter 6, Article 44:

(2) Every person has a duty to protect and improve the environment and foster cultural heritage.

(3) No person shall imperil or damage the environment, natural wealth and cultural heritage beyond the limits set by law.

SLOVENIA

Section 3, Article 73: "Everyone is obliged ... to protect natural points of interest and rarities and cultural monuments."

SOUTH SUDAN

Article 41: "Every person shall have the obligation to protect the environment for the benefit of present and future generations."

SPAIN

Title I, Chapter 3, Article 45(3): "For those who violate the provisions of the foregoing paragraphs [regarding environmental protection], penal or administrative sanctions ... shall be established and they shall be obliged to repair the damage caused."

SUDAN

Chapter 11(1): "The State and the citizens have the duty to preserve and promote the country's biodiversity."

SYRIA

Part II, Article 14: "The state undertakes to exploit and to supervise the administration of this property in the interest of the entire people. It is the duty of the citizens to protect this property."

TAJIKISTAN

Chapter 2, Article 44: "Protection of the nature, historical, and cultural monuments is an obligation of everyone."

TANZANIA

Chapter 1, Part III, Article 27(1): "Every person has the duty to protect the natural resources of the United Republic, the property of the state authority, all property collectively owned by the people, and also to respect another person's property."

Chapter 1, Part III, Article 27(2): "All persons shall be required by law to safeguard the property of the state authority and all property collectively owned by the people, to combat all forms of waste and squander, and to manage the national economy assiduously with the attitude of people who are masters of the destiny of their nation."

THAILAND

Chapter 4, Section 69: "Every person shall have a duty to . . . conserve natural resources and the environment . . ."

URUGUAY

Section 2, Chapter 2, Article 47: "The protection of the environment is of common interest. Persons should abstain from any act that may cause the serious degradation, destruction, or contamination of the environment."

UZBEKISTAN

Part II, Chapter 11, Article 50: "All citizens shall protect the environment."

Part III, Chapter 12, Article 54: "An owner shall possess, use and dispose of his property. The use of any property must not be harmful to the ecological environment, nor shall it infringe on the rights and legally protected interests of citizens, juridical entities or the state."

VANUATU

Chapter 2, Part II, Article 7(d): "Every person has the ... fundamental duties to himself and his descendants and to others ... to protect the Republic of Vanuatu and to safeguard the national wealth, resources and environment in the interests of the present generation and of future generations."

VIETNAM

Chapter 2, Article 29: "[I]ndividuals have the duty to implement state regulations on the rational use of natural resources and protection of the environment. All acts likely to bring about exhaustion of and cause damage to the environment are strictly prohibited."

YEMEN

Article 35: "Environmental protection is the collective responsibility of the state and the community at large. Each individual shall have a religious and national duty to protect the environment."

State environmental duties

AFGHANISTAN

Chapter 1, Article 15: "The State is obligated to adopt necessary measures for ... proper exploitation of natural resources and the improvement of ecological conditions."

ANDORRA

Title II, Chapter 5, Article 31: "The State has the task of ensuring the rational use of the soil and of all the natural resources, so as to guarantee a befitting quality of life for all."

ANGOLA

Article 39(2): "The state shall take the requisite measures to protect the environment and species of flora and fauna throughout national territory, maintain the ecological balance, ensure the correct location of economic activities and the rational development and use of all natural resources, within the context of sustainable development, respect for the rights of future generations and the preservation of species."

ARMENIA

Chapter 1, Article 10: "The State shall ensure the protection and reproduction of the environment and the rational utilization of natural resources."

BAHRAIN

Chapter 2, Article 9h: "The State shall take the necessary measures for the protection of the environment and the conservation of wildlife."

Chapter 2, Article 11: "All natural wealth and resources are State property. The State shall safeguard them and exploit them properly, while observing the requirements of the security of the State and of the national economy."

BANGLADESH

Part II, Article 18A: "The State shall endeavour to protect and improve the environment and to preserve and safeguard the natural resources, biodiversity, wetlands, forests and wild life for the present and future citizens."

BÉNIN

Title II, Article 27: "The State shall watch over the protection of the environment."

BRAZIL

Article 225:

The Government and the community have a duty to defend and to preserve the environment for present and future generations.

Section 1. To assure the effectiveness of this right, it is the responsibility of the Government to: I – preserve and restore essential ecological processes and provide for ecological management of species and ecosystems; II – preserve the diversity and integrity of the Country's genetic patrimony and to supervise entities dedicated to research and manipulation of genetic material; III – define, in all units of the Federation, territorial spaces and their components that are to be specially protected, with any change or suppression permitted only through law, prohibiting any use that compromises the integrity of the characteristics that justify their protection; IV – require, as provided by law, a prior environmental impact study, which shall be made public, for installation of works or activities that may cause significant degradation of the environment; V – control production, commercialization and employment of techniques, methods and substances that carry a risk to life, the quality of life and the environment; VI – promote environmental education at all levels of teaching and public awareness of the need to preserve the environment; VII – protect the fauna and the flora, prohibiting, as provided by law, all practices that jeopardize their ecological functions, cause extinction of species or subject animals to cruelty.

Section 2. Those who exploit mineral resources are obligated to restore any environmental degradation, in accordance with technical solutions required by the proper governmental agencies, as provided by law.

Section 3. Conduct and activities considered harmful to the environment shall subject the violators, be they individuals or legal entities, to criminal and administrative sanctions, irrespective of the obligation to repair the damages caused.

Section 4. The Brazilian Amazonian Forest, the Atlantic Forest, the Serra do Mar, the Pantanal of Mato Grosso, and the Coastal Zone are part of the national patrimony, and they shall be utilized, as provided by law, under conditions assuring preservation of the environment, including use of natural resources.

Section 5. Lands necessary to protect natural ecosystems, which are vacant or which have reverted to the States through discriminatory actions, are inalienable.

BULGARIA

Chapter 1, Article 15: "[The State must] ensure the protection and conservation of the environment, the sustenance of animals and the maintenance of their diversity, and the sensible utilization of the country's natural wealth and resources."

BURUNDI

Article 35: "The State shall ensure the proper management and rational use of natural resources while preserving the environment and conservation of these resources for future generations."

CAMBODIA

Chapter 5, Article 59: "The State shall protect the environment and balance of abundant natural resources and establish a precise plan of management of land, water, air, wind, geology, ecological system, mines, energy, petrol and gas, rocks and sand, gems, forests and forestry products, wildlife, fish and aquatic resources."

CAMEROON

Preamble: "The State shall ensure the protection and improvement of the environment . . ."

Part XII, Paragraph 65: "The Preamble shall be part and parcel of this Constitution."

CAPE VERDE

Part I, Title I, Article 7(j): State duties include those "To protect the land, nature, natural resources, and environment, as well as the historical-cultural and artistic national heritage . . ."

CHAD

Title II, Chapter 1, Article 48: "The State and the Decentralized Territorial Collectivities must see to the protection of the environment."

CHILE

Chapter 3, Article 19: "The Constitution guarantees to all persons . . .
. . .
(8) The right to live in an environment that is free from contamination. It is the duty of the State to see to that this right will not be affected and to guard the preservation of nature."

CHINA

Chapter 1, Article 9: "The state ensures the rational use of natural resources and protects rare animals and plants."

Chapter 1, Article 26: "The state protects and improves the living environment and the ecological environment, and prevents and remedies pollution and other public hazards. The state organizes and encourages forestation and the protection of forests."

COLOMBIA

Title II, Chapter 3, Article 79: "It is the duty of the State to protect the diversity and integrity of the environment, to conserve the areas of special ecological importance, and to foster education for the achievement of these ends."

Title II, Chapter 3, Article 80: "The State will plan the handling and use of natural resources in order to guarantee their sustainable development, conservation, restoration, or replacement. Additionally, it will have to caution and control the factors of environmental deterioration, impose legal sanctions, and demand the repair of any damage caused. In the same way, it will cooperate with other nations in the protection of the ecosystems located in the border areas."

CONGO, DEMOCRATIC REPUBLIC OF

Article 53: "The State sees to the protection of the environment and the health of the population."

COSTA RICA

Title V, Article 50: "Every person has the right to a healthy and ecologically balanced environment. The State shall guarantee, defend and preserve this right. The law will determine the corresponding responsibilities and sanctions."

CROATIA

Chapter 2, Section 3, Part III, Article 69: "The State shall ensure conditions for a healthy environment."

CUBA

Chapter 1, Article 27: "The State protects the environment and natural resources of the country. It recognizes their close link with the sustainable economic and social development for making human life more sensible, and for ensuring the survival, welfare, and security of present and future generations. It corresponds to the competent organs to implement this policy."

CZECH REPUBLIC

Article 7: "The state shall see to it that natural resources are used prudently and natural wealth is protected."

DOMINICAN REPUBLIC

Article 67: "The prevention of pollution, [and] the protection and maintaining of the environment for the benefit of the present and future generations, constitute duties of the State."

Article 67(4): "In the contracts celebrated by the State or in the permits that it grants that involve the use and exploitation of the natural resources, the obligation to preserve the ecological equilibrium, the access to technology and its transfer, as well as the reestablishment of the environment to its natural state, if it is altered [as a] result[,] will be considered [as] included."

EAST TIMOR

Part II, Title III, Section 61(3): "The State shall promote actions aimed at protecting the environment and safeguarding the sustainable development of the economy."

EGYPT

Part III, Article 59: "Safeguarding the environment is a national duty, and the law shall regulate the right to a good environment and the measures necessary to safeguard it."

EL SALVADOR

Title II, Chapter 2, Section 4, Article 69: "[T]he State shall control the quality of food products and the environmental conditions that may affect health and well-being."

EQUATORIAL GUINEA

Part I, Article 6: "The State shall ... ensure the conservation of nature."

ETHIOPIA

Chapter 10, Article 92(1): "Government shall endeavor to ensure that all Ethiopians live in a clean and healthy environment."

Chapter 10, Article 92(4): "Government and citizens shall have the duty to protect the environment."

Chapter 10, Article 92(2): "The design and implementation of programmes and projects of development shall not damage or destroy the environment."

FINLAND

Chapter 2, Section 20: "The public authorities shall endeavor to guarantee for everyone the right to a healthy environment."

FRANCE

Charter of the Environment, Article 9: "Research and innovation shall assist the preservation and utilization of the environment."

GAMBIA, THE

Chapter 20, 218: "The State and all the people of The Gambia shall strive to protect, preserve and foster the ... natural ... heritage of The Gambia."

GHANA

Chapter 6, Article 36(9): "The State shall take appropriate measures needed to protect and safeguard the national environment for posterity; and shall seek cooperation with other states and bodies for purposes of protecting the wider international environment for mankind."

GREECE

Part II, Article 24(1): "The protection of the natural and cultural environment constitutes a duty of the State."

GUATEMALA

Title II, Chapter 2, Section 7, Article 97: "The State ... [is] obliged to promote social, economic, and technological development that would prevent the contamination of the environment and maintain the ecological balance. It will issue all the necessary regulations to guarantee that the use of the fauna, flora, land, and water may be realized rationally, obviating their depredation."

GUINEA

Article 16: "The State sees to the protection of the environment."

HAITI

Title VIII, Chapter 2, Article 253: "[A]ny practices that might disturb the ecological balance are strictly forbidden."

Title VIII, Chapter 2, Article 254: "The State shall organize the enhancement of natural sites to ensure their protection and make them accessible to all."

Title VIII, Chapter 2, Article 257: "The law specifies the conditions for protecting flora and fauna, and punishes violations thereof."

HONDURAS

Title III, Chapter 7, Article 145: "The State shall maintain a satisfactory environment for the protection of everyone's health."

HUNGARY

Article 20: "(1) Every person shall have the right to physical and mental health. (2) Hungary shall promote the exercise of the right set out in Paragraph (1) by ensuring that its agriculture remains free from any genetically modified organism, by providing access to healthy food and drinking water ... and by ensuring environmental protection."

INDIA

Part IV, Article 48A: "The State shall endeavour to protect and improve the environment and to safeguard the forests and wild life of the country."

INDONESIA

Section 14, Article 33(3): "The land and the waters as well as the natural riches therein are to be controlled by the state to be exploited to the greatest benefit of the people.

(4): The organization of the national economy shall be based on economic democracy that upholds the principles of solidarity, efficiency along with fairness, sustainability, keeping the environment in perspective, self sufficiency, and that is concerned as well with balanced progress and with the unity of the national economy."

IRAN

Chapter 4, Article 50: "The preservation of the environment, in which the present as well as the future generations have a right to flourishing social existence, is regarded as a public duty in the Islamic Republic. Economic and other activities that inevitably involve pollution of the environment or cause irreparable damage to it are therefore forbidden."

IRAQ

Article 33(2): "The state guarantees protection and preservation of the environment and biological diversity."

KAZAKHSTAN

Section 2, Article 31(1): "The State sets objectives for the protection of the environment favorable for the life and health of the people."

KOREA, DEMOCRATIC PEOPLE'S REPUBLIC OF (NORTH)

Chapter 3, Article 57: "The State shall adopt measures to protect the environment in preference to production, preserve and promote the natural environment and prevent environmental pollution so as to provide the people with a hygienic environment and working conditions."

LATVIA

Chapter 8, Article 115: "The State shall protect the right of everyone to live in a benevolent environment by ... by promoting the preservation and improvement of the environment."

LITHUANIA

Chapter 4, Article 53: "The State ... must protect the environment from harmful influences."

LUXEMBOURG

Article 11.2: "The State guarantees the protection of the human and natural environment, working to establish a sustainable balance between nature conservation, especially its capacity for renewal, and satisfying the needs of present and future generations ... It promotes the protection and welfare of animals."

MACEDONIA

Chapter 1, Article 8: Requiring "proper urban and rural planning to promote a congenial human environment, as well as ecological protection and development."

MADAGASCAR

Title II, Sub-title II, Article 39: "The State, with the participation of the autonomous provinces, assures the protection, the conservation and the valorisation of the environment through appropriate means."

MALAWI

Chapter 3, Article 13(d): "The State shall actively promote the welfare and development of the people of Malawi by progressively adopting and implementing policies and legislation aimed at ... manag[ing] the environment responsibly in order to (i) prevent the degradation of the environment, (ii) provide a healthy living and working environment for the people of Malawi, (iii) accord full recognition to the rights of future generations by means of environmental protection and the sustainable development of natural resources, and (iv) conserve and enhance the biological diversity of Malawi.

MALDIVES

Chapter 2: "Every citizen [has] the following rights pursuant to this Constitution, and the State undertakes to achieve the progressive realisation of these rights by reasonable measures within its ability and resources: ... (d) a healthy and ecologically balanced environment."

MALI

Title I, Article 15: "The protection, defense and promotion of the environment are an obligation ... for the State."

MALTA

Chapter 2, Article 9: "The State shall safeguard the landscape ... of the Nation."

MAURITANIA

Title IV, Article 57: "The following shall be the domain of the law ... general regulation of water, mines and hydro-carbons, fishing and the merchant marine, fauna, flora and the environment."

MEXICO

Title I, Chapter 1, Article 27: "The Nation shall ... [take] necessary measures ... to prevent the destruction of natural resources."

MICRONESIA

Preamble: "[W]e affirm our common wish ... to preserve the heritage of the past, and to protect the promise of the future."

MONGOLIA

Chapter 1, Article 6(1): "The land, its subsoil, forests, water, fauna and flora and other natural resources shall be subject to national sovereignty and State protection."

Chapter 3, Part III, Article 38(2),(4): "Carrying out the State laws and directing the economic, social and cultural development of the country, the Government shall exercise the following powers ... To undertake measures on the protection of the environment and on the rational use and restoration of natural resources ..."

MONTENEGRO

Environment, Article 23: "Everyone, the state in particular, shall be bound to preserve and improve the environment."

MOROCCO

Article 31: "The State, the public establishments and the territorial collectivities work for the mobilization of all the means available [*disponibles*] to facilitate the equal access of the [citizens] to conditions that permit their enjoyment of the right ... to the access to water and to a healthy environment."

MOZAMBIQUE

Article 90(2): The State and the local authorities, with collaboration from associations for environmental protection, shall adopt policies to protect the environment and shall promote the rational use of all natural resources."

MYANMAR

Chapter 1, Article 45: "The Union shall protect and conserve natural environment."

NAMIBIA

Chapter 11, Article 95(1): "The State shall actively promote and maintain the welfare of the people by adopting, inter alia, policies aimed at ... maintenance of ecosystems, essential ecological processes and biological diversity of Namibia and utilization of living natural resources on a sustainable basis for the benefit of all Namibians, both present and future."

NETHERLANDS, THE

Chapter 1, Article 21: "It shall be the concern of the authorities to keep the country habitable and to protect and improve the environment."

NICARAGUA

Title VI, Chapter 1, Article 102: "The natural resources are national patrimony. The preservation of the environment, and the conservation, development and rational exploitation of the natural resources are responsibilities of the State."

NIGER

Article 35: "The State has the obligation to protect the environment in the interest of present and future generations."

NIGERIA

Part II, Article 20: "The State shall protect and improve the environment and safeguard the water, air and land, forest and wild life of Nigeria."

NORWAY

Section E, Article 110b: "Natural resources should be made use of on the basis of comprehensive long-term considerations whereby this right will be safeguarded for future generations as well."

OMAN

Chapter 2, Article 11: "All natural resources and revenues therefrom shall be the property of the State which will preserve and utilize them in the best manner taking into consideration the requirements of the State's security and the interests of national economy. No concession or investment in any of the public resources of the country may be granted except by virtue of a law and for a limited period, provided the national interests are safeguarded."

PALAU

Article 6: "The national government shall take positive action to . . . conserv[e] a beautiful, healthful and resourceful natural environment . . ."

PALESTINE

Chapter 1, Article (15): "The state strives to achieve a clean, balanced environment whose protection shall be an official and societal responsibility. Tampering with it is punishable by law." [Draft]

PANAMA

Title III, Chapter 7, Article 114: "The State has the fundamental obligation to guarantee that its population lives in a healthy environment, free of contamination (pollution), and where air, water, and foodstuffs satisfy the requirements for proper development of human life."

Title III, Article 115: "The State ... [has] the obligation of promoting economic and social development that prevents environmental contamination, maintains ecological balance, and avoids the destruction of ecosystems."

Title III, Article 116: "The State shall regulate, supervise, and apply, at the proper time, the measures necessary to guarantee rational use of, and benefit from, land, river and sea life, as well as forests, lands and waters, to avoid their misuse, and to ensure their preservation, renewal, and permanence."

Title III, Article 117: "Benefits gained from non-renewable natural resources shall be regulated by law, to avoid social, economic and environmental abuses that could result."

PAPUA NEW GUINEA

Chapter 1, Preamble, Section 4: "We declare our fourth goal to be for Papua New Guinea's natural resources and environment to be conserved and used for the collective benefit of all and be replenished for the benefit of future generations. We accordingly call for

(1) wise use to be made of natural resources and the environment ... in the interests of development and in trust for future generations; and
(2) the conservation and replenishment, for the benefit of ourselves and posterity, of the environment and its sacred, scenic, and historical qualities; and
(3) all necessary steps to be taken to give adequate protection to our valued birds, animals, fish, insects, plants and trees."

PARAGUAY

Part I, Title II, Chapter 2, Section 2, Article 7: "The preservation, recovery, and improvement of the environment, as well as efforts to reconcile these goals with comprehensive human development, are priority objectives ..."

PHILIPPINES

Article II, Section 16: "The State shall protect and advance the right of the people to a balanced and healthful ecology in accord with the rhythm and harmony of nature."

POLAND

Chapter 2, Article 74(2): "The protection of the environment is the duty of public authorities."

Chapter 2, Article 74(4): "Public authorities shall support the activities of citizens to protect and improve the quality of the environment."

PORTUGAL

Part I, Section 2, Chapter 1, Article 9(e): "Fundamental responsibilities of the State shall be ... To protect and enhance the cultural heritage of the Portuguese people, to protect nature and the environment, to conserve natural resources and to ensure the proper development of the national territory ..."

QATAR

Chapter 2, Article 33: "The State endeavors to protect the environment and its natural balance, to achieve comprehensive and sustainable development for all generations."

ROMANIA

Title IV, Article 135(2)(e): "The State is expected to ensure ... the restoration and protection of the environment, as well as the preservation of ecological balance."

RUSSIAN FEDERATION

Chapter 1, Article 9(1): "The land and other natural resources are utilized and protected in the Russian Federation as the basis of the life and activity of the peoples living on their respective territories."

RWANDA

Article 49: "The State shall ensure the protection of environment. An Organic Law shall determine the modalities for protecting, safeguarding and promoting the environment."

SAN MARINO

Declaration of Citizen Rights: "The Republic protects the historic and artistic heritage and the natural environment."

SAO TOMÉ AND PRÍNCIPE

Part II, Title III, Article 50(2): "[I]t is incumbent upon the State to promote the public health which has as objectives the physical and mental well-being of the populations and their balanced fitting into the socio-ecological environment in which they live."

SAUDI ARABIA

The Basic System of the Consultative Council (Decree A/90), 1992, Chapter 5, Article 32: "The State works toward protecting and improving the environment, as well as keeping it from being harmed."

SERBIA

Article 74: "Everyone, especially the Republic of Serbia and autonomous provinces, shall be accountable for the protection of environment."

SEYCHELLES

Chapter 3, Part I, Article 38: "The State recognises the right of every person to live in and enjoy a clean, healthy and ecologically balanced environment, and with a view to ensuring the effective realisation of this right the State undertakes – (a) to take measures to promote the protection, preservation and improvement of the environment; (b) to ensure a sustainable socioeconomic development of Seychelles by a judicious use and management of the resources of Seychelles; (c) to promote public awareness of the need to protect, preserve and improve the environment."

SLOVAKIA

Part II, Chapter 6, Article 44(4): "The State sees to the economical use of the natural resources and the economical balance and active care of the life environment and safeguards the protection of certain kinds of plants and freely living animals."

SLOVENIA

Section 3, Article 72: "The state promotes a healthy living environment. To this end, the conditions and manner in which economic and other activities are pursued are established by law. The law shall establish under which conditions and to what extent a person who has damaged the living environment is obliged to provide compensation. The protection of animals from cruelty shall be regulated by law."

SOUTH KOREA

Chapter 9, Article 120(2): "The land and natural resources shall be protected by the State, and the State shall establish a plan necessary for their balanced development and utilization."

SOUTH SUDAN

Article 41(4): "All levels of government shall develop energy policies that will ensure that the basic needs of the people are met while protecting and preserving the environment."

SPAIN

Title I, Chapter 3, Article 45(2): "The public authorities shall concern themselves with the rational use of all natural resources for the purpose of protecting and improving the quality of life and protecting and restoring the environment ..."

SRI LANKA

Chapter 6, Article 27(14): "The State shall protect, preserve and improve the environment for the benefit of the community."

SUDAN

Chapter 11(3): "The State shall promote, through legislation, sustainable utilization of natural resources and best practices with respect to their management."

SURINAME

Chapter 3, Article 6(g): "The social objectives of the State shall aim at ... creating and improving the conditions necessary for the protection of nature and for the preservation of the ecological balance."

SWEDEN

The Instrument of Government, Chapter 1, Article 2: "The public institutions shall promote sustainable development leading to a good environment for present and future generations."

SWITZERLAND

Title III, Chapter 2, Section 3, Article 65(1): "The Confederation collects the necessary statistical data concerning the status and evolution of ... the environment in Switzerland."

Title III, Chapter 2, Section 3, Article 74(1): "The Confederation legislates on the protection of humans and the natural environment against damaging and harmful influences."

TAIWAN (REPUBLIC OF CHINA)

Chapter 13, Section 6, Article 169: "The State shall actively undertake and foster the development of education, culture, communications, water conservancy, public health, and other economic and social enterprises among the various ethnic groups in the frontier regions. With respect to land utilization, the State shall, in the light of climatic conditions, nature of the soil, and the life and habits of the people, adopt measures for its protection and assist in its development."

TAJIKISTAN

Chapter 2, Article 38: "The State adopts measures for improvement of the environment, development of mass sport, physical culture, and tourism."

TANZANIA

Chapter 1, Part II, Article 9(1)(c): "The state authority and all its agencies are obliged to direct their policies and programmes towards ensuring ... that public affairs are conducted in such a way as to ensure that the national resources and heritage are harnessed, preserved and applied for the common good and also to prevent the exploitation of one person by another."

THAILAND

Chapter 5, Section 79: "The State shall promote and encourage public participation in the preservation, maintenance and balanced exploitation of natural resources and biological diversity and in the promotion, maintenance and protection of the quality of the environment in accordance with the sustainable development principle as well as the control and elimination of pollution affecting public health, sanitary conditions, welfare and quality of life."

TOGO

Title II, Subsection I, Article 41: "The State shall take care of the protection of the environment."

TURKEY

Part II, Chapter 3, Section 3, Part B, Article 44: "The state takes the necessary measures to maintain and develop efficient land cultivation, to prevent its loss through erosion, and to provide land to farmers with insufficient land of their own, or no land."

UGANDA

Preamble, XIII: "The State shall protect important natural resources, including land, water, wetlands, minerals, oil, fauna and flora on behalf of the people of Uganda."

Preamble, XXVII:

(i) The State shall promote sustainable development and public awareness of the need to manage land, air, water resources in a balanced and sustainable manner for the present and future generations.

(ii) The utilization of the natural resources of Uganda shall be managed in such a way as to meet the development and environmental needs of present and future generations of Ugandans; and in particular, the State shall take all possible measures to prevent or minimise damage and destruction to land, air and water resources resulting from pollution or other causes.

(iii) The State shall promote and implement energy policies that will ensure that people's basic needs and those of environmental preservation are met.

UNITED ARAB EMIRATES

Chapter 2, Article 23: "The natural resources and wealth in each Emirate shall be considered the public property of that Emirate. Society shall be responsible for the protection and proper exploitation of such natural resources and wealth for the benefit of the national economy."

UZBEKISTAN

Part III, Chapter 12, Article 55: "The land, its mineral, fauna and flora, as well as other natural resources shall constitute the national wealth, and shall be rationally used and protected by the state."

VENEZUELA

Title III, Chapter 9, Article 127: "It is a fundamental obligation of the State ... to guarantee that the population develops in an environment free of contamination, where the air, the water, the coasts, the climate, the ozone layer, the living species are especially protected in conformity with the law."

VIETNAM

Chapter 2, Article 29: "State organs, units of armed forces, economic organizations . . . have the duty to implement state regulations on the rational use of natural resources and protection of the environment. All acts likely to bring about exhaustion of and cause damage to the environment are strictly prohibited."

YEMEN

Article 35: "Environmental protection is the collective responsibility of the state and the community at large. Each individual shall have a religious and national duty to protect the environment."

ZAMBIA

Preamble: "We, The People of Zambia, Pledge to ourselves that we shall ensure that the State shall respect the rights and dignity of the human family, uphold the laws of the State and conduct the affairs of the State in such manner as to preserve, develop, and utilise its resources for this and future generations . . ."

Environmental policy directives

ALGERIA

Title II, Chapter 2, Article 122(19)–(25):

The Parliament legislates in the domains attributed to it by the Constitution as well as the following fields: . . .

(19) General rules relating to the environment and the standard of life and land management;
(20) General rules relating to the protection of the fauna and flora;
(21) The protection and safeguarding of the cultural and historic patrimony;
(22) The general system of forests and pasture lands;
(23) The general water system;
(24) The general system of mines and hydrocarbons.

ARMENIA

Chapter 5, Article 89(5): "The Government . . . shall ensure the implementation of state policies in the area . . . of . . . environmental protection."

AUSTRIA

Chapter 1, Part A, Article 10(1):

Legislation and its implementation is a Federal concern (Bundessache) in the following matters:

10. mining; forestry, including timber floating; water law, regulation and maintenance of waters for the safe diversion of floods or for the purpose of shipping and rafting operations; control of wild streams; construction and maintenance of waterways . . .

12. [m]easures to defend the environmental against dangerous stresses which originate from the violation of the emission limits . . .

BELIZE

Preamble (e): "Whereas the People of Belize . . . require policies of state . . . which protect the environment . . ."

EAST TIMOR

Part II, Title III, Section 61(2): "The State recognizes the need to preserve and rationalize natural resources."

ECUADOR

Section 2, Article 14:

The right of people to live in a healthy and ecologically balanced environment that ensures sustainability and good living, sumak kawsay. There is a public interest in environmental conservation, the protection of ecosystems, biodiversity and the integrity of the country's genetic assets, the prevention of environmental damage, and the recovery of degraded natural spaces are declared matters of public interest.

EGYPT

Article 59: "Safeguarding the environment is a national duty, and the law shall regulate the right to a good environment and the measures necessary to safeguard it."

FRANCE

Preamble, Charter of the Environment:

The French people recognizing that the natural resources and their balance have been the prerequisite for the emergence of mankind; that the future and the very existence of mankind cannot be separated from its natural environment; that the environment is the common heritage of human beings; that man exercises a growing influence on the conditions of life and on his own evolution; that biological diversity, the free development of the individual and the progress of human societies are affected by certain patterns of consumption or protection and by the excessive exploitation of natural resources; that the preservation of the environment must be pursued in the same way as the other fundamental interests of the Nation; that in order to achieve sustainable development, the choices made to meet the needs of the present shall not compromise the capacity of future generations and of other peoples to satisfy their own needs, proclaim:

Article 5:

Where the occurrence of a damage, even if it is uncertain in the light of scientific knowledge, could gravely and irreversibly affect the environment, the public authorities make sure, through application of the precautionary principle and within their respective fields of competences, that risk assessments are carried out and provisional and proportionate measures are adopted in order to prevent the occurrence of the damage.

GREECE

Part II, Article 24(1):

The State is bound to adopt special preventive or repressive measures for the preservation of the environment in the context of the principle of sustainability. Matters pertaining to the protection of forests and forest expanses in general shall be regulated by law. The compilation of a forest register constitutes an obligation of the State. Alteration of the use of forests and forest expanses is prohibited, except where agricultural development or other uses imposed for the public interest prevail for the benefit of the national economy.

INDONESIA

Articles 33(3), 33(4):

(3) The land and the waters as well as the natural riches therein are to be controlled by the state to be exploited to the greatest benefit of the people. (4) The organization of the national economy shall be based on economic democracy that upholds the principles of solidarity, efficiency along with fairness, sustainability, keeping the environment in perspective, self-sufficiency, and that is concerned as well with balanced progress and with the unity of the national economy.

ITALY

Part II, Title V, Article 117(s): "The state has exclusive legislative power with respect to ... the protection of the environment, [and] the ecosystem ..."

PERU

Title III, Chapter 2, Article 67: "The State determines national environmental policy. It promotes the sustainable use of its natural resources."

SYRIA

Part 2, Article 14: "The law regulates ownership, which is of three kinds:

(1) Public ownership includes natural resources, public utilities, and nationalized installations and establishments, as well as installations and establishments set up by the state. The state undertakes to exploit and to supervise the administration of this property in the interest of the entire people. It is the duty of the citizens to protect this property."

Sustainable development, future generations, and public trust

SUSTAINABLE DEVELOPMENT

Belgium

Title I BIS, Article 7bis: "In the exercise of their respective competences, the Federal State, the Communities and the Regions pursue the objective of sustainable development in its social, economic and environmental aspects, taking into account the solidarity between the generations."

Bénin

Article 27: "Every person has the right to a healthy, satisfactory and sustainable environment and has the duty to defend it. The State sees to the protection of the environment."

Bolivia

Title II, Chapter 1, Article 342: "It is the duty of the State and the population to conserve, protect and use natural resources and the biodiversity in a sustainable manner, as well as to maintain the equilibrium of the environment."

Article 346: "The natural assets are of public importance and of strategic character for the sustainable development of the country."

Colombia

Chapter 3, Article 80: "The State shall plan the handling and use of the natural resources in order to guarantee their sustainable development, their conservation, restoration, or substitution."

Ecuador

Section 2, Article 14: "The State shall protect the right of people to live in a healthy and ecologically balanced environment that ensures sustainability."

Eritrea

Chapter 2, Article 8(2): "The State shall work to bring about a balanced and sustainable development throughout the country, and shall use all available means to enable all citizens to improve their livelihood in a sustainable manner, through their participation."

Chapter 2, Article 8(3): "[T]he State shall be responsible for managing all land, water, air and natural resources and for ensuring their management in a balanced and sustainable manner."

Greece

Article 24(1): "The State is bound to adopt special preventive or repressive measures for the preservation of the environment in the context of the principle of sustainable development."

Montenegro

Preamble: "Stemming from . . . [t]he conviction that the state is responsible for the preservation of nature, sound, environment, sustainable development, balanced development of all its regions and the establishment of social justice."

Nepal

Part IV, Section 35(5): "Provision shall be made for the protection of the forest, vegetation and biodiversity, its sustainable use and for equitable distribution of the benefit derived from it."

Peru

Title III, Chapter 2, Article 67: "The State determines national environmental policy. It promotes the sustainable use of its natural resources."

Poland

Chapter 1, Article 5: "The Republic of Poland shall safeguard the independence and integrity of its territory and ensure the freedoms and rights of persons and citizens, the security of the citizens, safeguard the national heritage and shall ensure the protection of the natural environment, pursuant to the principles of sustainable development."

Serbia

Part IV, No. 9: "The Republic of Serbia shall organise and provide for … sustainable development, system of protection and improvement of environment; protection and improvement of flora and fauna."

Seychelles

Chapter 3, Part I, Article 38(b): "The State recognises the right of every person to live in and enjoy a clean, healthy and ecologically balanced environment with a view to ensuring the effective realisation of this right the State undertakes – to ensure a sustainable socio-economic development of Seychelles by a judicious use and management of the resources of Seychelles."

Somalia

Chapter 3, Article 43: "Land shall be held, used and managed in an equitable, efficient, productive and sustainable manner."

Sudan

Chapter 11(3): "The State shall promote, through legislation, sustainable utilization of natural resources and best practices with respect to their management."

Switzerland

Section 4, Article 73: "Sustainable Development. The Confederation and the Cantons shall endeavor to achieve a balanced and sustainable relationship between nature and its capacity to renew itself and the demands placed on it by the population."

Thailand

Part VIII, Section 85(5): "The State shall pursue directive principles of State policies in relation to land, natural resources and the environment, as follows: to prescribe rules on land which cover areas throughout the country, having regard to the consistency with natural surroundings, whether land areas, water surfaces, ways of life of local residents, and the efficient preservation of natural resources, and prescribe standards for sustainable land use provided that residents in areas affected by such rules on land use shall also have due participation in the decision making ... to provide town and country planning and carry out the development and action in the implementation of town and country plans in an efficient and effective manner in the interest of sustainable preservation of natural resources ... promote, maintain and protect the quality of natural resources in accordance with the sustainable development principle, control and eradiate polluted conditions affecting health, sanitary conditions, welfare and the quality of life of the public, provided that members of the public, local residents and local government organisations shall have due participation in determining the direction of such work."

FUTURE GENERATIONS

Andorra

Chapter 5, Article 31: "The State has the task of ensuring the rational use of the land and of all natural resources, so as to guarantee a fitting quality of life for all and for the sake of future generations, to restore and maintain a reasonable ecological balance in the atmosphere, water and land as well as to protect the autochthonous flora and fauna."

Argentina

Article 41: "All residents enjoy the right to a healthy, balanced environment fit for human development and by which productive activities satisfy current necessities without compromising those of future generations; and shall have the duty to preserve it."

Armenia

Chapter 2, Article 48, Number 10: "[A] basic [task] of the state in the economic, social and cultural spheres [is] ... to pursue the environmental security policy for present and future generations."

Bolivia

Article 33: "Everyone has the right to a healthy, protected, and balanced environment. The exercise of this right must be granted to individuals and collectives of present and future generations, as well as to other living things, so they may develop in a normal and permanent way."

Brazil

Chapter 6, Article 225: "Everyone has a right to an ecologically balanced environment, which is a public good for the people's use and is essential for a healthy life. The Government and the community have a duty to defend and preserve the environment for present and future generations."

Burundi

Article 35: "The State shall ensure the proper management and rational use of natural resources while preserving the environment and conservation of these resources for future generations."

Germany

Section 2, Article 20(a): "Mindful of its responsibility toward future generations, the state shall protect the natural foundations of life and animals by legislation and, in accordance with law and justice, by executive and judicial action, all within the framework of the constitutional order."

Guyana

Part I, Chapter 2, Article 36: "In the interests of the present and future generations, the State will protect and make rational use of its land, mineral and water resources, as well as its fauna and flora, and will take all appropriate measures to conserve and improve the environment."

Iran

Chapter 4, Article 50: "The preservation of the environment, in which the present as well as the future generations have a right to flourishing social existence, is regarded as a public duty in the Islamic Republic."

Kenya

Article 42: "Every person has the right to a clean and healthy environment, which includes the right – (a) to have the environment protected for the benefit of present and future generations through legislative and other measures, particularly those contemplated in Article 69; and (b) to have obligations relating to the environment fulfilled."

Lesotho

Chapter 2, Article 36: "Lesotho shall adopt policies designed to protect and enhance the natural and cultural environment of Lesotho for the benefit of both present and future generations and shall endeavor to assure to all citizens a sound and safe environment adequate for their health and well-being."

Luxembourg

Article 11.2: "The State guarantees the protection of the human and natural environment, working to establish a sustainable balance between nature conservation, especially its capacity for renewal, and satisfying the needs of present and future generations ... It promotes the protection and welfare of animals."

Namibia

Chapter 11, Article 95(l): "The State shall actively promote and maintain the welfare of the people by adopting, inter alia, policies aimed at ... maintenance of ecosystems, essential ecological processes and biological diversity of Namibia and utilization of living natural resources on a sustainable basis for the benefit of all Namibians, both present and future."

Niger

Section 2, Article 149: "The exploitation and the administration of the natural resources and of the subsoil must be done with transparency and taking into account the protection of the environment, [and] the cultural heritage as well as the preservation of the interests of present and future generations."

Norway

Section 110(b): "Every person has a right to an environment that is conducive to health and to a natural environment whose productivity and diversity are maintained. Natural resources shall be managed on the basis of comprehensive long-term considerations whereby this right will be safeguarded for future generations as well."

Poland

Chapter 2, Article 74(1): "Public authorities shall pursue policies ensuring the ecological safety of current and future generations."

South Africa

Chapter 2, Article 24: "Everyone has the right (a) to an environment that is not harmful to their health or well-being; and (b) to have the environment protected, for the benefit of present and future generations, through reasonable legislative and other measures . . ."

South Sudan

Chapter 41: "(2) Every person shall have the obligation to protect the environment for the benefit of present and future generations; (3) Every person shall have the right to have the environment protected for the benefit of present and future generations, through appropriate legislative action and other measures that: (a) prevent pollution and ecological degradation; (b) promote conservation; and (c) secure ecologically sustainable development and use of natural resources while promoting rational economic and social development so as to protect genetic stability and biodiversity; (4) All levels of government shall develop energy policies that will ensure that the basic needs of the people are met while protecting and preserving the environment."

Vanuatu

Part II, Chapter 2, Article 7(d): "Every person has the following fundamental duties to himself and his descendants and to others . . . to protect the Republic of Vanuatu and to safeguard the national wealth, resources and environment in the interests of the present generations and of future generations."

SUSTAINABLE DEVELOPMENT AND FUTURE GENERATIONS

Albania

Part II, Chapter V5, Article 59(1)(e)–(f): "The State, within its constitutional powers and the means at its disposal, aims to supplement private initiative and responsibility with ... (e) a healthy and ecologically adequate environment for the present and future generations; (f) and rational exploration of forests, waters, pastures and other natural resources on the basis of the principle of sustainable development."

Angola

Article 39(2): "The state shall take the requisite measures to protect the environment and species of flora and fauna throughout national territory, maintain the ecological balance, ensure the correct location of economic activities and the rational development and use of all natural resources, within the context of sustainable development, respect for the rights of future generations and the preservation of species."

"The fundamental tasks of the Angolan state shall be: to promote harmonious and sustainable development throughout national territory, protecting the environment, natural resources and the historic, cultural and artistic heritage of the nation."

"The state shall take the requisite measures to protect the environment and species of flora and fauna throughout national territory, maintain the ecological balance, ensure the correct location of economic activities and the rational development and use of all natural resources, within the context of sustainable development, respect for the rights of future generations and the preservation of species."

Cuba

Chapter 1, Article 27: "The State protects the environment and natural resources of the country. It recognizes their close link with the sustainable economic and social development for making human life more sensible, and for ensuring the survival, welfare, and security of present and future generations. It corresponds to the competent organs to implement this policy."

Dominican Republic

Chapter 4, Article 17: "The mineral and hydrocarbon deposits and, in general, the nonrenewable resources, can only be explored and exploited by individuals, under sustainable environmental criteria, by virtue of concessions, contracts, licenses, permits or quotas, in accordance with the conditions that the law determines."

"The prevention of the pollution [and] the protection and maintaining of the environment for the benefit of the present and future generations, constitute duties of the State. In Consequence: Every person has the right, both individually and collectively, to the sustainable use and enjoyment of the natural resources; to live in a healthy ecologically balanced and suitable environment for the development and preservation of the various forms of life, of the landscape and of nature."

East Timor

Part II, Sections 61(1) and (2): "Everyone has the right to a humane, healthy and ecologically balanced environment and the duty to protect it and improve it for the benefit of the future generations. The State should promote actions aimed at protecting the environment and safeguarding the sustainable development of the economy."

Eritrea

Chapter 2, Article 8(3): "In the interest of present and future generations, the State shall be responsible for managing all land, water, air and natural resources and for ensuring their management in a balanced and sustainable manner; and for creating the conditions to secure the participation of the people in safeguarding the environment."

France

Constitution preamble: "The French People, Considering that ... care must be taken to safeguard the environment along with the other fundamental interests of the Nation ... in order to ensure sustainable development, choices designed to meet the needs of the present generation should not jeopardise the ability of future generations and other peoples to meet their own needs, Hereby proclaim ... public policies shall promote sustainable development.

To this end they shall reconcile the protection and enhancement of the environment with economic development and social progress."

Charter of the Environment, Article 6: "The public policies shall promote sustainable development. To this effect, they reconcile protection and utilization of the environment, economic development and social progress."

Georgia

Article 37, Number 4: "With due regard to the interests of the current and future generations the State shall guarantee the protection of environment and the rational use of nature, sustainable development of the country according to the economic and ecological interests in order to ensure providing of safe environment for the individual."

Guyana

Part II, Title I, Article 149: "The State shall protect the environment, for the benefit of present and future generations, through reasonable legislative and other measures designed to ... secure sustainable development and use of natural resources while promoting justifiable economic and social development."

Malawi

Chapter 3, Article 13(d)(iii): "The State shall actively promote the welfare and development of the people of Malawi by progressively adopting and implementing policies and legislation aimed at achieving the following goals: To manage the environment responsibly in order to ... accord full recognition to the rights of future generations by means of environmental protection and the sustainable development of natural resources."

Maldives

Article 22: "The State has a fundamental duty to protect and preserve the natural environment, biodiversity, resources and beauty of the country for the benefit of present and future generations. The State shall undertake and promote desirable economic and social goals through ecologically balanced sustainable development and shall take measures necessary to foster conservation, prevent pollution, the extinction of any species and ecological degradation from any such goals."

Mozambique

Article 117(2)(d): "With a view to guaranteeing the right to the environment within the framework of sustainable development, the State shall adopt policies aimed at: ... guaranteeing the rational utilisation of natural resources and the safeguarding of their capacity to regenerate, ecological stability and the rights of future generations ..."

Namibia

Article 95(l): "The State shall actively promote and maintain the welfare of the people by adopting, *inter alia*, policies aimed at the following: ... maintenance of ecosytems, essential ecological processes and biological diversity of Namibia and utilization of living natural resources on a sustainable basis for the benefit of all Namibians, both present and future ..."

Qatar

Chapter 2, Article 33: "The State shall work to protect the environment and ecological balance so as to achieve sustainable development for the generations to come."

South Sudan

Part III, Chapter 1, Title XL1(3): "Every person shall have the right to have the environment protected for the benefit of present and future generations, through appropriate legislative action and other measures that: secure ecologically sustainable development and use of natural resources while promoting rational economic and social development so as to protect genetic stability and bio-diversity."

Sweden

Article 2: "The public institutions shall promote sustainable development leading to a good environment for present and future generations."

Zambia

Constitution, Part IX. Article 112(i): "The State shall promote sustenance, development and public awareness of the need to manage the land, air and water resources in a balanced and sustainable manner for the present and future generations."

PUBLIC TRUST

Ghana

Chapter 21, Article 211(1): "All public lands in Ghana shall be vested in the President, on behalf of, and in trust for, the people of Ghana."

Article 213: "Every mineral in its natural state in, under or upon any land in Ghana, rivers, streams, watercourses throughout Ghana, the exclusive economic zone and any area covered by the territorial sea or continental shelf is the property of the Republic of Ghana and shall be vested in the President, on behalf of, and in trust for, the people of Ghana."

Tanzania

Article 22, Preamble: "Whereas the Tanganyika African National Union believes ... That all citizens together possess all the natural resources of the country in trust for their descendants."

PUBLIC TRUST AND FUTURE GENERATIONS

Ethiopia

Article 130(b): "The natural resources in the waters, forests, land, air, lakes, rivers and ports of the Empire are a sacred trust for the benefit of present and succeeding generations of the Ethiopian people."

Papua New Guinea

Goal Number 4(1): "We declare our fourth goal to be for Papua New Guinea's natural resources and environment to be conserved and used for the collective benefit of us all, and be replenished for the benefit of future generations. We accordingly call for ... wise use to be made of our natural resources and the environment in or on the land and seabed, in the sea, under the land, and in the air, in the interests of our development and in trust for future generations."

SUSTAINABLE DEVELOPMENT, FUTURE GENERATIONS AND PUBLIC TRUST

Bhutan

Articles 5, 1 and 2(b): "Every Bhutanese is a trustee of the Kingdom's natural resources and the environment for the benefit of the future and present generations and it is the fundamental duty of every citizen to contribute to the protection of the natural environment, conservation of the rich biodiversity of Bhutan and prevention of all forms of ecological degradation including noise, visual and physical pollution through the adoption and support of environment friendly practices and policies."

"The Royal Government shall ... secure ecologically balanced sustainable development while promoting justifiable economic and social development."

Swaziland

Chapter 12, Article 210(2), Article 216(1), and Article 217(d): "In the interests of the present and future generations, the State shall protect and make rational use of its land, mineral and water resources as well as its fauna and flora, and shall take appropriate measures to conserve and improve the environment."

"From the date of commencement of this Constitution, all land (including any existing concessions) in Swaziland, save privately held title-deed land, shall continue to vest in *iNgwenyama* in trust for the Swazi Nation as it vested on the 12th April, 1973."

"All minerals and mineral oils in, under or upon any land in Swaziland shall, after the commencement of this Constitution, continue to vest in *iNgwenyama* in trust for the Swazi Nation as vested on the 12th April, 1973."

"Every person shall promote the protection of the environment for the present and future generations."

"Parliament shall make laws – ... for the protection of the environment including management of natural resources on a sustainable basis."

Uganda

Chapter 15, Article 245(b): "The State shall promote sustainable development and public awareness of the need to manage land, air and water resources in a balanced and sustainable manner for the present and future generations."

"The utilisation of the natural resources of Uganda shall be managed in such a way as to meet the development and environmental needs of present and future generations of Ugandans."

"The Government or a local government as determined by Parliament by law, shall hold in trust for the people and protect, natural lakes, rivers, wetlands, forest reserves, game reserves, national parks and any land to be reserved for ecological and touristic purposes for the common good of all citizens."

"Parliament shall, by law, provide for measure intended – ... to manage the environment for sustainable development."

Miscellaneous constitutional environmental provisions

CLIMATE CHANGE

Dominican Republic

Dominican Republic Constitution. Chapter 4, Article 17; Chapter 6, Article 67; Title IX, Chapter 1, Article 194: "The formulation and execution, through the law, of a plan of territorial ordering that assures the efficient and sustainable use of the natural resources or the Nation, in accordance with the need of adaption to climate change, is [a] priority of the State."

LIMITATIONS ON WASTE DISPOSAL AND HAZARDOUS ACTIVITIES

Dominican Republic

Article 67(2): "The introduction, development, production, possession, commercialization, transport, storage and use of chemical, biological and nuclear and agrochemical weapons [that are] internationally forbidden, is prohibited, as well as of nuclear residues [and] toxic and hazardous wastes."

Ecuador

Section 2, Article 14: "The development, production, ownership, marketing, import, transport, storage and use of chemical, biological and nuclear weapons, highly toxic persistent organic pollutants, internationally prohibited agrochemicals, and experimental biological technologies and agents and genetically modified organisms that are harmful to human health or that jeopardize food sovereignty or ecosystems, as well as the introduction of nuclear residues and toxic waste into the country's territory, are forbidden."

Haiti, Republic of

Title VIII, Chapter 2, Article 258: "No one may introduce into the country wastes or residues of any kind from foreign sources."

Hungary

Article 21(3): "No pollutant waste shall be brought into Hungary for the purpose of dumping."

Namibia

Chapter 11, Article 95(l): "[T]he Government shall provide measures against the dumping or recycling of foreign nuclear and toxic waste on Namibian territory."

Niger

Article 35: "The acquisition, the storage, the handling and the disposal of toxic wastes or pollutants originating from factories and other industrial or handwork sites, installed on the national territory[,] are regulated by the law. The transit, importation, storage, landfill, [and] dumping on the national territory of foreign pollutants or toxic wastes, as well as any agreement relating [to it] constitute a crime against the Nation, punished by the law."

Paraguay

Part I, Title II, Chapter 1, Section 2, Article 8: "Those activities that are likely to cause environmental changes will be regulated by law. Similarly, the law may restrict or prohibit those activities that are considered hazardous."

PROVISIONS IDENTIFYING RESPONSIBILITIES TO NATURE

Bangladesh

Part II, Article 18A: "The State shall endeavour to protect and improve the environment and to preserve and safeguard the natural resources, biodiversity, wetlands, forests and wild life for the present and future citizens."

Ecuador

Article 71 and Articles 72–4: "Nature, or Pachamama, where life is reproduced and created, has the right to integral respect for her existence, her maintenance, and for the regeneration of her vital cycles, structure, functions, and evolutionary processes."

Germany

Part II, Article 20a: "Mindful also of its responsibility toward future generations, the State protects also the natural bases of life and the animals within the framework of the constitutional order by legislation, and in accordance with law and justice, by executive and judicial power."

Kuwait

Part II, Article 21: "Natural resources and all revenues therefrom are the property of the State. It shall ensure their preservation and proper exploitation . . ."

Lithuania

Chapter 4, Article 54: "The State shall concern itself with the protection of the natural environment, its fauna and flora, separate objects of nature and particularly valuable districts, and shall supervise the moderate utilization of natural resources as well as their restoration and augmentation. The exhaustion of land and entrails of the earth, the pollution of waters and air, the production of radioactive impact, as well as the impoverishment of fauna and flora shall be prohibited by law."

Luxembourg

Article 11.2: "The State . . . promotes the protection and welfare of animals."

Nigeria

Part II, Article 20: "The State shall protect and improve the environment and safeguard the water, air and land, forest and wild life of Nigeria."

Sudan

Chapter 11(2): "The State shall not pursue any policy, or take or permit any action, which may adversely affect the existence of any species of animal or vegetative life, their natural or adopted habitat."

Syria

Part 2, Article 14: "Public ownership includes natural resources."

Yemen

Article 8: "All types of natural resources and sources of energy, whether above ground, underground, in territorial waters, on the continental shelf or the exclusive economic zone are owned by the State, which assure their exploitation for the common good of the people."

PROVISIONS PERTAINING TO ENERGY POLICY

Brazil

Article 225, Section 6: "Power plants with nuclear reactors shall be located as defined in federal law and may not be installed otherwise."

Dominican Republic

Article 67(3): "The State shall promote, in the public and private sectors, the use of alternative and clean [no contaminantes] technologies and energy."

Ecuador

Section 2, Article 15: "The State shall promote, in the public and private sectors, the use of environmentally clean technologies and nonpolluting and low-impact alternative sources of energy. Energy sovereignty shall not be achieved to the detriment of food sovereignty nor shall it affect the right to water."

LIMITATIONS ON PROPERTY RIGHTS

Australia

Chapter 4, Section 100: "The Commonwealth shall not, by any law or regulation of trade or commerce, abridge the right of a State or of the residents therein to the reasonable use of the waters or rivers for conservation or irrigation."

Liberia, Republic of

Chapter 2, Article 7: "The Republic shall, consistent with the principles of individual freedom and social justice enshrined in this Constitution, manage the national economy and the resources of Liberia."

Mauritius

Chapter 2, Section 8(4)(a): "[Making exceptions to the constitution's prohibition against the compulsory taking of property when:] (v) by reason of its being in a dangerous state or injurious to the health of human beings, animals, trees or plants . . . [or] (vii) for so long only as may be necessary for the purposes of any examination, investigation, trial or inquiry or, in the case of land, the carrying out on it (A) of work of soil conservation or the conservation of other natural resources; or (B) of agricultural development or improvement that the owner or occupier of the land has been required, and has, without reasonable and lawful excuse, refused or failed to carry out."

Mongolia

Chapter 1, Article 6(4): "The State shall have the right to hold responsible the landowners in connection with the manner the land is used, to exchange or take it over with compensation on the grounds of special public need, or confiscate the land if it is used in a manner adverse to the health of the population, the interests of environmental protection and national security."

RELATIONSHIP OF ENVIRONMENTAL RIGHTS
TO OTHER FREEDOMS

Chile

Chapter 3, Article 19: "The law can establish specific restrictions on the exercise of certain rights or freedoms in order to protect the environment."

Estonia

Chapter 2, Article 34: "All persons who are legally sojourning in Estonia shall have the right to freedom of movement and choice of residence. The right to freedom of movement may be restricted only in the cases and in accordance with procedures established by law . . . to protect the environment."

Madagascar, Republic of

Title II, Sub-title II, Article 37: "The State guarantees the freedom of enterprise within the limits of respect for the general interest, the public order and the environment."

RELATED PROVISIONS PERTAINING TO HEALTH

Comoros

Preamble: "[There is] the right of all Comorans to health . . ."

Croatia

Chapter 2, Section 3, Part III, Article 69: "Everyone shall have the right to a healthy life."

Guatemala

Title II, Chapter 2, Section 7, Article 93: "The right to health is a fundamental right of the human being without any discrimination."

Guinea-Bissau

Title I, Article 15: "The object of public health shall be to . . . encourage [the people's] balanced integration into the social ecological sphere in which they live."

Honduras

Title III, Chapter 7, Article 145: "The right to the protection of one's health is hereby recognized."

REQUIREMENTS TO CONSIDER ENVIRONMENTAL IMPACTS

Niger

Article 35: "The State sees to the evaluation and control of the impacts of any project and program of development on the environment."

REQUIREMENTS FOR ENVIRONMENTAL EDUCATION

France

Charter of the Environment, Article 8: "Education and training on the environment shall contribute to the exercise of the rights and obligations defined by this Charter."

SUBNATIONAL ENVIRONMENTAL POLICY

Australia

Chapter 4, Section 100: "The Commonwealth shall not, by any law or regulation of trade or commerce, abridge the right of a State or of the residents therein to the reasonable use of the waters or rivers for conservation or irrigation."

Bangkok

"The State shall follow the Policy Directive on Land, Natural Resources, and Environment as follows: Establish rules on land use to cover the whole country, by considering the consistency of the natural environment, including land area, water surface, ways of life of local communities, and the efficient conservation on the natural resources; provide the standard measures for sustainable land use, with regard to the joint decision making by the residents of the area affected by that land-use policy ... lay out a town and country planning effectively and efficiently for the interests of sustainable natural resource preservation ... promote, maintain, and protect the quality of environment on the principle of sustainable development." (Bangkok constitution. Part VIII, Sections 85[1][3] and [5]. English original text of the Constitution of 2007 as translated by IFES and the US Embassy in Bangkok for the Constitutional Court.)

Cape Verde

Part II, Title III, Article 70(2): "The state and municipalities, with the cooperation of associations for environmental protection, shall adopt policies for the protection and conservation of environment."

Part II, Title III, Article 70(3): "The State shall stimulate and support the creation of associations for the protection of the environment and protect natural resources."

Guatemala

Title II, Chapter 2, Section 7, Article 97: "[T]he municipalities ... of the national territory are obliged to promote social, economic, and technological development that would prevent the contamination of the environment and maintain the ecological balance."

Hong Kong

Basic Law of the Hong Kong Special Administrative Region of the People's Republic of China, Chapter 4, Section 5, Article 97: "District organizations which are not organs of political power may be established in the Hong Kong Special Administrative Region, to be consulted by the government of the Region on district administration and other affairs, or to be responsible for providing services in such fields as culture, recreation and environmental sanitation."

Chapter 5, Section 1, Article 119: "The Government of the Hong Kong Special Administrative Region shall formulate appropriate policies to promote and coordinate the development of various trades such as manufacturing, commerce, tourism, real estate, transport, public utilities, services, agriculture and fisheries, and pay regard to the protection of the environment."

Switzerland

Sustainable development. "The Confederation and the Cantons shall endeavor to achieve a balanced and sustainable relationship between nature and its capacity to renew itself and the demands placed on it by the population."

Switzerland constitution. Section 4, Article 73. English text of the Constitution of 1999 as amended by the Referendum of November 30, 2008.

DRAFT PROVISIONS

Tunisia (December, 2012)

Preamble: "Supporting the will of the people to be a maker of their own history, while believing in work as a sublime human value, seeking leadership, opting to contribute to civilisation by caring for the environment in such a manner that guarantees a safe sustainable life and better tomorrow for future generations, on the basis of peace, human solidarity and independence of the national decision."

Article 33: "Each person shall have the right to live in a peaceful and balanced environment and shall be entitled to sustainable development.

'Protection of environment and wise utilisation of natural resources shall be the responsibility of the state, institutions and people.'"

Article 34: "Every person shall have the right to water. The state shall protect water resources and rationalise the use thereof and distribute them fairly."

Rights to water

ENVIRONMENTAL RIGHTS

Andorra

Article 31: "The State has the task of ensuring the rational use of the soil and of all the natural resources, so as to guarantee a befitting quality of life for all and, for the sake of the coming generations, to restore and maintain a reasonable ecological balance in the atmosphere, water and land, as well as to protect the autochthonous flora and fauna."

Cambodia

Article 59: "The State shall protect the environment and balance of abundant natural resources and establish a precise plan of management of land, water, air, wind, geology, ecological systems, mines, energy, petrol and gas, rocks and sand, gems, forests and forestrial products, wildlife, fish and aquatic resources."

Eritrea

Article 8(3): "The State shall have the responsibility to regulate all land, water and natural resources and to ensure their management in a balanced and sustainable manner and in the interest of the present and future generations; and to create the right conditions for securing the participation of the people to safeguard the environment."

Guyana

Article 36: "In the interests of the present and future generations, the State will protect and make rational use of its land, mineral and water resources, as well as its fauna and flora, and will take all appropriate measures to conserve and improve the environment."

Kenya

Allocation of responsibilities to national government: 22. Protection of the environment and natural resources with a view to establishing a durable and sustainable system of development, including, in particular – (a) fishing, hunting and gathering; (b) protection of animals and wildlife; (c) water protection, securing sufficient residual water, hydraulic engineering and the safety of dams; and (d) energy policy."

Laos

Article 17: "All organisations and citizens must protect the environment and natural resources: land, underground, forests, fauna, water sources and atmosphere."

Lithuania

Article 54: "The State shall take care of the protection of the natural environment, wildlife and plants, individual objects of nature and areas of particular value and shall supervise a sustainable use of natural resources, their restoration and increase.

'The destruction of land and the underground, the pollution of water and air, radioactive impact on the environment as well as depletion of wildlife and plants shall be prohibited by law.'"

Nigeria

Article 20: "The State shall protect and improve the environment and safeguard the water, air and land, forest and wild life of Nigeria."

Philippines

Article 12, Section 2: "The State shall protect the nation's marine wealth in its archipelagic waters, territorial sea, and exclusive economic zone, and reserve its use and enjoyment exclusively to Filipino citizens."

Article 12, Section 4: "The Congress shall provide for such period as it may determine, measures to prohibit logging in endangered forests and watershed areas."

Samoa

Section 14: "Rights regarding property shall not be affected by general laws regarding . . . (k) Providing for the carrying out of work on land for the purpose of soil conservation or for the protection of water catchment areas."

South Korea

Article 120 [Natural resources]: "(1) Licenses to exploit, develop, or utilize minerals and all other important underground resources, marine resources, water power, and natural powers available for economic use may be granted for a period of time under the conditions as prescribed by law. (2) The land and natural resources are protected by the State, and the State establishes a plan necessary for their balanced development and utilization."

Taiwan (Republic of China)

Article 169: "The State shall also guarantee and provide assistance and encouragement for aboriginal education, culture, transportation, water conservation, health and medical care, economic activity, land, and social welfare, measures for which shall be established by law."

Tajikistan

Article 13: "The earth, its resources, water, the atmosphere, flora, fauna, and other natural resources are the exclusive property of the state, and the government guarantees their effective utilization in the interests of the people" (public trust doctrine).

Thailand

Directive principles, Section 84: "The state shall implement the land, natural resources, and environment policy as follows: (1) The state shall organize the system of land use in accordance with the natural environment in each locality – technically to be applied with land and water areas nationwide, arrange for town planning which is in harmony with the environment, and allow people in areas affected by the implementation of this policy to participate in decision-making process."

Uganda

Chapter 27: "(i) The State shall promote sustainable development and public awareness of the need to manage land, air and water resources in a balanced and sustainable manner for the present and future generations ... the State shall take all possible measures to prevent or minimise damage and destruction to land, air and water resources resulting from pollution or other causes."

HUMAN RIGHTS

Colombia

Article 366: "The general welfare and improvement of the population quality of life are social purposes of the state. A basic objective of the state's activity will be to address unsatisfied public health, educational, environmental, and potable water needs."

Ethiopia

Article 90: "1. Every Ethiopian shall be entitled, within the limits of the country's resources, to food, clean water, shelter, health, education and security of pension."

Gambia, The

Section 216(4): "The State shall endeavour to facilitate equal access to clean and safe water, adequate health and medical services, habitable shelter, sufficient food and security to all persons."

Iraq

Exclusive federal authority: "... Eighth: Plan policies relating to water sources from outside Iraq, and guarantee the rate of water flow to Iraq and its fair distribution, in accordance with international laws and norms."

Kenya

Chapter 43: "(1) Every person has the right – ... (d) to clean and safe water in adequate quantities."

Chapter 56: "The State shall put in place affirmative action programmes designed to ensure that minorities and marginalised groups – ... (e) have reasonable access to water, health services and infrastructure.

'Equalization Fund used to supply basic services including water to marginalized areas: 10. Implementation of specific national government policies on natural resources and environmental conservation, including – (a) soil and water conservation; and (b) forestry. 11. County public works and services, including – (a) storm water management systems in built-up areas; and (b) water and sanitation services.'"

Maldives

Article 23: "Every citizen [has] the following rights pursuant to this Constitution, and the State undertakes to achieve the progressive realisation of these rights by reasonable measures within its ability and resources: (a) adequate and nutritious food and clean water ..."

Paraguay

Article 163: "A departmental government will have jurisdiction: 1. To coordinate activities among the various municipalities within the department, to organize joint departmental services such as public works, power supply, potable water, and others that would serve more than one municipality; as well as to promote associations to promote cooperation among them."

South Africa

Article 27.1: "Everyone has the right to have access to – (b) sufficient food and water; enforced by regular reports on progressive realization."

Uganda

Chapter 14: "General social and economic objectives. The State shall endeavour to fulfill the fundamental rights of all Ugandans to social justice and economic development and shall, in particular, ensure that – ... (b) all

Ugandans enjoy rights and opportunities and access to education, health services, clean and safe water, work, decent shelter, adequate clothing, food security and pension and retirement benefits."

Chapter 21: "Clean and safe water. The State shall take all practical measures to promote a good water management system at all levels."

Representative subnational environmental constitutionalism in Brazil and the United States [Additional subnational provisions found at: www.environmentalconstitutionalism.org]

BRAZIL

(Provisions for Santa Catarina and São Paulo only. Remaining subnational provisions from Brazil are found in the "the website address above.")

Santa Catarina

Article 9: "It is incumbent upon the State, along with the Federal Union and the Municipalities, to:

III – protect the documents, works and other assets of historical, artistic and cultural value, monuments, notable natural areas and archaeological sites;

VI – protect the environment and fight pollution in any of its forms;

VII – preserve forests, fauna and flora;

XI – register, monitor and supervise concessions rights of research and exploitation of mineral and water resources within its territory;"

Article 10: "It is incumbent upon the State to legislate concurrently with the Union on:

VI – forests, hunting, fishing, wildlife, nature conservation, protection of soil and natural resources, environmental protection and pollution control;

VII – protection of the historical, cultural, artistic, tourist and landscape heritage;

VIII – liability for environmental damage, as well as consumer, material and immaterial rights of artistic, aesthetic, historic, touristic and landscape value;"

Article 181: "All have the right to an ecologically balanced environment, and both the Government and the community shall have the duty to defend and preserve it for present and future generations."

Article 182: "It is incumbent upon the State, in the manner prescribed by law, to:

I – preserve and restore essential ecological processes and provide the ecological management of species and ecosystems;

II – preserve the diversity and integrity of the genetic heritage of the State and supervise entities dedicated to research and manipulation of genetic material;

III – protect the fauna and flora, with prohibition of practices that may endanger their ecological function, cause the extinction species or subject animals to cruelty;

IV – define within the State, territorial spaces and its components to be specially protected, and the alteration and suppression can only be allowed by law, with prohibition of any use that compromises the integrity of attributes which justify their protection;

V – require for installation of work or activity that may potentially cause significant degradation of the environment, previous environmental impact studies, which shall be made public;

VI – control the production, sale and use of techniques, methods and substances that represent a risk to life, quality of life and the environment;

VII – promote environmental education in all levels of public and private education, as well as promote public awareness to preserve the environment, ensured joint action of the boards of education and performance in the environmental area;

VIII – systematically inform the public about the levels of pollution, the quality of the environment, the situations that impose accident risks and the presence of substances potentially harmful to health in water, air, soil and food;

IX – to protect domestic animals, historically related with man, that suffer the consequences of urbanization and of modernity.

1st Paragraph. The voluntary participation in programs and projects of environmental monitoring shall be considered relevant service accomplished for the State.

2nd Paragraph. The State shall establish, in the military police, special body of forest police."

Article 183: "The result of the State's participation in exploration of petroleum or natural gas, water and coal for purposes of generating electricity and other mineral resources in their territory, continental shelf, territorial sea or exclusive economic zone, is preferably applied in the mining and energy sector and in programs and projects for environmental monitoring, conservation and recovery."

Article 184: "The following areas are considered of special ecological interest, and its use shall require prior authorization by the competent bodies approved by the Legislature, preserved their special attributes:

I – the Mata Atlântica;
II – the Serra Geral;
III – the Serra do Mar;
IV – the Serra Costeira;
V – bands protecting surface waters;
VI – the slopes susceptible to landslides.

São Paulo

Article 192: "The execution of works, activities, processes and projects and the exploitation of natural resources of any kind, either by the public or by the private sector, shall be admitted if there is safeguard for the ecologically balanced environment.

1st Paragraph. The granting of the environmental permit, by body or governmental authority, part of a unified system shall be made in compliance with the general criteria laid down by law, and norms and standards set forth by the Government and in accordance with environmental planning and zoning.

2nd Paragraph. The environmental permit, renewed in the manner provided by law, for the implementation and operation mentioned in this article, when potentially harmful for the environmental, shall always be preceded, as per the criteria specified by the legislation, by the approval of a prior Environmental Impact Study and report, which shall be made public, being the public hearings guaranteed."

Article 197: "The following are considered permanent protection areas:

I – mangroves;
II – the springs, the wellsprings and the riparian areas;
III – areas that harbor rare specimens of fauna and flora, as well as those that serve as landing site or reproduction of migratory animals;
IV – the estuarine areas;
V – the remarkable landscapes;
VI – the natural underground cavities.

Water resources
Article 205: "The State shall establish, by law, the integrated management of water resources, bringing together state and local agencies and governments and civil society, and ensure financial and institutional means to:

I – the rational use of surface and groundwater and its priority for population supply;

III – the protection of waters against actions that could jeopardize the current and future use;"

Article 206: "The groundwater, deemed strategic reserves for economic and social development and valuable for public water supply, shall have a permanent program of conservation and protection against pollution and overexploitation, with guidelines established by law."

Article 208: "It is prohibited to discharge effluents and municipal and industrial sewage, without proper treatment, in any bay water resource.

Article 209: "The State shall adopt measures for erosion control, setting standards for soil conservation in agricultural and urban areas."

UNITED STATES

Alabama

Alabama constitution. Article 11, Section 219.07(1): "The Legislature of Alabama finds that Alabama is endowed with a rich diversity of natural areas having unique ecological systems, plant and animal life, geological formations, wildlife habitats, recreational values and scenic beauty. As a part of the continuing growth of the population and the economic development of the state, it is necessary and desirable that certain lands and waters be set aside, managed and preserved for use as state parks, nature preserves, recreation areas, and wildlife management areas."

California

California constitution. Article 10, Section 2: "It is hereby declared that because of the conditions prevailing in this State the general welfare requires that the water resources of the State be put to beneficial use to the fullest extent of which they are capable, and that the waste or unreasonable use or unreasonable method of use of water be prevented, and that the conservation of such waters is to be exercised with a view to the reasonable and beneficial use thereof in the interest of the people and for the public welfare. The right to water or to the use or flow of water in or from any natural stream or water course in this State is and shall be limited to such water as shall be reasonably required for the beneficial use to be served, and such right does not and shall not extend to the waste or unreasonable use or unreasonable method of use or unreasonable method of diversion of water. Riparian rights in a stream or water course attach to, but to no more than so much of the flow thereof as may be required or used consistently with this section, for the purposes for which such lands are, or may be made adaptable, in view of such reasonable and beneficial uses; provided, however, that nothing herein contained shall be construed as depriving any riparian owner of the reasonable use of water of the stream to which the owner's land is riparian under reasonable methods of diversion and use, or as depriving any appropriator of water to which the appropriator is lawfully entitled. This section shall be self-executing, and the Legislature may also enact laws in the furtherance of the policy in this section contained."

Colorado

Colorado constitution. Article 18, Section 6: "The general assembly shall enact laws in order to prevent the destruction of, and to keep in good preservation, the forests upon the lands of the state, or upon lands of the public domain, the control of which shall be conferred by congress upon the state."

Florida

Florida constitution. Article 2, Section 7: "It shall be the policy of the state to conserve and protect its natural resources and scenic beauty. Adequate provision shall be made by law for the abatement of air and water pollution and of excessive and unnecessary noise and for the conservation and protection of natural resources.

'Those in the Everglades Agricultural Area who cause water pollution within the Everglades Protection Area or the Everglades Agricultural Area shall be primarily responsible for paying the costs of the abatement of that pollution.'"

Hawaii

Hawaii constitution. Article 11, Section 9: "Each person has the right to a clean and healthful environment, as defined by laws relating to environmental quality, including control of pollution and conservation, protection and enhancement of natural resources. Any person may enforce this right against any party, public or private, through appropriate legal proceedings, subject to reasonable limitations and regulation as provided by law."

Idaho

Idaho constitution. Article 15, Section 1: "The use of all waters now appropriated, or that may hereafter be appropriated for sale, rental or distribution; also of all water originally appropriated for private use, but which after such appropriation has heretofore been, or may hereafter be sold, rented, or distributed, is hereby declared to be a public use, and subject to the regulations and control of the state in the manner prescribed by law."

Illinois

Illinois constitution. Article 11, Section 2: "Each person has the right to a healthful environment. Each person may enforce this right against any party, governmental or private, through appropriate legal proceedings subject to reasonable limitation and regulation as the General Assembly may provide by law."

Louisiana

Louisiana constitution. Article 9, Section 1: "The natural resources of the state, including air and water, and the healthful, scenic, historic, and esthetic quality of the environment shall be protected, conserved, and replenished insofar as possible and consistent with the health, safety, and welfare of the people. The legislature shall enact laws to implement this policy."

Massachusetts

Massachusetts constitution. Article 97: "The people shall have the right to clean air and water, freedom from excessive and unnecessary noise, and the natural, scenic, historic, and esthetic qualities of their environment; and the protection of the people in their right to the conservation, development and utilization of the agricultural, mineral, forest, water, air and other natural resources is hereby declared to be a public purpose.

'The general court shall have the power to enact legislation necessary or expedient to protect such rights.'"

Michigan

Michigan constitution. Article 13, Section 52: "The conservation and development of the natural resources of the state are hereby declared to be of paramount public concern in the interest of the health, safety and general welfare of the people. The legislature shall provide for the protection of the air, water and other natural resources of the state from pollution, impairment and destruction."

Minnesota

Minnesota constitution. Article 13, Section 12: "Hunting and fishing and the taking of game and fish are a valued part of our heritage that shall be forever preserved for the people and shall be managed by law and regulation for the public good."

Missouri

Missouri constitution. Article 3, Section 37: "The general assembly may authorize the contracting of an indebtedness on behalf of the state of Missouri and the issuance of bonds or other evidences of indebtedness not exceeding in the aggregate the sum of one hundred fifty million dollars for the purpose of providing funds for use in this state for the protection of the environment through the control of water pollution."

Montana

Montana constitution. Article 2, Section 3: "All persons are born free and have certain inalienable rights. They include the right to a clean and healthful environment and the rights of pursuing life's basic necessities, enjoying and defending their lives and liberties, acquiring, possessing and protecting property, and seeking their safety, health and happiness in all lawful ways. In enjoying these rights, all persons recognize corresponding responsibilities."

New Mexico

New Mexico constitution. Article 20, Section 21: "The state's beautiful and healthful environment is hereby declared to be of fundamental importance to the public interest, health, safety and the general welfare. The legislature shall provide for control of pollution and control of despoilment of the air, water and other natural resources of this state, consistent with the use and development of these resources for the maximum benefit of the people."

New York

New York constitution. Article 14, Section 1: "The lands of the state, now owned or hereafter acquired, constituting the forest preserve as now fixed by law, shall be forever kept as wild forest lands. They shall not be leased, sold or exchanged, or be taken by any corporation, public or private, nor shall the timber thereon be sold, removed or destroyed."

Article 14, Section 3: "Forest and wild life conservation are hereby declared to be policies of the state. For the purpose of carrying out such policies the legislature may appropriate moneys for the acquisition by the state of land, outside of the Adirondack and Catskill parks as now fixed by law, for the practice of forest or wild life conservation."

Article 14, Section 4: "The policy of the state shall be to conserve and protect its natural resources and scenic beauty and encourage the development and improvement of its agricultural lands for the production of food and other agricultural products. The legislature, in implementing this policy, shall include adequate provision for the abatement of air and water pollution and of excessive and unnecessary noise, the protection of agricultural lands, wetlands and shorelines, and the development and regulation of water resources. The legislature shall further provide for the acquisition of lands and waters, including improvements thereon and any interest therein, outside the forest preserve counties, and the dedication of properties so acquired or now owned, which because of their natural beauty, wilderness character, or geological, ecological or historical significance, shall be preserved and administered for the use and enjoyment of the people. Properties so dedicated shall constitute the state nature and historical preserve and they shall not be taken or otherwise disposed of except by law enacted by two successive regular sessions of the legislature."

North Carolina

North Carolina constitution. Article 14, Section 5: "It shall be the policy of this State to conserve and protect its lands and waters for the benefit of all its citizenry, and to this end it shall be a proper function of the State of North Carolina and its political subdivisions to acquire and preserve park, recreational, and scenic areas, to control and limit the pollution of our air and water, to control excessive noise, and in every other appropriate way to preserve as a part of the common heritage of this State its forests, wetlands, estuaries, beaches, historical sites, openlands, and places of beauty."

Ohio

Ohio constitution. Article 8, Section 2: "It is determined and confirmed that the environmental and related conservation, preservation, and revitalization purposes referred to in ... this section, and provisions for them, are proper public purposes of the state and local governmental entities and are necessary and appropriate means to improve the quality of life and the general and economic well-being of the people of this state; to better ensure the public health, safety, and welfare; to protect water and other natural resources; to provide for the conservation and preservation of natural and open areas and farmlands, including by making urban areas more desirable or suitable for development and revitalization; to control, prevent, minimize, clean up, or remediate certain contamination of or pollution from lands in the state and water contamination or pollution; to provide for safe and productive urban land use or reuse; to enhance the availability, public use, and enjoyment of natural areas and resources; and to create and preserve jobs and enhance employment opportunities."

Oregon

Oregon constitution. Article 11, Section 2: "In the manner provided by law and notwithstanding the limitations contained in sections 7 and 8, Article XI, of this Constitution, the credit of the State of Oregon may be loaned and indebtedness incurred in an amount not to exceed, at any one time, one percent of the true cash value of all taxable property in the state: (1) To provide funds to be advanced, by contract, grant, loan or otherwise, to any municipal corporation, city, county or agency of the State of Oregon, or combinations thereof, for the purpose of planning, acquisition, construction, alteration or improvement of facilities for or activities related to, the collection, treatment, dilution and disposal of all forms of waste in or upon the air, water and lands of this state."

Pennsylvania

Pennsylvania constitution. Article 1, Section 27: "The people have a right to clean air, pure water, and to the preservation of the natural, scenic, historic and esthetic values of the environment. Pennsylvania's public natural resources are the common property of all the people, including generations yet to come. As trustee of these resources, the Commonwealth shall conserve and maintain them for the benefit of all the people."

Puerto Rico

Puerto Rico constitution. Article 6, Section 19: "It shall be the public policy of the Commonwealth to conserve, develop and use its natural resources in the most effective manner possible for the general welfare of the community."

Rhode Island

Rhode Island constitution. Article 1, Section 17: "The people shall continue to enjoy and freely exercise all the rights of fishery, and the privileges of the shore, to which they have been heretofore entitled under the charter and usages of this state, including but not limited to fishing from the shore, the gathering of seaweed, leaving the shore to swim in the sea and passage along the shore; and they shall be secure in their rights to the use and enjoyment of the natural resources of the state with due regard for the preservation of their values; and it shall be the duty of the general assembly to provide for the conservation of the air, land, water, plant, animal, mineral and other natural resources of the state, and to adopt all means necessary and proper by law to protect the natural environment of the people of the state by providing adequate resource planning for the control and regulation of the use of the natural resources of the state and for the preservation, regeneration and restoration of the natural environment of the state."

Utah

Utah constitution. Article 18, Section 1: "The Legislature shall enact laws to prevent the destruction of and to preserve the Forests on the lands of the State, and upon any part of the public domain, the control of which may be conferred by Congress upon the State."

Virginia

Virginia constitution. Article 11, Section 2: "To the end that the people have clean air, pure water, and the use and enjoyment for recreation of adequate public lands, waters, and other natural resources, it shall be the policy of the Commonwealth to conserve, develop, and utilize its natural resources, its public lands, and its historical sites and buildings. Further, it shall be the Commonwealth's policy to protect its atmosphere, lands, and waters from pollution, impairment, or destruction, for the benefit, enjoyment, and general welfare of the people of the Commonwealth."

Procedural environmental rights: provisions regarding information, participation, and access to justice in environmental matters

INFORMATION

Albania

Article 56: "Everyone has the right to be informed about the status of the environment and its protection."

Argentina

Section 41: "The authorities shall provide for environmental information and education."

Armenia

Article 33.2: "The public officials shall be held responsible for hiding information on environmental issues and denying access to it."

Azerbaijan

Part II, Chapter 3, Article 39(11): "Everyone has the right to collect information on the environmental situation ..."

Belarus

Section 2, Article 34: "Citizens are guaranteed the right to receive, store and disseminate complete, reliable, and timely information ... on the state of the environment."

Chechnya

Section 1, Chapter 2, Article 39: "Everyone has the right to a decent environment, reliable information about its condition . . ."

Czech Republic

Charter of Fundamental Rights and Freedoms, Article 35(2): Everybody is entitled to timely and complete information about the state of the environment and natural resources."

Eritrea

Chapter 2, Article 8(2): "The State shall work to bring about a balanced and sustainable development throughout the country, and shall use all available means to enable all citizens to improve their livelihood in a sustainable manner, through their participation."

France

Charter of the Environment, Article 7: "Everyone has the right, subject to the conditions and within the limits defined by the law, to have access to the information relating to the environment held by the public authorities."

Georgia

Chapter 2, Article 37(5): "A person shall have the right to receive complete, objective and timely information on the state of his or her working and living environment."

Iceland (draft)

Article 35: "The public authorities shall inform the public on the state of the environment and nature and the impact of construction thereon. The public authorities and others shall provide information on an imminent danger to nature, such as environmental pollution. The law shall secure the right of the public to have the opportunity to participate in the preparation of decisions that have an impact on the environment and nature as well as the possibility to seek independent verdicts thereon. In taking decisions regarding Iceland's nature and environment, the public authorities shall base their decisions on the main principles of environmental law."

Kazakhstan

Section 2, Article 31(2): "Officials are held accountable ... for the concealment of facts and circumstances endangering the life and health of the people."

Latvia

Chapter 8, Article 115: "The State shall protect the right of everyone to live in a benevolent environment by providing information about environmental conditions and by promoting the preservation and improvement of the environment."

Moldova

Title II, Chapter 2, Article 37(2): "The State guarantees every person the right of free access to truthful information regarding the state of the natural environment, the living and working conditions and the quality of food products and household goods."

Montenegro

Article 23: "Everyone shall have the right to a sound environment. Everyone shall have the right to receive timely and full information about the status of the environment, to influence the decision-making regarding the issues of importance for the environment, and to legal protection of these rights."

Norway

Section E, Article 110b: "In order to safeguard their right [to a healthy environment] [citizens are to be] informed of the state of the natural environment and of the effects of any encroachments on nature that are planned or commenced."

Poland

Chapter 2, Article 74: "3. Everyone has the right to be informed of the condition and protection of the environment."

Russian Federation

Chapter 2, Article 42: "Everyone shall have the right to a favorable environment, [and] reliable information about its condition . . ."

Serbia

Article 74: "Everyone shall have the right to healthy environment and the right to timely and full information about the state of environment."

Ukraine

Chapter 2, Article 50: "Everyone is guaranteed the right of free access to information about the environmental situation . . . and also the right to disseminate such information."

Zambia

Section 302: "(o) the people shall have access to environmental information to enable them to preserve, protect and conserve the environment."

PARTICIPATION

Brazil

Title II, Chapter 4: " . . . require, as provided by law, a prior environmental impact study, which shall be made public, for installation of works or activities that may cause significant degradation of the environment."

Colombia

Title II, Chapter 3, Article 79: "Every individual has the right to enjoy a healthy environment. The law will guarantee the community's participation in the decisions that may affect it."

Ecuador

Article 71: "All persons, communities, peoples and nations can call upon public authorities to enforce the rights of nature."

Eritrea

Chapter 2, Article 8(3): "[T]he State shall be responsible ... for creating the right conditions to secure the participation of the people in safeguarding the environment."

Ethiopia

Chapter 10, Article 92(3): "People have the right to full consultation and to the expression of views in the planning and implementations of environmental policies and projects that affect them directly."

Finland

Chapter 2, Section 20: "The public authorities shall endeavor to guarantee ... for everyone the possibility to influence the decisions that concern their own living environment."

France

Charter of the Environment, Article 7: "Everyone has the right, subject to the conditions and within the limits defined by the law ... to participate in the making of public decisions which have an impact on the environment."

Iceland (draft)

Article 35: "The law shall secure the right of the public to have the opportunity to participate in the preparation of decisions that have an impact on the environment and nature as well as the possibility to seek independent verdicts thereon. In taking decisions regarding Iceland's nature and environment, the public authorities shall base their decisions on the main principles of environmental law."

Kosovo

Articles 52(2) and (3): "2. Everyone should be provided an opportunity to be heard by public institutions and have their opinions considered on issues that impact the environment in which they live. 3. The impact on the environment shall be considered by public institutions in their decision making processes."

Poland

Chapter 2, Article 74: "4. Public authorities shall support the activities of citizens to protect and improve the quality of the environment."

Thailand (revoked)

Ra tta'tamma noon Ha'eng Raatcha anaaja'k Tai [Constitution] Part XII, Section 67: "Any project or activity which may seriously affect the quality of the environment, natural resources and biological diversity shall not be permitted, unless its impacts on the quality of the environment and on health of the people in the communities have been studied and evaluated and consultation with the public and interested parties have been organized, and opinions of an independent organization, consisting of representatives from private environmental and health organizations and from higher education institutions providing studies in the field of environment, natural resources or health, have been obtained prior to the operation of such project or activity."

Zambia

Section 302: "(n) the people shall be involved and participate in the development of relevant policies, plans and programmes."

JUSTICE

Angola

Article 39(3): "Acts that endanger or damage conservation of the environment shall be punishable by law."

Article 74 (right to popular action): "Every citizen, either individually or through associations representing specific interests, shall have the right to take legal action in the cases and under the terms established by law, with the aim of annulling acts which are harmful to ... the environment ... the legality of administrative acts and any other collective interests."

Azerbaijan

Part II, Chapter 3, Article 39(11): "Everyone has the right ... to get compensation for damage rendered to the health and property due to the violation of ecological rights."

Bolivia

Article 34: "Any person, in his own right or on behalf of a collective, is authorized to take legal actions in defense of environmental rights, without prejudice to the obligation of public institutions to act on their own in the face of attacks on the environment."

Brazil

Title II, Chapter I, Article 5, Paragraph 73: "[A]ny citizen has standing to bring a popular action to annul an act injurious to the public patrimony or the patrimony of an entity in which the State participates ... to the environment ..."

Burkina Faso

Title I, Chapter 4, Article 30: "Every citizen has the right to initiate an action or to join a collective action under the form of a petition against the acts ... affecting the environment or the cultural or historic patrimony."

Chechnya

Section 1, Chapter 2, Article 39: "Everyone has the right to a decent environment ... and compensation for damage caused to their health or property as a result of ecological violations of the law."

Chile

Chapter 3, Article 20: "Anybody who, due to arbitrary or illegal actions or omissions, suffers privation, disturbance or threats in the legitimate exercise of the rights and guarantees established in Article 19 [including a "right to live in an environment that is free from contamination"] ... (24) ... may ... approach the respective Court of Appeal which shall immediately adopt the measures that it deems necessary to re-establish the rule of law and to ensure the due protection of the affected person without prejudice to other rights which he/she might invoke before the competent authorities or courts. The action of for the protection of fundamental rights shall always lie in the case of numeral 8 of Article 19, when the right to live in an environment free from contamination has been affected by an illegal act or omission imputable to an authority or specific person."

Costa Rica

Title V, Article 50: "Every person has the right to a healthy and ecologically balanced environment. Due to this, the person is justified to denounce those acts which infringe this right and to claim reparation for harm caused. The state shall guarantee, defend and preserve this right. The law will determine the corresponding responsibilities and sanctions."

Dominican Republic

Article 67(5): "The public powers shall prevent and control the factors of environmental degradation [deterioro], will impose the legal sanctions, [and] the objective responsibility for damages caused to the environment and to the natural resources and will require reparation [of] them. Likewise, they will cooperate with other nations in the protection of the ecosystems along the maritime and terrestrial frontier."

Finland

Chapter 2, Section 20: "The public authorities shall endeavor to guarantee for ... everyone the possibility to influence the decisions that concern their own living environment."

Kazakhstan

Section II, Article 31(2): "Officials are held accountable ... for the concealment of facts and circumstances endangering the life and health of the people."

Kenya

Chapter 42: "Every person has the right to a clean and healthy environment, which includes the right ... (b) to have obligations relating to the environment fulfilled under Article 70." [Article 70 provides that any person may apply to a court for redress of damage to the environment.]

Kyrgyzstan

Section 1, Chapter 2, Section 3, Article 35(1): "[C]itizens of the Kyrgyz Republic have the right to a favorable and healthy natural environment and to compensation for the damage caused to health or property by the activity in the area of nature exploitation."

Madagascar

Title II, Sub-title II, Article 35: "The Fokonolona can take the appropriate measures tending to oppose acts susceptible to destroy their environment, dispossess them of their land, claim the traditional spaces allocated to their herds of cattle or claim their ceremonial heritage, unless these measures may undermine the general interest or public order."

Mozambique

Article 81: "1. All citizens shall have the right to popular action in accordance with the law, either personally or through associations for defending the interests in question. 2. The right of popular action shall consist of: (a) the right to claim for the injured party or parties such compensation as they are entitled to; (b) The right to advocate the prevention, termination or judicial prosecution of offences against the public health, consumer rights, environmental conservation and cultural heritage."

Paraguay

Part I, Title II, Chapter 1, Section 2, Article 8: "A law will define and establish sanctions for ecological crimes. Any damage to the environment will entail an obligation to restore and to pay for damages."

Portugal

Part I, Section 2, Chapter 2, Article 52(3): "To all is conferred – personally or through associations that purport to defend the interests in issue – the right of popular action in the cases and under the conditions specified by law, including the right to advocate on behalf of the aggrieved party or parties . . . to promote the prevention, the suppression and the prosecution of offenses against . . . the preservation of the environment."

Russian Federation

Chapter 2, Article 42: "Everyone shall have the right to . . . compensation for the damage caused to his or her health or property by ecological violations."

Bibliography

PRIMARY SOURCES

Cases

African Commission on Human and Peoples' Rights

Social and Economic Rights Action Center 155/96 (African Commission on Human and Peoples' Rights, October 27, 2001).

Antigua

The Barbuda Council v. Attorney General. No. 456 of 1988. High Court of Justice, Antigua and Barbuda Civil, September 10, 1993.

Argentina

Defensoria de Menores Nro 3 v. Poder Ejecutivo Municipal, Agreement 5 (Argentina Superior Court of Justice. Neuquen, March 2, 1999a.
Expediente: – 6706–2009 (Argentine Supreme Court, 2010), Libro de Acuerdos N° 53, F° 364/380, N° 118.
Irazu Margarita v. Copetro S.A. Camara Civil y Comercial de la Plata, Ruling of May 10, 1993.
Kattan, Alberto E. Y. Otro C. Gobierno Nactional- Poder Ejecutivo. Juzgado Nacional de 1a Instancia en lo Contencioso administrativo Federal No. 2 (JNFed Contencioso administrativo), May 10, 1983. Mendoza Beatriz Silva et al. v. State of Argentina et al. M.1569.XL (Supreme Court of Argentina, July 8, 2008).
Sociedad De Fomento Barrio Félix v. Camet Y Otros. Cámara De Apelaciones Y Garantías En Lo Penal De Mar Del Plata, Sala I. No. LLBA, 2000–991, September 9, 1999.

Bangladesh

BELA v. *Bangladesh*. No. Writ. Pet. 7465. Supreme Court of Bangladesh. 2006.

Farooque v. *Sec'y, Ministry of Commc'n, Gov't of the People's Republic of Bangl. and Twelve Other*. Writ. Pet. 300 H.C.D (1995).

Farooque v. *Bangladesh and Others*. 48 D.L.R. 1996 (Supreme Court of Bangladesh Appellate Division [Civil]).

Farooque v. *Bangladesh*. Writ. Pet. 300 of 1995 (2002.02) (Supreme Court of Bangladesh High Court Division, February 2002).

Farooque v. *Bangladesh*. Writ. Pet. No. 891 of 1994 (2007.07.15) (Supreme Court of Bangladesh High Court Division, July 15, 2007).

Farooque v. *Bangladesh*. 30 CLC (HCD) (Supreme Court of Bangladesh High Court Division, July 15, 2001).

Farooque v. *Government of Bangladesh*. Writ. Pet. 998 of 1994, Civil Action 24 of 1995 (July 25, 1996) (Supreme Court of Bangladesh High Court Division, August 28, 1997).

Botswana

Mosetlhanyane and Others v. *Attorney General of Botswana*. Civil Appeal No. CACLB-074-10. Court of Appeal in Lobatse, January 27, 2011.

Canada

Quebec Attorney General v. *Moses*. 1 S.C.R. 557. Supreme Court of Canada, May 14, 2010.

Chile

Alejandro Papic Dominguez Con Comunidad Indigena Aymara Chuzmiza y Usmagama. No. 2840/2008 (Chile Supreme Court, November 25, 2009).

Antonio Horvath Kiss y Otros v. *Nat'l Comm'n for the Env't*. (Supreme Court of Chile, March 19, 1997).

Aurelio Vargas y otros v. *Municipalidad de Santiago y otros* (The Lo Errazuriz Case) Chile Supreme Court (May 27, 1987).

CODEFF v. *Ministro de Obras Públicas y otros Corte de Apelaciones*. Court of Appeals of Arica and Supreme Court of Arica. 1985.

Comunidad de Chañaral v. *Codeco División el Saldor* (1988) S/ Recurso de Protecion. Corte Suprema (Chile).

Pablo Orrego Silva y Otros v. *Empresa Electrica Pange SA*. Supreme Court of Chile. August 5, 1993.

Pedro Flores et al. v. *Codelco, División Salvador*. No. Rol. 2.052. Copiaco Court of Appeals. June 23, 1988.

Pedro Flores y Otros v. *Corporación Del Cobre, Codelco, División Salvador*. No. Rol. 12.753 FS. 641. Supreme Court of Chile, July 28, 1988.

Trillium. Decision No. 2.732-96. Supreme Court of Chile. March 19, 1997.

Colombia

Auto 275/11. Colombia Constitutional Court 2011.
Castrillion Vega v. *Federación Nacional de Algodoneros y Corporacion Autonoma Regional del Cesar.* No. Acción de Tutela Case 4577. Colombia. November 19, 1997.
Expediente D-8019. Colombia Constitutional Court. 2010.
José Cuesta Novoa v. *The Secretary of Public Health of Bogota.* Constitutional Court of Colombia, May 17, 1995.
María Elena Burgos v. *Municipality of Campoalegre. Sentencia T-095/97.* Colombia Constitutional Court. February 27, 1997.
Marlene Beatriz Duran Comacho v. *Republic of Colombia.* Colombia Constitutional Court, September 26, 1996.
Sentencia C-703/10. Colombia Constitutional Court. 2010.
Sentencia T-724/11. Colombia Constitutional Court. 2011.
Sentencia T-291/06. Colombia Constitutional Court. April 23, 2009.
Sentencia T-291/09. Colombia Constitutional Court. 2010.
Sentencia T-608/11. Colombia Constitutional Court, 2011.
Sentencia C-632/11. Colombia Constitutional Court, 2011.
Sentencia T-616/10. Colombia Constitutional Court. 2010.

Costa Rica

Decision 1700-03. (Costa Rica Constitutional Chamber).

Ecuador

Case No. 224/90, *Arco Iris* v. *Instituto Ecuatoriano de Mineria.* Judgment No. 054-93-CP (Constitutional Court of Ecuador).
Case Nos. 337/90, 378/90, 379/90, 380/90 combined, *Fundacion Natura* v. *Petroecuador.* Resolution No. 230-92-CP (Tribunal of Constitutional Guarantees, October 15, 1992).
Federación Independiente del Pueblo Shuar del Ecuador (FIPSE) c. *Arco Oriente s/ Amparo [ENG].* Tribunal Constitucional de Ecuador, Sala Primera. April, 2000.
Wheeler c. *Director de la Procuraduria General Del Estado de Loja,* Juicio No. 11121-2011-0010, available at http://therightsofnature.org/first-ron-case-ecuador

European Court of Human Rights

Guerra v. *Italy.* Case 14967/89 (European Court of Human Rights, February 19, 1998).
Lopez Ostra v. *Spain.* 20 Eur. Ct. H.R. 277 (European Court of Human Rights, 1995).
Taskin and Others v. *Turkey.* Application No. 46117/99 (European Court of Human Rights, 2004).

Hong Kong

Clean Air Foundation Ltd. and Another v. *Government of HKSAR.* 2007 WL 1824740.
Court of First Instance. July 26, 2007.
Ng Ngau Chai v. *Town Planning Board.* No. 64 of 2007. Hong Kong.

Hungary

Alkotmánybíróság. MK. No. 1994/Decision 28. Hungary Constitutional Law
Court, 1994.
Magyar Közlöny. No. 1994/ No. 55. Hungarian Constitutional Court. 1994.

India

Ashoka Kumar Thakur v. *Union of India.* No. Writ. Pet. 265 of 2006. Supreme Court
of India. 10 April 2008.
Bandhua Mukti Morcha v. *Union of India.* 3 S.C.C. 161. Supreme Court of
India. 21 February 1984.
Bombay Environmental Action Group v. *Pune Cantonment Board.* No. Writ. Pet.
No. 2733. Bombay High Court, 1986.
Charan Lal Sahu v. *Union of India.* A.I.R. 1990 S.C. 1480. Supreme Court of
India. 22 December 1989.
Francis Coralie v. *Administrator, Union Territory of Delhi and Ors.* No. Writ. Pet. 3042
of 1980. Supreme Court of India. January 13, 1981.
Indian Council for Enviro-Legal Action v. *Union of India.* No. 3 SCC 212. Supreme
Court of India. 1996.
Indian Council for Enviro-Legal Action v. *Union of India.* Writ Petition (C) No. 664 of
1993 (Supreme Court of India, April 18, 1996).
Indra Sawhney v. *Union of India.* No. A.I.R. 1993 S.C. 447. Supreme Court of
India. 16 November 1992.
Intellectuals Forum, Tirupathi v. *State of Andhra Pradesh and Others.* Civil Appeal
1251 of 2006. Supreme Court of India, February 23, 2006.
Karnataka Industrial Areas Development Board v. *C. Kenchappa and Others.*
No. AIRSCW 2546. Supreme Court of India. 2006.
L. Krishnan v. *State of Tamil Nadu.* Writ. Pet. No. 20186 of 2000. Madras High Court.
June 27, 2005.
M.C. Mehta v. *Kamal Nath and Others,* 1 SCC 388. Supreme Court of
India. 1997.
M.C. Mehta v. *Union of India.* Writ Petition No. 3727 of 1985. Supreme Court of
India, January 12, 1988.
M.C. Mehta v. *Union of India.* No. Writ. Pet. 13029 of 1985. 26 March 2001.
M.C. Mehta v. *Union of India.* No. 4 SCC 463. (Supreme Court of India, 1987).
M.C. Mehta v. *Union of India.* AIR 1988 SC 1115 (Supreme Court of India).
M.C. Mehta v. *Union of India.* No. Writ. Pet. 860 of 1991. 11 November 1991.
M.C. Mehta v. *Union of India.* AIR 1997 SC 723 (India).

M.C. Mehta v. *Union of India and Others (Oleum Gas Case 3)*
1987 AIR 1086; 1987 SCR (1) 819; 1987 SCC (1) 395; JT 1987 (1) 1; 1986 SCALE (2) 1188.

M.C. Mehta v. *Union of India and Others.* 1991 SCR (1) 866 1991 SCC (2) 353 JT 1991 (1) 620 1991 SCALE (1) 427 at 4.

M.R. Balaji and Others v. State of Mysore. Supreme Court of India. 28 September 1962.

Municipal Council, *Ratlam v. Vardhichand.* No. 1980 AIR 1622, 1981 SCR (1) 97. Supreme Court of India. July 29, 1980.

Narmada Bahao Andolan v. Union of India. No. 10 S.C.C. 664. Supreme Court of India. 2000.

Perumatty Grama Panchayat v. State of Kerala. No. 2004 (1) KLT 731. Kerala High Court. December, 16, 2003.

Reliance Petrochemicals Ltd. v. Indian *Express.* No. 1989 AIR 190, 1988 SCT Supl. (3) 212. Supreme Court of India. September 23, 1988.

Rural Litigation and Entitlement Kendra (RLEK) v. State of Uttar Pradesh. No. AIR 1987, SC 359. Supreme Court of India. March 12, 1985.

Samatha v. State of Andhra Pradesh and Others. No. AIF 1997 SC 3297. Supreme Court of India. July 11, 1997.

Satyapal v. CPIO, TCIL. No. ICPB/A-1/CIC/2006. Central Information Commission, 2006.

S.P. Gupta v. President of India and Others. No. AIR 1982 SC 149. Supreme Court of India. December 30, 1981.

Susetha v. State of Tamil Nadu and Others. Civil Appeal No. 3418 of 2006. Supreme Court of India. August 8, 2006.

Subhash Kumar v. State of Bihar. No. 1991 A.I.R. 420, 1991 SCR (1) 5. Supreme Court of India, January 9, 1991.

Thangal v. Union of India. COU-144405 (Kerala High Court, September 17, 2002).

Tirupur Dyeing Factory Owners v. Noyyal River A. Protection Association (2009).

T.N. Godavarman Thirumulpad v. Union of India and Others. Writ. Pet. No. 202 of 1995. Supreme Court of India. September 26, 2005.

Vellore Citizens' Welfare Forum v. Union of India. Writ. Pet. No. 914 of 1991. Supreme Court of India. April 26,1996.

Vellore Citizens Welfare Forum v. Union of India AIR 1996 SC 2715. Supreme Court of India. August 28, 1996.

Israel

Abu Masad v. Water Commissioner. Civil App. No. 9535/06 (Israel Supreme Court, 2011).

Kenya

Ogiek People v. District Commissioner. Case No. 238/1999 (Kenya High Court, March 23, 2000).

Latvia

Amoliņa v. Garkalne Pagasts Council, No. 2006-09-03 (Latvia Constitutional Court, 2007) (Latvijas Republikas Satversmes tiesa).

Balams v. Ādaži Parish Council, No. 2007-12-03 (Latvia Constitutional Court, 2007) (Latvijas Republikas Satversmes tiesa).

Baldzēns v. Cabinet of Ministers, No. 2002-14-04 (Latvia Constitutional Court, 2003) (Latvijas Republikas Satversmes tiesa).

Coalition for Nature and Cultural Heritage Protection v. Riga City Council, No. 2007-11-3 (Latvia Constitutional Court, 2008) (Latvijas Republikas Satversmes tiesa).

Gruba v. Jurmala City Council, No. 2008-38-03 (Latvia Constitutional Court, 2009) (Ecolex)

Zandbergs v. Kuldīga District, No. 2005-10-03 (Latvia Constitutional Court, 2005) (Latvijas Republikas Satversmes tiesa).

Nepal

Advocate Kedar Bhakta Shrestha v. HMG, Department of Transportation Management. Writ. No. 3109 of 1999 (Supreme Court of Nepal, 1999).

Advocate Prakash Mani Sharma and Others v. Nepal Drinking Water Corporation and Others. WP 227/1990 (Supreme Court of Nepal, Joint Bench, July 10, 2001).

Advocate Prakash Mani Sharma for Pro Public v. His Majesty Government Cabinet Secretariat and others. WP 2991/1995 (Nepal Supreme Court, Joint Bench, 1997.06.09).

Dhungel v. Godawari Marble Indus. Writ Pet. 35/1992 (Supreme Court of Nepal, October 31, 1995).

Yogi Narahari Nath v. Honorable Prime Minister Girija Prasad Koirala and Others, 33 N.L.R. (Supreme Court of Nepal, 1955) in *UNEP Summaries*.

Pakistan

Anjum Irfan v. Lahore Development Authority. Writ Petition No. 25084 of 1997 (P.L.D. 2002 Lahore 555, Ch. Ijaz Ahmad, J., June 14, 2002).

Human Rights Case No. 31-K/92(Q) (*Environment Pollution in Balochistan*). P.L.D. 1994 S. C. 102 (1992), *in U.N. Environment Programme [UNEP], Compendium of Judicial Decisions in Matters Related to Environment: National Decisions*, vol. I, 280 (1998).

Shelhla Zia v. WAPDA. Human Rights case No. 15-K of 1992, P L D 1994 Supreme Court 693 (Supreme Court of Pakistan, February 12, 1994).

Peru

Proterra v. Ferroaleaciones San Roman S.A. Judgment No. 1156–90 (Supreme Court of Peru, November 19, 1992).

Sociedad Peruana de Derecho Ambiental contra *Ministerio de Energia y Minas* (Habeus Data), Expediente No. 1658–95, Dictramen Fiscal No. 122–96 (Sala de Derecho Constitucional 19 de junio de 1996).

Philippines

A.M. No. 09-6-8-SC, Rules of Procedure for Environmental Cases. (Supreme Court of the Philippines, April 13, 2010).

Henares v. Land Transportation and Franchising and Regulatory Board. G.R. No. 158290, 505 S.C.R.A. 104 (Philippines, October 23, 2006).

Juan Antonio Oposa et. al. v. The Honorable Fulgencio S. Factoran, Jr., G.R. No. 101083, 224 S.C.R.A. 792 (Supreme Court of Philippines, July 30, 1993), reprinted in 33 I.L.M. 173, 187 (1994).

Metropolitan Manila Development Authority v. Concerned Residents of Manila Bay. G.R. Nos. 171947-48 (Supreme Court of Philippines, December 18, 2008).

Social Justice Society v. Atienza. G.R. No. 156052, 517 S.C.R.A. 657 (Supreme Court of the Philippines, March 7, 2007).

Social Justice Society v. Atienza. G.R. No. 156052, 545 S.C.R.A. 92 (Supreme Court of the Philippines, February 13, 2008).

Tano v. Socrates. G.R. No. 110249, 278 S.C.R.A. 154 (Supreme Court of the Philippines, August 21, 1997).

South Africa

Director: Mineral Development, Gauteng Region and Another v. Save the Vaal Environment and others, Case No. 133 of 98 (Supreme Court of Appeal of South Africa, March 12, 1999).

Fuel Retailers Association of South Africa Ltd. v. Director-General Environmental Mangagement, Department of Agriculture, Conservation and Environment, Mpumalanda and Others. [2007] ZACC 13 Case CCT 67/06 (South Africa Constitutional Court, June 7, 2007).

Lindiwe Mazibuko and Others v. City of Johannesburg and Others. CCT 39/09 2009 ZAC 28 (Constitutional Court of South Africa).

Residents of Bon Vista Mansions v. Southern Metropolitan Local Council. 01/12312 (High Court of South Africa, September 2001).

Van Huyssteen v. Minister of Environmental Affairs and Tourism, 1996 (1) SA 283 (C) (High Court of South Africa, June 28, 1996).

Sri Lanka

Bulankulama and Six Others v. Ministry of Industrial Development and Seven Others. S.C. Application No 884/99 (F.R) (Supreme Court of the Democratic Socialist Republica of Sri Lanka).

Salley v. Colombo Municipal Council and Others. Application No. 252/2007 (Supreme Court of Sri Lanka, 2007).

Tanzania

Felix Joseph Mavika v. Dar es Salaam City Commission. Civil Case No. 316 of 2000 (High Court of Tanzania, October 23, 2000).

Turkey

Senih Özay v. Ministry of the Environment, Ankara and Eurogold Madencilik AS. Ref. No. 1996/5477; Ruling No. 1997/2311 (Sixth Chamber, Higher Adminstrative Court, Turkey, May 13, 1997).

Uganda

Advocates Coalition for Development and Environment v. Attorney General. Miscellaneous Cause No. 0100 of 2004 (High Court of Uganda, July 13, 2005).
Greenwatch v. Uganda Wildlife Authority. Miscellaneous Application No. 92 of 2004 (High Court of Uganda in Kampala, 2004) (arising from Miscellaneous Cause No. 15 of 2004).

United States of America

Association for the Protection of the Adirondacks v. MacDonald, 253 N.Y. 234, 242 (1930)
Baker v. Carr. 369 U.S. 186, 217 (Supreme Court of the United States, 1962).
Blue Mountain Preservation Association v. Township of Eldred, 867 A.2d 692 (Pennsylvania Commonwealth Court, 2005).
Borough of Moosic v. Pennsylvania Public Utility Commission, 429 A.2d 1237, 1239 (Pennsylvania Commonwealth Court, 1981)
Butler Township Board of Supervisors v. Commonwealth of Pennsylvania, Department of Environmental Resources, 99 Pennsylvania Commonwealth Court, 239, 249, 513 A.2d 508 (1986).
Cape-France Enterprises v. Estate of Peed, 29 P.3d 1011 (Montana, 2001).
Central Valley Chrysler-Jeep, Inc. v. Witherspoon. 2007 WL 135688 (E.D. Cal., 2007).
Central Valley Chrysler-Jeep v. Witherspoon. 456 F. Supp. 2d 1160 (E.D. Cal., 2006).
Clark Fork Coal. v. Montana Department of Environmental Quality, 197 P.3d 482 (Montana, 2008).
Clean Air Foundation Ltd. and Another v. Government of HKSAR. 2007 WL 1824740 (Court of First Instance, July 26, 2007).
Community College of Delaware County v. Fox, 342 A.2d 468, 482 (Pennsylvania Commonwealth Court, 1975).
Commonwealth v. Blair, 805 N.E.2d 1011, 1018 (Massachusetts Appeal Court, 2004).
Commonwealth of Pennsylvania v. National Gettysburg Battlefield Tower, Inc., 454 Pa. 193, 205, 311 A.2d 588, 594–5 (Supreme Court of Pennsylvania, 1973).
Concerned Citizens for Orderly Progress v. Commonwealth of Pennsylvania, 36 Pennsylania Commonwealth Court, 192, 387 A.2d 989 (1978).

Coeur Alaska, Inc. v. *Southeast Alaska Conservation Council.* 129 S. Ct. 2458 (Supreme Court of the United States, 2009).

Davis v. *Burke.* 179 U.S. 399 (Supreme Court of the United States, 1900).

Del-AWARE Unlimited Inc. v. *Commonwealth of Pennsylvania,* 96 Pennsylvania Commonwealth Court 361, 508 A.2d 348 (1986).

Enos v. *Secretary of Environmental Affairs,* 731 N.E.2d 525 (Supreme Judicial Court of Massachusetts, 2000).

Entergy Corp. v. *Riverkeeper, Inc.* 129 S. Ct. 1498 (Supreme Court of the United States, 2009).

Envtl. Def. v. *Duke Energy Corp.* 549 U.S. 561 (Supreme Court of the United States, 2007).

Federated Conservationists of Westchester County, Inc. v. *Reid,* 377 N.Y.S.2d 380 (Supreme Court of New York, 1975).

Flores v. *Southern Peru Copper Corp.,* 343 F.2d 140, 160 (2d Cir., 2003).

Florida Wildlife Federation v. *State Department of Environmental Regulation.* 390 So.2d 64 (Supreme Court of Florida, 1980).

Glisson v. *City of Marion.* 720 N.E.2d 1034 (Illinois, 1999).

Green Mountain Chrysler Plymouth Dodge Jeep v. *Crombie.* 508 F. Supp. 2d 295, 340 (D. Vt., 2007).

Green Mountain Chrysler Plymouth Dodge Jeep v. *Crombie.* Nos. 2:05-CV-302, 2:05-CV-304, 2006 WL 4761053, para 65 (D. Vt., August 14, 2006).

Hamilton v. *Diamond,* 42 A.2d 465, 349 N.Y.S.2d 146, 148–9 (Appellate Division of the Supreme Court of the State of New York, 1973).

Illinois Pure Water Committee, Inc. v. *Director of Public Health,* 104 Ill.2d 243, 470 N.E.2d 988 (Illinois Supreme Court, 1984).

Kleppe v. *Sierra Club.* 427 U.S. 390 (Supreme Court of the United States, 1976).

Klink v. *Department of Transportation,* 29 Pennsylvania Commonwealth Court 106, 370 A.2d 379 (1977).

Lawrence v. *Texas,* 539 U.S. 558 (2003).

Leland v. *Moran,* 235 F. Supp. 2d 153, 154–5 (New York Northern District Court, 2002).

Life of the Land v. *Land Use Commission,* 623 P.2d 431 (Hawaii, 1981).

Lincoln Dodge, Inc. v. *Sullivan.* 558 F. Supp. 2d 224 (D. R.I., 2008).

Lohmeier v. *Gallatin County,* 135 P.3d 775, 777 (Montana, 2006).

Marbury v. *Madison.* 5 U.S. (1 Cranch) 137, 177 (Supreme Court of the United States, 1803).

Massachusetts v. *EPA.* 549 U.S. 497 (Supreme Court of the United States, 2007).

Meech v. *Hillhaven W.,* 238 Montana 21, 776 P.2d 488 (Montana, 1989).

Montana Environmental Information Center v. *Department of Environmental Quality,* 988 P.2d 1236, 1246 (Montana, 1999).

National Association of Home Builders v. *Defenders of Wildlife.* 551 U.S. 644 (Supreme Court of the United States, 2007).

NBD Bank v. *Krueger Ringier, Inc.,* 686 N.E.2d 704, 709–710 (Illinois Appeal Court, 1997).

Northern Plains Resource Council v. *Montana Board of Land Commissioners,* 288 P.3d 169 (Montana, 2012).

Payne v. *Kassab,* 11 Pennsylvania Commonwealth Court, 14, 29–30, 312 A.2d 86, 94 (1973), affirmed 468 Pa. 226, 361 A.2d 263 (Supreme Court of Pennsylvania, July 6, 1976).

Payne v. *Kassab*, 468 Pa. 226, 245, 361 A.2d 263 (Supreme Court of Pennsylvania, July 6, 1976).

Pfost v. *State*, 219 Montana 206, 216, 713 P.2d 495, 505 (Montana, 1985).

Robertson v. *Methow Valley Citizens Council.* 490 U.S. 332 (Supreme Court of the United States, 1989).

Robinson Township et al. v. *Commonwealth of Pennsylvania*, Pennyslvania Commonwealth Court, 52 A.3d 463 (2012).

Robinson Township et al. v. *Commonwealth of Pennsylvania*, Supreme Court of Pennsylvania, No. J-127A-D-2012 (decided December 19, 2013) (plurality opinion).

Roper v. *Simmons*, 543 U.S. 551 (2005).

Sierra Club v. *Department of Transportation*, 115 Hawaii 299, 320, 167 P.3d 292 (Supreme Court of Hawaii, 2007).

Sierra Club v. *Morton.* 405 U.S. 727, 741 (Supreme Court of the United States, 1972) (Douglas, J., dissenting).

Snelling v. *Department of Transportation*, 366 A.2d 1298 (Pennsylvania Commonwealth Court, 1976).

State v. *General Development Corporation*, 448 So. 2d 1074 (Florida District Court of Appeal, 1984), aff'd.

State v. *General Development Corporation*, 469 So. 2d 1381 (Florida, 1985).

Sullivan v. *Resisting Environmental Destruction on Indigenious Lands*, 311 P.3d 625 (Alaska, 2013).

Summers v. *Earth Island Institute.* 129 S. Ct. 1142 (Supreme Court of the United States, 2009).

United Haulers Association v. *Oneida-Herkimer Solid Waste Management.* Auth. 550 U.S. 330 (Supreme Court of the United States, 2007).

Winter v. *Natural Res. Def. Council.* 129 S. Ct. 365 (Supreme Court of the United States, 2008).

Venezuela

Donato Furio Giodano v. *Ministry of Environment and Renewable Natural Resources.* Supreme Court of Justice, Venezuela. November 25, 1999.

Jesús Manuel Vera Rivera v. *Ministry of Environment and Renewable Natural Resources* (Supreme Court of Justice, September 21, 1999), available at www.unep.org/delc/Portals/119/UNEPCompendiumSummariesJudgementsEnvironment-relatedCases.pdf

Legislative sources and other primary documents

African Charter on Human and Peoples' Rights. UNTS 1520 (1981): 217.

African (Banjul) Charter on Human and Peoples' Rights. ILM 21 (1982): 58, available at www.achpr.org/instruments/achpr,

American Convention on Human Rights, Article 13.

Antarctic Environment Protocol, 30 ILM 849 (1992).

ASEAN Human Rights Declaration (adopted November 18, 2012), available at www.asean.org/news/asean-statement-communiques/item/asean-human-rights-declaration

Case on the Constitutionality of Election Campaign Using Loudspeaker, 2006 Hun-Ma 711 (July 31, 2008), translated by Professor Jibong Lim, Sogang University College of Law.

Convention on Access to Information, Public Participation in Decision-Making and Access to Justice in Environmental Matters, 2161 UNTS 447 (*opened for signature* June 25, 1998).

Declaration of the United Nations Conference on the Human Environment, Stockholm Conference, Princ. 1, U.N. Doc. A/CONF.48/14/rev.1 (adopted June 16, 1972).

European Climate Change Programme, http://ec.europa.eu/clima/policies/eccp/index_en.htm

European Convention for the Protection of Human Rights and Fundamental Freedoms, 213 UNTS 222, Articles 6, 10 (1950).

European Union, *Consolidated Version of the Treaty on the Functioning of the European Union*, 13 December 2007, 2008/C 115/01, art. 191, available at www.unhcr.org/refworld/docid/4b17a07e2

European Parliament and of the Council. "Directive 2000/60/EC." October 23, 2000. OJ L 327, 22.12.2000.

Fiji, *Draft Constitution: The Explanatory Report*. The Constitution Commission 527 (2012, available at www.fijileaks.com/uploads/1/3/7/5/13759434/thursday_the_explanatory_report_two-4.pdf

GA resolution A/RES/63/117, Optional Protocol to the International Covenant on Economic, Social and Cultural Rights (December 10, 2008), Article 2.

Gateway to the United Nation's Systems on Climate Change, Climate Change at a Glance.

Global Water Security. *Intelligence Community Assessment*. ICA 2012-08, at iii. 2012.

Human Development Report 2006, Beyond Scarcity: Power, Poverty, and the Global Water Crisis. United Nations Development Programme, 2006, reprinted in Shelton, Donald K Anton and Dinah L. Environmental Protection and Human Rights. Cambridge University Press, 2011.

International Covenant on Civil and Political Rights, 999 UNTS 171, arts. 19, 25 (1966).

República del Ecuador Asamblea Nacional, Comisión de la Biodivesidad y Recursos Naturales. Acta de Sesión No. 66 (June 15, 2011), available at http://asambleanacional.gov.ec/blogs/comision6/files/2011/07/acta-66.pdf

"Rio Declaration on Environment and Development." 31 ILM 874. 1992.

"Stockholm Declaration on the Human Environment." 11 ILM 1416. 1972.

Transcript of Montana Constitutional Convention, Vol. V, 1971–1972, at 1243–4 (March 1, 1972), available at http://ia360606.us.archive.org/2/items/montanaconstituto5mont/montanaconstituto5mont.pdf

United Nations Comm'n on Human Rights, Sub-Comm'n on Prevention of Discrimination and Protection of Minorities, Human Rights and the Environment, prepared by Fatma Zohra Ksentini, U.N. Doc. E/CN.4/Sub.2/1994/9 at para. 248 (July 6, 1994).

United Nations Conference on Environment and Development, Annex II. "Agenda 21: A Programme for Action for Sustainable Development." UN Doc.A./Conf. 151/26. August 12, 1992.

United Nations Conference on Environment and Development, *Rio Declaration on Environment and Development*, Principle 1, UN Doc.A/CN.17/1997/8 (1992).

United Nations Conference on Sustainable Development. "The Future We Want, A/CONF.216/L.1*." June 20–2, 2012. Para. 3.

United Nations Declaration on Environment and Development ("Rio Declaration") U.N. Doc A/CONF.151/5/Rev. 1 (1992).

United Nations Economic and Social Council. "General Comment no. 15: The Right to Water." E/C.12/2002/11, at para 1, January 20, 2003.

United Nations Framework Convention on Climate Change, Article 6 (1992).

United Nations Human Rights Council. "Human Rights and Access to Safe Drinking Water and Sanitation." A/HRC/RES/15/8, at para 9(a) and (f), September 30, 2010.

United Nations Human Rights Council. "Fact Sheet No. 35." August 2010, 40, 41.

United Nations. "Millennium Development Goals, Goal 7, Target 3," 2000.

Universal Declaration of Human Rights, GA Res 217 (AIII), UN GAOR, UN Doc A/810 (December 10, 1948).

The Universal Declaration of the Rights of Nature, available at http://therightsofnature. org/universal-declaration

United States, America's Climate Security Act of 2007, S. 2191, 110th Cong. (2007), available at http://usclimatenetwork.org/federal/lieberman-warner-bill/ACSA.pdf

United States Freedom of Information Act, 5 U.S.C. sec. 552.

United States Global Warming Reduction Act of 2007, S. 485, 110th Cong. (2007).

United States Low Carbon Economy Act of 2007, S. 1766, 110th Cong. (2007).

United States National Environmental Policy Act, 42 U.S.C. 4321–4347 (NEPA).

Washington State, Department of Ecology, www.ecy.wa.gov/climatechange/effects.htm

Secondary sources

Aarhus Convention on Access to Information. "Public Participation in Decisionmaking and Access to Justice in Environmental Matters." ILM 38 (June 1998): 517.

Abate, Randall S. "Kyoto or Not, Here We Come: The Promise and Perils of the Piecemeal Approach to Climate Change Regulation in the United States." *Cornell Journal of Law and Public Policy* 15 (2006): 369, 372.

"Climate Change, the United States, and the Impacts of Arctic Melting: A Case Study in the Need for Enforceable International Environmental Human Rights." *Stanford Journal of International Law* 43A (2007): 3, 10, 27.

Akhmouch, Aziza. "Water Governance in Latin America and the Caribbean: A Multi-Level Approach." *OECD Regional Development Working Papers* 2012/04. (OECD Publishing), 2012: 31.

Anderson, Michael R. "Human Rights Approaches to Environmental Protection: An Overview." In *Human Rights Approaches to Environmental Protection*, by Alan E. Boyle and Michael R. Anderson (eds.). Oxford University Press, 1998.

"Individual Rights to Environmental Protection in India." In *Human Rights Approaches to Environmental Protection*, by Alan E. Boyle and Michael R. Anderson (eds.). Oxford University Press, 1998.

Ankersen, Thomas T. "Shared Knowledge, Shared Jurisprudence: Learning to Speak Environmental Law Creole (Criollo)." *Tulane Environmental Law Journal* 16 (2003): 807, 820, 822–3.

Annus, Taavi. "Comparative Constitutional Reasoning: The Law and Strategy of Selecting the Right Arguments." *Duke Journal of Comparative and International Law* 14 (2004): 301.

Ansari, Abdul Haseeb, Abdulkadir B. Abdulkadir and Shehu Usman Yamusa. "Protection of Environmental Rights for Sustainable Development: An Appraisal of International and National Laws." *Australian Journal of Basic and Applied Sciences* 6 (2012): 258–72.

Anton, D. and D. Shelton. "Problems in Environment Protection and Human Rights: A Human Right to the Environment." *ANU College of Law Research Paper No. 11–17* (June, 2011): 357.

Environmental Protection and Human Rights. Cambridge University Press, 2011.

Atapattu, Sumudu. "The Right to a Healthy Life or the Right to Die Polluted? The Emergence of a Human Right to a Healthy Environment Under International Law." *Tulane Environmental Law Journal* 16 (2002): 65.

Aylwin, Jose. *The Ralco Dam and the Pehuenche People in Chile: Lessons from an Ethno-Environmental Conflict*. Institute of Indigenous Studies, University of la Frontera, 2002.

Bandi, Gyula. "The Right to Environment in Theory and Practice: The Hungarian Experience." *Connecticut Journal of International Law* 8 (1993): 439, 450–65.

Banisar, David. *Freedom of Information Around the World 2006: A Global Survey of Access to Government Information Laws*. Privacy International, 2006.

Barak, Aharon. "Response to the Judge as Comparatist: Comparison in Public Law." *Tulane Law Review* 80 (2005): 195, 197.

Proportionality: Constitutional Rights and their Limitations. Cambridge Studies in Constitutional Law, 2012.

Belbase, Nayaran. *Environmental Rights and the New Constitution*. IUCN Policy Brief, 2009, available at http://cmsdata.iucn.org/downloads/environmental_rights_in_the_new_constitution.pdf

Bell, S. and D. McGillivray. *Environmental Law*, 7th edn. Oxford University Press, 2008: 94–5.

Biagiotti, Isabelle. "Emerging Corporate Actors in Environment and Trade Governance: New Vision and Challenge for Norm-setting Processes." In *Participation for Sustainability in Trade*, by S. Thoyer and B. Martimort-Asso (eds.), 121, 122. Aldershot: Ashgate, 2007.

Blackstone, William. *Commentaries on the Laws of England*. Vols. 2, 4. The Lawbook Exchange, 1766.

Borgeaud, Charles. *Adoption and Amendment of Constitutions in Europe and America*. Edited by John Martin Vincent. Charles Downer Hazen trans. New York: Macmillan, 1895: 35.

Boyd, David R. "The Implicit Constitutional Right to Live in a Healthy Environment." *Review of European Community and International Environmental Law* 20(2) (July, 2011): 171–9.

The Environmental Rights Revolution: A Global Study of Constitutions, Human Rights, and the Environment. UBC Press, 2012.

"The Constitutional Right to a Healthy Environment." *Environment: Science and Policy for Sustainable Development* 54(4) (July–August, 2012): 3–15, available at www.environmentmagazine.org/Archives/Back%20Issues/2012/July-August% 202012/constitutional-rights-full.html

The Right to a Healthy Environment: Revitalizing Canada's Constitution. UBC Press, 2012: 61–6.

Boyle, Alan E. "The Role of International Human Rights Law in the Protection of the Environment." In *Human Rights Approaches to Environmental Protection*, by Alan E. Boyle and Michael R. Anderson (eds.). Oxford University Press, 1998.

"Human Rights and the Environment: A Reassessment." *Fordham Environmental Law Review* 18 (revised, 2010): 471.

"Human Rights and the Environment: Where Next?" *European Journal of International Law* 23 (2012): 613–42.

Boyle, Alan E. and Michael R. Anderson (eds.). *Human Rights Approaches to Environmental Protection*, 1st edn, Clarendon Press, 1996; 2nd edn, Oxford University Press, 1998.

Brandl, Ernest and Hartwin Bungert. "Constitutional Entrenchment of Environmental Protection: A Comparative Analysis of Experiences Abroad." *Harvard Environmental Law Review* 16 (1992): 1, 4–5, 82, Table I.

Brewer-Carías, Allan R. *Constitutional Protection of Human Rights in Latin America: A Comparative Study of Amparo Proceedings.* Cambridge University Press, 2009: 199.

Brooks, Richard O. "A Constitutional Right to a Healthful Environment." *Vermont Law Review* 16 (1992): 1063, 1103–5, 1109.

Brown, Donald A. "The U.S. Performance in Achieving its 1992 Earth Summit Global Warming Commitments." *Environmental Law Reporter* 32 (2002): 10,741.

Brown, Elizabeth F. *In Defense of Environmental Rights in East European Constitutions.* Vol. 1. University of Chicago Law School Roundtable, 1993: 191, available at http://papers.ssrn.com/sol3/papers.cfm?abstract_id=995326

Bruch, Carl, Wole Coker, and Chris VanArsdale. *Constitutional Environmental Law: Giving Force to Fundamental Principles in Africa.*, 2nd edn. Environmental Law Institute Research Report, 2007.

Bruckerhoff, Joshua J. "Giving Nature Constitutional Protection: A Less Anthropocentric Interpretation of Environmental Rights." *Texas Law Review* 86 (2008): 615, 625–6, 638, 645.

Bruinsma, James. "Environmental Law: Brazil Enacts New Protections for Amazon Rain Forest." *Harvard International Law Journal* 30 (1989): 503–05.

Bruyninckx, Hans, Sander Happaerts, and Karoline Van Den Brande. *Sustainable Development and Subnational Governments: Policy Making and Multi-Level Interactions.* Palgrave Macmillan, 2012.

Bryce, James. *Constitutions.* Oxford University Press, 1905: 37–8.

Buchanan, James M. "Why do Constitutions Matter?" In *Why Constitutions Matter*, by Niclas Berggren, Nils Karlson, and Joakim Nergelius (eds.), 1, 12. New Brunswick, NJ: Transaction Publishers, 2002.

Burhenne, W.E. (ed.). *International Environmental Soft Law. Collection of Relevant Instruments.* The Netherlands, Kluwer Academic, 1996.

Cassuto, D.N. and Romulo S.R. Sampaio. "Water Law in the United States and Brazil – Climate Change and Two Approaches to Emerging Water Poverty." *William and Mary Environmental Law and Policy Review* 35 (2011): 371, 400.

Center for International Environment Law (CIEL). *Chilean Supreme Court Rejected Controversial Trillium Logging Project* (March 21, 1997).

Chirisa, I. and Muzenda, A. "Environmental Rights as a Substantive Area of the Zimbabwean Constitutional Debate: Implications for Policy and Action." *Southern Peace Review Journal* 2(2) (September 2013): 104–21.

Cho, H.S. and O.W Pedersen. "Environmental Rights and Future Generations." In *Routledge Handbook of Constitutional Law*, by M. Tushnet, T. Fleiner and C. Saunders (eds.). Abingdon, Oxon, and New York: Routledge, 2013.

Chuabi, Sanjay. "Environmental Law in India." In *International Environmental Law and Regulation*, by Andrew J. Schlickman, Thomas M. McMahon, and Nicoline Van Riel (eds.). Salem, NH: Butterworth Legal Publishers, 1995. Vol II.

Churchill, Robin. "Environmental Rights in Existing Human Rights Treaties." In *Human Rights Approaches to Environmental Protection*, by Alan E. Boyle and Michael R. Anderson (eds.). Oxford University Press, 1998.

"Court: Individuals can Sue over Endangered Species." *St. Louis Post-Dispatch* (July 6, 1998): 4.

Craig, Robin Kundis. "Should There be a Constitutional Right to a Clean/Healthy Environment?" *Environmental Law Report* 34(12) (2004): 11013.

"A Comparative Guide to the Eastern Public Trust Doctrine: Classifications of States, Property Rights, and State Summaries," available at http://papers.ssrn.com/sol3/papers.cfm?abstract-id=1008161

"A Comparative Guide to the Western States' Public Trust Doctrines: Public Values, Private Rights, and the Evolution Toward an Ecological Public Trust," available at http://papers.ssrn.com/sol3/papers.cfm?abstract_id=1405822

Cramer, Benjamin W. "The Human Right to Information, the Environment and Information About the Environment: From the Universal Declaration to the AARHUS Convention." *Communication, Law and Policy* 14 (2009): 73, 74, 86, 90.

Cusack, Mary Ellen. "Judicial Interpretation of State Constitutional Rights to a Healthful Environment." *Boston College Environmental Affairs Law Review* 20(1) (1993): 173, 181, 193.

Daly, Erin. *Environmental Human Rights: A Paradigm of Indivisibility*, Widener L. Legal Studies Research Paper no. 11-05 (2011).

Dignity Rights: Courts, Constitutions, and the Worth of the Human Person. University of Pennsylvania Press, 2012.

Constitutional Protection for Environmental Rights: The Benefits of Environmental Process," 17 Int'l J. Peace Studies 71 (2012).

"The Ecuadorian Exemplar: The First Ever Vindications of the Constitutional Rights of Nature." *RECIEL* 21(1): 63 (2012). ISSN 0962 8797, available at http://celdf.live2.radicaldesigns.org/downloads/The_Ecuadorian_Exemplar_The_First_Ever_Vindications_of_Constitutional_Rights_of_Nature.pdf

Daly, Erin and May, James. "Constitutional Environmental Rights and Liabilities." *Environmental Liability* 3 (2012): 75, available at Social Science Research Network (SSRN): http://ssrn.com/abstract=2221561

Dam, Shubhankar and Vivek Tewary. "Polluting Environment, Polluting Constitution: Is a 'Polluted' Constitution Worse than a Polluted Environment?" *Journal of Environmental Law* 17 (2005): 383, 389.

Dannenmaier, Eric. "Environmental Law and the Loss of Paradise." *Columbia Journal of Transnational Law* 49 (2011): 463, 467.

Davenport, Paula M. "Plan for Dam Sparks Dispute in Marion." *St. Louis Post-Dispatch* (April 15, 1991): 11.

Davis, Thomas. "Illinois House Votes to Allow Development on Some Land with Endangered Species." *State Journal-Register* (May 22, 1999): 20.

Deimann, Sven and Bernard Dyssli (eds.). *Environmental Rights: Law, Litigation and Access to Justice.* Gaunt, 1995.

Dernbach, John C. "Taking the Pennsylvania Constitution Seriously When it Protects the Environment: Part I – An Interpretive Framework for Article I, Section 27." *Dickinson Law Review* 103 (1999): 693.

"Taking the Pennsylvania Constitution Seriously When it Protects the Environment: Part II – Environmental Rights and Public Trust." *Dickinson Law Review* 104 (1999): 97.

Stumbling Toward Sustainability. Washington, DC: Environmental Law Institute, 2002.

Agenda for a Sustainable America. Washington, DC: ELI Press, Environmental Law Institute, 2009, 2–3.

Dicey, Albert Venn. *Introduction to the Study of the Law of the Constitution,* 10th edn. Palgrave Macmillan, 1959.

Dorsen, Norman, Michel Rosenfeld, András Sajó and Susanne Baer. *Comparative Constitutionalism: Cases and Materials.* St. Paul, MN: West Group, 2003, 1313–14.

Douglas-Scott, S. "Environmental Rights in European Union: Participatory Democracy or Democratic Deficit?" In *Human Rights Approaches to Environmental Protection,* by Alan E. Boyle and Michael R. Anderson (eds.). Oxford University Press, 1998.

Dupre, Catherine. *Importing the Law in Post-Communist Transitions: The Hungarian Constitutional Court and the Right to Human Dignity.* Hart Publishing, 2003.

EarthJustice. "*Environmental Rights Report 2008,*" available at http://earthjustice.org/sites/default/files/library/reports/2008-environmental-rights-report.pdf

Ebrahim, Hassen. *The Soul of a Nation: Constitution-making in South Africa.* Oxford University Press, 1998.

Elkins, Zachary, Tom Ginsburg and Beth Simmons. "Getting to Rights: Treaty Ratification, Constitutional Convergence, and Human Rights Practice." *Harvard International Law Journal* 54(1) (2013): 61–95.

"Environmental and Natural Resources Provisions in State Constitutions." *Journal of Land, Resources, and Environmental Law* 22 (2002): 73, 74.

Environmental Law Alliance Worldwide (ELAW). *Valuing Biodiversity in Costa Rica* (July, 1999), available at www.elaw.org/node/866

Eurick, Janelle P. "The Constitutional Right to a Healthy Environment: Enforcing Environmental Protection Through State and Federal Constitutions." *International Legal Perspectives* 11 (2001): 185.

European Climate Change Programme, available at http://ec.europa.eu/clima/policies/eccp/index_en.htm check elsewhere

Ewald, Sylvia. "State Court Adjudication of Environmental Rights: Lessons from the Adjudication of the Right to Education and the Right to Welfare." *Columbia Journal of Environmental Law* 36 (2011): 413, available at http://columbiaenvironmentallaw.org/assets/pdfs/36.2/Ewald.pdf

Fabra, Adriana. "Indigenous Peoples, Environmental Degradation and Human Rights: A Case Study." In *Human Rights Approaches to Environmental Protection*, by Alan E. Boyle and Michael R. Anderson (eds.). Oxford University Press, 1998.

Fabra, Adriana and Eva Arnal. "Review of Jurisprudence on Human Rights and the Environment in Latin America." Joint UNEP-OHCHR Expert Seminar on Human Rights and the Environment, Background Paper No. 6. Office of the United Nations High Commissioner for Human Rights. Geneva, January 14–16, 2002, available at www2.ohchr.org/english/issues/environment/environ/bp6.htm

Ferlo, Albert M., Karin P. Sheldon, and Mark Squillace (eds.). *The NEPA Litigation Guide*, 2nd edn. American Bar Association, 2014.

Fernandes, Edesio. "Constitutional Environmental Rights in Brazil." In *Human Rights Approaches to Environmental Protection*, by Alan E. Boyle and Michael R. Anderson (eds.), 265–84. Oxford University Press, 1998.

Fernandez, José L. "State Constitutions, Environmental Rights Provisions, and the Doctrine of Self-Execution: A Political Question?" *Harvard Environmental Law Review* 17 (1993): 333.

Finer, S.E., Vernon Bogdanor, and Bernard Rudden. *Comparing Constitutions*. Oxford University Press, 1995.

Fitzmaurice, Malgosia. "The Human Right to Water." *Fordham Environmental Law Review* 18 (2007): 537.

Fontana, David. "Refined Comparativism in Constitutional Law." *UCLA Law Review* 49 (2001): 539.

"The Rise and Fall of Comparative Constitutional Law in the Postwar Era." *Yale Journal of International Law* 36(1) (2011).

Foreman, Elaine F. "Protecting the Antarctic Environment: Will a Protocol be Enough?" *American University International Law Review* 7(4) (1992): 849.

Francis, Rose. "Water Justice in South Africa: Natural Resources Policy at the Intersection of Human Rights, Economics, and Political Power." *Georgetown International Environmental Law Review* 18 (2005): 149, 186.

Franco, Guido. "California Energy Commission, Climate Change Impacts and Adaptation in California." *Integrated Energy Policy Report* 7 (2005), available at www.ccap.org/docs/resources/427/Climate_Change_Impacts_and_Adaptation_in_California.pdf

Frankenberg, Günter. "Comparing Constitutions: Ideas, Ideals, and Ideology – toward a layered narrative." *International Journal of Constitutional Law* 4 (2006): 439.

Gardner, James A. *Interpreting State Constitutions: A Jurisprudence of Function in a Federal System*. University of Chicago Press, 2005.

In Search of Subnational Constitutionalism. Prepared for Seventh World Congress, International Association of Constitutional Law, Athens, Greece, June 11–15, 2007, available at available at http://papers.ssrn.com/sol3/papers.cfm?abstract_id=1017239

Gatmaytan-Mango, Dante. "Judicial Restraint and the Enforcement of Environmental Rights in the Philippines." *Oregon Review of International Law* 12 (2010): 1.

Gellers, Joshua. "Righting Environmental Wrongs: Assessing the Role of Legal Systems in Redressing Environmental Grievances." *Journal of Environmental Law and Literature* 26(2) (2011): 461.

"Greening Constitutions with Environmental Rights: Testing the Isomorphism Thesis" (2011), available at http://papers.ssrn.com/sol3/papers.cfm?abstract_id=1902346

"Survival of the Greenest: A Statistical Analysis of Constitutional Environmental Rights" (2012), available at http://papers.ssrn.com/sol3/papers.cfm?abstract_id=2103960

"Expecting the Elephant but Getting the Mouse: Analyzing the Adoption of a Constitutional Environmental Right in Nepal" (2013), available at http://papers.ssrn.com/sol3/papers.cfm?abstract_id=2238073

Gelling, Peter. "Focus of Climate Talks Shifts to Helping Poor Countries Cope." *New York Times* (December 13, 2007): A31.

Giga Quotes. *Earth*, available at www.giga-usa.com/quotes/topics/earth_t001.htm.

Ginsburg, Tom. Constitutionmaking.org option reports, environmental provisions (November 6, 2009), available at www.iconnectblog.com/2009/11/new-report-on-constitutional-treatment-of-the-environment

Glazewski, Jan. "The Environment, Human Rights and a New South African Constitution." *South African Journal for Human Rights* 7 (1991): 167.

Glicksman, Robert L. "Global Climate Change and the Risks to Coastal Areas from Hurricanes and Rising Sea Levels: The Costs of Doing Nothing." *Loyola Law Review* 52 (2006): 1127, 1179.

Global Alliance for the Rights of Nature. *Turkey Calling for Ecological Constitution*, available at http://therightsofnature.org/rights-of-nature-laws/turkey-ecological-constitution

Gormley, Paul W. *Human Rights and the Environment: The Need for International Cooperation.* Sijthoff, 1976.

Hassan, Parvez and Azim Azfar. "Securing Environmental Rights Through Public Interest Litigation in South Asia." *Virginia Environmental Law Journal* 22 (2004): 215, 242, 244.

"Securing Environmental Rights Through Public Interest Litigation in South Asia." *Virginia Environmental Law Journal* 22 (2004): 215, 242.

Hayward, Tim. *Constitutional Environmental Rights.* Oxford University Press, 2005.

"'Healthful Environment' Doesn't Include Protecting Animals." *State Journal-Register* (October 22, 1999): 34.

Hernandez, Antonio Maria. *Sub-National Constitution Law in Argentina.* Kluwer Law International, 2011.

Heyer, Eric. "Latin American State Secrecy and Mexico's Transparency Law." *George Washington International Law Review* 38 (2006): 437.

Higgins, Rosalyn. "Natural Resources in the Case Law of the International Court." In *International Law and Sustainable Development: Past Achievements and Future Challenges*, by Alan Boyle and David Freestone (eds.), 87, 111. Oxford: Oxford University Press, 1999.

Hill, Barry E., Steve Wolfson, and Nicholas Targ. "Human Rights and the Environment: A Synopsis and Some Predictions." *Georgetown International Environmental Law Review* 16 (2004): 361.

Hirshl, Ran. "The Question of Case Selection in Comparative Constitutional Law." *American Journal of Comparative Law* 53 (2005): 125.

"From Comparative Constitutional Law to Comparative Constitutional Studies." *International Journal of Constitutional Law* 11(1) (2013): 1–12.

Hiskes, Richard P. *The Human Right to a Green Future: Environmental Rights and Intergenerational Justice*. Cambridge University Press, 2008.

Hodkova, Iveta. "Is There a Right to a Healthy Environment in the International Legal Order?" *Connecticut Journal of International Law* 7 (1991): 65, 67.

Houck, Oliver A. "Light from the Trees: The Stories of *Minors Oposa* and the Russian Forest Cases." *Georgetown International Environmental Law Review* 19 (2007): 321, 326.

"A Case of Sustainable Development: The River God and the Forest at the End of the World." *Tulsa Law Review* 44 (2008): 275, 305.

Taking Back Eden: Eight Environmental Cases that Changed the World, 1st edn. Washington DC: Island Press, 2011.

Howard, A.E.D. "The Indeterminacy of Constitutions." *Wake Forest Law Review* 31 (1996): 383–410, available at http://heinonline.org/HOL/LandingPage?handle= hein.journals/wflr31&div=21&id=&page=194

Hudson, Blake. "Federal Constitutions, Global Governance, and the Role of Forests in Regulating Climate Change." *Indiana Law Journal* 87 (2012): 1455–515.

"What Kind of Constitutional Design is Optimal for Environmental Governance?" *Environmental Law Professor Blog* (February 6, 2012), available at http://law-professors.typepad.com/environmental_law/2012/02/what-kind-of-constitutional-design-is-optimal-for-environmental-governance.html

Jackson, V.C. "Methodological Challenges in Comparative Constitutional Law." *Penn State International Law Review* 28 (2009): 319.

Jacobson, Philip. "In Jakarta, a Fight Over Money and Water." *Jakarta Globe*. (December 27, 2011), available at www.thejakartaglobe.com/news/jakarta/in-jakarta-a-fight-over-money-and-water

Constitutional Engagement in a Transnational Era. Oxford University Press, 2010.

Johnston, Barbara Rose (ed.). *Life and Death Matters: Human Rights, Environment and Social Justice*. Left Coast Press, 2011: 11.

Jörgensen, Kirsten. *Climate Initiatives at the Subnational Level of the Indian States and their Interplay with Federal Policies*. 2011 ISA Annual Convention, March 16–19, 2011, Montreal, available at www.polsoz.fu-berlin.de/polwiss/forschung/systeme/ffu/pub-likationen/2011/11_joergensen_montreal/isa11_joergensen_draft.pdf?1367711988

Jung, Courtney and Evan Rosevear. "Economic and Social Rights Across Time, Regions, and Legal Traditions: A Preliminary Analysis of the TIESR Dataset." *Nordic Journal of Human Rights* 30 (2012): 372, 376.

Justinian, Caesar Flavius. "Of the Different Kind of Things." In *The Institutes of Justinian*, Book II, Title I. trans. J.B. Moyle, available from Project Gutenberg, 1893.

Kay, Richard S. "American Constitutionalism." In *Constitutionalism: Philosophical Foundations*, by Larry Alexander (ed.), 16, 27. Cambridge University Press, 1998.

Keefe, Patrick Radden. "Reversal of Fortune: A Crusading Lawyer Helped Ecuadorans Secure a Huge Environmental Judgment against Chevron. But Did He Go Too Far?" *The New Yorker* (January 9, 2012): 38.

Kelly, Michael J. "The Kurdish Regional Constitution within the Framework of the Iraqi Federal Constitution: A Struggle for Sovereignty, Oil, Ethnic Identity, and the Prospects for a Reverse Supremacy Clause." *Penn State Law Review* 114 (2009–10): 784.

Kerr, Richard A. "Latest Forecast: Stand by for a Warmer, but not Scorching, World." *Science* 312 (April 21, 2006): 351, available at www.sciencemag.org/cgi/content/full/312/5772/351a

Khanna, Leela. *Open Drainage Throughout Delhi: Who Will Take Responsibility?* New Delhi: Centre for Social Research (July 2, 2012), available at http://csrindia.org/blog/2012/07/02/open-drainage-throughout-delhi-who-will-to-take-responsibility

Kiss, Alexandre Charles and Dinah Shelton. *International Environmental Law*, 2nd edn. New York: Transnational Publishers, 2000.

Klabbers, J., A. Peters, and G. Ulfstein. *The Constitutionalization of International Law.* Oxford University Press, 2009.

Klipsch, Ronald E. "Aspects of a Constitutional Right to a Habitable Environment: Towards an Environmental Due Process." *Indiana Law Journal* 49 (1974): 203.

Kotzé, Louis J. "Arguing Global Environmental Constitutionalism." *Transnational Environmental Law* 1 (2012): 199.

"Sustainable Development and the Rule of Law for Nature: A Constitutional Reading." In *Rule of Law for Nature: New Dimensions and Ideas in Environmental Law*, by C. Voigt (ed.), 130–45. Cambridge University Press, 2013.

Kotzé, Louis J. and Anél du Plessis. "Some Brief Observations on Fifteen Years of Environmental Rights Jurisprudence in South Africa." *Journal of Court Innovation* 3 (2010): 157, 163–4.

Kravchenko, Svitlana. "Citizen Enforcement of Environmental Law in Eastern Europe." *Widener Law Review* 10 (2004): 475, 484.

"The Aarhus Convention and Innovations in Compliance and Multilateral Environmental Agreements." *Colorado Journal of International Environmental Law and Policy* 18(1) (2007): 1–50.

Kravchenko, Svitlana and John E. Bonine. *Human Rights and the Environment: Cases, Law and Policy.* Carolina Academic Press, 2008.

Kury, Franklin L. "The Environmental Amendment to the Pennsylvania Constitution: Twenty Years Later and Largely Untested." *Villanova Environmental Law Journal* 1 (1990): 123, 124.

Kysar, Douglas A. "Global Environmental Constitutionalism: Getting There from Here." *Transnational Environmental Law* 1 (2012): 83, 87.

Larsen, J.L. "Importing Constitutional Norms from a 'Wider Civilization': *Lawrence* and the Rehnquist Court's Use of Foreign and International Law in Domestic Constitutional Interpretation." *Ohio State Law Journal* 65 (2004): 1283.

Lau, Martin. "Islam and Judical Activism: Public Interest Litigation and Environmental Protection in the Islamic Republic of Pakistan." In *Human Rights Approaches to Environmental Protection*, by Alan E. Boyle and Michael R. Anderson (eds.). Oxford University Press, 1998.

Laxman, Lekha and Abdul Haseeb Ansari. "The Interface between TRIPS and CBD: Efforts towards Harmonization." *Journal of International Trade Law and Policy* 11 (2012): 108– 132.

Lazarus, Richard J. "Restoring What's Environmental about Environmental Law in the Supreme Court." *UCLA Law Review* 47 (2000): 703, 708.

The Making of Environmental Law. London: University of Chicago Press, 2004.

Leitao, Kevin. "Rhode Island's Forgotten Bill of Rights." *Roger Williams University Law Review* 1 (1996): 31, 58, n.68.

Leng, Ang Hean. "Constitutional Rights Adjudication in Asian Societies." *The Law Review* (Sweet and Maxwell) (2011): 229, 241.

Leopold, Aldo. *A Sand County Almanac*. Random House Digital Inc., 1986.

MacDonald, Karen E. "Sustaining the Environmental Rights of Children: An Exploratory Critique." *Fordham Environmental Law Review* 18 (2006): 1, 5, 7.

McLaren, Robert A. "Environmental Protection Based on State Constitutional Law: A Call for Reinterpretation." *University of Hawaii Law Review* 12 (1990): 123, 149.

MacLaren, V., A. Morris, and S. Labatt. "Engaging Local Communities in Environmental Protection with Competitiveness: Community Advisory Panels in Canada and the United States." In *Sustainability, Civil Society and International Governance*, by J.J. Kirton and Peter Hajnal (eds.), 31, 36. Farnham: Ashgate, 2006.

Mairal, Hector A. *Collective and Class Actions in Argentina, National Report*, The Globalization of Class Actions Conference Proceedings, December, 2007, available at http://globalclassactions.stanford.edu/sites/default/files/documents/Argentina_ National_Report.pdf

Marko, Joseph. *Federalism, Sub-national Constitutionalism, and the Protection of Minorities*, available at http://camlaw.rutgers.edu/statecon/subpapers/marko.pdf

May, James R. "Of Development, daVinci and Domestic Legislation: The Prospects for Sustainable Development in Asia and its Untapped Potential in the United States." *Widener Law Symposium Journal* 3 (1998): 197.

"The Availability of State Environmental Citizen Suits." *Natural Resources and Environment* 18 (2004): 53.

"The North American Symposium on the Judiciary and Environmental Law: Constituting Fundamental Environmental Rights Worldwide." *Pace Environmental Law Review* 23 (2005/2006): 113, Appendix B.

"U.S. Supreme Court Decisions: Review for 2006–2007 and Outlook." *Environment Reporter* 38 (BNA), No. 34 (August 24, 2007): 1851.

"Climate Change, Constitutional Consignment, and the Political Question Doctrine." *Denver University Law Review* 85 (2008): 919.

"The Intersection of Constitutional Law and Environmental Litigation." In *Environmental Litigation: Law and Strategy*, by Cary R. Perlman (ed.), 359. ABA, 2009.

"Not at All: Environmental Sustainability in the Supreme Court." *Sustainable Development Law and Policy* 10 (2009): 20.

"U.S. Supreme Court Environmental Cases 2008–2009: A Year Like No Other." *Environment Reporter* 40 (BNA), No. 36 (September 11, 2009): 2154.

Constitutional Directions in Procedural "Environmental Rights", 28 *J. Envtl. Law and Litigation* 27 (2013).

May, James R. and Erin Daly, "Vindicating Fundamental Environmental Rights Worldwide, Symposium: The Confluence of Human Rights and the Environment" *Oregon Review of International Law* 11 (2009): 365.

"New Directions in Earth Rights, Environmental Rights and Human Rights: Six Facets of Constitutionally Embedded Environmental Rights Worldwide." *IUCN Academy of Environmental Law E-Journal* (2011): 13–25.

"Constitutional Environmental Rights Worldwide." In *Principles of Constitutional Environmental Law*, by James R. May. ABA Publishing, Environmental Law Institute, 2011.

"Global Constitutional Environmental Rights." In *Routledge Handbook of International Environmental Law*, by Shawkat Alam, Jahid Hossain Bhuiyan, Tareq M.R. Chowdhury, and Erika J. Techera (eds.). Routledge, 2012.

May, James R. and Robert L. Glicksman. "Justice Rehnquist and the Dismantling of Environmental Law." *Environmental Law Report* 36 (2006): 10585.

May, James R. and William Romanowicz. "Environmental Rights Embedded in State Constitutions." In *Principles in Constitutional Environmental Law*, by James R. May. ABA Publishing, Environmental Law Institute, 2011.

Merrills, J.G. "Environmental Protection and Human Rights: Conceptual Aspects." In *Human Rights Approaches to Environmental Protection*, by Alan E. Boyle and Michael R. Anderson (eds.). Oxford University Press, 1998.

Morrow, K. "Worth the Paper that They are Written on? Human Rights and the Environment in the Law of England and Wales." *Journal of Human Rights and the Environment* 1 (2010): 66.

Mova Al'Afghani, Mohamad. "Constitutional Court's Review and the Future of Water Law in Indonesia." *Law, Environment and Development Journal* 2(1) (2006):1, available at www.lead-journal.org/content/06001.pdf

Mudd, Michelle Bryan. "A 'Constant and Difficult Task': Making Local Land Use Decisions in States with a Constitutional Right to a Healthful Environment." *Ecology Law Quarterly* 38 (2011): 1.

Nanda, Ved P. and George Pring. *International Environmental Law and Policy for the 21st Century*, 2nd edn, revised. Martinus Nijhoff Publishers, 2013.

Nedelsky, Jennifer. *Law's Relations: A Relational Theory of Self, Autonomy, and the Law*. New York: Oxford University Press, 2011.

Nelson, Antria. "Steering Sustainability: What, When, and Why." In *Steering Sustainability in an Urbanizing World: Policy Practice and Performance*, by A. Nelson (ed.), 1, 2–3. Farnham: Ashgate, 2007.

Onzivu, William. "International Environmental Law, The Public's Health, and Domestic Environmental Governance in Developing Countries." *American University International Law Review* 21 (2006): 597, 672.

Open Society Justice Initiative. *Constitutional Rights of the Right to Information*, available at http://right2info.org/constitutional-protections-of-the-right-to (internal citation omitted).

Osiatynski, Wiktor, "Paradoxes of constitutional borrowing." *International Journal of Constitutional Law* 1(2) (2003): 244.

Pallemaerts, Marc. "The Human Right to a Healthy Environment as a Substantive Right." In *Human Rights and the Environment: Compendium of Instruments and Other International Texts on Individual and Collective Rights Relating to the Environment in the International and European Framework*, by Maguelonne DéJeant-Pons and Marc Pallemaerts. Council of Europe, 2002.

Panjabi, R.K.L. *The Earth Summit at Rio: Politics, Economics, and the Environment*. New England: Northeastern University Press, 1997: 17.

Parmesan, Camille and Hector Galbraith. *Observed Impacts of Global Climate Change in the U.S.* Pew Center on Global Client Change, 2004.

Peczenik, Aleksander. "Why Constitution? What Constitution? Contraints on Majority Rule." In *Why Constitutions Matter*, by Niclas Berggren, Nils Karlson, and Joakim Nergelius (eds.), 17, 21–2, 36. New Brunswick, NJ: Transaction Publishers, 2002.

Pedersen, Ole W. "European Environmental Human Rights and Environmental Rights: A Long Time Coming?" *George Washington International Law Review* 21(1) (2008): 73, available at http://ssrn.com/abstract=1122289

  "A Bill of Rights, Environmental Rights and the British Constitution." *Public Law* (2011): 577.

Peters, Anne. "Are we Moving towards Constitutionalization of the World Community?" In *Realizing Utopia: The Future of International Law*, by Antonio Cassese (ed.), 126. Oxford University Press, 2012, available at http://law.huji.ac.il/upload/Peters_Constitutionalization_in_Cassese.2012.pdf

Pettigrew, Harry W. "A Constitutional Right of Freedom from Ecocide." *Environmental Law* 2 (1971): 1, 1–41.

Piet, Bame. "Four boreholes for CKGR Basarwa" (June 21, 2011), Mmegionline, available at www.mmegi.bw

Polémica Medida Cautelar en favor de los Derechos de la Naturaleza, available at http://mariomelo.wordpress.com/2011/06/28/polemica-medida-cautelar-en-favor-de-los-derechos-de-la-naturaleza

Pontin, Ben. "Environmental Rights under the UK's 'Intermediate Constitution.'" *Natural Resources and Environment* 17 (2002): 21–3, 64–5.

Pring, George (Rock) and Catherine (Kitty) Pring. *Greening Justice: Creating and Improving Environmental Courts and Tribunals*, with an Introduction by Lalanath de Silva, The Access Initiative (2009), available at www.law.du.edu/documents/ect-study/greening-justice-book.pdf

Rai, Dewain. "Naturally Nepal: Protecting the Natural Environment is Protecting the Nation." *Nepali Times* (May 22–8, 2009).

Razzaque, Jona. "Public Participation in Water Governance." In *The Evolution of the Law and Politics of Water*, by J.W. Dallepenna and J. Gupta (eds.), 355, 364–5. Springer, 2009.

  "Information, Public Participation, and Access to Justice." In *Routledge Handbook of International Environmental Law*, by Shawkat Alam, Jahid Hossain Bhuiyan, Tareq M.R. Chowdhury, and Erika J. Techera (eds.). Oxford University Press, 2012.

Real Climate: Climate Science from Climate Scientists. Available at www.realclimate.org

Regassa, Tsegaye. "Sub-national Constitutions in Ethiopia: Towards Entrenching Constitutionalism at State Level." *Mizan Law Review* 2 (2009): 1. Available at www.ajol.info/index.php/mlr/article/viewFile/54006/42550

Reid, C. and Ross, A. "Environmental Governance in the UK." In *Environmental Protection in Multi-layered Systems: Comparative Lessons from the Water Sector*, by M. Alberton and F. Palermo (eds.), 161–85. Leiden: Martinus Nijhoff, 2012 (Studies in territorial and cultural diversity governance).

Ristroph, Elizabeth Barrett and Ilya Fedyaev. "Obstacles to Environmental Litigation in Russia and the Potential for Private Actions." *Environs* 29 (2006): 221.

Rosencranz, Armin, Edward Boenig, and Brinda Dutta. "The *Godavarman* Case: The Indian Supreme Court's Breach of Constitutional Boundaries in Managing India's Forests." *Environmental Law Reporter* 37 (2007): 10032.

Rosenn, Keith S. "Brazil's New Constitution: An Exercise in Transient Constitutionalism for a Transitional Society." *American Journal of Comparative Law* 38 (1990): 773, 796–7.

Ross, A. "Why Legislate for Sustainable Development?" *Journal of Environmental Law* 20 (2008): 35–68.

"It's Time to Get Serious – Why Legislation is Needed to Make Sustainable Development a Reality in the UK." *Sustainability* 2 (2010): 1101–27, available at www.mdpi.com/2071-1050/2/4/1101

Ruhl, J.B. "The Metrics of Constitutional Amendments: And why Proposed Environmental Quality Amendments don't Measure up." *Notre Dame Law Review* 74 (1999): 245.

Sachs, Aaron. "What do Human Rights have to do with Environmental Protection? Everything." *Sierra Magazine* (November–December, 1997), available at www.sierraclub.org/sierra/199711/humanrights.asp

Sands, Philippe. *Principles of International Environmental Law*, 2nd edn. Cambridge University Press, 2003.

Saunders, Cheryl. "The Use and Misuse of Comparative Constitutional Law." *Indiana Journal of Global Legal Studies* 13 (2006): 37.

Sax, Joseph L. *Defending the Environment: A Strategy for Citizen Action*. New York: Alfred A. Knopf, Inc., 1971: 159.

"The Search for Environmental Rights." *Journal of Land Use and International Law* 93 (1990).

Scanlon, John, Angela Cassar, and Noémi Nemes. "Water as a Human Right?" *IUCN Environmental Policy and Law Paper No. 51* (2004).

Schlickman, Andrew J., Thomas M. McMahon, and Nicoline Van Riel (eds.). *International Environmental Law and Regulation*. Salem, NH: Butterworth Legal Publishers, 1995. Vol II.

Schochet, Gordon J. "Introduction: Constitutionalism, Liberalism, and the Study of Politics." In *Nomos XX 1*, by J. Roland Pennock and John W. Chapman (eds.), 1–2. New York University Press, 1979.

"Introduction to Constitutionalism." In *Constitutionalism*, by J. Roland Pennock and John W. Chapman (eds.). New York University Press, 1979.

Scottish Government, The. *Scotland's Future* (2013), Chapter 8, available at www.scotland.gov.uk/Publications/2013/11/9348

Sharma, Binod Prasad. "Constitutional Provisions Related to Environment Conservation: A Study." *IUCN policy brief.* (September, 2010), available at http://cmsdata.iucn.org/downloads/constitutional_provisions_related_to_environment_conservation___final.pdf

Shelton, Dinah. "Human Rights, Environmental Rights, and the Right to the Environment." *Stanford Journal of International Law* 28 (1991): 103, 112–13, 116.

Symposium. "Earth Rights and Responsibilities: Human Rights and Environmental Protection." *Yale Journal of International Law* 18 (1993): 215–411.

"Human Rights and the Environment." *Yearbook of International Environmental Law* 13 (2002): 199.

"Human Rights and the Environment: What Specific Environmental Rights Have Been Recognized?" *Denver Journal of International Law and Policy* 35 (2006): 128, 163.

Shemshuchenko, Y. "Human Rights in the Field of Environmental Protection in the Draft of the New Constitution of the Ukraine." In *Environmental Rights: Law, Litigation and Access to Justice*, by Sven Deimann and Bernard Dyssli. Gaunt, 1995.

Slaughter, A-M. "A Typology of Transjudicial Communication." *University of Richmond Law Review* 29 (1994): 99.

"Judicial Globalization." *Virginia Journal of International Law* 40: (2000): 1103.

Social Watch Report 2006, "National Reports, Colombia: A Resource Allocation that will not meet the MDGs," 195, n.3, available at www.socialwatch.org/node/10994

Sripati, Vijayashri. "Human Rights in India – Fifty Years after Independence." *Denver Journal of International Law and Policy* 26 (1997): 100.

Staveland-Saeter, Kristi. "Can Litigation Clean Rivers? Assessing the Policy Impact of 'the Mendoza Case' in Argentina." CHR Michelsen Institute, *CMI Brief* 11(3) (May, 2012), available at www.cmi.no/publications/file/4467-can-litigation-clean-rivers.pdf

Stec, Stephen. "Ecological Rights Advancing the Rule of Law in Eastern Europe." *Journal of Environmental Law and Litigation* 13 (1998): 275, 320–1.

Stec, Stephen and Susan Casey-Lefkowitz. *The Aarhus Convention: An Implementation Guide*. United Nations, 2000.

Steinhardt, Ralph G. "The Role of International Law as a Canon of Domestic Statutory Construction." *Vanderbilt Law Review* 43 (1990): 1103.

Stern, Sir Nicholas. *Stern Review on the Economics of Climate Change* (2006), available at http://webarchive.nationalarchives.gov.uk/+/http:/www.hm-treasury.gov.uk/sternreview_index.htm

Stone, Christopher D. "Should Trees Have Standing? Toward Legal Rights for Natural Objects." *Southern California Law Review* 45 (1972): 450.

Should Trees Have Standing? Law, Morality, and the Environment, 3rd edn. Oxford University Press, 2010.

Study on Carbon Governance at Sub-national Level in the Philippines. Ateneo School of Government (November 16, 2011), available at http://pub.iges.or.jp/modules/envirolib/upload/3514/attach/carbon%20governance%20sub-national%20level%20philippines.pdf

"The Right to Information Act, 2005," *Gazette of India, Extraordinary*, Part II, Section 1 (June 21, 2005), available at www.iitb.ac.in/legal/RTI-Act.pdf

Thompson, Barton H. Jr. "Environmental Policy and State Constitutions: The Potential Role of Substantive Guidance." *Rutgers Law Journal* 27 (1996): 863, 871.

"Constitutionalizing the Environment: The History and Future of Montana's Environmental Provisions." *Montana Law Review* 64 (2003).

Thorme, Melissa. "Establishing Environment as a Human Right." *Denver Journal of International Law and Policy* 19 (1991): 301.

Tucker, John C. "Constitutional Codification of an Environmental Ethic." *Florida Law Review* 52 (2000): 299.

Turner, Stephen J. *A Substantive Environmental Right. An Examination of the Legal Obligations of Decision-makers Towards the Environment*. Kluwer Law International, 2008.

Velasco, Presbitero J. "Manila Bay: A Daunting Challenge in Environmental Rehabilitation and Protection." *Oregon Review of International Law* 11 (2009): 441, 444, 445.

Vidal, John. *Bolivia Enshrines Natural World's Rights with Equal Status for Mother Earth*, available at www.guardian.co.uk/environment/2011/apr/10/bolivia-enshrines-natural-worlds-rights

Walker, Sandra. "The Ontario Environmental Bill of Rights." In *Environmental Rights: Law, Litigation and Access to Justice*, by Sven Deimann and Bernard Dyssli, 20–32. Gaunt, 1995.

Warner, Jeroen. *Flood Planning: The Politics of Water Security*. New York: I.B. Taurus, 2011: 135.

Washington State, Department of Ecology. Available at www.ecy.wa.gov/climate-change/effects.htm (last visited March 22, 2008).

Weiss, Edith Brown. *International Environmental Law and Policy*. Aspen Law and Business, 1998.

Weiss, Edith Brown, Daniel Barstow Magraw, and Paul C. Szasz. *In Fairness to Future Generations: International Law, Common Patrimony, and Intergenerational Equity*. United Nations University, 1989.

Weston, Burns H. and David Bollier. *Green Governance: Ecological Survival, Human Rights, and the Law of the Commons*. Cambridge University Press, 2013 (Table of contents and Prologue), University of Iowa Legal Studies Research Paper No. 13–13, available at http://ssrn.com/abstract=2207977

Wilkinson, Charles F. "The Public Trust Doctrine in Public Land Law." *U.C. Davis Law Review* 14 (1980): 269, 315.

Wilson, Bryan P. "State Constitutional Environmental Rights and Judicial Activism: Is the Big Sky Falling?" *Emory Law Journal* 53 (2004): 627.

Wilson, Edward O. "The Current State of Biodiversity." In *Biodiversity*, by Edward O. Wilson. Washington, DC: National Academy Press, 1988.

Woolley, Craig and Tina Costas. "Directors' Liability and Environmental Law." *Juta's Business Law* 13 (2005): 2.

World Commission on Environment and Development. *Our Common Future*. New York: Oxford University Press, 1987.

Yang, Tseming and Adam Moser. *Environmental Tort Litigation in China* (2011), available at http://digitalcommons.law.scu.edu/facpubs/434

Yang, Tseming and Robert V. Percival. "The Emergence of Global Environmental Law." *Ecology Law Quarterly* 36 (2009).

Yost, Nicholas. *The Nepa Litigation Guide*, 2nd edn. American Bar Association, 2012.

Zillman, Donald M, Alistair Lucas, and George (Rock) Pring. *Human Rights in Natural Resource Development: Public Participation in the Sustainable Development of Mining and Energy Resources*. Oxford University Press, 2002.

Index

Printed in Great Britain
by Amazon